VISUAL QUICKSTART GUIDE

PHOTOSHOP ELEMENTS 2

FOR WINDOWS AND MACINTOSH

Craig Hoeschen and Christopher Dahl

 Peachpit Press

Visual QuickStart Guide

Photoshop Elements 2 for Windows and Macintosh

Craig Hoeschen and Christopher Dahl

Peachpit Press

1249 Eighth Street
Berkeley, CA 94710
510/524-2178
800/283-9444
510/524-2221 (fax)

Find us on the World Wide Web at: http://www.peachpit.com
To report errors, please send a note to errata@peachpit.com

Peachpit Press is a division of Pearson Education
Copyright © 2003 by Craig Hoeschen and Christopher Dahl

Editor: Karen Reichstein
Production Editor: Connie Jeung-Mills
Copyeditor: Judy Ziajka
Compositor: Owen Wolfson
Indexer: James Minkin
Cover design: The Visual Group

Notice of Rights

Notice of Liability

The information in this book is distributed on an "As Is" basis, without warranty. While
every precaution has been taken in the preparation of the book, neither the author nor
Peachpit Press, shall have any liability to any person or entity with respect to any loss or
damage caused or alleged to be caused directly or indirectly by the instructions contained
in this book or by the computer software and hardware products described in it.

Trademarks

Visual QuickStart Guide is a registered trademark of Peachpit Press, a division of
Pearson Education.

Throughout this book, trademarks are used. Rather than put a trademark symbol in
every occurrence of a trademarked name, we state that we are using the names in an
editorial fashion only and to the benefit of the trademark owner with no intention of
infringement of the trademark.

Adobe is a registered trademark, and Photoshop Elements is a trademark of Adobe
Systems, Inc.

ISBN 0-201-79974-X

9 8 7 6 5 4 3

Printed and bound in the United States of America

Thanks to our families, whose endless support, encouragement, love, and patience helped make this book possible. We could never have done it without you.

To Karen, Bethany, and Heather, who endured my all-night writing binges, midday naps, and all-too-frequent dinner table absences with a patience and good humor that I most surely did not deserve. I am truly blessed, and profoundly grateful for the three of you. —Craig

To Annette, Amanda, and Sarah, who patiently waited to leave on vacation while I finished charging the digital cameras, and who pretended to be interested while we discussed pixels and image compression at the dinner table. The smiles and memories we collected over the past few months will be cherished forever. —Chris

Acknowledgements

Special thanks to our editor, Karen Reichstein, for her guidance, patience, and insightful questions throughout the process of creating this book, and to our production editor, Connie Jeung-Mills, and compositor, Owen Wolfson, who ultimately brought it all together. Thanks also to our copyeditor, Judy Ziajka, for her careful review and suggestions, to James Minkin, for creating the index, and to the rest of the folks at Peachpit for their technical review and production assistance. We would never have had the unique opportunity of working with this talented team without the initial support and guidance of Marjorie Baer, Serena Herr, and Rebecca Ross. Thanks for your advice and assistance in putting the plan together. Finally, we owe a huge debt of gratitude to our good friend and colleague Paul Carew, who created and documented the wonderful, special projects used in Chapter 12 and featured in the color section of this book.

TABLE OF CONTENTS

TABLE OF CONTENTS

INTRODUCTION

With the release of Photoshop Elements, Adobe's consumer-level image-editing program, hobbyists as well as professional photographers and artists were provided many of the same powerful tools and features found in Adobe Photoshop (long the industry standard), but packaged in an easier-to-use and more accessible, intuitive workspace. Photoshop Elements' friendly user interface, combined with its bargain-basement price, has made an instant hit with the new wave of amateur digital photographers and home users lured by the recent proliferation of sophisticated, low-cost digital cameras and scanners.

Never content to rest on its laurels, Adobe recently introduced Photoshop Elements 2.0. While retaining the power and ease of use of its predecessor, the new version provides new tools and workspace enhancements that not only help stretch the bounds of your creativity, but that help to make your quick photo corrections and creative retouching even simpler and more fun than before.

In the next few pages, we'll briefly discuss some of Photoshop Elements' features (both old and new) and then provide instructions to help you get the software properly installed and set up on your computer. Finally, we'll share a few thoughts to help you get the most from this book, so that you can be on your way to mastering Photoshop Elements' simple, fun, and sophisticated image-editing tools.

Introducing Photoshop Elements

Photoshop Elements makes it easy to retouch your digital photos; apply special effects, filters, and styles; prepare images for the Web; and create wide-screen panoramas from a series of individual photos. And Photoshop Elements provides some completely unique features not present in Adobe Photoshop. Of particular note are two user-friendly palettes that not only introduce you to every major tool and feature, but help lead you step-by-step through a variety of common projects and tasks.

The **Hints palette** contains illustrated explanations of every image editing tool and palette. It's *context sensitive*, meaning that it knows which tool you're using. So each time you select a new tool (or simply hover over a palette with the pointer), the Hints palette changes accordingly and provides helpful information and tips for using that particular tool or palette. In addition, the Hint palette's More button contains links that send you directly to Photoshop Elements' built-in help system. There, you'll find even more detailed help and instruction for any tool, palette, or feature you're interested in learning more about.

The **How To palette** features collections of *recipes* designed to take you step by step through tasks as diverse as creating special text effects and animating graphics for your Web page. At the same time, these recipes are designed as a reference, so that over time you'll learn how to perform these tasks on your own. The How To palette recipes provide a great way to quickly learn sophisticated image editing techniques while completing your own projects.

What's new in version 2.0?

If you've worked with Photoshop Elements in the past, version 2.0 should feel much the same. While you may notice some subtle aesthetic changes as you scan the interface, most of the tools and palettes remain in their original locations, and the palette well and options bar still figure prominently on the desktop. A few notable items have been added or have undergone a significant change for the better.

The Welcome screen

A new Welcome screen has replaced the Quick Start screen from version 1.0. The former screen's text-cluttered and rather unintuitive interface has been replaced by a logical, friendly arrangement of buttons. From the Welcome screen, you can create a new file, browse for an existing file on your hard disk, or automatically download an image from a digital camera or scanner. Additional buttons direct you to either the How To palette and its selection of common photo-retouching tasks or to Photoshop Elements' built-in tutorials.

The improved File Browser

The File Browser, a tool for previewing, organizing, and getting information about your photos, realizes its full potential with a dramatic redesign in 2.0. The new File Browser is a full-featured searching, sorting, and viewing wonder. In addition to simply previewing files, you can now rotate, rename, and even delete your photos directly from the File Browser. By applying a number of file name, size, and creation date options, you can sort the order in which the previews appear. In addition, the File Browser now features a panel that can display comprehensive technical information about any photo, including its creation date, color settings, file format, and even the make and model of camera used to capture the original photo.

Video frame capture

Photoshop Elements 2.0 now offers the ability to capture individual frames of video, letting you edit and save them just like any other still digital image. The new Frame From Video dialog box features a control bar with the same functions as your video camera or VCR. You can play, fast-forward, or rewind to any frame in a video clip, then save that frame with just the click of a button. You can capture a single video frame to save as a stand-alone image, or capture a series of frames from which you can create simple Web animations.

PDF Slideshow

With PDF Slideshow, you can save a series of photos as a self-running, self-contained presentation, complete with sophisticated transitions and timing options. Your slideshow is created in Adobe Acrobat's PDF format, so anyone with Acrobat Reader—distributed as a free download from Adobe—can easily view your presentation. And because PDF files are naturally quite small, you can share a slideshow with your family and friends by simply including it as an e-mail attachment.

The Quick Fix dialog box

The Quick Fix dialog box contains an assortment of the most common photo correction tools in one handy place, so you don't have to search through different menus to make your individual image adjustments one by one. You'll find tools for correcting brightness, color correction, focus, and rotation, all accompanied by a list of options specific to each task. The Brightness tool, for example, lets you add a lighting effect to help bring out details in the shadow areas of a foreground subject. And in the Rotation category, you can rotate an image in 90-degree increments, or flip it horizontally or vertically.

The Selection brush

The Selection brush gives you a completely new method of selecting specific areas of your photos. As its name implies, you make a selection by "painting" through an area of an image using any of Photoshop Elements' vast array of brush shapes. Any area touched by the brush is instantly selected. Because you select with an actual brush shape, your selection acquires all the attributes of that brush, be it a soft, wet-edged watercolor brush or a stylized scattering of maple leaves. Used together with the other selection tools, the Selection brush allows you to adjust and fine-tune selections with a degree of precision not possible before.

Glossary of terms

The new glossary, accessible from the Help menu, provides easy-to-understand definitions of nearly 200 terms. Although this glossary is specifically written for use with Photoshop Elements, it also serves as a good general digital photography and image editing resource. Alongside the software-specific topics like *brush type* and *canvas size*, you'll also find excellent working definitions of concepts diverse as *bit depth*, *PostScript*, and *RGB color*.

System Requirements

Before you install Photoshop Elements, you will want to make sure that your system can run the software effectively. Following are the minimum system recommendations.

For Macintosh Systems

◆ PowerPC processor

◆ Mac OS 9.1, 9.2.x, or Mac OS X v.10.1.3-10.1.5.

◆ Microsoft Internet Explorer 4.0, 5.0, or 5.5.

◆ 64MB of RAM with virtual memory on

◆ 150 MB of available hard disk space

◆ Color monitor with 256-color (8-bit) or greater video card

◆ 800 x 600 or greater monitor resolution

◆ CD-ROM drive

For Windows Systems

◆ Intel Pentium–class processor

◆ Windows 98/ 98 SE/Me, 2000 /XP

◆ Microsoft Internet Explorer 4.0, 5.0, or 5.5.

◆ 64 MB of RAM

◆ 150 MB of available hard disk space

◆ Color monitor with 256-color (8-bit) or greater video card

◆ 800 x 600 or greater monitor resolution

◆ CD-ROM drive

Memory and Photoshop Elements

For simple color correction and quick retouching, you can probably get by with the bare minimum amount of RAM (computer memory) required to run Photoshop Elements. But to really get the most out of Photoshop Elements, we suggest that you consider installing at least 128 MB of memory into your computer. Some features, like Photomerge (which you'll use to create panoramas) are very memory dependent. And as you become more comfortable with Photoshop Elements, adding increasingly more layers, filters, typography, and other effects to your work, your files are likely to become larger and require more memory to support them. You'll find that the relatively small, up-front cost of investing in some extra memory is more than worth the aggravation saved by avoiding those troublesome and annoying "low on memory" warning boxes.

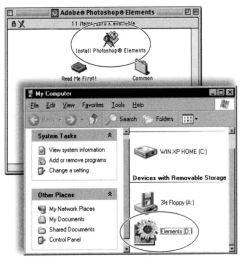

Figure i.1 The Photoshop Elements 2.0 installer icon as it appears in the Macintosh (upper left) and Windows XP (lower right) desktop window.

Installing and Starting Photoshop Elements

To get started, you need to install Photoshop Elements from the Photoshop Elements CD onto your computer's hard disk. The installer includes screens that guide you step-by-step through the entire installation. Once the installation is complete, be sure to look at the other information and resources included on the installation CD. (Let's face it—once the CD is back in its box and shelved, you're probably not going to remember what's on it.)

It's possible that Photoshop Elements came preinstalled on your computer or bundled with a digital camera or scanner. If that's the case, you might want to peek inside the Photoshop Elements application folder on your hard drive, just to see exactly what has been installed.

To install Photoshop Elements:

1. Insert the Photoshop Elements CD in the CD-ROM drive.

   The Photoshop Elements CD icon appears on the desktop.

2. Double-click the CD icon.

   A window containing the Photoshop Elements installer appears (**Figure i.1**).

3. Double-click the installer icon.

   The Photoshop Elements installer splash screen appears.

   Some Windows systems are configured to automatically start installer applications. If this is the case, you won't need to double-click the installer icon.

continues on next page

4. In the installer window, click the Continue button and follow the onscreen instructions.

The Easy Install option is the best means of ensuring that all required files are installed in their proper locations. But if you have limited hard drive space or just prefer not to include certain files (like the Tutorials, for example), you can choose the Custom Install option from the pop-up menu (**Figure i.2**), then select what files you want to install.

✔ Tips

■ The CD also includes a Goodies folder, which contains an impressive collection of free stock photography images for you to practice on or to use in your own projects. If hard disk space isn't a concern, you many want to consider copying all or some of the stock image files to your hard disk. The complete collection will occupy about 80 MB of space.

■ Also included in the Goodies folder is the Stock Art Catalog (**Figure i.3**), a thumbnail gallery of every stock image included in the Goodies folder. You can view or print the catalog from Adobe's Acrobat Reader, also included on the Photoshop Elements CD. Acrobat Reader is automatically loaded along with Photoshop Elements' other program files when you choose the Easy Install option.

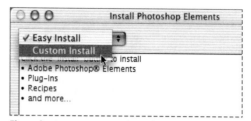

Figure i.2 As you progress through the installation, you have the option of performing either an Easy or Custom install.

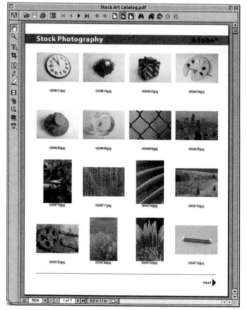

Figure i.3 Stock photographic images and an accompanying PDF catalog are available in the Goodies folder on the Photoshop Elements installation CD.

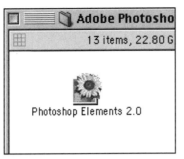

Figure i.4 The Photoshop Elements 2.0 application icon.

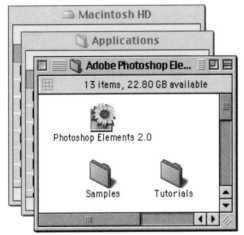

Figure i.5 On the Macintosh, you may have to navigate through several levels of folders to find the application icon.

Figure i.6 The Photoshop Elements Welcome screen.

To start Photoshop Elements:

1. Locate the Photoshop Elements application icon on your hard disk (**Figure i.4**).

   As part of the installation process, most Windows systems automatically place a shortcut icon directly on your desktop. To locate the icon on a Macintosh, you may have to navigate to the folder in which you chose to place the application files during installation (**Figure i.5**).

2. Double-click the Photoshop Elements icon.

   Photoshop Elements launches and opens the Welcome screen (**Figure i.6**).

3. To begin working, choose from the list of options on the button panel on the left side of the screen.

INSTALLING AND STARTING PHOTOSHOP ELEMENTS

✔ Tips

- In Mac OS 9, you can create an *alias* for Photoshop Elements. An alias, similar to a shortcut in Windows, is a duplicate of the original application icon. When you double-click the alias, the original file opens. Simply select the Photoshop Elements icon and choose Make Alias from the File menu. From there, you can drag the alias to your desktop or to the folder of your choice, wherever is most convenient for you.

- In Mac OS X, you can create an alias simply by dragging the application icon to the dock (**Figure i.7**).

To exit Photoshop Elements:

Do one of the following:

- From the File menu (Windows), choose Exit (Ctrl+Q).

- From the File menu (Mac OS 9), choose Quit (Command+Q).

- From the Photoshop Elements menu (Mac OS X), choose Quit (Command+Q).

Figure i.7 In Mac OS X, drag Photoshop Elements' application icon into the dock to create an alias for quick access.

INSTALLING AND STARTING PHOTOSHOP ELEMENTS

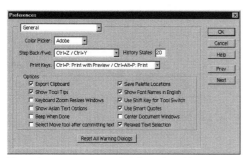

Figure i.8 You can customize Photoshop Elements' tools, palettes, and settings within its series of specialized Preferences dialog boxes.

Figure i.9 Move from one Preference dialog box to the next by choosing different options from the pop-up menu.

Personalizing Photoshop Elements

Because no two users work quite the same way, Photoshop Elements gives you the freedom to customize its tools and palettes to suit your own personal work habits, expertise, and aesthetic. You can create favorite sets of brush types, swatch libraries, and patterned fills, and you can set preferences for save options, transparency, ruler units, and grid color. Slightly more advanced options help you set the way the program manages memory and displays and prints color. Additionally, since it supports Adobe's plug-in file format, Photoshop Elements can be a constantly evolving work-in-progress as you add new plug-ins for everything from custom filter effects to digital camera image browsers that allow you to view your camera's stored photos onscreen.

Setting Preferences

Preferences are settings that let you control and modify the way that Photoshop Elements looks, works, and behaves. The Preferences dialog box is divided into eight windows, each one focusing on a specific aspect of the application: general display properties, file saving options, cursor display and behavior, transparency settings, rulers and units of measurement, grid appearance and behavior, and scratch disks and cache for managing memory (**Figure i.8**). You can change preferences at any time by choosing Preferences from the Edit menu or by navigating through the dialog box using the pop-up menu (**Figure i.9**).

About Presets

Presets are collections of brush styles, swatch colors, gradient fills, and patterns organized into sets, or *libraries* (**Figure i.10**). At any time during your work session, you can load different preset libraries using either the Preset Manager, or the palette menus on the options bar or Swatches palette.

About Plug-ins

Photoshop Elements makes great use of Adobe's extendable plug-ins format. Plug-in modules are little software programs that add functionality to the main application. For instance, the different filters and effects that you access from Photoshop Elements' Filter menu are all plug-in modules. Plug-ins are stored in folders inside a Plug-ins folder, where additional folders and plug-ins can be added at any time.

Plug-ins are worth special mention, because you aren't limited to just those included with Photoshop Elements. In cooperation with Adobe, developers of both software and hardware have created compatible plug-ins that install and run seamlessly with Photoshop Elements. If you've recently purchased a digital camera or scanner, its browser or scanning software may very well include plug-ins to help the devices communicate with Photoshop Elements.

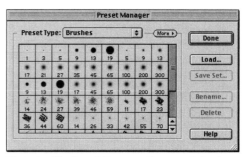

Figure i.10 The Preset Manager allows you to load custom brushes, color swatches, gradients, and patterns.

Downloading Plug-Ins

To download additional plug-ins from Adobe, first make sure your computer is connected to the Internet. In Photoshop Elements, choose File > Online Services to view an updated collection of plug-ins available for you to download.

How to Use This Book

This Visual QuickStart Guide, like others in the series, is a task-based reference. Each chapter focuses on a specific area of the application and presents it in a series of concise, illustrated steps. We encourage you to follow along using your own images or those provided with Photoshop Elements. We believe the best way to learn is by doing, and this Visual QuickStart Guide is the perfect vehicle for that style of learning.

This book is meant to be a reference work, and though it's not expected that you'll read through it in sequence from front to back, we've made an attempt to order the chapters in a logical fashion. The first couple of chapters take you on a tour of the work area and provide a foundation for the basics of image editing and creation. From there you explore color, selections, layers, effects, painting, and typography and then learn a variety of techniques for saving and printing images, including special formatting options for distributing images over the Web. The book concludes with a selection of advanced techniques and projects, organized as short tutorials that we hope will provide further creative inspiration as you work with your own images. This book is suitable for the beginner just starting in digital photography and image creation, as well hobbyists, photo enthusiasts, intermediate-level photographers, illustrators, and designers.

Keyboard Shortcuts

Many of the commands that you access from Photoshop Elements' menu bar have a keyboard equivalent (or shortcut) that appears beside each command name in the menu. Keyboard shortcuts are great time savers and save you from having to constantly refocus your energy and attention as you jump from image window to menu bar and back again. When this book introduces a command, the keyboard shortcut is also listed. The Windows shortcut is always listed first, followed by the Macintosh shortcut. For example, the keyboard shortcut for the Copy command is displayed as (Ctrl+C/Command+C). You'll find a complete list of Photoshop Elements' keyboard shortcuts in the appendix of this book.

Cross-Platform Issues

Adobe has traditionally done a wonderful job of cross-platform interface design, and Photoshop Elements is no exception. You'll find little difference between the look and functionality of the Windows and Macintosh versions of this software. Throughout this book, illustrations containing Photoshop Elements' interface are weighted evenly among the Windows, Mac OS 9, and Mac OS X platforms. On the rare occasion when significant differences do exist, each platform is illustrated, with accompanying platform-specific procedures.

THE BASICS

Before you start working in Photoshop Elements, take a look around the work area to familiarize yourself with the program's tools and menus. When you first launch Photoshop Elements, you immediately see the Welcome screen, which allows you to quickly open and create new files or download images from a digital camera or scanner. The work area includes the document window, where you'll view your images, along with many of the tools, menus, and palettes you'll use as you get better acquainted with the program.

This chapter presents a quick tour of the palettes and menus you'll use when you first create or open a new file in Photoshop Elements. You'll learn more about how to use these tools in subsequent chapters of this book.

Understanding the Work Area

The Photoshop Elements work area is designed to make the tools easy to find and use. Just as with a well-organized workbench, the menus, palettes, and tools are intuitively arranged in a way that makes them easy to find where and when you need them.

The Welcome screen

When you first start Photoshop Elements, the Welcome screen automatically appears on your desktop (**Figure 1.1**). Think of this screen as a handy launching pad for creating or opening new files, pasting contents from the clipboard, or acquiring images from a digital camera or scanner. The Welcome screen also includes links to common issues and tutorials. But if you find the display of this screen annoying, simply click the Exit Welcome Screen button at the bottom of the screen to shoo it away.

✔ Tip

■ If you don't want to see the Welcome screen each and every time you launch Photoshop Elements, click the check box in the lower left corner that reads Show This Screen at Startup to remove the check mark and turn it off. If you change your mind and want to see it again, just choose Welcome from the Window menu and check the box to automatically display this screen at startup.

UNDERSTANDING THE WORK AREA

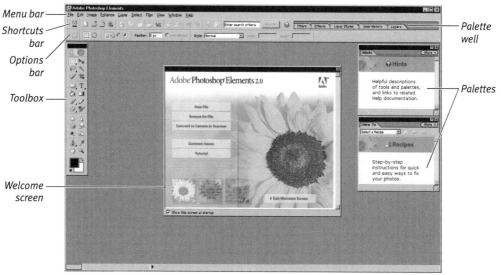

Menu bar

Shortcuts bar

Options bar

Toolbox

Welcome screen

Palette well

Palettes

Figure 1.1 The Photoshop Elements Welcome screen provides a simple and fast way to open, create, and import files.

File	
New...	⌘N
New from Clipboard	
Open...	⌘O
Browse...	⇧⌘O
Open Recent	▶
Create Photomerge...	
Close	⌘W
Close All	⌥⌘W
Save	⌘S
Save As...	⇧⌘S
Save for Web...	⌥⇧⌘S
Revert	
Attach to E-mail...	
Create Web Photo Gallery...	
Online Services...	
Place...	
Import	▶
Export	▶
Batch Processing...	
Automation Tools	▶
File Info...	
Page Setup...	⇧⌘P
Print Preview...	⌘P
Print...	⌥⌘P
Print Layouts	▶

Figure 1.2 The menu bar offers myriad pull-down menus.

Figure 1.3 The shortcuts bar gives you handy access to some of Photoshop Elements' most common tasks, such as creating, browsing, and printing files.

Menus, tools, and palettes

The Photoshop Elements work area may look familiar if you've used other Adobe products, and for good reason. Adobe has worked hard to maintain a consistent interface across its software product lines—so if you've ever used Adobe Photoshop, you'll be pleased to know that you don't have to learn a whole new program; Photoshop Elements retains much of the look and feel of its bigger, more powerful cousin.

The **menu bar** offers drop-down menus for performing common tasks, editing images, and organizing your work area. Each menu is organized by topic. For example, the File menu offers commands for importing, saving, and batch processing your images (**Figure 1.2**).

The **shortcuts bar** (**Figure 1.3**) displays buttons for performing routine Photoshop Elements commands, such as creating, browsing, and printing files. Of course, you can perform these same tasks by navigating through the menu bar, but the shortcuts bar offers easier access to the most common file management tasks.

continues on next page

UNDERSTANDING THE WORK AREA

The **toolbox** (**Figure 1.4**) is the unofficial workhorse of Photoshop Elements, as it contains most of the tools you'll use for editing and enhancing your images. These are arranged in the general order you'll be using them, with the most commonly used selection tools at the top, followed by painting, drawing, and color selection tools toward the bottom.

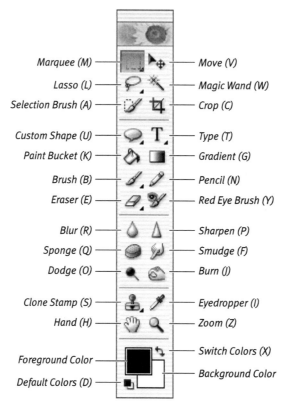

Marquee (M) — — Move (V)
Lasso (L) — — Magic Wand (W)
Selection Brush (A) — — Crop (C)

Custom Shape (U) — — Type (T)
Paint Bucket (K) — — Gradient (G)
Brush (B) — — Pencil (N)
Eraser (E) — — Red Eye Brush (Y)

Blur (R) — — Sharpen (P)
Sponge (Q) — — Smudge (F)
Dodge (O) — — Burn (J)

Clone Stamp (S) — — Eyedropper (I)
Hand (H) — — Zoom (Z)

Switch Colors (X)
Foreground Color —
Background Color
Default Colors (D) —

Figure 1.4 The toolbox contains most of the tools you'll use to edit your images.

Figure 1.5 The options bar changes its display depending on the tool you select in the toolbox.

Figure 1.6 Palettes can be used from within the palette well (as shown) or moved to your work area.

Figure 1.7 When palettes are in the work area, you can place them anywhere you want for easy access.

The **options bar**, located right below the shortcuts bar, provides unique settings and options for each tool in the toolbox. For example, when you're using either the Lasso or Marquee selection tool, you can choose to add to or subtract from the current selection, and when you're using the Brush tool, you can change the brush size and opacity (**Figure 1.5**).

The **palette well**, located at the upper right of the desktop, contains an impressive collection of filters and special effects to apply to your photos, along with the handy Undo History and Layers palettes (**Figure 1.6**). The Hints and How To palettes can also be stored in the palette well, although by default they appear in your work area when you start Photoshop Elements for the very first time.

Palettes are designed to work the way *you* want to work. You can work with palettes from within the palette well simply by clicking the tab for the palette (**Figure 1.7**), or you can drag them to the main work area for easier access. Palettes can also be grouped together or docked below one another, depending on your organizational mood.

UNDERSTANDING THE WORK AREA

Browsing, Opening, and Closing Files

Before you can do any image editing in Photoshop Elements, you need to find and open your photo files. The File Browser offers you a convenient and intuitive method of finding them. From here, you can easily search, sort, and preview all of your images. You can also change the size of your image previews, sort your files, and even rotate the image thumbnails.

The File Browser offers the easiest way to browse and open files. However, you can also open files using the File > Open command from the main menu bar or the Open file shortcut on the shortcuts bar. In these cases, you'll end up using the Open dialog box to find and open your image. The dialog box includes options for limiting your search to specific file formats, showing or hiding a preview of the image, and finding a file by typing the file name.

To open a file using the File Browser:

1. To open the File Browser, *do one of the following:*
   - ▲ Click the Browse for File tab, located on the Welcome screen (**Figure 1.8**).
   - ▲ From the File menu, choose Browse (**Figure 1.9**); or press Shift+Ctrl+O/ Shift+Command+O.
   - ▲ Click the Browse icon on the shortcuts bar (**Figure 1.10**).

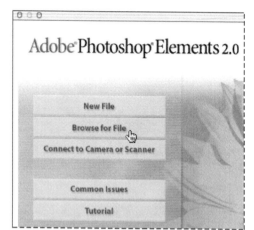

Figure 1.8 Click the Browse for File tab on the Welcome screen to open the File Browser.

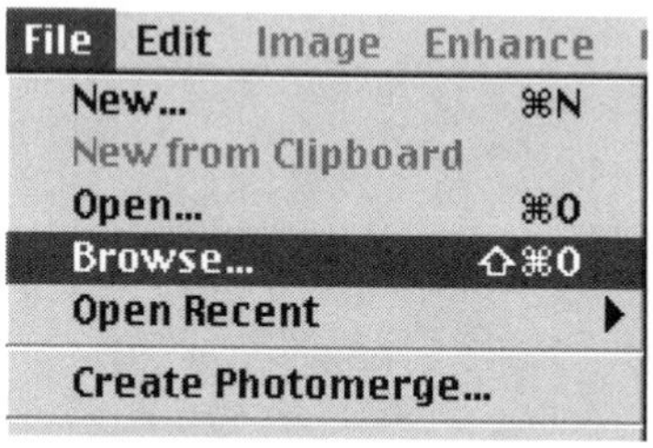

Figure 1.9 Choosing File > Browse also opens the File Browser.

Figure 1.10 You'll also find a shortcut to the File Browser on the shortcuts bar.

The File Browser window opens, and you can browse through your files and view detailed information about them (**Figure 1.11**).

continues on next page

File structure

Image preview

File information

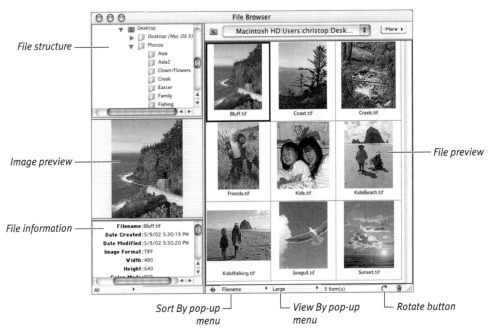

File preview

Sort By pop-up menu

View By pop-up menu

Rotate button

Figure 1.11 The File Browser lets you browse for images, sort and rename image files, and view detailed information about each file.

2. To browse for a folder or file, *do one of the following*:

   ▲ Navigate through your hard drive's contents in the file structure window, which displays the files in a manner similar to your Windows or Macintosh operating system (**Figure 1.12**).

   ▲ Use the navigation pop-up menu located above the file preview window (**Figure 1.13**).

3. Click any image to see an enlarged version in the image preview window on the left.

   Once you've clicked on an image, you can view extremely detailed information about that image (such as file type, size, and creation date) by viewing the file information window, located below the image preview window (**Figure 1.14**).

4. To open an image file, double-click it from anywhere in the File Browser.

   The image appears in the document window.

Figure 1.12 You can navigate through the file structure to find image folders and files.

Figure 1.13 The navigation pop-up menu offers another way to access folders and files.

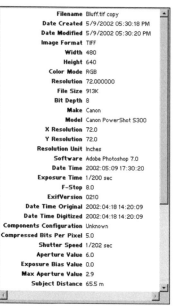

Figure 1.14 The file information window displays detailed information on an image's file size, type, color mode, resolution, format, and more.

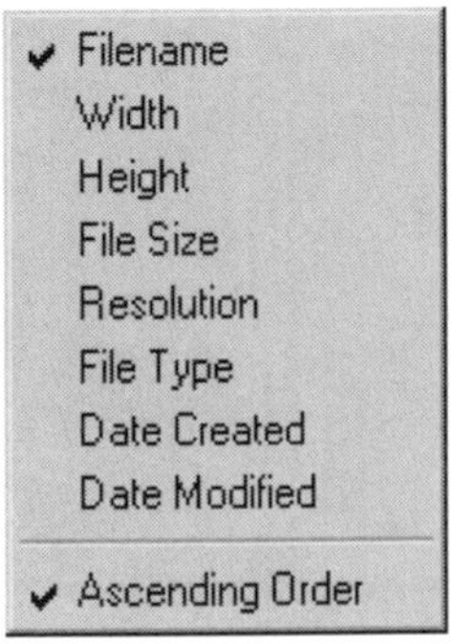

✔ Filename
Width
Height
File Size
Resolution
File Type
Date Created
Date Modified

✔ Ascending Order

Figure 1.15 You can sort files based on eight different criteria and also reverse the sorting order.

Bluff.tif copy
Coast.tif copy
Creek.tif copy
Friends.tif copy
Kids.tif copy
KidsBeach.tif copy
KidsWalking
Seagull.tif copy
Sunset.tif copy

Figure 1.16 Choosing small thumbnail previews allows you to keep the browser window as narrow as possible.

To sort files using the File Browser:

◆ Select a sorting option from the Sort By pop-up menu at the bottom of the File Browser (**Figure 1.15**).

As you choose different options, the browser automatically resorts and redisplays images based on your choice.

✔ Tips

■ To reverse the sorting order, select Ascending order to remove the check mark; images will now appear in reverse order. To restore the original order, select Ascending order again, so that this option is again checked.

■ You can rename files right in the File Browser. For example, if you want a series of images to appear in a particular order, you can rename them 01, 02, 03, and so on; then, when you sort them, they'll appear in numerical order. (Note: If you don't place the zero before numbers 1 through 9, images numbered 10 and higher will not be sorted correctly.)

To change thumbnail previews:

◆ Select an option from the View By pop-up menu at the bottom of the File Browser.

▲ **Small** displays the smallest thumbnails in one column. This is a good choice if you want to scroll quickly through all of your folders and files (**Figure 1.16**).

▲ **Medium** displays thumbnails at a medium size.

continues on next page

BROWSING, OPENING, AND CLOSING FILES

▲ **Large** is the default option and is the best choice for detailed viewing of your images.

▲ **Details** includes file information about each image, such as creation date, file size, resolution, file type, and color mode (**Figure 1.17**).

✔ Tips

■ You can rotate images in the File Browser by clicking on the Rotate button (**Figure 1.18**). Simply select an image and click the button to rotate the image 90° clockwise. To rotate the image 90° counterclockwise just Alt-click (Windows) or Option-click (Mac) the Rotate button. *Note:* for some strange reason, the Rotate button can't be applied to images that reside directly on your desktop. Your image must be nestled inside a folder (or stored within your hard drive directory) before you can rotate it.

■ If you like, you can customize the File Browser further by resizing any of its windows. To do this, position your pointer directly on the dividing line between any two of the File Browser's windows. The pointer turns into a double-headed arrow. Depending on the window location, you can drag left, right, up, or down to resize the window. This is particularly handy for enlarging the image preview window so you can see more detail in your images.

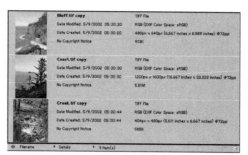

Figure 1.17 The Details option displays important file information for each image.

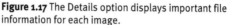

Figure 1.18 Click the Rotate button (it's almost hidden at the right-hand bottom of the File Browser) to rotate an image while you preview it.

Figure 1.19 Choose File > Open to open an image file.

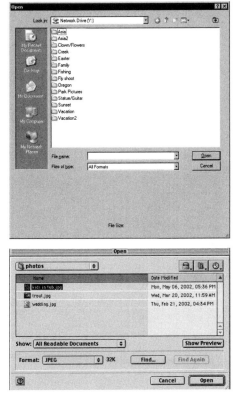

Figure 1.20 You can also open a file by clicking the Open icon on the shortcuts bar.

To open a file from the Open dialog box:

1. To find and open a file, *do one of the following:*

   ▲ From the File menu, choose Open (**Figure 1.19**); or press Ctrl+O/ Command+O.

   ▲ On the shortcuts bar, click the Open file icon (**Figure 1.20**).

   The Open dialog box appears (**Figure 1.21**).

2. Browse to the folder that contains your images (**Figure 1.22**).

3. To open the file you want, *do one of the following:*

   ▲ Double-click the file name.

   ▲ Select the file name and click the Open button.

   The image appears in your document window.

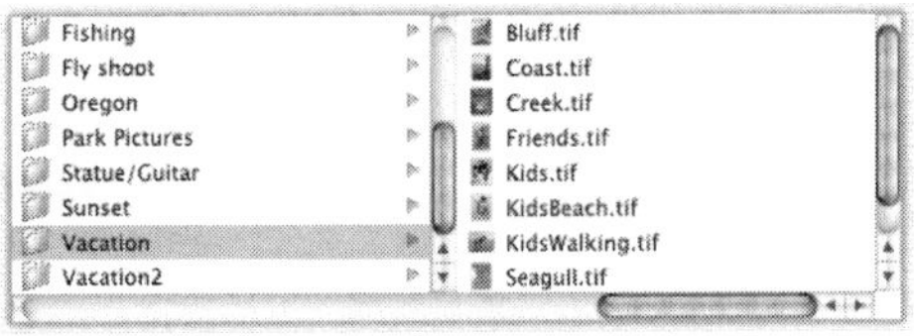

Figure 1.21 The Open dialog box (Windows, top; Mac OS 9, bottom) lets you browse for specific file types.

Figure 1.22 Browse to navigate to any folder or file.

To close a file:

Do one of the following:

- Click the close icon on the title bar for the active window (**Figure 1.23**).

- From the File menu, choose Close; or press Ctrl+W/Command+W (**Figure 1.24**).

- To close all open files at once, from the Window menu, choose Close All; or press Shift+Ctrl+W/Shift+Command+W.

✔ Tip

- If your document contains unsaved changes, Photoshop Elements asks you if you'd like to save those changes. Read on for more information on saving files.

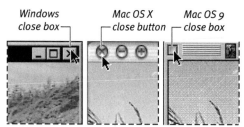

Figure 1.23 Click the close button in the upper right (Windows) or upper left (Mac) corner of the title bar.

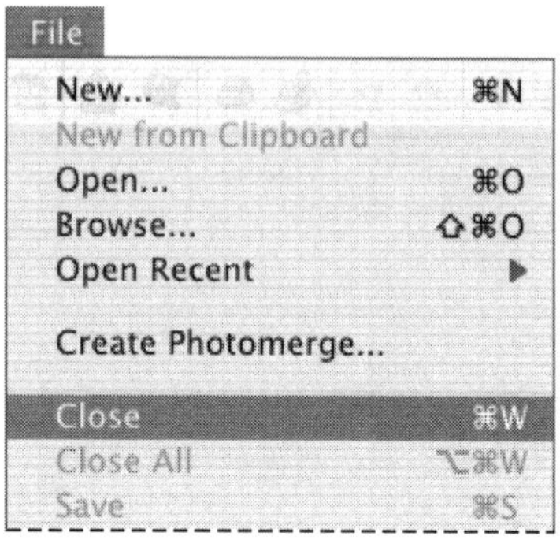

Figure 1.24 From the File menu, choose Close.

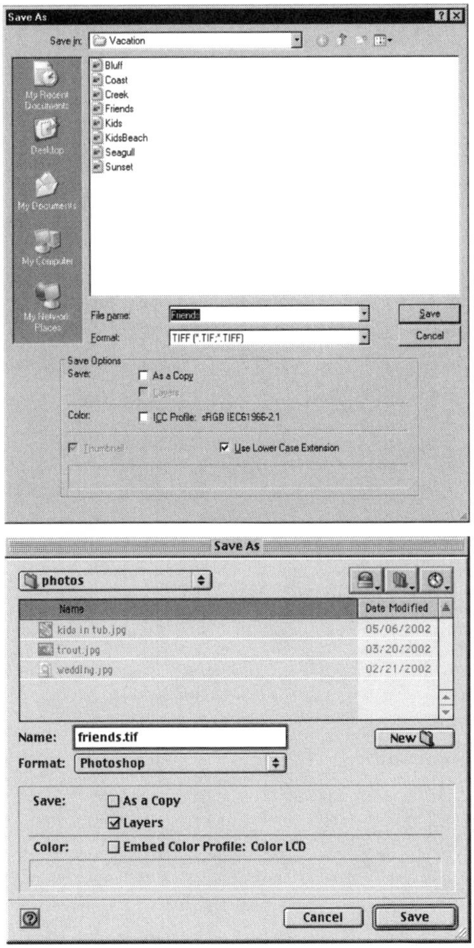

Figure 1.25 The Save As dialog box in Windows (top) and Mac OS 9 (bottom).

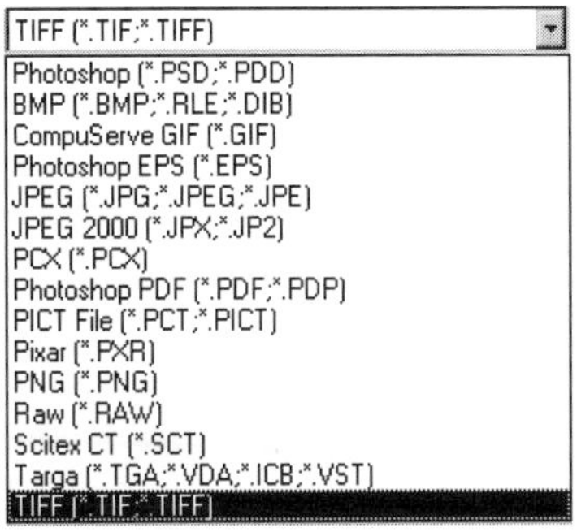

Figure 1.26 If the default format is not what you need, you can choose a different file format for your file.

Saving Files

As you work on an image, it's good practice to periodically save the file to a disk or to your hard drive. When you save a file, you can choose from a number of file formats. (For detailed information on the file formats you can choose, see Chapter 11, "Saving and Printing Images.")

If you're interested in showing off your photos on the Web, you can also choose the Save for Web option. Saving your images for the Web involves its own set of unique operations; these are covered in detail in Chapter 10, "Preparing Images for the Web."

To save a file for the first time:

1. From the File menu, choose Save As; or press Ctrl+S/Command+S.

The Save As dialog box appears (**Figure 1.25**).

2. Choose a destination for the file.

In Windows, browse to the location in the Save In field. On the Macintosh, use the directory pop-up menu at the top of the dialog box.

3. In the File Name (Windows) or Name (Mac) field, type a name for the file.

4. From the Format menu, choose a format, if necessary, from the list of options (**Figure 1.26**).

Photoshop Elements automatically chooses a default file format for you, depending on the origins of your image. For now, it's perfectly fine to stick with the default format—you can always change it later. But if you're not sure what format to choose, choose either the native Photoshop format (PSD), which is the best all-purpose format, or choose the JPEG format, which works especially well with digital photos. When saving an image as a JPEG file, choose the highest quality setting possible.

continues on next page

SAVING FILES

5. If you want to retain the original file without altering it, select As a Copy.

Choosing As a Copy creates and saves a duplicate file, which now becomes the working file open on your desktop. This selection protects your original file from changes as you edit the duplicate file.

6. To include the color profile information currently assigned to your display, select the Color box.

You can assign color profiles to an image to ensure that colors are printed accurately on specific printers or monitors. At this point, you don't need to worry too much about setting color profiles, but for more detailed information on this topic, see Chapter 10, "Preparing Images for the Web."

7. When your settings are complete, click Save.

✔ Tips

■ To save changes to a file in subsequent operations, simply choose File > Save or press Ctrl+S/Command+S.

■ Saving using the As a Copy option is a good idea if you're experimenting with various changes and want to ensure that you keep your original version intact. It's also handy if you want to save an image in more than one file format, which is useful if you want to save a high-quality copy for printing and keep a smaller-sized file for e-mailing to friends.

■ For more detailed information on file formats, see Chapter 10, "Preparing Images for the Web."

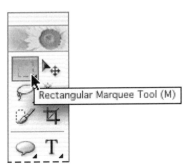

Figure 1.27 Hover the pointer over any tool icon to see a tip that displays the tool's name and keyboard shortcut.

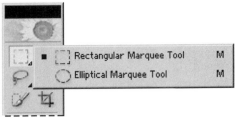

Figure 1.28 A small triangle next to a tool icon indicates additional tools. Right-click (Windows) or Control-click (Mac) to see a menu of these hidden tools.

Figure 1.29 When the Rectangular Marquee tool is selected, the pointer changes to crosshairs as it moves over the document window.

Selecting Tools

The toolbox contains tools for creating and editing images. You can use them to paint, draw, and view various parts of your images, for example. To view information about a tool, rest the pointer over it. A tool tip appears showing the name and keyboard shortcut (if any) for that tool (**Figure 1.27**). Additional information about the tool also appears on the Hints palette; see "Using the Hints Palette" later in this chapter.

To use a tool, you must first select it from the toolbox. Some tools have additional tools hidden beneath them, as indicated by a small triangle at the lower right of the tool icon (**Figure 1.28**).

To select a tool from the toolbox:

◆ Click the tool icon in the toolbox.

When you move your pointer into the document window, the pointer changes appearance to reflect the tool you have selected (**Figure 1.29**).

To select a hidden tool:

1. Click and briefly hold down the mouse button, or right-click (Windows) or Control-click (Mac) a tool icon that displays a small triangle.

   A menu of the hidden tools appears (**Figure 1.30**).

2. Click the tool you want to use.

✔ Tips

■ Once you've familiarized yourself with the toolbox, it's even easier to use keyboard shortcuts to access tools. Shortcuts are displayed in tool tips, on the printed Quick Reference card included in the product box, and in the online help. For example, if you look at the tool tip for the Type tool, you'll see the letter T in parentheses (**Figure 1.31**). That's the keyboard short-cut for the Type tool. If you press T on your keyboard, even when another tool is chosen, the Type tool becomes activated. (Note that when you press the letter T to select the Type tool, Photoshop Elements automatically selects the Type tool that was most recently used.)

■ To cycle through hidden tools, hold down the Shift key and repeatedly press the tool's shortcut key. Each tool option is displayed in turn.

To hide or display the toolbox:

◆ To hide the toolbox, from the Window menu, choose Hide Tools.

◆ To display toolbox, from the Window menu, choose Show Tools.

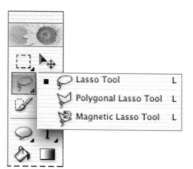

Figure 1.30 the mouse button to view hidden tools.

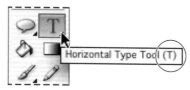

Figure 1.31 Tool tips display the keyboard shortcut for each tool.

Gripper bar

Options bar

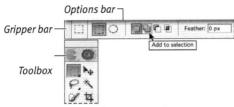

Toolbox

Figure 1.32 Use the options bar to customize the tool you've selected.

Figure 1.33 The shortcuts bar provides easier access to common commands than does the menu bar.

Using the Options and Shortcuts Bars

Think of the options bar as a natural extension of the toolbox. After you select a tool, you can adjust any of its settings using the options bar. The buttons on the options bar change depending on what tool is selected, so if you're using the Paintbrush tool, for example, you can use the options bar to choose different brush sizes and saturation and opacity settings.

The shortcuts bar gives you easy access to some of the most frequently used menu commands. Instead of navigating through the File menu to open, save, and preview your image, you can accomplish the same tasks with an easy click on the shortcuts bar. A couple of the handiest shortcuts are the two little arrows that allow you to undo each change you've made to an image or restore a change if you change your mind.

To use the options bar:

1. From the toolbox, select a tool.

2. View the options bar to see the available options for that tool (**Figure 1.32**).

   Click through the tools to see the options for each tool.

To use the shortcuts bar:

◆ On the shortcuts bar, click the icon for the desired command (**Figure 1.33**).

   The command is launched, just as if you'd chosen it from the menu bar.

To move the options or shortcuts bar:

◆ Click the gripper bar at the left edge of the options or shortcuts bar and drag the bar to a new location.

When you drag the options or shortcuts bar out into the work area, the gripper bar changes to a solid bar. This indicates that the bar can now be collapsed and expanded.

To collapse or expand the options or shortcuts bar:

◆ To collapse either the options or shortcuts bar when it is not docked at the top or bottom of the application, double-click the bar at its left edge.

On the shortcuts bar, only the Adobe logo remains visible. On the options bar, the icon for the selected tool remains visible.

◆ To redisplay the full bar, double-click the bar at the left edge again.

To hide or display the options or shortcuts bar:

◆ To hide either the options or shortcuts bar, choose Options or Shortcuts from the Window menu (**Figure 1.34**).

A check mark means that the item will appear, and no check mark means that it won't.

◆ To redisplay the bar, choose Show Options or Show Shortcuts, as appropriate, from the Window menu.

✔ Tip

■ When you hide the shortcuts bar, the palette well disappears as well. You must choose Show Shortcuts from the Window menu to display the palette well once more.

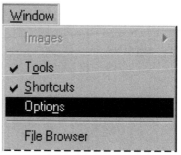

Figure 1.34 If you prefer less clutter in your workspace, choose Options (or Shortcuts) to make the check mark disappear and to hide the selected bar.

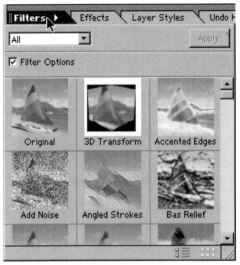

Figure 1.35 Simply click a palette's tab to view its contents; click again to close the palette.

Working with Palettes

Photoshop Elements offers 11 palettes, all of which are accessible from the palette well and the desktop. They can be used as stand-alone tools, or you can combine several palettes to better organize your workflow. They can be both a blessing and a curse, allowing you to customize your workspace on the one hand, or, if you go overboard in displaying them, taking up so much space that you can't see your image. Many palettes include handy drop-down menus, located in the upper right corner, that allow you to perform additional tasks directly from the palette.

To display a palette:

Do one of the following:

◆ In the palette well, click the palette's tab (**Figure 1.35**).

◆ From the Window menu, choose any palette to display it in your work area (**Figure 1.36**).

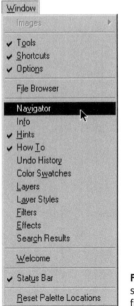

Figure 1.36 You can show or hide any palette from the Window menu.

WORKING WITH PALETTES

To close a palette:

Do one of the following:

◆ If the palette is open in the palette well, click its tab again or click outside the palette.

◆ If the palette is open in your work area (outside the well), click the close box on the palette title bar (**Figure 1.37**).

✔ Tip

■ To show or hide all palettes, press Shift-Tab. This is a handy way to temporarily remove palettes from view.

To move a palette out of the palette well:

1. Select the desired palette tab.

2. Drag the tab until the palette is in the desired location in your work area (**Figure 1.38**).

   The palette is now a floating palette on the desktop.

✔ Tip

■ To return a palette to the well, click the palette's tab and drag the palette back into the well.

Figure 1.37 To close a palette, you can click the close icon on the title bar. On the Macintosh, the close icon is in the upper left corner. In Windows, the close icon is on the right.

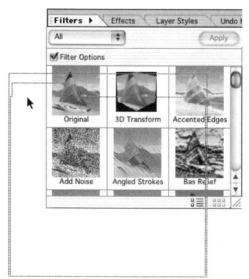

Figure 1.38 To move a palette from the well, just drag the tab to place the palette anywhere on your desktop.

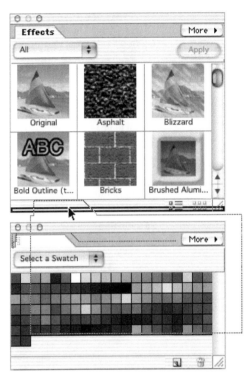

Figure 1.39 Drag a palette tab into another open palette to form a palette group.

To group palettes:

1. Make sure you can see the tabs of all of the palettes you want to group. At least one of the palettes (the target palette) must be outside of the palette well.

2. Drag a palette tab into the window of the target palette (**Figure 1.39**).

   A thick line appears around the window of the target palette to let you know that the palettes have been grouped.

✔ Tips

- To ungroup a palette, simply select the palette's tab and drag it out of the palette group.

- From the Window menu, you can choose to hide any stand-alone palettes. If you hide a palette in a palette group, the other palettes in the group will remain open.

To dock palettes:

- Drag any palette's tab to the bottom of any palette outside of the palette well (**Figure 1.40**).

   You must drag the palette by its tab (not its title bar) to successfully dock it to another palette. A double line appears at the bottom of the target palette to let you know that the palettes have been docked.

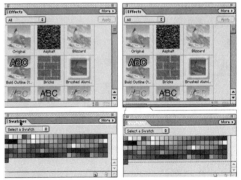

Figure 1.40 Docking one palette below another helps avoid clutter on your desktop.

WORKING WITH PALETTES

To use palette menus:

Do one of the following:

◆ If the palette is inside the palette well, click the More button triangle at the top of the palette tab (**Figure 1.41**).

◆ If the palette is outside the palette well, click the More button in the upper right corner of the palette (**Figure 1.42**).

The More button may look a little different, depending on whether a palette is located inside or outside the palette well. Inside the palette well, the More button is represented by a sideways triangle in the palette tab.

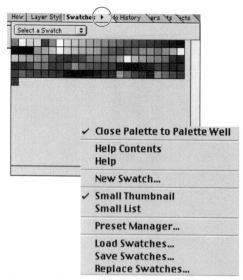

Figure 1.41 When a palette is docked in the palette well, click the More button, which looks like a sideways triangle, to access the palette menu.

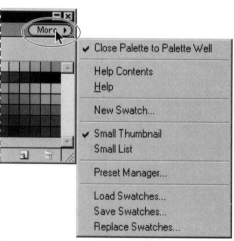

Figure 1.42 When a palette is outside the well, the More button looks a little different, but works the same.

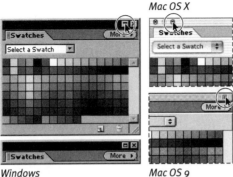

Mac OS X

Windows   *Mac OS 9*

Figure 1.43 Click the minimize/maximize box to collapse a palette group.

Figure 1.44 If you make a mess of your desktop, don't panic: you can reset the original palette locations to restore all of the palettes to their default locations.

✔ Tips

■ A quick way to return a palette to the palette well is to click its close box with the Close Palette to Palette Well palette menu option selected (you probably won't need to select this option, as it's already selected by default). If the palettes are docked or grouped together, the palettes will all end up back in the palette well, which might become a little crowded. If you find your palette well is too clogged for you to work efficiently, just choose Reset Palette Locations from the Window menu to get some breathing room again.

■ To collapse a stand-alone palette or a palette group, click the minimize/maximize box (Windows) or the zoom box (Mac) (**Figure 1.43**) or double-click the palette tab or title bar.

To return palettes to their default positions:

◆ Select Window > Reset Palette Locations (**Figure 1.44**).

Using the Zoom Tool

You can magnify and reduce your view by using the Zoom tool, which is available from the toolbox, or by using keyboard shortcuts. Since you'll often want to zoom in and out while simultaneously using other tools, you will often find the shortcuts handier and so should become familiar with them. The current level of magnification is shown in the document title bar and also in the status bar at the bottom of the document window (yet another location where you can adjust the magnification, in this case by clicking the value in the status bar and deleting it and then entering a specific zoom percentage of your choice).

Figure 1.45 The Zoom tool, located near the bottom of the toolbox, resembles a tiny magnifying glass.

Figure 1.46 To zoom in on an image, click the Zoom In button on the options bar.

To zoom in:

1. In the toolbox, select the Zoom tool (**Figure 1.45**); or press Z on the keyboard.

   The pointer changes to a magnifying glass when you move it into the document window.

2. Be sure that a plus sign appears in the center of the magnifying glass. If you see a minus sign instead, click the Zoom In button on the options bar (**Figure 1.46**) to switch the pointer.

3. Click the area of the image that you want to magnify.

   Each time you click, the magnification increases by a factor of two.

Figure 1.47 Drag with the Zoom tool to zoom in on a specific area of an image.

To zoom out:

1. In the toolbox, select the Zoom tool; or press Z on the keyboard.

2. Be sure that a minus sign appears in the center of the magnifying glass. If you see a plus sign instead, click the Zoom Out button on the options bar to switch the pointer.

3. Click the area of the image that you want to reduce.

    Each time you click, the magnification decreases by a factor of two..

To zoom in on a specific area:

1. In the toolbox, select the Zoom tool; if necessary, click the Zoom In button on the options bar to display the Zoom tool with a plus sign.

2. Drag over the area of the image that you want to zoom in on (**Figure 1.47**).

    A selection marquee appears around the selected area. When you release the mouse button, the selected area is magnified and appears centered in the image window.

3. To move the view to a different area of the image, hold down the spacebar; then, when the hand pointer appears, drag to the area that you want to see.

To display an image at 100 percent:

To display an image at 100 percent (also referred to as displaying actual pixels), *do one of the following:*

◆ In the toolbox, double-click the Zoom tool.

◆ In the toolbox, select either the Zoom or Hand tool and click Actual Pixels on the options bar (**Figure 1.48**).

◆ From the View menu, choose Actual Pixels (**Figure 1.49**).

◆ Enter 100 in the status bar at the bottom of the document window and then press Enter (Windows) or Return (Mac) (**Figure 1.50**).

✔ Tips

■ You can temporarily select the Zoom tool by holding down Ctrl+spacebar/ Command+spacebar to zoom in, or Alt+ spacebar/Option+spacebar to zoom out.

■ To change the magnification of the entire image, press Ctrl++ /Command++ (Control or Command plus the plus sign) to zoom in or Ctrl+- /Command+- (Control or Command plus the minus sign) to zoom out.

■ Toggle the Zoom tool between zoom in and zoom out by holding down the Alt/Option key as you click.

■ Photoshop Elements lets you change the magnification to a specific percentage in the status bar at the bottom of the document window. Just click the zoom value in the status bar and enter a specific zoom percentage of your choice.

■ You can automatically resize the document window to fit the image (as much as possible) when zooming in or out. On the options bar, select Resize Windows to Fit. To maintain a constant window size, deselect the Resize Windows to Fit option.

Figure 1.48 Clicking the Actual Pixels button on the options bar returns the image view to 100 percent.

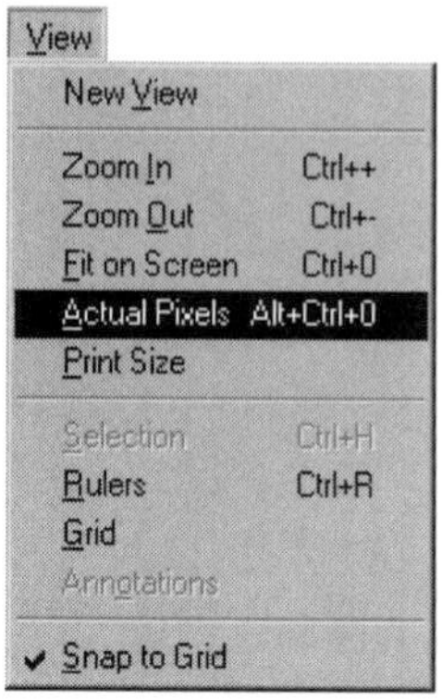

Figure 1.49 If the options bar is hidden, choose Actual Pixels from the View menu.

Figure 1.50 If you like, you can also type a specific view percentage in the status bar at the bottom of the document window.

Figure 1.51 Drag with the Hand tool to quickly view a different area of the same image.

Figure 1.52 Click the arrows or drag the scroll bars to move around an image.

Moving the View Area

When working in Photoshop Elements, you'll often need to change your view area to work on another part of your image. This can happen when you're zoomed in on a part of the image or when your image is too large to be completely visible on your screen. Luckily, Photoshop Elements offers you multiple features for changing your viewing area. Two of the most common are the Hand tool and the Navigator palette. (For more information on how to manage views, see Chapter 2, "Creating and Managing Images.")

To view another area of the image:

Do one of the following:

- From the toolbox, select the Hand tool and drag to move to another area of the image (**Figure 1.51**).

- Use the scroll arrows at the bottom and right side of the document window to scroll to the left or right and up or down. You can also drag the scroll bars to adjust the view (**Figure 1.52**).

To change the view using the Navigator palette:

1. Choose Window > Show Navigator, or in the palette well, click the Navigator tab.

2. Drag the view box in the thumbnail of the image (**Figure 1.53**).

   The view in the document window changes accordingly.

✔ Tips

- If you're using another tool, pressing the spacebar gives you temporary access to the Hand tool.

- You can drag the slider bar at the bottom of the Navigator palette to adjust the level of magnification.

Figure 1.53 As you move the view box on the Navigator palette, the image view in the document window changes to match.

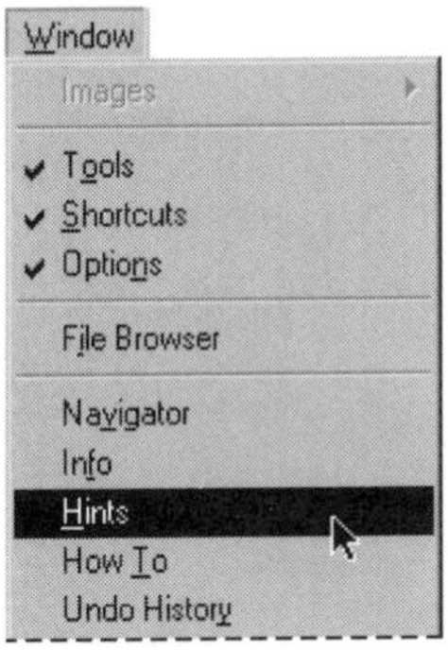

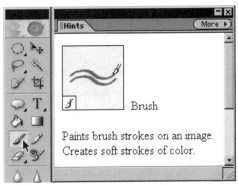

Figure 1.54 The Hints palette gives you instant information about the tool you're currently using.

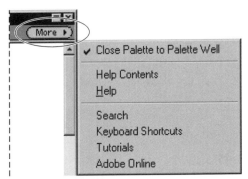

Figure 1.55 When you move the pointer over a tool or palette, the Hints palette displays a description of the tool and its uses.

Figure 1.56 Click the More button to open the help system to the page for the selected item.

Using the Hints Palette

The Hints palette is a handy, compact help window that introduces each tool and palette and displays a brief description of its use and function.

To use the Hints palette:

1. In the palette well, click the Hints tab; or choose Window > Hints (**Figure 1.54**).

2. Position the pointer over a tool or palette; then look at the Hints palette to see the description of that item (**Figure 1.55**).

3. Click the More button; then choose Help from the palette menu to get more detailed information on the tool or palette (**Figure 1.56**).

   Choosing Help from the palette menu opens the Photoshop Elements' help system directly to the page for that tool or palette.

✔ Tip

- When using the Hints palette, you must remember to *hover* your pointer over the palette or tool in question. If you select a tool or click a palette tab, the Hints palette disappears.

Selecting Recipes from the How To Palette

The How To palette provides step-by-step instructions—referred to as recipes—for many commonly performed Photoshop Elements tasks, such as adding a drop shadow to an image or removing red-eye from a photograph. Most recipes also offer a Play button with some steps; just click, and Photoshop Elements performs those steps for you.

To use the How To palette:

1. Choose Window > How To, or if the How To palette is visible in the well, click its tab.

   The How To palette drops down from the palette well (**Figure 1.57**).

2. From the Select a Recipe drop-down menu, choose a category; then select a recipe from the list that appears (**Figure 1.58**).

3. Follow the step-by-step recipe instructions. If a step includes a Play button, click it, and Photoshop Elements will complete that step for you (**Figure 1.59**).

Figure 1.57 Choose Window > How to, or click the How To tab in the palette well to open the palette containing recipes.

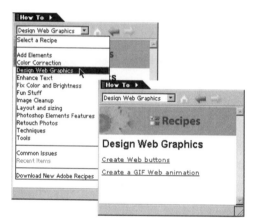

Figure 1.58 Select a category; then choose a recipe from the category list.

Figure 1.59 Click the Play button to watch Photoshop Elements complete a step for you.

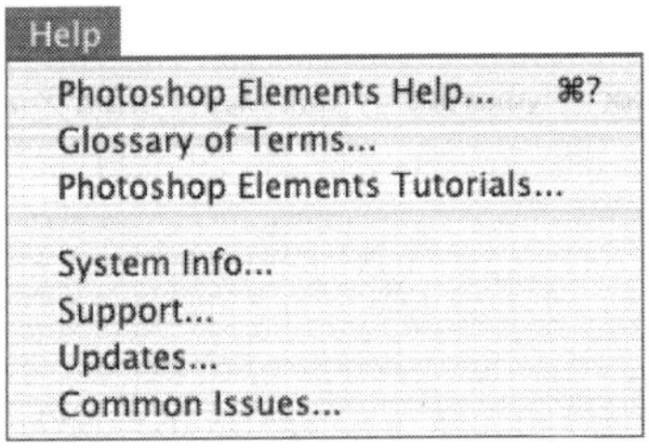

Help

Photoshop Elements Help...   ⌘?
Glossary of Terms...
Photoshop Elements Tutorials...

System Info...
Support...
Updates...
Common Issues...

Figure 1.60 The Help menu includes links to the help system, a glossary, and tutorials.

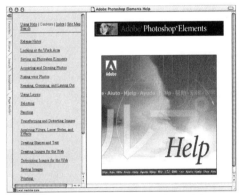

Figure 1.61 If you need assistance with a task in Photoshop Elements or want more information about a feature, use the built-in help system.

Using the Help System

Photoshop Elements includes a comprehensive help system containing the complete text of the *Photoshop Elements User Guide*, keyboard shortcuts for both Windows and Macintosh platforms, and a small collection of tutorials. You'll need a current version of either the Internet Explorer or Netscape Communicator Web browser to view the help system. Although the help system uses a Web browser for viewing, you don't actually need a live Internet connection to use the help system, as all of the help files are automatically installed on your hard disk during the Photoshop Elements installation process.

Photoshop Elements 2.0 also includes a search field located right on the shortcuts bar. If you have a question, you can just type a topic, and Photoshop Elements will search through both the help contents and recipes to find all of the appropriate links in the help system. There's even a glossary that includes an extensive list of terms you're likely to run across while working on your images.

In addition, the application CD includes PDF versions of the user guide and a quick reference guide to tools and palettes. If you want to use these bonus materials, simply reinsert the installation CD into your computer and copy these files to your hard drive.

To use the help system:

1. From the Help menu (**Figure 1.60**), choose Photoshop Elements Help; or press F1 (Windows only).

   The Photoshop Elements help system opens in your browser (**Figure 1.61**).

continues on next page

USING THE HELP SYSTEM

2. To find information, *do one of the following:*

▲ Select Using Help to view information on how to use the help system.

▲ Select Contents to see the table of contents for the help system.

▲ The help contents are organized in the same manner as the user guide.

▲ Select Index to search for terms alphabetically as you would in a book's index.

▲ Select Search to enter and search for a specific topic.

To search for help using the shortcuts bar:

1. Type a topic in the Search field on the shortcuts bar (**Figure 1.62**); then click Search.

Photoshop Elements finds all topics that include the word or words you entered (**Figure 1.63**).

2. Sort the search results using one of the following options (**Figure 1.64**):

▲ Select All Search Results to see all related recipes and help topics.

▲ Select Results for Recipes to see just related recipes.

▲ Select Results for Help to see just the results from the online help system.

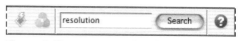

Figure 1.62 You can type a topic in the Search field located on the shortcuts bar.

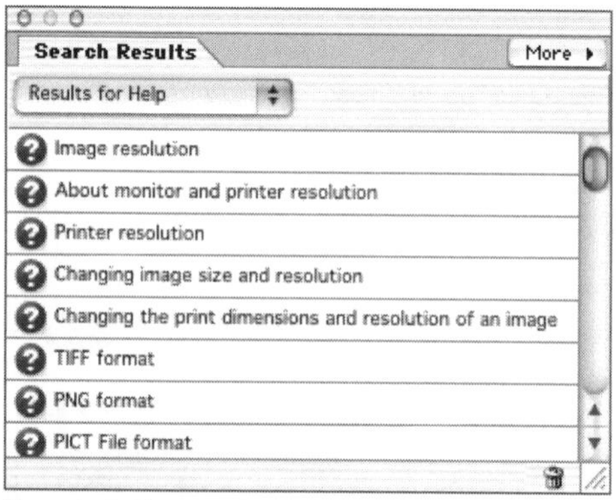

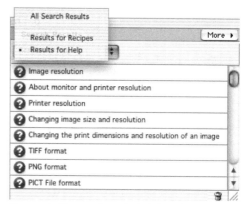

Figure 1.63 The search results list all topics that include the word or words you enter.

Figure 1.64 The search can include just the contents of the help system, recipes, or both.

CREATING AND MANAGING IMAGES

One of the first things you'll be doing in Photoshop Elements is setting up your image. This involves creating a new file (or importing a photo or image from a digital camera, camcorder, or scanner), setting its dimensions and size, and arranging it on your desktop in a way that works best for you. Photoshop Elements can seem a little overwhelming at first, presenting you with almost *too* many settings choices when you first start working on an image. While you're welcome to adjust your image's resolution and print size to your heart's desire, you can also choose to skip this information for now if you just want to start correcting or retouching your photos. That's the beauty of Photoshop Elements. It offers an enormous amount of control and precision over your images, no matter how large or small the task.

This chapter shows you how to get your images into Photoshop Elements, and offers some basic guidelines on adjusting an image's size and resolution, depending on whether you want to print it, e-mail it, or put it up on the Web. You'll also learn the different methods for viewing additional information about your images.

Understanding Resolution and Image Size

Resolution and image size are frequently used and often misunderstood terms.

Resolution simply refers to the number of physical *pixels*, or picture elements—tiny, square, building blocks—that are packed into a digital image.

Image size refers to both the print size and resolution of an image. Depending on whether you want to print a photograph, post it on a Web page, or e-mail it to a friend, you'll need to adjust its image size and resolution accordingly. This section explains the important relationship between image resolution and image size, and how to control these options to get the results you want.

Pixel basics

Everything you do in Photoshop Elements involves controlling and changing pixels. Pixels—individual, tiny squares, or *picture elements*—make up your entire image and are typically not visible as individual elements until you zoom in on your picture (**Figure 2.1**). In fact, Photoshop Elements may even have derived its name at least in part from these small but powerful image structures.

Image at 100%   Image at 800%

Figure 2.1 Pixels become visible as you increase the magnification of your image.

1600 x 1200 pixels, 1000 KB

1024 x 768 pixels, 300 KB

640 x 480 pixels, 300 KB

Figure 2.2 Examples of common digital camera resolutions and associated file sizes, all viewed at 100% (also referred to as *actual pixels*). Higher-resolution images, like the photo on top, provide a sharper, clear picture that's excellent for printing. Lower-resolution images, like the middle and bottom photos, lack sufficient pixel information for printing purposes, but work fine for posting on the Web or e-mailing to friends.

As you work in Photoshop Elements, you'll find that you need to adjust the size of your images for different projects. If you want to send a photo to a friend via e-mail, you'll want the file size to be as small as possible for easy delivery—so you'll want to create a low-resolution image, which means it contains a smaller number of pixels. If you're planning to print high-quality images on your ink-jet printer, then you'll want to maintain as high a resolution as your printer can handle (meaning a greater density of pixels), to ensure a crisp, clear print.

Images are often described using pixels as the unit of measure. For example, a common setting for many digital cameras is 1600 x 1200 pixels (the *x* is pronounced "by," just as in "3 x 5 photo"). Multiplying 1600 times 1200 gives us the total number of pixels in the image, which in this case is 1.92 million pixels.

Digital cameras often include preset resolution modes. These settings determine both the physical dimensions and file size of the image (**Figure 2.2**).

Displaying and printing images

Any discussion of resolution and output can be confusing, but you need to keep just a few basic details in mind. Image resolution is described in *pixels* per inch, or *ppi*. When you print your file, the printer resolution setting (or multiple settings) is usually described in *dots* per inch, or *dpi*.

The ideal amount of detail and level of resolution depend on how you intend to use an image. If you're going to be displaying your photos on the Web, keep in mind that large files take forever to download and view, so you'll want to stick with a lower resolution of 72 ppi (72 ppi is the most common image resolution for monitor displays).

Three factors affect the way that an image is displayed on a computer monitor: the number of pixels in the image, the screen resolution, and the screen size (**Figure 2.3**). The size of each pixel is determined by the resolution and size of the monitor. For example a 17-inch monitor set to a resolution of 1024 x 768 pixels would have 82 pixels per inch (**Figure 2.4**). The same monitor set to a resolution of 640 x 480 would have fewer pixels per inch, so each pixel takes up more screen space (**Figure 2.5**). If you change your monitor resolution to a lower resolution setting, the images and icons become bigger on your screen. This is because fewer pixels occupy the same space, and so the size of each pixel becomes bigger.

Printer resolution is usually described by the number of dots per inch that the printer is capable of printing. If you want to print a high-quality flyer or photo, you may need a resolution as high as 300 ppi. Fortunately, a wide range of resolutions are available that work well for different types of situations, and Photoshop Elements includes some automatic functions (such as the Save for Web command) that take the guesswork out of the process.

17-inch monitor at 1600 x 1200 resolution

Figure 2.3 The display of an on-screen image is based on the resolution of the image, the size of the monitor, and the monitor resolution.

Figure 2.4 A monitor set to 1024 x 768 is a much more common setting, and allows program menus to be seen more easily.

Figure 2.5 The same monitor set to 640 x 480 displays fewer pixels per inch, so less of the image appears on your screen.

Figure 2.6 Click the New File button on the Welcome screen to create a new image.

Figure 2.7 The New File icon on the shortcuts bar offers another quick way to get started with a new file.

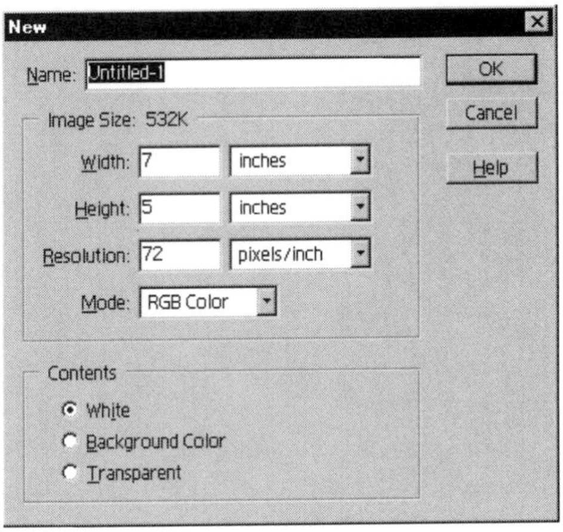

Figure 2.8 The New Image dialog box lets you name your new image and set its dimensions, resolution, and color mode.

Creating a New Image

Remember the many alternatives for opening files mentioned in Chapter 1? You have almost as many alternatives for *creating* a new file. Either way, you end up using the New Image dialog box to set up the basic dimensions, image resolution, and color mode. Creating a new file is like starting with a blank canvas. You can create your own work of art using Photoshop Elements' many painting and drawing tools, or you can assemble a collage of multiple images. But for now, we'll stick with the basics.

To create a new image:

1. To create a new image, click New File on the Welcome screen (**Figure 2.6**),

   or do one of the following:

   ▲ From the File menu, select New, or press Ctrl+N/Command+N.

   ▲ On the shortcuts bar, click the New file icon (**Figure 2.7**).

   The New file dialog box appears, presenting you with options for changing size, resolution, and file type.

2. In the New file dialog box, enter a file name; then enter dimensions for the width and height (**Figure 2.8**).

   The default size is 7x5 inches, which works perfectly fine as a starting point. You can always change it later.

3. Set the resolution and color mode.

   By default, Photoshop Elements automatically chooses a preset resolution and color mode for you. When you're first creating a new file, it's fine to use these default settings, as you can always change them later. If you want more information on color modes, see Chapter 3, "Changing and Adjusting Colors."

   continues on next page

CREATING A NEW IMAGE

4. Select one of the Contents radio buttons to choose the appearance for the bottom (or background) layer of the image.

White is the default background option and creates a pure white background layer for the image. This option is just fine for most purposes.

Background Color fills the background with the current background color, making this setting useful if you're creating a Web graphic and want it to match the background color of your Web page.

Transparent makes the first layer transparent and results in an image with no background at all—a good choice if you're creating an image for the Web and want it to appear transparent on the page.

For more information on Layers, see chapter 5, "Working with Layers."

✔ Tip

- Don't be intimidated by the sheer number of size, resolution and transparency settings available when you first create a new image. We'll cover all these in more detail as we progress through the book. If you're brand-new at Photoshop Elements, creating a new image is really just as simple as pressing Ctrl+N/ Command+N, accepting the default settings, and charging bravely ahead.

Importing Images from Cameras and Scanners

Digital cameras have revolutionized photography and are one of the main forces driving the need for products like Photoshop Elements. Over the past couple of years, the prices have dropped, while quality (as measured by higher resolution) has risen dramatically. Typically, these cameras come with their own software to help you browse and manage photos. You can choose to download these photos to your hard disk and then open them in Photoshop Elements, or you can connect directly to the camera from within Photoshop Elements and then select individual images for downloading.

Photoshop Elements even lets you capture frames from digital videos, with the new Frame From Video command. In order to capture video frames, you'll need to make sure your video is in a format that can be recognized. Supported Windows formats include .avi, .mpg, and .mpeg, and Macintosh formats include QuickTime and .mpeg.

Similar to digital cameras, scanners offer another way to get images into Photoshop Elements. They're ideal for getting family photos and other paper documents into the computer. You're not limited to photos, either. As long as you can fit it onto your flatbed scanner, you can scan almost anything your heart desires: letters, buttons, fabric, leaves, or clip art. You can also scan an image from within Elements itself, as long as your scanner's appropriate plug-in is located inside the Import/Export folder; this folder is inside the Plug-ins folder, which is located within the Photoshop Elements application folder on your hard drive.

Using Adobe's Online Services

You can use Adobe's Online Services feature to check for additional Photoshop Elements plug-ins and recipes. As long as you're connected to the Internet while you're working in Photoshop Elements, choose File > Online Services to view a list of new plug-ins and recipes, which you can then select and download to your computer. It's a good idea to check this feature from time to time, as Adobe frequently updates this service with new files.

You can also use this feature to upload your photos to an online photo service entirely within Photoshop Elements—you don't even have to launch your Web browser. For more information on uploading your photos to an online photo service, see "Using Online Photo Services" in Chapter 11, "Saving and Printing Images."

To import images from a digital camera:

1. Connect your digital camera to your computer using the instructions provided by the camera manufacturer.

Figure 2.9 The Import icon on the Shortcuts bar provides quick access to your digital camera.

2. To import images from a digital camera, click Connect to Camera or Scanner on the Welcome screen, *or do one of the following:*

   ▲ On the shortcuts bar, click the Import icon (**Figure 2.9**).

   ▲ From the File menu, choose Import.

   If you choose Connect to Camera or Scanner from the Welcome screen or use the shortcuts bar, you'll see a Select Import Source menu, and if you go to the File menu, the Import menu appears. Both work the same way.

3. Select your digital camera software from the menu list (**Figure 2.10**).

   Depending on your individual digital camera software and plug-ins, you may see a different menu choice here.

   Your camera software launches, displaying your photos (**Figure 2.11**).

4. Following your camera software directions, import and then open the digital images in Photoshop Elements.

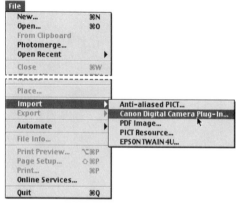

Figure 2.10 Choosing File > Import is another way for you to download photos from your camera.

Figure 2.11 Digital cameras usually include software to browse and select images, as with the Canon Image Browser shown here.

✔ Tips

■ If your camera software is not visible from the File > Import menu, check to make sure that your digital camera's plug-in is located in the Photoshop Elements Plug-ins folder.

■ When shooting pictures with your digital camera, it's always better to shoot it at the highest resolution possible. That way, you always start out with a high-quality original file, and you can always reduce the image resolution and file size later for output to the Web or a printer.

Compact Storage Cards

Almost all digital cameras ship with some sort of *compact storage card*—it's a thin, plastic card that stores your camera's digital data. The most common variety is the CompactFlash card; other compact storage cards include SmartMedia, Secure Digital Card (SD), and the MultiMedia Card (MMC). Sony uses its own proprietary storage format, called a Memory Stick.

As you snap photos, your digital camera's compact storage card acts as a virtual holding space for all your images. When you delete (or transfer and then delete) images from your camera, that memory space is freed up on your storage card, giving you more room for additional photos.

Most digital cameras include a cable that connects your camera to your computer for easy photo transferring. An alternate way to get photos into your computer is via a *storage card reader,* which you connect to your PC or Macintosh via a USB cable. Once you've installed the card reader software on your computer, just insert your compact storage card into the card reader to import your photos from your camera to your computer with a minimum of fuss.

To capture frames from video footage:

1. To capture still video frames, click Connect to Camera or Scanner on the Welcome screen, *or do one of the following:*

   ▲ On the shortcuts bar, click the Import icon and select Frame From Video.

   ▲ From the File menu, choose Import > Frame From Video (**Figure 2.12**).

   The Frame From Video dialog box appears (**Figure 2.13**).

2. Click the Browse button to locate the file you want, and then click Open to see the video footage (**Figure 2.14**).

   The video clip appears in the Frame From Video dialog box (**Figure 2.15**).

3. To view your footage, click the Play button. When you see the frame you want, click the Grab Frame button.

   In order the grab the frame you want, you can also use the Pause button to stop the video at the desired frame. Another useful option is to simply move the slider to the correct frame in the video.

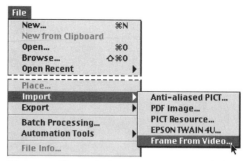

Figure 2.12 Choose the Import > Frame From Video command to convert movie footage into Photoshop Elements image files.

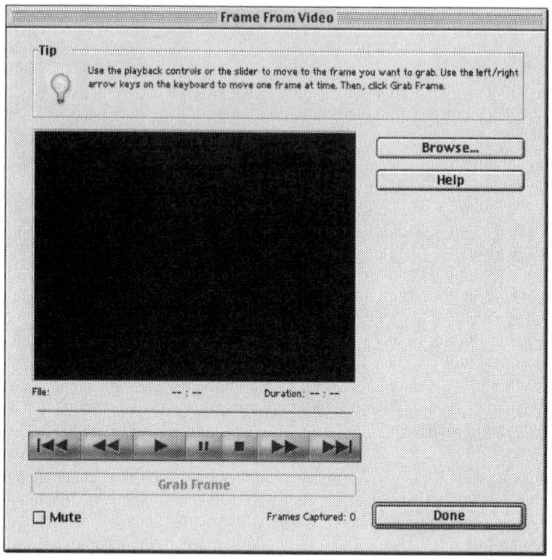

Figure 2.13 The Frame From Video dialog box lets you browse for and play movie files.

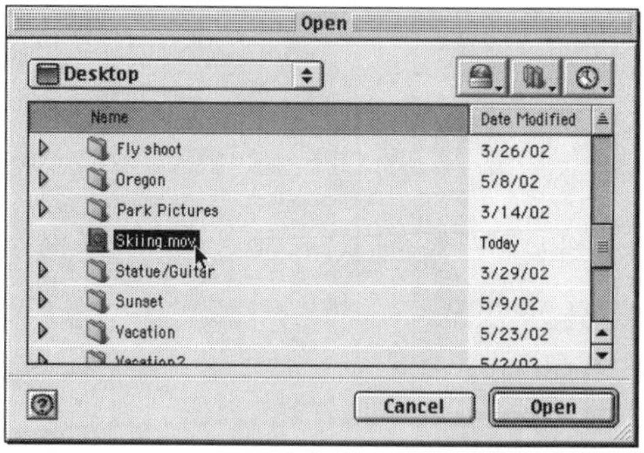

Figure 2.14 You can open any supported movie file format. Supported Windows formats include .avi, .mpg, and .mpeg, and Mac formats include QuickTime and mpeg.

Play button ─┐   ┌─ Pause button

Grab Frame button

Figure 2.15 After you open a movie file, it appears in the Frame From Video dialog box, where you can play, pause, and grab movie frames.

Figure 2.16 Captured frames automatically appear as Photoshop Elements images in your work area.

4. Grab as many video frames as you want, one by one, then click Done.

As you click the Grab Frame button, you will see the images appear as Photoshop Elements files in your work area (**Figure 2.16**).

5. Once you've captured the frames, you can save and edit them just like any other images.

✔ Tip

■ You'll likely have a greater variety of exposure problems with video frames than with the still shots you take with a digital camera. You can easily fix bad contrast and dark tones with a few of Photoshop Elements' correction tools, which we'll explore more in Chapter 3, "Changing and Adjusting Colors" and Chapter 6, "Fixing and Retouching Photos."

To scan an image into Photoshop Elements:

1. Connect the scanner to your computer using the instructions provided by the scanner manufacturer.

2. To scan the image, click Connect to Camera or Scanner on the Welcome screen, *or do one of the following*:

   ▲ On the shortcuts bar, click the Import icon.

   ▲ From the File menu, choose Import (**Figure 2.17**).

3. Select your scanner software from the menu list, and then follow your scanner's directions to complete the scan.

4. Import and open the digital images within Photoshop Elements.

✔ Tip

■ If you're planning to use only part of an image, you'll save yourself a lot of time if you use your scanning software to crop your image *before* importing it into Photoshop Elements (**Figure 2.18**).

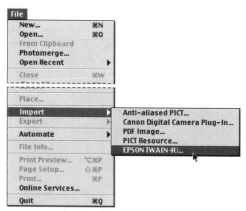

Figure 2.17 Choose File > Import to connect to your scanner.

Figure 2.18 Most scanning software allows you to choose a specific area of an image to crop to (left), so that your scan is already cropped when you open it in Photoshop Elements (right).

IMPORTING IMAGES FROM CAMERAS AND SCANNERS

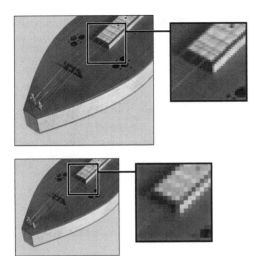

Figure 2.19 Here, an image was duplicated (top) then reduced 70% (bottom). Notice in the zoom views, that the reduced image isn't as detailed as the original. That's because though both have the same number of pixels per inch, the reduced image contains fewer pixels overall.

Changing Image Size and Resolution

Pixel dimensions, image dimensions, and resolution are all adjusted using the Image Size dialog box. Since you will often capture one image and then use it for different purposes, it's important to understand how these adjustments affect your image file.

For the Web and other on-screen viewing, it's common to adjust the pixel dimensions, or number of pixels, to control the resolution and/or file size of the image. This is known as *resampling*. The Resample Image check box is probably the most important feature to understand. When this box is checked, the pixel dimensions change—that is, the pixels will increase or decrease in number as the image is resampled (**Figure 2.19**). When the box is *not* checked, the pixel dimensions are locked in, and no resampling can occur— you can change the *document* size (the size the image will print) but the size the image displays onscreen will stay the same.

Recommended Resolutions

There are no absolute rules for the best resolution to use when scanning your images for the Web or for printing. The best approach is to try a couple of settings, using the following guidelines, and see what works well for your specific situation. Following are some typical situations and recommended resolution ranges:

◆ For on-screen viewing of Web images, 72 ppi is a standard and safe resolution.

◆ For color images printed on color ink-jet printers, a range of up to 150 ppi is often ideal. The exact resolution will depend on your printer and the type of paper on which you are printing.

◆ For color images to be used in printed materials, like a brochure or newsletter, you'll want a higher resolution, usually between 150 and 300 ppi.

If you want to create higher-quality professional projects, such as magazine or print design work, be aware that Photoshop Elements is not capable of producing CMYK files (the color-separated files used for high-end printing). If you need an image-editing program that can handle these kinds of jobs, you should consider buying the full version of Adobe Photoshop.

To resize an image for onscreen viewing:

1. From the Image menu, choose Resize > Image Size to bring up the Image Size dialog box.

2. Make sure the Resample Image box is checked (**Figure 2.20**) and choose an option from the Resample Image drop-down menu.

   When you resample an image, its pixels are transformed using a process known as an *interpolation*. Interpolation is a computer calculation used to estimate unknown values based on existing known values—in this case, pixel color values. So, when you resample an image in Photoshop Elements, its existing pixels are changed using one of three interpolation methods (**Figure 2.21**):

   Bicubic is the default option, and generally produces the best results and smoothest gradations.

   Bilinear produces medium-quality results.

   Nearest-Neighbor is the fastest method, but may produce jagged effects.

   Unless you're resampling a large number of files, then the resampling speed in not a major issue, so we recommend using the Bicubic option in almost all situations.

3. To maintain the current width-to-height ratio, make sure Constrain Proportions is checked.

4. Enter new values in the Pixel Dimensions fields. You can enter values in pixels or as a percentage (**Figure 2.22**).

   If you choose percentage, then you can enter a percentage amount (1-100) in either the Height or Width box to automatically scale the image to that percentage. The new file size for the image is displayed at the top of the dialog box (along with the old file size in parentheses).

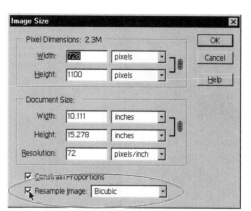

Figure 2.20 The Resample Image box includes three options for specifying how the resampling occurs.

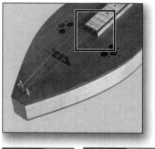

Figure 2.21 You can resample an image using one of three calculation methods: Bicubic (left), Bilinear (center), or Nearest Neighbor (right). Bicubic does the best job at retaining detail, and anti-aliasing, while Nearest Neighbor creates images with a rougher quality.

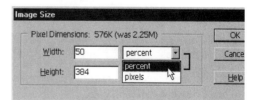

Figure 2.22 Pixel dimensions can be entered as pixels or as a percentage.

Figure 2.23 If you want to reduce an image's file size *and* display size, you can resize it by reducing its pixel dimensions, making it smaller for posting on the Web or e-mailing to friends.

5. Click OK to complete the change.

The image is resized larger or smaller, depending on the pixel dimensions or percentage you entered (**Figure 2.23**).

✔ Tip

■ When you change an image's size onscreen (by changing its pixel dimensions), you also change its print size, as indicated by the changed width and height dimensions in the Document Size fields of the Resize Image dialog box. While these images are acceptable as quick test prints, you may be disappointed with their printed quality. That's because you're discarding image information by resampling (see "Downsampling vs. Upsampling" sidebar, below) and in so doing, lose some sharpness and detail. If you're resizing an image mainly for print purposes, see "To resize an image for print" later in this chapter.

Downsampling vs. Upsampling

In Photoshop Elements, changing the resolution and/or size of an image by adjusting the number of its pixels is known as *resampling*.

Downsampling, which is the term for decreasing resolution by *removing* pixels from your photo, is one of the easiest and most common ways to make your files smaller. If you take an 8x10 photograph of your grandmother and shrink it to a 4 x 5 image by reducing its pixel count, you've just downsampled it. Photoshop Elements "throws away" unneeded pixels intelligently, with little or no visible impact to the quality of your image.

But *upsampling*, which is the term for increasing resolution by *adding* new pixels to your photo, should be avoided whenever possible. If you take a 4x5 photograph and try to enlarge it to 8 x10, then Photoshop Elements has to add pixels to your photograph. Since it has to manufacture those pixels out of thin air, so to speak, they add no real detail to your image. The end result? A distorted, jagged-edge, pixelated photo.

Since downsampling rarely detracts from the quality of your images, you should capture all your original files at the highest resolution possible, whether you're scanning an image or snapping a digital photo.

To resize an image for print:

1. From the Image menu, choose Resize > Image Size.

2. To maintain the current width-to-height ratio, select Constrain Proportions.

3. Uncheck the Resample Image box.

4. Choose a unit of measure (or choose percent to scale by a percentage) and then enter new values (**Figure 2.24**) for the width and/or height in the Document Size portion of the dialog box

   In the Document Size portion of the dialog box, the resolution value will change accordingly. For instance, if you enter width and height values of half the original image size, the resolution value will double, making the image appear clearer and sharper. That's because you're compressing the same number of pixels into a smaller space. So, when scaled at 50%, an image 4 inches wide with a resolution of 150 pixels per inch (ppi) becomes 2 inches wide with a resolution of 300 ppi.

5. Click OK to complete the change.

   The image's print size will be changed, but since it still contains the same number of pixels, it will appear to be unchanged on your screen. You can, however, view a preview of the final print size onscreen.

6. From the View menu, choose Print Size.

   The image will be resized on your screen to approximate its final, printed size (**Figure 2.25**).

7. From the View menu, choose Actual Pixels, or press Alt+Ctrl+0/Option+Command+0 to return the display size on your screen to 100%.

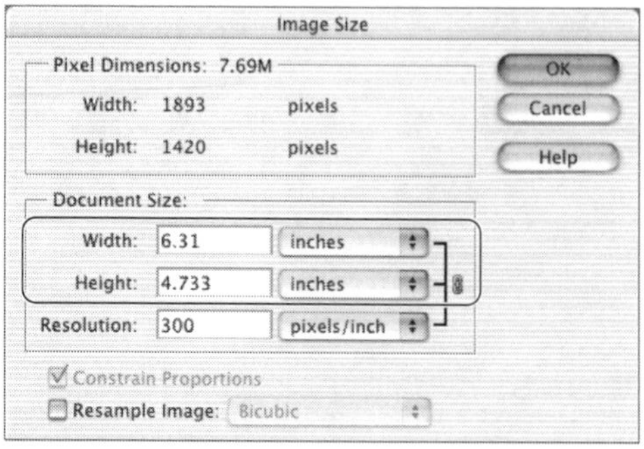

Figure 2.24 Enter new width and height values to change an image's print size.

Figure 2.25 An image can be viewed at an approximation of its final print size, even when its resolution differs from the computer's display.

✔ Tip

■ If things get really messed up and you want to return the dialog box to original settings, press Alt (Windows) or Option (Mac OS) to change the Cancel button into a Reset button. Then click Reset.

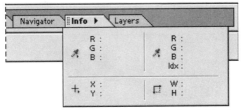

Figure 2.26 To view the Info palette, choose View > Show Info (as shown here) or click the Info palette tab.

Figure 2.27 The Info palette opens from its position in the palette well.

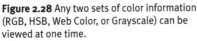

Figure 2.28 Any two sets of color information (RGB, HSB, Web Color, or Grayscale) can be viewed at one time.

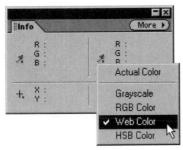

Figure 2.29 Color mode displays can be changed at any time from pop-up lists in the info palette.

Getting Information About Your Image

The Info palette displays measurement and color information as you move a tool over an image in the image window. In combination with the Eyedropper tool, you can use it to view the RGB (red/green/blue), Grayscale, and HSB (hue/saturation/brightness) values of your image. The Info palette is a very handy tool if you want to sample and then enter specific color values in the Color Picker (covered in detail in Chapter 3, "Changing and Adjusting Colors"). When an area is selected, this palette shows the position, angle of rotation, and scale, allowing you to control the precise placement and movement of selections.

The status bar displays file and image information, and in addition, the Windows version provides instructions on how to use any selected tool.

To use the Info palette:

1. To show the Info palette, click the Info palette tab or choose Window > Info (**Figure 2.26**).

   The Info Palette opens in the palette well (**Figure 2.27**).

2. To work in an image and view its information simultaneously, move the Info palette out of the palette well.

3. Select the desired tool and then move the pointer over the image. Depending on the tool you are using, the following types of information appear:

   ▲ The numeric values for the color beneath the pointer. You can view any two sets of color modes at the same time (**Figure 2.28**). Information for different color modes can be displayed at anytime by clicking either of the eyedropper cursor buttons in the Info palette (**Figure 2.29**).

continues on next page

▲ The x and y coordinates of the pointer, and the starting x and y coordinates of a selection or layer, along with the change in distance as you move the pointer over your image (**Figure 2.30**).

▲ The width and height of a selection or shape and the values relating to transformations, such as the percentage of scale, angle of rotation, and skew (which distorts a selection along the horizontal or vertical axis) (**Figure 2.31**).

✔ Tip

■ It can be quicker to change units of measure using the Info palette rather than by using the Preferences menu. Simply click the XY cursor icon (it looks like a plus sign) at the lower left of the palette to pick from a list of measurement options.

Figure 2.30 The x and y coordinates of the pointer are shown in the Info palette.

Figure 2.31 Any change in the scale or transformation of a selection or layer is visible in the Info palette.

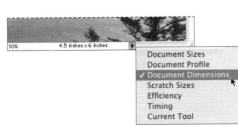

Figure 2.32 Here's the Status bar as it appears in the Macintosh version of Photoshop Elements. When you select an information option, the status bar (at the left of the selection) automatically changes to show the new information.

Figure 2.33 The Windows version of the status bar also includes helpful instructions on any selected tool.

To use the status bar:

1. On the status bar, click the triangle to open the drop-down menu (**Figure 2.32**).

2. From the drop-down menu, choose an option.

   You can view a variety of information options. Here are some of the most useful ones:

   Document Sizes displays information relating to the file's size. The first number represents the approximate size of the file if flattened (all layers combined into one) and saved. The second number represents the current file size, with layers.

   Document Profile displays the color mode of the image.

   Document Dimensions displays the width and height of the image.

   Scratch Sizes displays the amount of memory needed to process the image. The first number represents the memory currently used to display all open images. The second number represents the total, available RAM. If you think you're running into memory problems and need to add RAM, viewing the information here will help you evaluate the problem. (See Appendix B for more information on memory and scratch disks.)

✔ Tips

- Click the middle (blank) area of the status bar to quickly view a pop-up menu displaying the image dimensions, color mode, and resolution of your image.

- The Windows version of the status bar provides instructions on how to use any active tool (**Figure 2.33**).

GETTING INFORMATION ABOUT YOUR IMAGE

Opening and Arranging Multiple Views

The image window is where your image appears in Photoshop Elements. You can open multiple windows with different images, or, if you prefer, you can open multiple views of the same image. This is a very handy way to work on a detailed area of your image while viewing the full-sized version of the image at the same time. It's especially useful when you're doing touch-up work, such as correcting red eye or erasing a blemish in a photo.

Figure 2.34 Multiple image views let you work on a detailed area while viewing the overall results at the same time. Here, the zoomed image on the right offers better access for retouching the tree branches, while the image on the left lets us preview our changes in the full-sized photo.

To open multiple views of an image:

1. From the View menu, choose New View.

2. Drag the title bar to move the additional window(s) as necessary to view them simultaneously.

   You can set different levels of magnification for each window to see both details and the big picture at the same time (**Figure 2.34**).

Figure 2.35 Cascading windows overlap from the upper left to the lower right. They allow you to maintain many open images at one time without cluttering the work space.

Figure 2.36 In Windows, tiled windows are arranged side by side. Tiled windows let you work in multiple views of the same image simultaneously.

Figure 2.37 On the Macintosh, tiled windows are arranged in a stack, from top to bottom.

To arrange multiple views:

Do one of the following:

◆ To create cascading, overlapping windows from the upper left to the lower right of your screen, from the Window menu, choose Images > Cascade (**Figure 2.35**).

◆ (Windows only) To display windows side by side, from the Window menu, choose Images > Tile (**Figure 2.36**).

◆ (Macintosh only) To display windows stacked, from the Window menu, choose Images > Tile (**Figure 2.37**).

To close all windows:

Do one of the following:

◆ In the active window, click the close button on the title bar.

◆ To Close all document windows, from the File menu, choose Close All or press Shift+Ctrl+W/Shift+Command+W.

◆ To quickly switch from one open document to the next, press Ctrl+Tab.

OPENING AND ARRANGING MULTIPLE VIEWS

Using Rulers

Customizable rulers, along the top and left sides of the document window, can help you scale and position Photoshop Elements graphics and selections. The rulers are helpful if you are combining photos with text (for a greeting card, for example) and want to be precise in placing and aligning the various elements. Interactive tick marks in both rulers provide constant feedback, displaying the position of any tool or pointer as you move it through the window. You can also change the ruler origin, also known as the *zero point*, to measure different parts of your image.

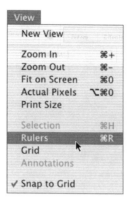

Figure 2.38 Choose Rulers from the View menu to toggle the rulers on and off.

To show or hide the rulers:

◆ From the View menu, choose Rulers to turn the rulers on and off, or press Ctrl+R/ Command+R (**Figure 2.38**).

Ruler units number down and to the right, starting from the zero point, where the two rulers intersect. To measure from a given spot in an image, you can move the zero point to anywhere within the document window.

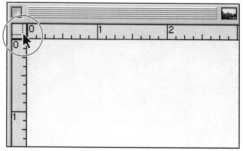

Figure 2.39 The rulers' zero point establishes the origin of the rulers.

To change the zero point:

1. Place the pointer over the zero point crosshairs, in the upper-left corner of the document window (**Figure 2.39**).

2. Drag the zero point to a new position in the document window.

   As you drag, a set of crosshairs appears, indicating the new position of the zero point (**Figure 2.40**).

3. Release the mouse button to set the new zero point.

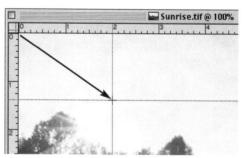

Figure 2.40 Drag the zero point to a new location anywhere in the document window.

✔ Tip

■ To reset the zero point to its original location, double-click the zero point crosshairs in the upper-left corner of the document window.

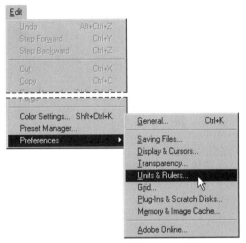

Figure 2.41 Choose Edit > Preferences > Rulers & Units to open the Rulers & Units dialog box.

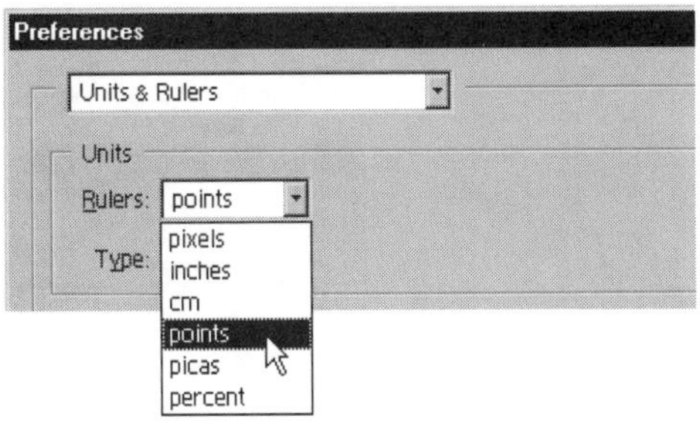

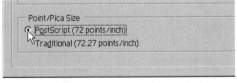

Figure 2.42 Rulers can be displayed in any of seven measurement systems.

Figure 2.43 Designate points in either PostScript or Traditional units.

To change the units of measure:

1. Open the Units & Rulers dialog box. To do so, *do one of the following:*

   ▲ Double-click a ruler in the document window.

   ▲ From the Edit menu, choose Preferences > Units & Rulers (**Figure 2.41**).

   In Mac OS X, Preferences is located under the Photoshop Elements menu.

2. In the Units area, from the Rulers pop-up menu, choose a unit of measure (**Figure 2.42**).

   The default setting is Inches. You can choose Pixels, to view the actual pixel dimensions in your image, in addition to other various unit options.

3. For the Point/Pica size, *choose one of the following:*

   ▲ PostScript (72 points/inch) (**Figure 2.43**).

   ▲ Traditional (72.27 points/inch).

4. Click OK.

✔ Tips

- With the advent of PostScript printing, the traditional measures of points and picas have become all but irrelevant. Most graphic design software companies base units of measure on PostScript settings rather than traditional points. Unless some special circumstance presents itself, you should leaving the Point/Pica Size option set to PostScript (72 points/inch).

- You can quickly change the rulers' units of measure without having to open the Preferences dialog box. Right-click (Windows) or Contol+click (Mac OS) on either ruler. You'll see a pop-up menu appear, and you can then choose a new measurement unit.

USING RULERS

55

Setting Up the Grid

The nonprinting, customizable grid appears as an overlay across the entire document window. As with the rulers, it can be used for scaling and positioning, but it can be especially helpful for maintaining symmetry in your layout and design, or for occasions when you'd like objects to snap to specific points in the window.

To show or hide the grid:

◆ From the View menu, choose Grid to turn the grid on and off (**Figure 2.44**).

To change the grid settings:

1. From the Edit menu, choose Preferences > Grid to open the Grid Preferences dialog box (**Figure 2.45**).

2. From the Color pop-up menu, choose a preset grid color, or choose Custom (**Figure 2.46**).

    Choosing Custom displays the color picker, where you can select a custom grid color.

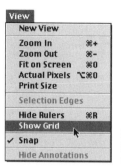

Figure 2.44 Choose View > Show Grid to display the document grid.

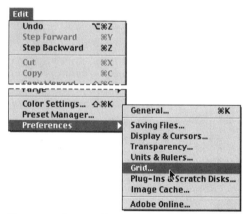

Figure 2.45 Choose Edit > Preferences > Grid to open the Grid Preferences dialog box.

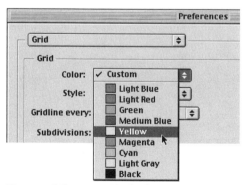

Figure 2.46 Choose a grid color from the list of preset colors or create a custom color.

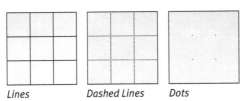

Lines   Dashed Lines   Dots

Figure 2.47 Examples of grid line styles.

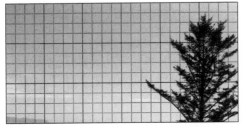

Figure 2.48 This figure shows a document grid with major grid lines set every inch, subdivided by four minor grid lines.

3. From the Style pop-up menu, choose a line style for the major grid lines (**Figure 2.47**).

4. In the Gridline Every pop-up menu, choose a unit of measure; then enter a number in the accompanying field to define the spacing of the major grid lines.

5. In the Subdivisions field, enter a number to define the frequency of minor grid lines (**Figure 2.48**).

6. Click OK.

SETTING UP THE GRID

CHANGING AND ADJUSTING COLORS

Almost any photograph can benefit from some simple color or lighting corrections. For example, you might find that a vivid sunset you photographed ends up looking more red than orange, or that an outdoor snapshot is too dark to make out any details. Luckily, with Photoshop Elements, you're never stuck with a roll of bad-looking film. Photoshop Elements provides a surprisingly powerful set of color correction tools, with both manual and automatic adjustments, so you can fine-tune your images as much as you want.

In this chapter, we review Photoshop Elements' color options and when you'll most likely want to use them. We also show you how to make sure colors display and print accurately (also known as *color management*) and how to correct the colors and tones in your images. Along the way, we also shed some light on why the most obvious color-enhancement options are not always the best choices for improving the color in your image.

About Computers and Color Models

No matter how your images got into the computer, whether from a scanner or a digital camera or copied from a stock art CD-ROM, the version of the image stored in the computer can only *approximate* the colors of the original scene. A computer, at its core, is only capable of dealing with numbers, so it somehow has to come up with numerical equivalents of the colors perceived by our eyes.

How does your computer come up with a number to represent color? There are several ways to do this, called *color models,* and one of the most common is the RGB color model. In this model, the color of each pixel is described as combinations of different amounts of the colors red, green, and blue. These colors were chosen because the cells in our eyes that respond to color, the "cones," come in three varieties; some are sensitive to red, some to green, and some to blue. Therefore, the RGB model tries to characterize colors in a way that's similar to the way the human eye works.

Again, the most important thing to remember is that color models, at best, can only *approximate* the colors in your image. No color model is as sensitive (or as opinionated) as the human eye.

Working with Color Modes

As you work in Photoshop Elements, you'll find that you may want to save your image in a different *color mode*. A color mode determines which color *model* will be used to display and print your images. Photoshop Elements includes four different color modes—roughly half the number of color modes included in Adobe Photoshop. This may seem like a significant limitation, but actually, you can create almost all of the same effects with just these few modes.

Most of the time you'll work in the RGB mode, as it's the standard, default mode in Photoshop Elements (as well as the most versatile), but you can convert to other color modes whenever necessary. For example you may want to convert an RGB image to grayscale to reduce its file size if you know the image will only be printed in back and white. And a grayscale image can be converted to a bitmap to create a more graphic, stylized look, and then colored or altered from there. Indexed color is used when you want to prepare images for viewing on the Web, and reduces the millions of colors possible in RGB mode to just 256 colors optimized for Web viewing.

RGB mode

As we mentioned earlier in this chapter, RGB stands for Red, Green, and Blue, which are the three color channels in your image (**Figure 3.1**). Not coincidentally, these are also the three color phosphors used in your computer monitor to display color. The combination of these three channels, viewed simultaneously, brings the full color in your image to life. It's important to understand this concept, as many of your color selection and correction options allow you to adjust these colors independently. (See the color plate section of this book for a full-color example of RGB mode.)

Red   *Green*   *Blue*

Figure 3.1 An RGB image is made up of 3 separate color channels: Red, Green, and Blue.

Grayscale mode

A grayscale image is not black and white, but is actually made up of 256 unique shades of gray. If you're creating an image that's destined to be printed in black and white, there are many advantages to converting it to grayscale. First, the conversion reduces the image down to just one color channel, and so the resulting image file size is about 1/3 of the RGB version. The result is that image-editing and printing within Photoshop Elements will all go a bit faster. Secondly, when you work on the image in Grayscale mode, it's easier to predict what the final black and white image will look like when printed.

Bitmap mode

An image converted to bitmap mode really *is* a black and white image, as during the conversion, each little pixel must make up its mind on whether it's black or white. The result is an image with a very graphic look that can be effective on its own, or modified even further with the painting and drawing tools (**Figure 3.2**). The Bitmap mode is also an effective approach if you're preparing an image for printing on a lower resolution, black and white printer.

Figure 3.2 You can convert any Grayscale image to a bitmapped image.

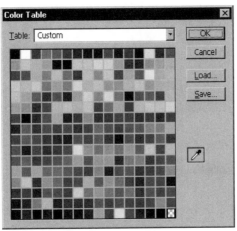

Figure 3.3 Indexed images are made up of 256 colors, as represented in the Color Table above.

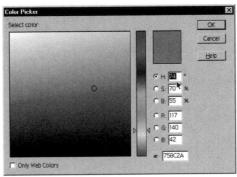

Figure 3.4 The Color Picker includes access to the Hue, Saturation, and Brightness (HSB) of your image.

Indexed mode

The indexed color version of an image is limited to a maximum of 256 colors, and is used when you're preparing images for viewing on computer monitors. Limiting the number of colors reduces the file size, allowing quick loading and display of images on Web pages. When you convert an image from RBG to indexed mode, Photoshop Elements creates a color table for the image, designed to represent the color palette of the image as accurately as possible. When the image contains colors not included in the color table, Photoshop Elements chooses the closest available color (**Figure 3.3**).

✔ Tip

- Ever wonder about the origin of those "millions of colors" described in all that marketing literature? Each of the red, green, and blue color channels contains 256 different color possibilities. When you multiply 256 x 256 x 256, the result is over 16 million colors.

The HSB Color Model

The RGB model isn't the only way to translate and interpret color. For some purposes, it's useful to describe color in terms of the HSB model. H represents the color's overall *hue* (how you'd characterize it in the color spectrum, such as "purple" or "teal"). S stands for *saturation*, the purity of the color, and B stands for *brightness*, or how light or dark the color is. Although you can't convert an image to HSB mode, you can make color selections and changes using either RGB or HSB within the *Color Picker* (**Figure 3.4**) and many of the color-adjustment tools covered later in this chapter. Say, for example, you want to color something bluish-green. How do you describe that in terms of red, green, and blue? If you're working in the HSB model, it's relatively easy. In the toolbox, click the foreground or background color selection box to access the Color Picker. Using the Color Picker, just click the H button, then find the basic color on the Hue slider, then choose the specific shade from the large square on the left, which shows all the variations of saturation and brightness within that hue.

Changing Color Modes

Before converting your file to a different color mode, it's a good idea to save a "master" version of your photo first. That way, no matter what changes you make to your image, you always have an untouched backup version, just in case.

To convert an image to grayscale:

1. From the Image menu, select Mode > Grayscale (**Figure 3.5**).

    A message appears asking "Discard color information?"

2. Click OK (**Figure 3.6**).

    The conversion discards all color information, resulting in an image with up to 256 shades of gray. (See the color plate section of this book for a full-color example.)

✔ Tip

- It's usually a good idea to save the RGB version of your image before converting to grayscale. But if you forget, and want to revert to the RGB mode to regain all that lost color information, just choose Edit > Undo Grayscale or press Alt+Ctrl+Z/ Option+Command+Z.

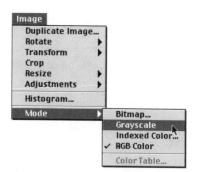

Figure 3.5 Choose Image > Mode > grayscale to convert an RGB image to grayscale. A Grayscale image is only about 1/3 the size of a RGB image.

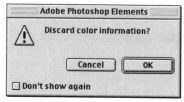

Figure 3.6 In order to convert from RGB to grayscale, you will discard the color information. Save a separate color version of your image to preserve colors.

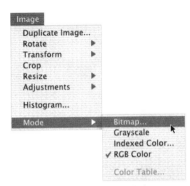

Figure 3.7 Choose Image > Mode > Bitmap to convert an image to bitmap (black and white) mode.

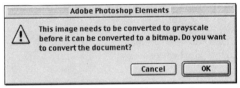

Figure 3.8 Before converting to bitmap mode, your image is converted to grayscale.

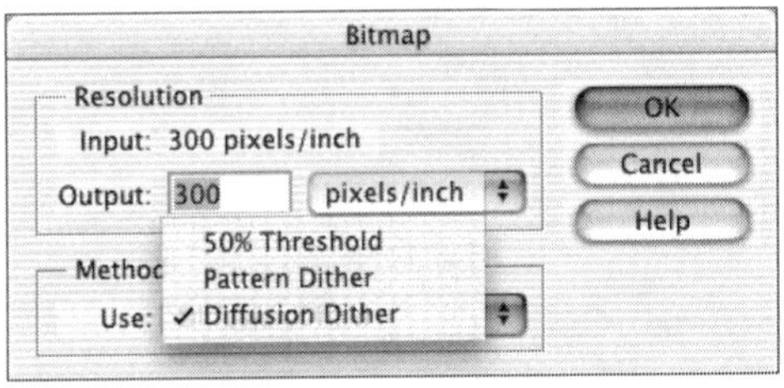

Figure 3.9 The Bitmap dialog box.

To convert an image to bitmap:

1. From the Image menu, select Mode Bitmap (**Figure 3.7**).

2. Click OK to convert the image to grayscale (**Figure 3.8**).
   The Bitmap dialog box appears (**Figure 3.9**).

3. If desired, enter a value for the output resolution.
   The default value is the current resolution of the image, which is usually fine for most purposes, and need not be changed during this conversion.

   continues on next page

4. Choose from one of the following three conversion methods to complete the bitmap conversion:

▲ **50% Threshold** converts pixels above medium gray to white, and below medium gray to black, resulting in a high-contrast image (**Figure 3.10**).

▲ **Pattern Dither** converts areas of gray into geometric patterns (**Figure 3.11**).

▲ **Diffusion Dither** results in a grainy, graphic look (**Figure 3.12**).

Figure 3.10 50% Threshold results in a high-contrast image.

Figure 3.11 Pattern Dither creates geometric patterns based on areas of gray.

Figure 3.12 Diffusion Dither results in a grainy, posterized look.

The History of Web-Safe Color

If you're familiar with the creation of graphics or images specifically for the Web, you may already know about Web-safe or browser-safe colors. For those of you new to this buzzword, Web-safe colors are the 216 colors that can be accurately displayed on all color computer monitors, regardless of age or platform. Here's the background.

Back in the pioneer days of the Web—in the mid 1990s—a lot of computer systems still used 256-color cards (also known as 8-bit color). This meant that the monitors on these systems could display only 256 colors at any given time. You (or your kids) may even still have a few CD-ROM games designed around this limitation; you'll know them because they ask you to change the display to 256 colors—in other words, to use the Web-safe palette.

But even though the palette consists of 256 colors, only 216 of those colors are considered Web safe. That's because Windows and Macintosh computers share only 216 colors, each reserving the remaining colors for system use. Thus, we're left with 216 colors that are guaranteed to appear with absolute accuracy, regardless of platform. Surprisingly, even using just these 216 colors, your images can come out looking pretty good.

Today, even the most basic PCs come out of the box with the ability to display thousands—or, more often, millions—of colors, and there are very few 8-bit systems still in use. However, because Windows and Macintosh computers display some colors a little bit differently, using the Web-safe palette is the only way to ensure that your colors look completely accurate on *both* systems.

Bottom line? If you're not concerned about folks running older computer systems, or the slight color differences in PC and Macintosh systems, then use all of the colors your glorious system came with. But if you want to make sure that absolutely *all* viewers can see your images in the exact colors you intended, stick to the Web-safe color palette.

To convert an image to indexed color:

1. From the Image menu, select Mode > Indexed Color (**Figure 3.13**).

   The Indexed Color dialog box appears.

2. Choose Palette, Dithering, and other options displayed in the dialog box (**Figure 3.14**).

   Palette options allow you to choose the best color palette, taking into account where the image will ultimately be viewed. See the sidebar "Indexed Color Palette Options" for a summary of the different Palette options.

   The **Forced** option lets you lock in specific colors so that they are not changed in the conversion process. You can choose to lock in **Black and White,** which is particularly useful if you have a large area of white or black in the background, as well as **Primaries** (white, red, green, blue, cyan, magenta, yellow, and black). Choosing the **Forced Web** option protects all 216 "Web-safe" colors in the palette from being altered.

✔ Tip

■ If all you want to do is convert your images for posting on the Web, you don't have to mess around with the Indexed Color dialog box. Instead, try using Photoshop Elements' Save for Web command, which takes a lot guesswork out of the process. See chapter 11, "Saving and Printing Images," for more information.

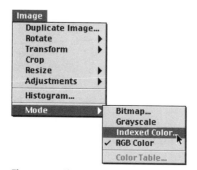

Figure 3.13 Choose Image > Mode > Indexed Color to convert an RGB image to Indexed Color.

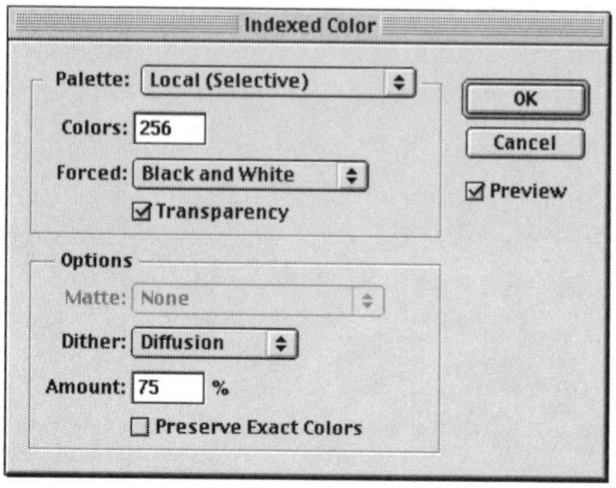

Figure 3.14 The Indexed Color dialog box includes options for choosing colors, palettes, and dithering. This figure shows the dialog box on a Macintosh.

Indexed Color Palette Options

Exact Choosing this option means that Photoshop Elements uses the exact same colors in your image to construct the color table. But this option appears only if your image contains fewer than 256 colors (such as an image in Grayscale mode).

System (Mac OS or **Windows)** Choose one of these options if you know that a majority of your users will be viewing your images on a specific computer system. (Macintosh and Windows monitors display the same colors slightly differently). This is also a useful option if you just want to see how your image will look when viewed on a computer system different from your own.

Web When you choose the Web palette, your image is limited to the 216 colors recognized by most Web browsers. Your image's colors will stay consistent, no matter whether it's viewed using Internet Explorer, Netscape Communicator, AOL, or any other Web browsers.

Uniform The Uniform color palette relies on its own even (uniform) sampling of 216 colors to make up its color palette. Unlike other color palettes, it doesn't look to your original image to try and approximate those colors.

Adaptive (Local and Master) This palette creates a color table based on the most frequently-occurring colors in your image. For example, if your image contains mostly red and orange colors, then the adaptive color palette will be composed of mostly reds and oranges. Use the **Local** setting if you're working on a single image. You'll rarely have to use the **Master** setting, unless you're working on multiple open images all sharing the same color palette.

Perceptual (Local and Master) This palette relies on color to which the human eye has the most sensitivity. Just as with the Adaptive palette, use the Local setting when working on a single image; use the Master setting when working on multiple open images all sharing the same color palette.

Selective (Local and Master) Places selective emphasis on Web-safe colors, which results in images with the best color integrity. This is the best choice for most images, and you'll find that this palette often appears as the default choice on the Palette pop-up menu. As with the Adaptive and Perceptual palettes, use the Local setting when working on a single image; use the Master setting when working on multiple open images all sharing the same color palette.

Custom Use this choice if you want to create your own custom color palette.

Managing Color

We've covered some color basics, but before going any further you may want to do a couple things to ensure that the color you see on your monitor will be reasonably accurate when you decide to print or send images to the Web. Luckily, color management in Photoshop Elements is very simple, and doesn't require any labor-intensive chores on your part.

First, you should make sure that the colors you see on the monitor are reasonably accurate, and represent with others will see on their monitors. Calibrating your monitor is a particularly good idea if you have an older monitor, or inherited it from a friend or relative (you don't know what they might have done to the monitor settings). If you have a newer monitor, it probably came with an accurate calibration from the factory. In that case, as you go through the steps below, you may find that no changes are needed.

If you prefer, you can also choose color settings optimized for either Web graphics or color printing.

To calibrate your monitor with Adobe Gamma (Windows and Mac OS 9):

1. In Windows, start Adobe Gamma which is located either in the Program Files/Common Files/Adobe/Calibration folder (Windows XP) (**Figure 3.15**), or in the Control Panels folder (Windows 2000 and earlier). On the Macintosh, select Apple menu > Control Panels > Adobe Gamma.

   The Adobe Gamma start screen appears. If you've calibrated your monitor before, you may be launched to the Gamma control panel directly. If so, go to step 3.

Figure 3.15 In Windows XP, the Adobe Gamma control panel is buried inside the Calibration folder in your hard drive.

Figure 3.16 The Adobe gamma utility can be used to calibrate your monitor for Windows and Mac OS 9. It includes a Step by Step mode which guides you through the monitor calibration process.

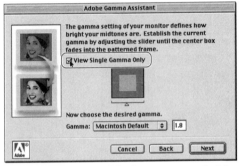

Figure 3.17 Setting up Adobe Gamma ensures that the color images on your screen are represented accurately. In this Macintosh dialog box, unchecking View Style Gamma Only lets you adjust the red, green, and blue values on your monitor.

color sliders ⌐

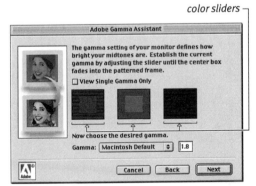

Figure 3.18 To make adjustments to the red, green, and blue values, move the color slider back and forth until the inside and outside boxes match as closely as possible. Usually the colors will match closest around the midpoint of the sliders range.

2. From the Adobe Gamma start screen, *do one of the following:*

▲ In Windows, click Step by Step (Wizard). On the Macintosh, click Step by Step (Assistant) to adjust your color settings using the on-screen instructions (**Figure 3.16**).

▲ Choose Control Panel, click Next, and follow the steps below.

3. When you come to the gamma settings screen, uncheck the View Single Gamma Only check box (**Figure 3.17**).

Three color boxes appear, representing the red, green, and blue colors displayed by your monitor (**Figure 3.18**).

4. Using the sliders, match the inner colors to the outer colors in the boxes.

5. Click OK (Windows), or click the close box (Mac OS 9) or close button (Mac OS X) in the upper left hand corner of the dialog box, then choose Save (Mac) to save your changes.

The monitor profile is saved in the profiles folder.

✔ Tip

■ It's very possible that you'll discover that your monitor settings were fine. In that case, you can choose Cancel (Windows) or Don't Save (Mac OS) when exiting the Adobe Gamma dialog box.

MANAGING COLOR

Color Management Is an Imperfect Science

As you start selecting and adjusting colors in Photoshop Elements, it's important to understand that the term *color management* can be a little misleading.

Color management operates under the assumption that we're creating artwork at our calibrated monitors under specific, controlled lighting conditions, and that our desktop printers work at peak performance at all times. In other words, it assumes controlled, uncompromised perfection.

At the time of this writing, the late afternoon sun is casting some lovely warm reflections off the blinds of the window and onto the wall directly behind my computer monitor, and is competing for attention with the glow from the 40-watt, soft-white bulb in my desk lamp. And therein lies the problem: the vast majority of Photoshop Elements users are working in similarly imperfect conditions.

In addition to trying to make a perfect science out of a host of imperfect variables, color management all but ignores one of the most imperfect sciences of all: our very human, very subjective perception. I may print out an image I find perfectly acceptable, while you may look at the same image and decide to push the color one way or another to try and create a different mood or atmosphere. That's what makes everything we create so different. That's what makes it art. And that's (at least in part) what makes color management an imperfect science. So, as you read through this chapter, keep in mind that your images will never look *precisely* the same when viewed by different users on different monitors.

And that's perfectly all right.

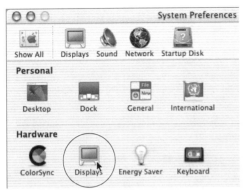

Figure 3.19 For Mac OS X, you can use the Display Calibration Assistant to calibrate your monitor. First click Displays on the System Preferences window.

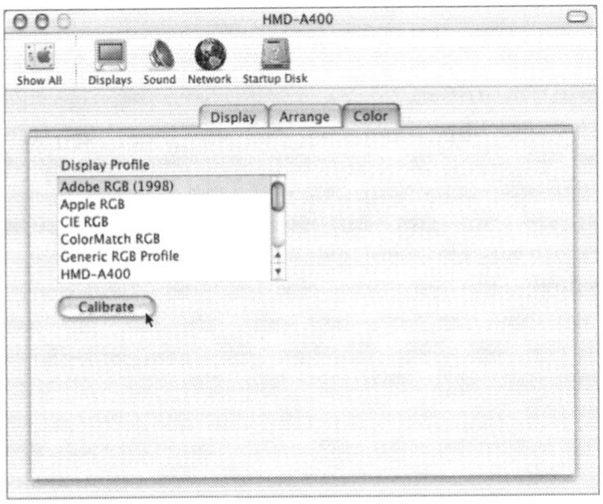

Figure 3.20 Click on the Color tab and then click Calibrate to start the Display Calibration Assistant.

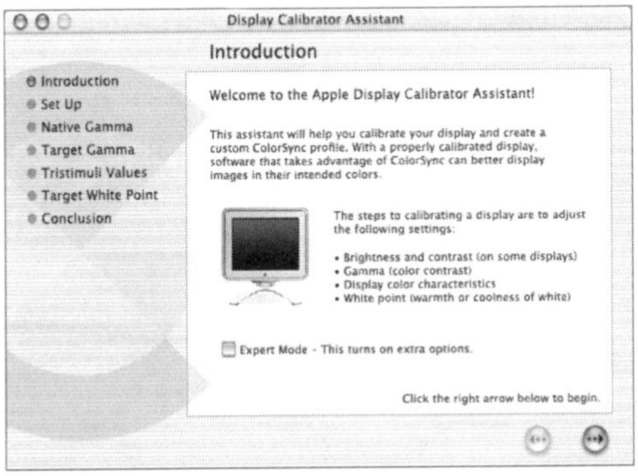

Figure 3.21 The Display Calibration Assistant guides you through the steps to calibrate your monitor.

To calibrate your monitor with the Apple calibration utility (Mac OS X):

1. From the System Preferences window, click Displays (**Figure 3.19**).

2. Click on the Color tab on the Displays window and then click Calibrate (**Figure 3.20**).

   The Display Calibration Assistant appears (**Figure 3.21**).

3. Follow the step-by-step instructions to calibrate your monitor.

✔ Tip

■ To ensure accurate calibration of your monitor, make sure that it's been on for at least 30 minutes. The colors may display slightly differently until the monitor is completely "warmed up".

MANAGING COLOR

To choose color settings:

◆ From the Edit menu, choose Color Settings (**Figure 3.22**).

The Color Settings dialog box appears, with three color-management options (**Figure 3.23**).

▲ If you have been using Photoshop Elements, are happy with the colors you're seeing, and don't want to change anything, then choose **no color management**. This is the default setting (and a perfectly acceptable option).

▲ If you are creating images which will be seen mostly on the Web, choose **limited color management**. You may want to try this option if you're not happy with the colors of your images when viewed on different monitors.

▲ To ensure that you get the most accurate colors for your printed images, choose **full color management**.

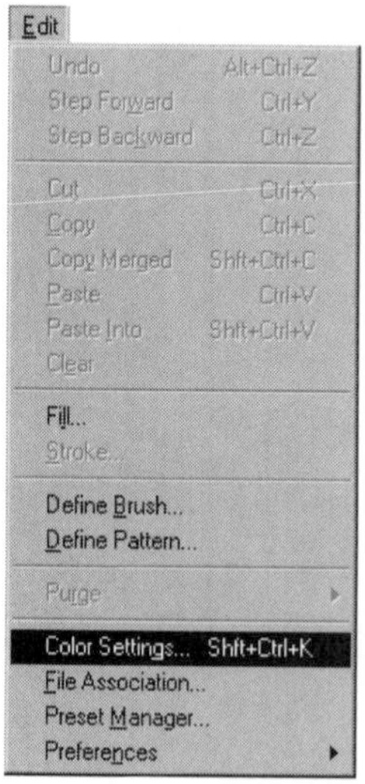

Figure 3.22 Choose Edit > Color Settings to bring up the Color Settings dialog box.

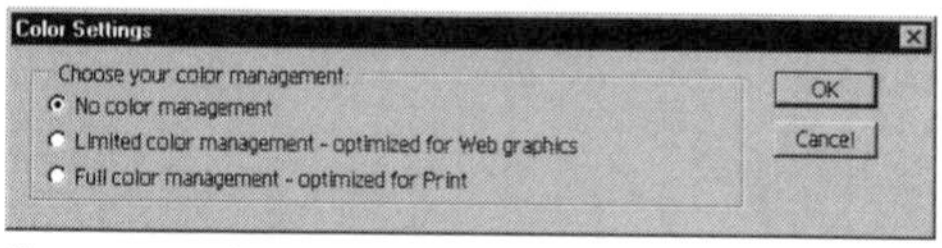

Figure 3.23 Choose a color management option best suited to the final output of your image.

About Tonal Correction

Tonal correction tends to be one of the least understood (and therefore most intimidating) features of Photoshop Elements. Mention levels and histograms and white points to even seasoned graphics professionals, and you'll see a number of eyes begin to glaze over. That's a shame, because there's really no special magic involved, and once understood, tonal correction can be one of the simplest and most instantly gratifying steps you can take to improving an image.

In plain terms (and whether you're working with a grayscale or color image) correcting tonal range simply comes down to adjusting brightness and contrast. Photoshop Elements offers several ways to make automatic brightness and contrast adjustments (see "Adjusting Levels Automatically" later in this chapter) but the most precise and intuitive method is by way of the Levels dialog box; and the heart of the Levels dialog box is the histogram.

Understanding histograms

The **histogram** is a graphic representation of the tonal range of an image. The lengths of the bars represent the number of pixels at each brightness level: from the darkest, on the left, to the lightest, on the right. If the bars on both sides extend all the way to the left and right edges of the histogram box, then the darkest pixels in the image are black, the lightest pixels are white, and the image is said to have a *full tonal range* (**Figure 3.24**). If, as in many images, the bars stop short of the edges, then the darkest and lightest pixels are some shade of gray, and the image may lack contrast (**Figure 3.25**). In extreme circumstances, the bars may be weighted heavily to the left or right, with the tonal range favoring either the shadows or highlights. Whatever the tonal range, the brightness and contrast of an image can be adjusted using sliders located beneath the histogram in the Levels dialog box (see "Adjusting Levels Manually" later in this chapter).

Figure 3.24 A photo displaying full tonal range, and its accompanying histogram. Note how the histogram extends all the way to the left and right, indicating that pure blacks are present in the darkest shadow areas and pure whites are present in the lightest highlight areas. The fairly uniform peaks and valleys throughout the middle portion of the histogram also indicates that there is sufficient pixel data present in the midtones.

Figure 3.25 Here's the same image, this time with insufficient contrast. Note how the histogram doesn't extend all the way to the left and right. This is an indication that both the darkest and lightest areas of the image are shades of gray, rather than pure blacks and whites. The shortage of high-contrast pixel data makes the image appear rather washed out.

Figure 3.26 The photo on the top lacks sufficient tonal range, particularly in the highlight and lighter midtone areas. The photo on the bottom, corrected with the Auto Levels command, reveals more detail in both the shadow and highlight areas as the pixels have been distributed across the full tonal range.

Adjusting Levels Automatically

Photoshop Elements gives you the option of applying a quick fix to image levels and contrast with the Auto Levels and Auto Contrast commands. Though we recommend working with the histogram in the Levels dialog box, the auto commands can be a good jumping off point before launching into more controlled, manual image correction. The auto commands tend to be most successful when applied to photographs that contain an *average tonal range*; one where most of the image detail is concentrated in the *midtones*. Midtones are those tonal values that fall about halfway between the darkest and lightest values. Midtone areas tend to contain more image information—more visible detail, that is—than extremely dark or light areas. That's why photographs with predominant midtones—whether in grayscale or in color—are usually the best candidates for auto correction. Severely over- or underexposed images may be beyond help. If the camera or scanner didn't capture the detail in the first place, it's not there to be corrected.

To apply Auto Levels to an image:

1. From the Enhance menu, choose Auto Levels, or press Shift+Ctrl+L/ Shift+Command+L.

   Photoshop Elements instantly adjusts the image's tonal range (**Figure 3.26**).

2. If you're not happy with the result, select Edit > Undo Auto Levels, or press Alt+Ctrl+Z/Option+Command+Z.

To apply Auto Contrast to an image:

1. From the Enhance menu, choose Auto Contrast (**Figure 3.27**), or press Alt+Shift+Ctrl+L/ Option+Shift+Command+L. Photoshop Elements instantly adjusts the image's contrast (**Figure 3.28**).

2. To undo, choose Edit > Undo Auto Contrast, or press Alt+Ctrl+Z or Option+Command+Z.

✔ Tip

■ As mentioned earlier, the auto commands work best in rather specific circumstances (as when the when the image's tonal range favors the midtones) and so should be used sparingly. The Auto Levels command, in particular, can yield some surprising and unexpected color shifts. In some instances it seems to overcompensate by swapping out one undesirable color cast for another, while in others it may ignore the color altogether in favor of throwing the contrast way out of whack. Give these a try, but be prepared to commit those Undo keyboard shortcuts to memory.

Enhance	
Quick Fix...	
Auto Levels	⇧⌘L
Auto Contrast	⌥⇧⌘L
Auto Color Correction	⇧⌘B
Adjust Lighting	▶
Adjust Color	▶
Adjust Brightness/Contrast	▶

Figure 3.27 Choose Enhance > Auto Contrast to apply an instant contrast fix to your image.

Figure 3.28 The photo on the top lacks sufficient contrast, so detail is lost in both the shadow and highlight areas. The photo on the bottom, corrected with Auto Contrast and containing both strong blacks and whites, reveals detail not present in the original.

ADJUSTING LEVELS AUTOMATICALLY

Figure 3.29 The Levels dialog box.

Figure 3.30 Moving the left slider underneath the left edge of the histogram spreads the darker pixels more evenly into the dark areas of the midtones and shifts the darkest pixels to black.

Adjusting Levels Manually

The Levels dialog box can do more to improve the overall tonal quality of your image than any other workspace in Photoshop Elements. Many images, whether scanned or imported from a digital camera, don't contain the full tonal range, and as a result lack sufficient contrast. That lack of contrast translates into loss of detail, usually most noticeably in the shadow and highlight areas. Using the histogram and sliders in the Levels dialog box, you darken the darkest pixels and lighten the lightest ones to improve contrast, then adjust the brightness levels in the midtones.

To adjust the tonal range:

1. From the Enhance menu, choose Adjust Brightness/Contrast > Levels, or press Ctrl+L/Command+L to open the Levels dialog box (**Figure 3.29**).

2. With the Preview box selected, drag the slider on the left until it rests directly below the left edge of the histogram graph (**Figure 3.30**).

   The image darkens as the darkest pixels in the image move closer to black.

continues on next page

ADJUSTING LEVELS MANUALLY

3. Drag the slider on the right until it rests directly below the right edge of graph (**Figure 3.31**).

The image lightens as the lightest pixels in the image move closer to white.

4. Drag the middle slider to the left or right to adjust the brightness level of the pixels that fall in the midtones.

5. Click OK to close the Levels dialog box.

✔ Tip

■ You may have noticed a topic conspicuous by its absence: The Brightness/Contrast command. That's because we never use it, and neither should you. Unlike Levels, which affects pixels in specific tonal ranges, Brightness/Contrast indiscriminately lightens or darkens pixels across the entire tonal range, typically creating more problems (such as contrast that's either too weak or too severe) than it solves.

Figure 3.31 The right slider affects the lightest pixels in the image. Moving the right slider underneath the right edge of the histogram spreads the lighter pixels more evenly into the light areas of the midtones and shifts the lightest pixels to white, resulting in more detail in the highlight areas.

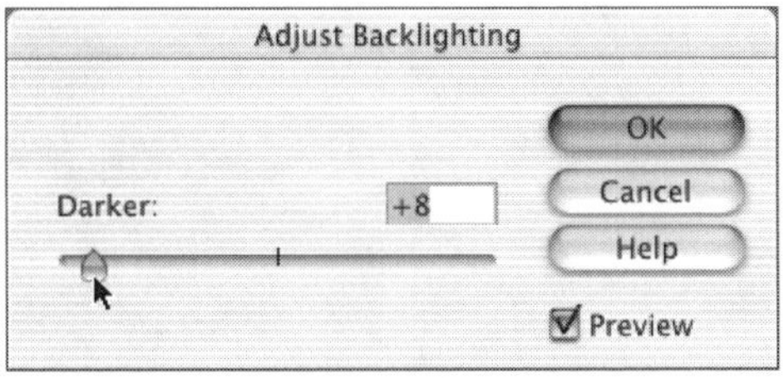

Adjust Backlighting

OK

Darker: +8   Cancel

Help

☑ Preview

Figure 3.32 The Adjust Backlighting dialog box.

Figure 3.33 The photo on the left suffers from an overexposed background. Applying the Adjust Backlighting command restores the detail of the background, mountains, and sky (right).

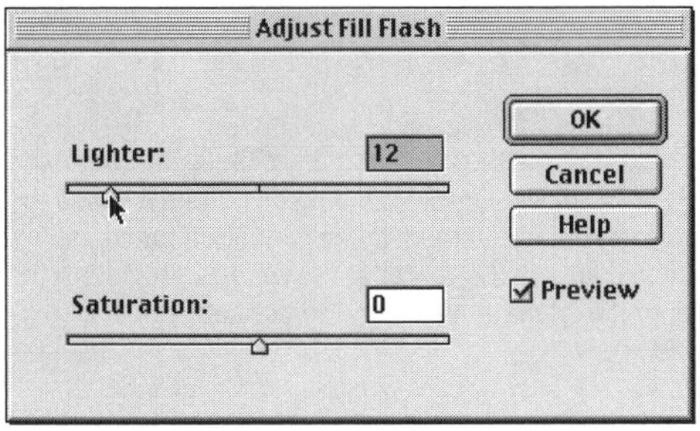

Adjust Fill Flash

OK

Lighter: 12   Cancel

Help

☑ Preview

Saturation: 0

Figure 3.34 The Fill Flash dialog box.

Lighting Your Image

Overexposed background images and under-exposed foreground subjects are a common problem for most amateur photographers. Photoshop Elements provides a couple of elegant little tools to help salvage your otherwise perfect compositions. Much like levels, they operate on pixels in specific tonal ranges (either highlights or shadows) while leaving the other tonal ranges alone. Adjust Backlighting darkens and adds detail to washed out background images, while the Fill Flash lightens and adds detail to areas in shadow.

To adjust the backlighting:

1. From the Enhance menu, choose Adjust Lighting > Adjust Backlighting.

   The Adjust Backlighting dialog box appears (**Figure 3.32**).

2. In the Adjust Backlighting dialog box, drag the Darker slider to the right until you're satisfied with the contrast and detail in the background or other brightly lit areas.

3. Click OK.

   The image now reflects your backlighting adjustments (**Figure 3.33**).

To use the Fill Flash:

1. From the Enhance menu, choose Adjust Lighting > Fill Flash, or press Shift+Ctrl+F/ Shift+Command+F (**Figure 3.34**).

continues on next page

LIGHTING YOUR IMAGE

81

2. In the Fill Flash dialog box, drag the Lighter slider to the right until you're satisfied with the contrast and detail in the foreground subject or other areas in shadow (**Figure 3.35**).

   As you use the Lighter slider, the color in the shadow areas may become a little washed out or faded. A second slider control is provided to help you make some subtle color correction.

3. Again in the Fill Flash dialog box, drag the Saturation slider until you're satisfied with the quality of the color in the image.

4. Click OK.

✔ Tip

■ Don't hesitate to use both Adjust Backlighting and Fill Flash on the same image. Photos with brightly lit skies and foreground subjects in shadow, for instance, are perfect candidates for applying both commands.

Figure 3.35 The photo on the left is a little underexposed in the foreground, and so the little girls' faces are hidden in shadow. Applying the Fill Flash command selectively brightens those areas in shadow to reveal the detail in their faces.

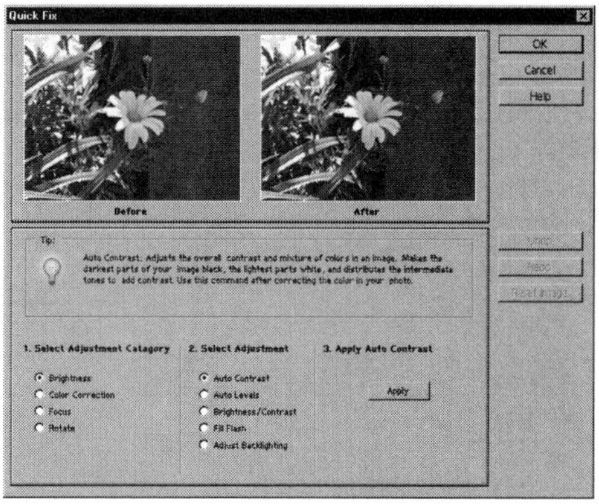

Figure 3.36 The Quick Fix dialog box offers a space to perform many common image correction functions. The Tip area in the center of the window provides helpful explanations of each adjustment you select and apply.

Image Correction One-Stop Shopping

New to Photoshop Elements 2.0 is the **Quick Fix** dialog box (**Figure 3.36**). Adobe has grouped a cross-section of some of the more commonly used commands and functions into one convenient, interactive workspace. Open the Quick Fix dialog box by clicking the Quick Fix button in the shortcuts bar, or choose Enhance > Quick Fix from the File menu. You select an adjustment category (like Brightness), then a specific adjustment (like Fill Flash), then use the supplied sliders or buttons to apply the adjustment to your image. Before and After views at the top of the dialog box help you monitor your progress, and buttons along the side provide multiple undo and redo functions, as well as the ability to reset the image and start over. In addition to Brightness and Color Correction, you'll also find adjustment categories for Focus and Rotation.

Figure 3.37 Choose Auto Color Correction from the Enhance menu to automatically remove color cast from your image.

Removing Color Cast

Color cast refers to a general shift of color to one extreme or another: an image can be said to have a yellow or red cast, for instance. While sometimes introduced into images intentionally (to create a certain mood or effect), colorcasts are usually unhappy accidents. They can result from any number of circumstances, from a scanner in need of calibrating to tired chemicals in a film developer's lab.

Thankfully, Photoshop Elements gives you a couple of ways to deal with color cast: a wonderful little automatic menu command, and a dialog box that allows you to manually color-correct your image by adding and subtracting color values in small increments.

To remove color cast with the Auto Color Correction command:

◆ From the Enhance menu, choose Auto Color Correction, or press Shift+Ctrl+B/Shift+Command+B (**Figure 3.37**).

That's it. Photoshop Elements does some elegant, behind-the-scenes magic, examining the image's color channels and histogram, then does a little math and *voilà*—no more color cast. (See the color plate section of this book for a full-color example or removing color cast.)

✔ Tip

■ We use this little feature all the time before starting into any other image correction. We're constantly amazed at how well this simple menu command works, and usually give it a try even if we don't perceive a color cast. It almost always offers some degree of improvement to the color.

To remove color cast with the Color Variations dialog box:

1. From the Enhance menu, choose Adjust Color > Color Variations.

2. Determine the color cast of your image.

   As Elements doesn't offer any help in determining color cast, you're pretty much on your own here. Look for clues to color cast in objects or areas you are familiar with and can make good, educated guesses on. Ask yourself if that bright blue sky is looking a little yellow, or if those leafy greens have a little pink tinge to them, then work from there.

3. In the lower portion of the dialog box, click on the thumbnail with the description that most describes what you need to do (Increase Red, Decrease Blue, and so on) while referring to the After view in the top half of the dialog box (**Figure 3.38**).

4. Continue to click any combination of thumbnails, as many times as necessary, until the After view looks the way you like.

5. Click OK, to close the Color Variations dialog box and view your corrected image.

✔ Tips

- To a large degree, using the Color Variations dialog box a matter of trial and error, and to a lesser degree a rather subjective process. And as much as we'd like to be able to provide some little hints or formulas, experience and experimentation are the real keys to success with this dialog box.

- If you find yourself completely lost, or just want to start over, click the Before thumbnail in the upper-left corner, or the Reset Image button along the right-hand side to reset the entire dialog box.

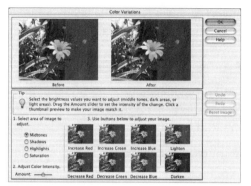

Figure 3.38 The core of the Color Variations dialog box is the lower, thumbnail button area. Each time you click a thumbnail you apply a slight color shift to your image. The thumbnails can be clicked any number of times and in any combination.

- The lower-left portion of the Variations dialog box can be all but ignored. The Shadows, Highlights, and Saturation modes can be a little unpredictable, so we tend to just stay with the default of Midtones.

- The Amount slider may be the one exception to the above tip. It controls the degree of change applied each time you click one of the thumbnails, and so can be helpful if you want to make subtle or extreme color changes.

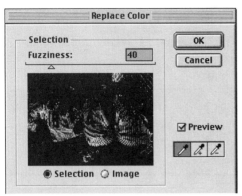

Figure 3.39 Buttons under the image preview box, let you choose whether to view your color selections or the image itself.

Figure 3.40 Click the actual image in the image window to make a color selection.

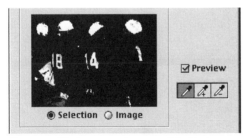

Figure 3.41 The image preview area of the Replace Color dialog box shows selected colors as white or shades of gray.

Replacing Color

The Replace Color command does just what you would expect it to do, and does it very well indeed. In a nutshell, it allows you to select a specific color, either across an entire image or in an isolated area of an image, then change not only the color, but its saturation and lightness values as well. Eyedropper tools let you add and subtract colors to be replaced, while a slider control softens the transition between the colors you choose and those around them. We've seen this used to great effect on projects varied as experimenting with different color schemes before painting a house's trim, to changing the color of a favorite uncle's tie so that it no longer clashes with his suit. (See the color plate section of this book for a full-color example.)

To replace color across an entire image:

1. From the Enhance menu, choose Adjust Color > Replace Color.

2. In the Replace Color dialog box, click the Selection button under the image preview box (**Figure 3.39**).

   When the Replace Color dialog box is open, your pointer will automatically change to an eyedropper tool when you move it over your image.

3. With the eyedropper tool, click in the image to select the color you want to change (**Figure 3.40**).

   The color selection appears as a white area in the image preview of the Replace Color dialog box (**Figure 3.41**).

4. To expand the selection and include similar colors, drag the Fuzziness slider to the right. To contract the selection and exclude similar colors, drag the Fuzziness slider to the left.

continues on next page

You may want to expand or contract your selection beyond the limits of the Fuzziness slider. If parts of a selection fall too heavily in shadow or highlight, or have very reflective surfaces, you may need to make additional color selections or deletions.

5. To add a color to the selection, Shift+click the eyedropper tool (Windows and Mac) in another area of the image. To subtract a color from the selection, press Alt+Click/Option+Click.

   The dialog box contains separate add and subtract eyedropper tools, but the keyboard shortcuts provide a much more efficient way to modify your color selections.

6. With the Preview check box selected, drag the Hue, Saturation, and Lightness sliders (**Figure 3.42**) until you achieve the desired color effect.

   These sliders operate just like the ones in the Hue/Saturation dialog box. The Hue slider controls the actual color change; the Saturation slider controls the intensity of the color, from muted to pure; and the Lightness slider controls the color's brightness value, adding either black or white.

7. Click OK to close the Replace Color dialog box and view your corrected image.

To replace color in a specific area of an image:

1. In the image window, make a selection around the specific area or object you want to apply the color change to (**Figure 3.43**) (see "Chapter 4: Selecting Areas of your Image").

2. From the Enhance menu, choose Adjust Color > Replace Color.

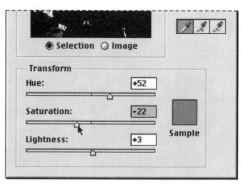

Figure 3.42 Drag the Hue, Lightness, and Saturation sliders until you capture the right color effect. You may have to experiment a little until you get it just right.

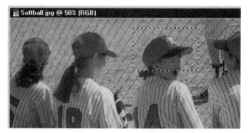

Figure 3.43 Any selections you make are reflected in the Replace Color dialog box.

Figure 3.44 Click the image within the Replace Color dialog box to make a color selection.

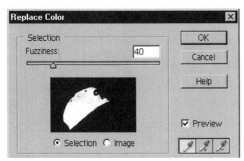

Figure 3.45 When the Selection button is clicked, the image in the preview box changes to show the selected colors as white or shades of gray.

3. In the Replace Color dialog box, click the Image button under the image preview box.

 A detail view of your selection appears in the image preview box.

 When the Replace Color dialog box is open, your pointer will automatically change to an eyedropper tool when you move it over your image in either the image window or the image area of the dialog box.

4. With the eyedropper tool, click in the image preview box of the Replace Color dialog box to select the color you want to change (**Figure 3.44**).

5. Click the Selection button to toggle to the Selection view.

 The color selection appears as a white area in the image preview (**Figure 3.45**).

6. To add or subtract a color from the selection, click the Image button to toggle back to that view, then use the keyboard shortcuts, as described in the previous procedure, to adjust the selection.

7. Use the Fuzziness slider to further fine-tune your selection.

8. With the Preview check box selected, drag the Hue, Saturation, and Lightness sliders until you achieve the desired color effect.

9. Click OK to close the Replace Color dialog box.

✔ Tip

- You can always choose to make your color selection in the actual image in the image window, just as we did in the previous procedure. But if the selections you're making are small, relative to the total size of your image, it's often easier to work within the confines of the Replace Color dialog box.

REPLACING COLOR

MAKING
SELECTIONS

Photoshop Elements offers many sophisticated options for enhancing and retouching your image—colors, filters, resizing tools, vignettes, and all sorts of special effects. But before you can start tinkering, you'll need to learn how to make selections. Once you've selected a specific area of an image, you can change its color, copy and paste it into another image, or change its size and rotation.

You can also use selections to create a protective mask for portions of your image. It's just as easy to select an area of your image and then apply changes to the rest of your image, keeping the selected area unchanged.

In this chapter, you learn about all of Photoshop Element's selection tools and when to choose one tool over another. You also learn how to use these tools in tandem to make the quickest and most accurate selections, depending on your specific needs.

About the Selection Tools

Often, you'll want to make changes and adjustments to just a part of an image. For example, you may want to eliminate a distracting element in your photo, or you may want to change the color of a specific item in a photograph or adjust the brightness of the background. Photoshop Elements gives you an almost unlimited number of selection tools from which to choose.

The selection tools are all grouped under three main icons on the toolbar (**Figure 4.1**). You make rectangular and elliptical selections with the **marquee** tools. When you select a marquee tool, the selection area is indicated by a row of moving dots, like the sign outside a movie theater, which is why these are called *marquee* tools (**Figure 4.2**).

You select freeform, or irregular, areas with the **lasso** tools (**Figure 4.3**). These include the regular Lasso tool; the Polygonal lasso, which is great for selecting areas that include straight sections; and the Magnetic lasso, which is good for selecting high-contrast areas in your image.

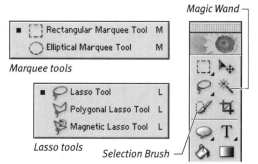

Marquee tools

Lasso tools   Selection Brush

Figure 4.1 The selection tools appear under three icons on the toolbar.

Figure 4.2 A selection border is represented by a row of moving dots, called a *marquee*.

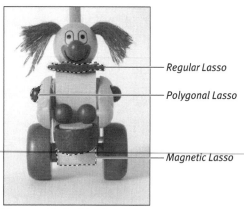

— Regular Lasso

— Polygonal Lasso

— Magnetic Lasso

Figure 4.3 Each of the three lasso tools works best in a particular situation.

Figure 4.4 The Magic Wand lets you selects areas based on their color.

Tolerance: 5   *Tolerance: 50*

Figure 4.5 The Magic Wand also lets you set the tolerance, or range of colors selected.

The **Magic Wand** lets you select areas with the same (or similar) color in your image. This is probably the most difficult tool to master, but with a little practice it allows you to make selections that are impossible to make with any of the other tools (**Figure 4.4**). For example, if your photo displays a field of yellow poppies, you can change all the poppies to red (or any color) without selecting each individual flower. The Magic Wand is a useful tool for making widespread color changes in your image.

While the selection tools often work well on their own, many times the area you want to edit will include all sorts of angles and edges. In these situations, you can use the tools together to expand and change the selection area.

You can also expand or contract a selection area using the same tool with different settings. For example, the Magic Wand allows you to alter the range of your selection by adjusting the tolerance using the options bar (**Figure 4.5**).

continues on next page

ABOUT THE SELECTION TOOLS

When your photo includes an object surrounded by a large background area, it's often easier to select the background and then invert the selection to select the object. Once the selection is made, you can copy and paste it into another composition or make any other changes (**Figure 4.6**).

You can adjust your selection area by adding to or subtracting from the selection. You'll often find it easiest to use one tool to make your initial selection and then edit the selection area with another selection tool (**Figure 4.7**).

Figure 4.6 Here, the white background was selected with the Magic Wand, and then the selection was inverted to capture the clown.

Figure 4.7 Here, the Elliptical Marquee tool was used to select the clown's head, and then the Lasso tool was used to select the clown's mouth.

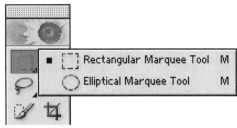

Figure 4.8 Simple geometric selections can be made with the Rectangular or Elliptical Marquee tools.

Figure 4.9 The default setting on the options bar creates a new selection.

Figure 4.10 After selecting one of the marquee tools, just click and drag to make a selection.

Using the Marquee Tools

The Rectangular and Elliptical Marquee tools are the easiest and most straightforward selection tools to use. With these tools, you can select rectangular or oval (elliptical) areas. You can also select a perfectly square or circular area. You will often want to move the selection area (or marquee) to get it aligned perfectly, and Photoshop Elements offers a couple ways to do this quickly and easily.

To make a rectangular or elliptical selection:

1. From the toolbar, choose either the Rectangular Marquee (M) or Elliptical Marquee (Shift-M) tool (**Figure 4.8**).

   The default setting on the options bar creates a new selection (**Figure 4.9**). See "Adjusting Selections" later in this chapter for more information on other options when creating selections.

2. Click and drag to choose the selection area (**Figure 4.10**).

continues on next page

USING THE MARQUEE TOOLS

✔ Tips

- To select a perfect square or circle, hold down the Shift key while making your selection (**Figure 4.11**).

- You can draw the marquee from the center outward by holding down Alt/Option (**Figure 4.12**).

- To toggle between marquee tools, press Shift+M. In fact, this works for any tool with hidden tools—simply hold down the Shift key while you press the keyboard shortcut to toggle through all of the choices.

- To select all pixels on a layer, press Ctrl+A/Command+A. This creates a selection around your entire image window, and is useful when you want to make universal color corrections or special effects to your image.

Figure 4.11 To select a perfect square or circle, hold down the Shift key while dragging.

Figure 4.12 To draw a selection from the center outward, hold down the Alt/Option key.

USING THE MARQUEE TOOLS

Figure 4.13 To move the selection area, position the pointer within the selection boundary.

Figure 4.14 Drag the selection border to a new location.

Original Position   *Repositioned*

Figure 4.15 To move the border during a selection, just press the spacebar while holding down the mouse button and adjust the border's location.

To reposition a selection border:

1. Once you've made a selection, and with the New selection icon active, position the pointer anywhere inside the selection area.

   The pointer becomes an arrow with a small selection icon next to it (**Figure 4.13**). Note that if the Add to, Subtract from, or Intersect with icons are active, then the pointer indicates that choice and the selection can't be moved.

2. Click and drag to reposition the selection area.

   The pointer arrow changes to solid black as you move the selection (**Figure 4.14**).

✔ Tip

■ You can use the arrow keys on your keyboard to move a selection in 1-pixel increments. Holding down the Shift key changes the movement to 10-pixel increments.

To reposition a selection border while making a selection:

1. Click and drag to create the selection area.

2. While keeping the mouse button pressed, press the spacebar.

3. Move the selection area to the desired location and release the spacebar and mouse button (**Figure 4.15**).

USING THE MARQUEE TOOLS

Selecting Areas with the Lasso Tools

You'll find yourself using the lasso tools to select areas with irregular shapes. The standard Lasso tool lets you draw or trace around an object or area in a freehand manner, much as you would draw with a pencil. This method takes patience, but with practice you can make very accurate selections with it.

The Polygonal Lasso tool is useful for selecting areas that include straight edges—and you can toggle between the freehand and straight-edge mode when your object includes both irregular and straight edges.

With the Magnetic Lasso tool, you trace around an area, and the tool automatically "snaps" the selection border to the edge of the area by looking for a change in color and contrast in the pixels. For this reason, this tool works best on high-contrast images. You'll want to experiment with the settings on the options bar to master this particular tool.

To select with the Lasso tool:

1. From the toolbar, choose the Lasso tool (L or Shift-L).

2. Keeping the mouse button pressed down, drag all the way around an object or area in your image (**Figure 4.16**).

   When you release the mouse button, the open ends of the selection automatically join together (**Figure 4.17**).

✔ Tip

■ Normally, if you lift the mouse button during a selection, the selection area will automatically close. To prevent this, hold down the Alt/Option key while you make your selection.

Figure 4.16 Select any area by tracing over it with the Lasso tool.

Figure 4.17 When you release the mouse button, the ends of the selection automatically join together.

Figure 4.18 The Polygonal Lasso tool creates a border made of straight-line segments.

Figure 4.19 If you make a mistake, just press Backspace/Delete to remove the last line segment.

Figure 4.20 For selection with both freehand and straight lines, press Alt/Option to switch between the regular Lasso and Polygonal Lasso tools.

To select with the Polygonal Lasso tool:

1. From the toolbar, choose the Polygonal Lasso tool (L or Shift-L).

2. Click points along the edge of the object to create straight-line segments for your selection (**Figure 4.18**).

3. Click the starting point to join the open ends of the selection.

   You can also Ctrl+click/Command+click or double-click anywhere on the image to close up the selection.

✔ Tips

- Be warned; the Polygonal Lasso tool can sometimes slip out of your control, creating line segments where you don't want them to appear. If you make a mistake or change your mind about a line selection, you can erase line-segment selections starting with the most recent one. Just press the Backspace/Delete key during the selection process, and one by one the segments will be removed (**Figure 4.19**).

- To use both the regular Lasso and Polygonal Lasso tools together, hold down Alt/Option when using either tool to toggle between the two modes (**Figure 4.20**).

To select using the Magnetic Lasso tool:

1. From the toolbar, choose the Magnetic Lasso tool (L or Shift-L).

2. Click on or very close to the edge of the area you want to trace to establish the first fastening point (**Figure 4.21**).

3. Move the pointer along the edge you want to trace.

   The Magnetic Lasso tool traces along the selection border to the best of its ability and places additional fastening points along the way (**Figure 4.22**).

4. If the selection line jumps to the edge of the wrong object, place the pointer over the correct edge and click the mouse button to establish an accurate fastening point (**Figure 4.23**).

5. To close the selection line, click the starting point, or *do one of the following:*

   ▲ Ctrl+click/Command+click.

   ▲ Double-click anywhere on the image.

   ▲ Press Enter/Return.

✔ Tip

■ Alt+click/Option+click to use the Polygonal Lasso tool while the Magnetic Lasso tool is selected. Alt+drag/Option+ drag to use the Lasso tool.

Figure 4.21 To start a selection border with the Magnetic Lasso tool, click the edge of the area you want to trace to create the first fastening point.

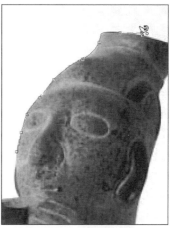

Figure 4.22 As you trace with the Magnetic Lasso tool, it places additional fastening points along the edge of the selection.

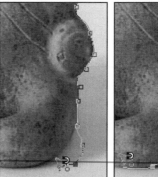

Selection off course   Selection reset

Figure 4.23 Sometimes the Magnetic Lasso tool jumps to another edge. To correct the path, just click the correct edge to bring the border back to the right location.

Figure 4.24 Look at the options bar while the Magnetic Lasso tool is selected; you'll find options that are unique to this tool.

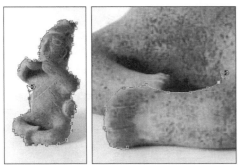

Width: 10 pixels   Width: 3 pixels

Figure 4.25 The Width option lets you set the width of the edge that the tool looks for to determine the selection edge.

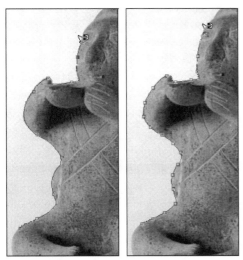

Frequency: 1   Frequency: 10

Figure 4.26 The Frequency option lets you determine how closely the fastening points are spaced.

To set Magnetic Lasso tool options:

1. Select the Magnetic Lasso tool.

2. Set any of the options visible on the options bar (**Figure 4.24**).

   ▲ Width sets the size of the area that the tool scans as it traces the selection line.

     You can set this option to a value from 1 to 40 pixels. Wide widths work well for high-contrast images, and narrow widths work well for images with subtle contrast and small shapes that are close to each other (**Figure 4.25**).

   ▲ Edge Contrast establishes the amount of contrast required between shapes for an edge to be recognized and traced.

     This option is indicated by the percentage of contrast (from 1 to 100 percent). Try higher numbers for high-contrast images, and lower numbers for flatter, low-contrast images (just as with the Width option).

   ▲ Frequency specifies how close the fastening points are to each other.

     For Frequency, enter a number from 1 to 100. In general, you will need to use higher frequency values when the edge is very ragged or irregular (**Figure 4.26**).

   ▲ If you are using a stylus tablet, you can select Stylus Pressure to increase the stylus pressure and so decrease the edge width. That's right: with the box checked, pressing on the stylus yields a smaller, more precise edge.

Using the Selection Brush Tool

The Selection Brush tool, new to Photoshop Elements 2.0, lets you brush over areas to make a selection. The brush options are very similar to the normal Brush tool, allowing you to choose from a wide range brush styles and sizes. So once you get familiar with either of these brush tools, you should feel pretty comfortable with the other.

The Selection Brush works a bit differently than the other selection tools. For one, when you are in Selection mode you can brush over any areas of your image to add to the selection. No need to click on an "Add to selection" icon, as these options aren't even included in the Options bar. And unlike the other selection tools, the Selection Brush includes a Mask mode, which allows you to create a "protected" or unselected area. To make it easier to work with masked areas, you can control the opacity and color of the mask overlay. The two modes can also be used together with great results. You will often find it easiest to make your initial selection, and then change to Mask mode to make final adjustments to your selection.

To make a selection with the Selection Brush:

1. From the toolbar, choose the Selection Brush (**Figure 4.27**).

2. On the options bar, choose to be in Selection mode (**Figure 4.28**).

3. Choose a brush style (**Figure 4.29**) and then enter values for the brush size and hardness.

   You can either enter specific values for the size and hardness, or just drag the slider (**Figure 4.30**) until you get the size you want.

Figure 4.27 The new Selection Brush tool is located on the toolbar.

Figure 4.28 To make a selection, choose the Selection mode option.

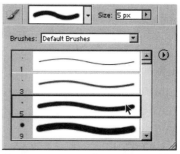

Figure 4.29 You can choose from a wide variety of pre-built brushes.

Figure 4.30 The brush size can be set from the options bar.

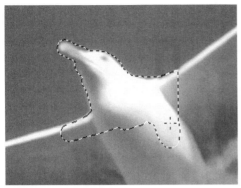

Figure 4.31 To make a selection, just "paint" over your image with the Selection brush.

Expand the selection   *New selection area*

Figure 4.32 You can expand the selection slightly by brushing next to the existing selection edge, or you can select a whole new area.

Figure 4.33 To make a mask, first select the Mask mode option.

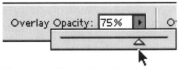

Figure 4.34 The opacity of your mask overlay can be set with the slider or entered into the text box.

4. Drag the brush tool over your image to make a selection (**Figure 4.31**).

To expand your original selection, just brush on the edge of the original area. To make a selection in another portion of your image, just move to that area and start brushing (**Figure 4.32**).

To make a mask with the Selection Brush:

1. From the toolbar, choose the Selection Brush.

2. On the options bar, choose to be in Mask mode (**Figure 4.33**).

3. Choose a brush style and then enter values for the brush size and hardness.

4. Set the overlay opacity with the slider, or enter a percentage in the text box (**Figure 4.34**).

continues on next page

5. Set the overlay color by clicking the Overlay Color box in the options bar, and then choose a color from the Color Picker (**Figure 4.35**).

The default color is red, and if your selection area is also red it may be hard to see. Just choose a color that works for you.

6. Drag the brush tool over your image to make a mask (**Figure 4.36**).

As soon as you select another tool, the mask overlay area changes to a selection border. The area is protected from any changes you apply to the image (**Figure 4.37**). Just as in Selection mode, you can paint over additional area in the Mask mode to expand the masked areas.

✔ Tip

■ The mask overlay is a very handy tool for inspecting your selections, and can be used with any selection tool. Whenever you have an active selection, just click on the Selection Brush tool and select the Mask option to see the masked area. When you're done viewing it in Mask mode, choose Selection from the pop-up menu.

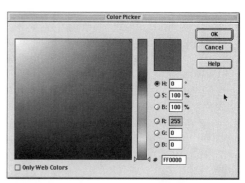

Figure 4.35 The mask overlay color can be changed from the default (red) to any color with the Color Picker.

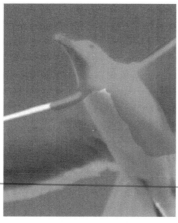

Figure 4.36 When you paint with the Mask option on, the area becomes filled with the mask overlay.

Figure 4.37 When you select another tool, the mask overlay changes appearance and becomes a selection area.

Figure 4.38 You can use a large brush size to quickly rough out your original selection.

Figure 4.39 When you change to Mask mode, the selection area becomes a mask.

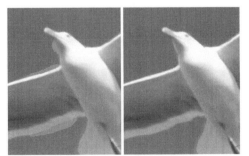

Before adjustments   *After adjustments*

Figure 4.40 In Mask mode, it's easy to see where the edge of your selection needs to be adjusted.

To adjust a selection using a mask:

1. From the toolbar, choose the Selection Brush, and make sure you're are in Selection mode.

2. Choose a brush style and enter values for the brush size and hardness.

3. Drag the brush over a selection area, in order to establish a quick, rough selection (**Figure 4.38**).

4. Change to Mask mode to see the mask overlay (**Figure 4.39**).

5. Fine-tune the edge of your mask, adjusting the brush size and hardness as necessary (**Figure 4.40**).

6. To edit the masked area, press Alt (Windows) or Option (Mac OS) while using the Selection Brush. You can remove any "painted" areas by working back and forth with the brush in this manner (**Figure 4.41**).

7. When you're satisfied with the mask, choose the Selection mode on the options bar.

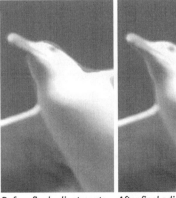

Before final adjustments   *After final adjustments*

Figure 4.41 You can toggle between mask editing modes pressing Alt (Windows) or Option (Mac OS). This allows you to quickly add to or remove the masked area.

USING THE SELECTION BRUSH TOOL

Making Selections by Color

The Magic Wand tool allows you to make selections based on a selected color. This tool can seem truly magical—or wildly unpredictable—at first. When you click an image with this tool, it selects all pixels within a color range close to the pixel you select. You control how closely the color must match (also known as the *tolerance*) to be included in the selection.

In addition to the tolerance, you can set options for anti-aliasing (smoothing), con-tiguousness (whether the pixels need to be connected to that first selected pixel), and whether all layers are included in the selection.

The Grow and Similar commands, found in the Select menu, can be used with the Magic Wand to expand the selection area. The Grow command expands the range of adjacent pixels, and the Similar command expands the selection based on the pixel colors.

To use the Magic Wand:

1. From the toolbar, choose the Magic Wand (W) (**Figure 4.42**).

2. On the options bar, choose whether to create a new selection, add to or subtract from an existing selection, or select an area where two selections intersect (**Figure 4.43**).
   The default setting on the options bar creates a new selection.

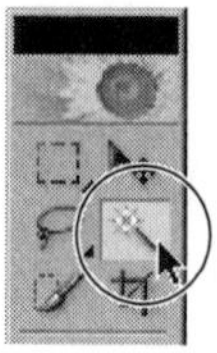

Figure 4.42 The Magic Wand icon is located right next to the Lasso tools on the toolbar.

Figure 4.43 The Magic Wand options bar.

MAKING SELECTIONS BY COLOR

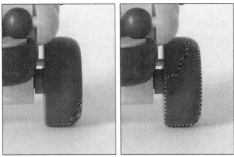

Tolerance: 5   Tolerance: 50

Figure 4.44 The Tolerance setting determines how wide a range of colors is included in the selection.

Contiguous on   Contiguous off

Figure 4.45 Choose Contiguous if you want the selection to include only adjacent pixels. Uncheck the box if you want to select all colors throughout the image.

3. Select the tolerance (a range of pixels from 0 to 255) to establish how wide a color range you want to include in your selection.

The default tolerance level is 32 pixels. To pick colors very close to the selected pixel, choose lower numbers. Entering higher numbers results in a wider selection of colors (**Figure 4.44**).

4. If you want your selection to have a smooth edge, select Anti-aliased.

5. If you want only pixels adjacent to the original pixel to be included in the selection, select Contiguous (**Figure 4.45**).

6. If you want the selection to include pixels on all the layers, select Use All Layers.

7. Click a color or shade in the image. Based on your settings, you will now see the selected pixels highlighted, which can now be edited as you like.

✔ Tip

■ When you make your original selection with the Magic Wand, it takes a color "sample" from your image. You can adjust the sample size with the Eyedropper tool. The Eyedropper options bar lets you sample 1 pixel, or the average of a 3-by-3-pixel area (9 pixels total), or a 5-by-5-pixel area (25 pixels total). Whatever option is active determines how the Magic Wand establishes the sample color.

MAKING SELECTIONS BY COLOR

To expand the selection area:

1. From the toolbar, choose the Magic Wand tool.

2. Click a color or shade in the image.

3. From the Select menu, choose Grow to expand the selection of adjacent pixels.

   Each time you select Grow, the selection is expanded by the tolerance amount displayed on the Magic Wand options bar (**Figure 4.46**).

✔ Tip

- You can also access the Grow command by right-clicking/Ctrl+clicking once you have made a selection with the Magic Wand. This brings up a dialog box with many other useful selection options (**Figure 4.47**).

Original selection: Contiguous unchecked

First Grow command: Contiguous unchecked, tolerance 50 pixels

Second Grow command: Contiguous unchecked, tolerance 50 pixels

Third Grow command: Contiguous checked, tolerance 20 pixels

Figure 4.46 In this example we set the tolerance to 50 pixels, with Contiguous unchecked for the first two Grow commands. To fine-tune the selection, we checked the Contiguous box, and reduced the tolerance to 20 pixels.

| Add To Selection |
| Subtract From Selection |
| Intersect Selection |
| Grow |
| Similar |
| Deselect |
| Select Inverse |
| Feather... |
| Layer via Copy |
| Layer via Cut |
| Last Filter |

Figure 4.47 After making a selection with the Magic Wand tool, right-click/Ctrl+click to access selection options.

Figure 4.48 Choose Select > Similar to add pixels to your selection.

To include similar colors:

1. From the toolbar, choose the Magic Wand.

2. Click a color or shade in the image.

3. From the Select menu, choose Similar to expand the selection of nonadjacent pixels.

   The selection is expanded by the tolerance amount set on the Magic Wand options bar (**Figure 4.48**).

Adjusting Selections

You can probably tell by now that creating most selections involves a little fine-tuning to get things just right. For example, imagine you're using the Polygonal Lasso tool to trace the outline of a face, but then realize you didn't include the ear in your selection. Rather than start all over again from scratch, you can simply add to or subtract from your selection until you've captured all the detail. Photoshop Elements also allows you to select the intersection (or overlapping area) of two independent selections. This comes in handy when making a selection, as the overlapping area may be something you'll want to work on independently.

Figure 4.49 To add to the current selection, either click Add to Selection on the options bar, or hold down the Shift key while making another selection.

To add to a selection:

1. Make a selection in your image with any of the selection tools.

2. With the selection still active, *do one of the following:*

   ▲ If desired, select a different selection tool, then click the Add to Selection icon (**Figure 4.49**) on the options bar.

     If the Add to Selection icon is already highlighted, skip to step 3.

   ▲ Hold down the Shift key, and, if desired, select a different selection tool.

     A plus sign appears, indicating that you are adding to the current selection.

3. Make a new selection in your image. If you want to add to your existing selection, make sure your new selection overlaps the original. If you want to create an additional selection, make sure you click outside of your original selection.

   The selection area expands based on the latest selection (**Figure 4.50**).

Figure 4.50 In this example, we added to the original selection using both the Magic Wand and Magnetic Lasso tools.

Figure 4.51 To subtract from the current selection, either click Subtract from Selection on the options bar, or hold down Alt/Option while selecting the area you want to subtract.

Figure 4.52 After the clown's nose is selected, it's removed from the selection.

Figure 4.53 For you to select an intersection, two selections must overlap.

Figure 4.54 Only the area of intersection remains.

To subtract from a selection:

1. Make a selection with any of the selection tools.

2. With the selection still active, *do one of the following*:

   ▲ Select the Subtract from Selection icon on the options bar and, if desired, choose any of the selection tools (**Figure 4.51**).

   ▲ Hold down the Alt /Option key.

   A minus sign appears, indicating that you are subtracting from the current selection.

3. Drag the pointer around the area you want to subtract.

   The selected area decreases based on the latest selection (**Figure 4.52**).

To select the intersection of two selections:

1. Make a selection with any of the Marquee or Lasso selection tools.

2. With the selection still active, *do one of the following*:

   ▲ Select the Intersect with Selection icon on the options bar and create a new selection that overlaps the current selection (**Figure 4.53**).

   ▲ Hold down Alt+Shift/Option+Shift and create a new selection that overlaps the current selection. An X appears, indicating that you are selecting an area of intersection.

3. A new selection area is formed based on the intersection of the two selections (**Figure 4.54**).

To deselect the current selection:

◆ From the Select menu, choose Deselect, or press Ctrl+D/Command+D.

To reselect the last selection:

◆ Choose Select > Reselect, or press Ctrl+Shift+D/Command+Shift+D.

To delete a selection:

Do one of the following:

◆ From the menu bar, choose Edit > Cut, or press Ctrl+X/Command+X.

◆ Choose Edit > Clear.

◆ Press Backspace/Delete.

When you delete a selection, the portion of the image within your selection disappears entirely, leaving a hole in your image (**Figure 4.55**). If you accidentally delete a selection, click the Undo icon on the shortcuts bar or press Ctrl+Z/Command+Z.

To hide a selection border:

◆ From the View menu, uncheck Selection, or press Ctrl+H/Command+H.

Sometimes, after you've made a selection, you will want to temporarily turn off the selection marquee in order to edit the image without the selection border obscuring your view. Be sure to press the same keyboard shortcut to display the selection once more—otherwise, you might go crazy trying to figure out where your selection went.

Figure 4.55 When you delete a selection, the selected area disappears, and your current background color shows through.

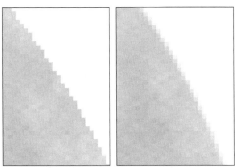

Anti-aliasing Off   *Anti-aliasing On*

Figure 4.56 Anti-aliasing automatically smoothes a selection edge by adding pixels that blend the color transition.

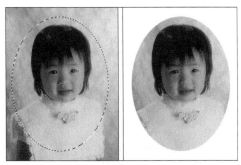

Figure 4.57 To use anti-aliasing, you must choose Anti-aliased on the options bar before making a selection. The resulting border is perfect for compositing with other images.

Softening the Edges of a Selection

When working with selections, you will often want to smooth or soften the edges of your selection before copying and pasting it into your final image. Anti-aliasing smoothes out the jagged edges of a selection by creating a color transition in the pixels along the edge (**Figure 4.56**). You will generally want to leave the Anti-aliased option on, to leave nice smooth edges on your selections. This is especially true if you are creating a composite (combination) image by copying and pasting selections from a number of photos.

Feathering blurs the edges of a selection. You set the amount of blurring on the options bar, in the Feather box. Unlike anti-aliasing, which affects only the edge and results in no loss of detail, feathering has more visible results, creating a soft, old-fashioned effect.

To smooth jagged edges with anti-aliasing:

1. From the toolbar, choose any selection tool.

2. Select Anti-aliased on the options bar. You must have anti-aliasing active before making your selection

3. Make a selection using the desired tool.

4. Cut or Copy and then paste the selection into a new file.

   The resulting selection edge is automatically smoothed, with no jaggies (**Figure 4.57**).

To feather the edge of a selection:

1. From the toolbar, choose from any of the Marquee or Lasso tools.

2. On the options bar, enter a value for the feather radius (from 1 to 230 pixels).

3. Make a selection.

   The resulting edge appears blurred, based on the number you entered for the Feather option (**Figure 4.58**).

✔ Tips

■ Unlike with anti-aliasing, you can apply feathering *after* you make a selection. With your selection active, from the File menu choose Select > Feather (Alt+Ctrl+D/Option+Control+D); then enter a feather radius.

■ You can also apply feathering effects to your image by applying the Vignette effect, available in the Effects palette. For more detail, see "To apply an effect" in chapter 7.

Figure 4.58 To get the vignette effect shown above, use the Elliptical Marquee tool to create a border. Then choose Select > Inverse to select the background. Next choose Select > Feather and enter a radius of about 10 pixels. Then, press Ctrl+Backspace (Windows) or Command+Delete (Mac OS) to complete the effect.

SOFTENING THE EDGES OF A SELECTION

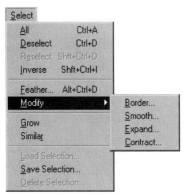

Figure 4.59 Choose Select > Modify to use the Border, Smooth, Expand, and Contract tools.

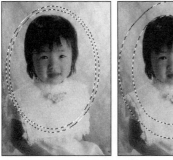

Border: 10 pixels   *Border: 40 pixels*

Figure 4.60 The Border command lets to control the width of a selection border. Normally, the border width is set to 1 pixel.

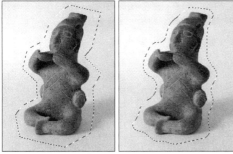

Smoothing: 1 pixels   *Smoothing: 10 pixels*

Figure 4.61 You can smooth the edge of a border with the Smooth command.

Modifying Selection Borders

You can make subtle—or significant—changes to a selection border with four options found on the Select > Modify menu (**Figure 4.59**). The *Border* command lets you change the width of the selection border. The *Smooth* command smoothes out a jagged or irregular selection edge. To make a slight increase in the size of a selection, use the *Expand* command. To reduce the selection area, use the *Contract* command.

To change the width of the border:

1. Make a selection in your image with any of the selection tools.

2. From the File menu, choose Select > Modify > Border.

3. Enter a value for the border width. The selection border changes based on the number you enter (**Figure 4.60**).

To smooth the edge of the border:

1. From the File menu, choose Select > Modify > Smooth.

2. Enter a value for the radius of the border. The radius value can range from 1 to 100 and defines how far away from the current edge the new outline can move to create a smooth edge. Lower numbers, from 2 to 5 or so, typically give good results (**Figure 4.61**).

MODIFYING SELECTION BORDERS

113

To expand or contract the selection area:

1. From the File menu, choose Select > Modify; then choose Expand or Contract.

2. Enter a value for the number of pixels by which you want to change the area.

   The selection border will expand or contract based on the pixel value you enter (**Figure 4.62**).

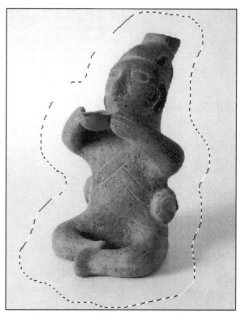

Expand: 20 pixels

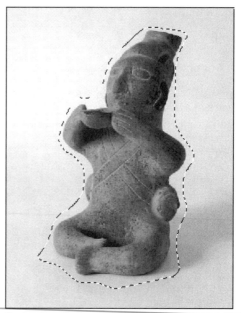

Contract: 10 pixels

Figure 4.62 You can smooth the edge of a border with the Smooth command.

WORKING WITH LAYERS

Photoshop Elements allows you to work on individual layers within your photos and to create, reorder, and rename these layers to your liking. As you get more comfortable with how layers work, you'll likely start to do more advanced tasks such as merging and grouping layers, and using adjustment layers to experiment with color adjustments without permanently changing the pixels in your images.

In this chapter, you explore how layers are created and how you work with them to get the results you want. The chapter concludes with a comprehensive look at the Undo History palette, which lets you undo any changes and return to saved states in the history of your image.

Understanding Layers

When you first import or scan an image into Photoshop Elements, it consists of just one default layer. You may find that in many cases, you'll just want to make a few simple changes to your photo and don't want to mess around with multiple layers. That's fine. But when you start working on images with any level of complexity, you'll find that layers make things a whole lot easier.

Layers act like clear, transparent sheets stacked on top of each other, and yet, when you view your image, they often appear as one unified picture (**Figure 5.1**). As you copy and paste selections, you may have noticed that these operations automatically create new layers in your image. You can edit only one layer at a time, which allows you to select and modify specific parts of your photo without affecting the information on other layers. This is the real beauty of layers: being able to work on and experiment with one part of your image while leaving the rest of it is completely untouched. One exception to this rule is Adjustment layers. These let you make color and tonal corrections to individual *or* multiple layers without changing the actual pixels.

Figure 5.1 Layers act like clear acetate sheets, where transparent areas let you see through to the layers below.

Figure 5.2 Selections float above your image in a sort of temporary layer, but once they're deselected, they become part of your image as a brand-new layer.

Floating Selections

When you make a selection in your photo, the active area is called a *floating* selection. A floating selection is like a temporary layer to which you can apply all sorts of transformations and effects. However, once the area is deselected, it must become a part of the image as a layer—it can be merged with an existing layer or become a new layer on its own (**Figure 5.2**).

UNDERSTANDING LAYERS

Figure 5.3 By default, an image with layers consists of a background layer, with additional layers named Layer 1, Layer 2, and so on.

Using the Layers Palette

When you launch Photoshop Elements for the first time, the Layers palette automatically appears on the right side of your screen, which is a good indication of how important layers really are.

Layers appear on the Layers palette in the same order as they appear in your image. The top layer of your image is the first layer listed on the Layers palette, and the Background layer is positioned at the bottom of the list (**Figure 5.3**).

If you spend any time at all working with layers, you'll find yourself constantly using the Layers palette. This is where you view and change the active layer, display and hide multiple layers, and lock layers to prevent changes (**Figure 5.4**).

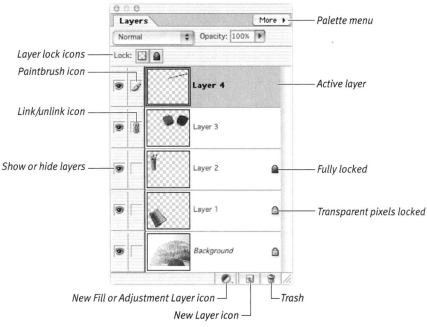

Figure 5.4 The Layers palette shows stacked layers exactly as they're arranged in your image, with the active layer on top. This palette gives you complete control over the stacking order of your layers, whether they're visible or hidden.

You can also view and change layer names and adjust the size of the thumbnail representations of those layers. On the Layers palette, you can select blending modes and set the opacity (transparency) of a layer. The palette includes quick access to many of the same commands found on the Layer menu.

To view the Layers palette:

Do one of the following:

◆ Choose Window > Layers.

◆ Click the Layers palette tab in the palette well.

You can choose to work with the open palette in the well, or drag it into your work area.

◆ Choose Window > Reset Palette Locations to return all of the palettes to their default locations, including Layers, which appears at the right.

To view the Layers palette menu:

Do one of the following:

◆ Click the triangle in the top right corner of the Layers palette.

◆ If the Layers palette is outside of the palette well, click on the More button (**Figure 5.5**).

◆ Select a command from the menu.

✔ Tip

■ To change the appearance of the layer thumbnail views, choose Palette Options from the Layers palette menu and click the size you want (**Figure 5.6**). The smaller the icon, the more layers you're able to view at one time on the palette. So if you find yourself working on images with lots of layers, the smallest thumbnail may work best.

Figure 5.5 Click the More button to display the Layers palette menu.

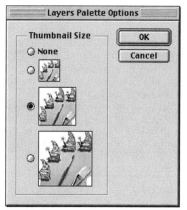

Figure 5.6 You can choose the size of the thumbnail views from the Layers Palette Options menu.

USING THE LAYERS PALETTE

Figure 5.7 Default layer names are Layer 1 for the first layer you create, Layer 2, Layer 3, and so on. You can enter a new name when creating a layer, or you can rename it later.

Layer Basics

When you first start working with layers, you need to master a few fundamental tasks. First, you can create and name a new layer and then add images (or parts of images) to it.

Once your image has multiple layers, you must first select a layer to work on the image. Keep in mind that any changes you make will affect only the selected, or *active* layer, and that only one layer can be active at a time.

To work more easily on your image, you can choose to show or hide any of its layers from the Layers palette.

To create a new layer:

1. From the Layer menu, select New > Layer, or press Shift+Ctrl+N/ Shift+Commmand+N.

2. In the New Layer dialog box, choose from the following options:

   ▲ Rename the layer with a more meaningful and intuitive name related to its contents. The default names are Layer 1, Layer 2, Layer 3, and so on (**Figure 5.7**).

   ▲ Choose a blending mode for the layer. The default blending mode is Normal, meaning that no change will be applied to the layer. This option is fine for most purposes. You'll often decide to experiment with blending modes later, by selecting the layer and making adjustments from the Layers palette.

   ▲ Choose the level of opacity for the layer. Again, opacity is something that's often adjusted later, from the Layers palette, so it's perfectly fine to stick with the default opacity mode (100%) for now.

To select a layer:

Do one of the following:

◆ On the Layers palette, click the Layer icon or name to make that layer active.

A paintbrush icon appears in the left column, indicating that this is the active layer (**Figure 5.8**).

If you've just imported an image from a digital camera or scanner, then by default it will only have one layer—the background layer, which is selected by default.

◆ Select the Move tool and right-click/ Control-click a location in your image.

A context-sensitive menu appears, showing all of the layers containing pixels in that specific spot (**Figure 5.9**). Select the desired layer from the context-sensitive menu.

✔ Tip

■ When you try to select or make changes to an area in your image, you sometimes may keep getting weird and unexpected results. For example, your selection can't be copied, or you apply a filter but nothing happens. More often than not, this is because you don't have the correct layer selected. Just refer to the Layers palette to see if this is the case. Remember that the active layer always has a paintbrush icon to its left.

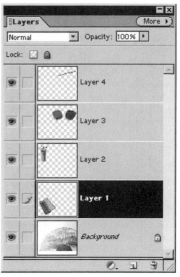

Figure 5.8 Click the layer name or thumbnail to make it the active (editable) layer.

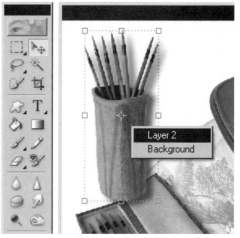

Figure 5.9 Right-click (Windows) or Control-click (Mac OS) to view and select layers from the context menu.

LAYER BASICS

Figure 5.10 Click the eye icon to hide a layer; click again to make the layer visible.

Figure 5.11 Choose Layer > Delete Layer from the Layer menu (or Layers palette) to delete a selected layer.

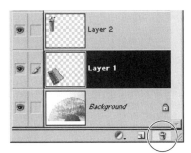

Figure 5.12 Clicking the trash icon also removes the selected layer.

To show or hide a layer:

◆ On the Layers palette, click the eye icon to hide the layer (the eye disappears). Click again to make the layer visible in your image (the eye reappears; see **Figure 5.10**).

✔ Tips

■ You can quickly show or hide multiple layers by simply dragging through the eye column.

■ To quickly display just one layer, Alt-click/ Option-click the eye icon for the desired layer. Alt-click/Option-click again to show all of the layers.

To delete a layer:

1. Select a layer on the Layers palette.

2. *Do one of the following:*

   ▲ From the Layer menu or the palette menu, choose Delete Layer (**Figure 5.11**).

   ▲ Click the Trash icon on the Layers palette (**Figure 5.12**) and then click Yes.

   ▲ Drag the layer to the Trash icon.

LAYER BASICS

Changing the Layer Order

The layer stacking order determines which layers are on top of the others and so plays a big role in determining how your image looks. As you build a composition, you may find that you want to change the layer order to work more easily on a particular layer and to get the final result you want. The actual, visible overlapping of elements is determined by the layer order, so you made find that you need to reorder layers frequently when you work on more complex images.

There are two main ways to change the stacking order of your layers. The most common and versatile approach is to drag the layer wherever you want in the layer stack. The second way is to select the Layer > Arrange menu and then choose commands such as Bring to Front and Send to Back— a method similar to what you use to arrange objects in a drawing program.

To change the layer order by dragging:

1. On the Layers palette, select the layer you want to move.

2. Drag the layer up or down on the Layers palette (**Figure 5.13**).

   You will see a thick highlight line between the layers, indicating the new layer position.

3. Release the mouse button when the layer is in the desired location.

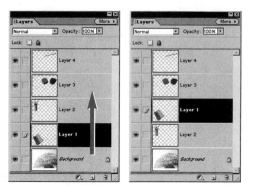

Figure 5.13 Drag a layer either up or down on the Layers palette to change its stacking order.

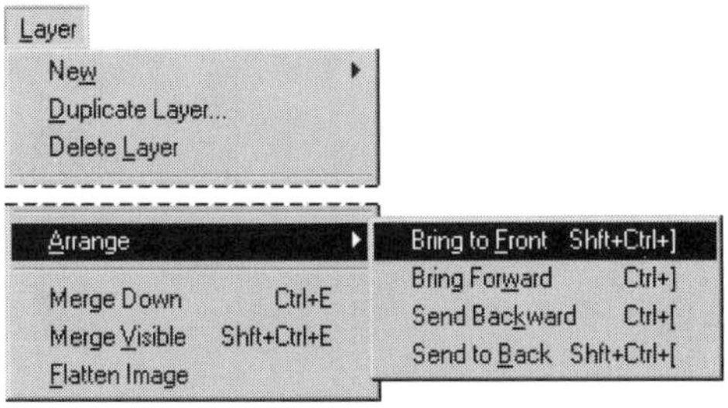

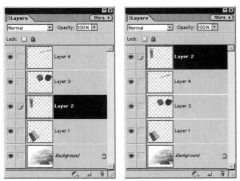

Figure 5.14 You can also change a layer's position using the options on the Layer > Arrange menu.

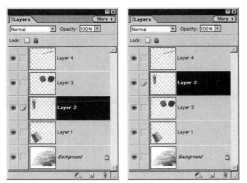

Figure 5.15 The Bring to Front command moves the layer to the top of the palette and to the top level in your image.

Figure 5.16 The Bring Forward command moves the layer up just one level.

To change the layer order by arranging:

1. Select the layer you want to move on the Layers palette.

2. From the Layer menu, choose Arrange and select one of the following options from the submenu, or use the keyboard shortcuts noted for each (**Figure 5.14**).

   ▲ Bring to Front (Shift+Ctrl+]/Shift+Command+]) moves the layer to the top of the Layers palette (and the image; see **Figure 5.15**).

   ▲ Bring Forward (Ctrl+]/Command+]) moves the layer up by one step in the stacking order (**Figure 5.16**).

   ▲ Send Backward (Ctrl+[/Command+[) moves the layer down by one step in the stacking order.

   ▲ Send to Back (Shift+Ctrl+[/Shift+Command+[) makes the layer the bottom layer on the Layers palette.

✔ Tip

■ If your image contains a background layer and you choose the Send to Back command, you'll find that the background layer stubbornly remains at the bottom of your Layers palette. By default, background layers are locked in place and can't be moved. To get around this, just double-click and rename the background layer to convert it to a functional layer, and then move it wherever you like.

Managing Layers

Photoshop Elements includes many of the same layer management tools found in Adobe Photoshop. As you add layers to an image, Elements assigns them a default numerical name (Layer 1, Layer 2, and so on). As your image becomes more complex, you'll usually find that renaming your layers takes a lot of guesswork out of managing your workflow. If you're adding a sky layer to your vacation photo, it's much easier to find a cloud image on a layer called *clouds* than it is to remember that the clouds are on Layer 14, for example.

You can also link layers together, so that any changes, such as moving and resizing, happen to two or more layers together.

And you can protect layers by locking them, to prevent changes. All layers can be fully locked, so that no pixels can be changed, or you can lock just the transparent pixels, so that any painting or other editing can happen only where there are already opaque (non-transparent) pixels present. This partial locking is useful if you've set up your image with areas you know you want to preserve as transparent, like for a graphic you want to incorporate into a Web page. And locking an image protects it in other ways, too: you can move a locked layer's stacking position on the Layers palette, but the layer can't be deleted.

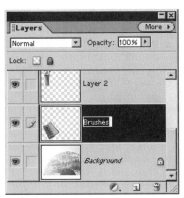

Figure 5.17 To rename a layer, just double-click its name on the Layers palette.

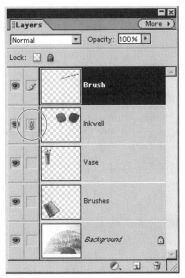

Figure 5.18 To link layers, first select a layer and then click in the link column for the layers you want linked.

To rename a layer:

1. Double-click the layer's name on the Layers palette to display the text cursor and make the name editable (**Figure 5.17**).

2. Enter a new name for the layer and press the Enter/Return key.

   The new name now appears on the Layers palette.

✔ Tip

- If you prefer, you can also use the Rename Layer command available on both the Layer menu and the Layers palette menu.

To link layers:

1. Select a layer on the Layers palette.

2. Click in the second column at the left of any layers you want linked to the active layer (**Figure 5.18**).

   The link icon appears in the column for the newly linked layer. You'll notice that this column is also used to display the paintbrush icon, which indicates the active layer The icon changes between the paintbrush and link icons, depending on the state of the layer.

MANAGING LAYERS

To lock all pixels on a layer:

1. Select the layer on the Layers palette.

2. Click the Lock All icon at the top of the Layers palette (**Figure 5.19**).

   The Lock All icon appears next to the layer name on the Layers palette (**Figure 5.20**).

To lock transparent pixels on a layer:

1. Select the layer on the Layers palette.

2. Click the Lock Transparent Pixels icon at the top of the Layers palette (**Figure 5.21**).

   The Lock Transparent Pixels icon appears next to the layer name on the Layers palette (**Figure 5.22**).

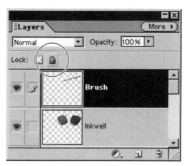

Figure 5.19 Select a layer and click the Lock All icon to prevent changes to any pixels.

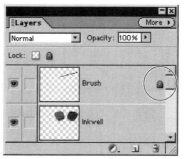

Figure 5.20 The Lock All icon indicates that the layers pixels are completely locked.

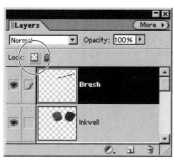

Figure 5.21 Select a layer and click the Lock Transparent Pixels icon to prevent changes to any transparent pixels in your image.

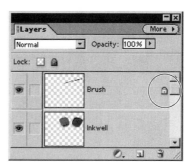

Figure 5.22 The Lock Transparent Pixels icon indicates that the transparent pixels are locked.

MANAGING LAYERS

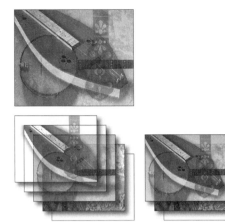

Figure 5.23 This photo collage (above left) was originally composed of three separate folk instrument layers, plus two background layers (lower left). To simplify the file, the three instrument layers were merged into a single layer (lower right). The finished collage will look the same, but because it's composed of fewer layers, its file size will be significantly smaller.

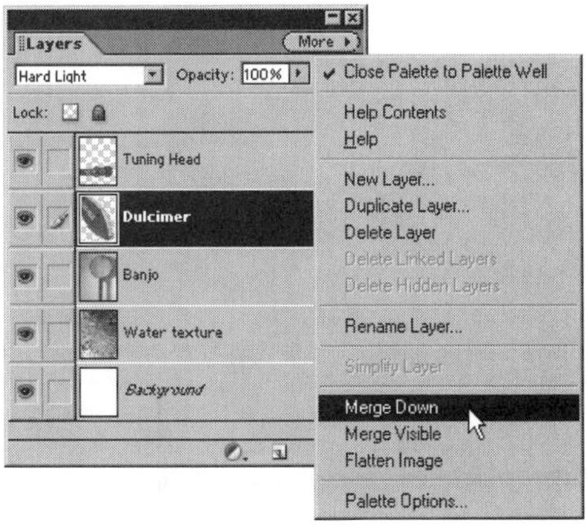

Figure 5.24 Combine a single layer with the layer below it by using the Merge Down command.

Merging Layers

Once you begin to create projects of even moderate complexity, the number of layers in your project can add up fairly quickly. While Photoshop Elements lets you create an almost unlimited number of layers, there are a couple of reasons why you may want to consolidate some or all of them into a single layer (**Figure 5.23**). For one thing, it's just good housekeeping. It doesn't take long before the Layers palette begins to fill up, and you find yourself constantly scrolling up and down in search of a particular object or text layer. And every layer you add drains a little more from your system's memory. Continue to add layers, and depending on available memory, you may notice a decrease in your computer's performance.

Photoshop Elements offers three approaches to merging image layers. You can merge just two at a time, merge multiple layers, or flatten your image into a single background layer.

To merge one layer with another:

1. On the Layers palette, identify the two layers you want to merge; then select the topmost of the two layers.

   Photoshop Elements will only merge two layers when one is stacked directly above the other. If you want to merge two layers that are separated by one layer or more, you'll need to rearrange their order in the Layers palette before they can be merged.

2. From the More menu on the Layers palette, choose Merge Down (**Figure 5.24**), or press Ctrl+E/Command+E.

   The two layers are merged into one layer.

MERGING LAYERS

To merge multiple layers:

1. On the Layers palette, identify the layers you want to merge, checking that the Visibility (eye) icon is on for each layer you want to merge.

2. From the More menu on the Layers palette, choose Merge Visible (**Figure 5.25**), or press Shift+Ctrl+E/Shift+Command+E. All of the visible layers are merged into one layer.

✔ Tip

■ You can create a new layer and then place a merged *copy* of all of the visible layers on that layer by holding down Alt/Option while choosing Merge Visible from the Layers palette's More menu. The visible layers themselves aren't merged and so remain separate and intact (**Figure 5.26**). This technique offers you a way to capture a merged snapshot of your current file without actually merging the physical layers. It can be a handy tool for brainstorming and comparing different versions of the same layered file. For instance, take a snapshot of a layered file, change the opacity and blending modes of several layers, and then take another snapshot. You can then compare the two snapshots to see what effect the different settings have on the entire file.

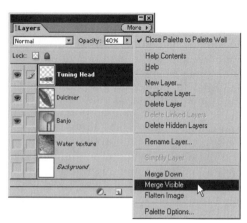

Figure 5.25 Combine any number of layers using the Merge Visible command.

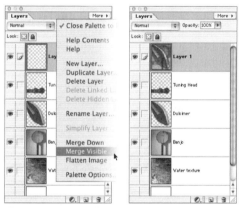

Figure 5.26 On the left, a new layer has been created at the top of the Layers palette. If you hold down Alt/Option while selecting Merge Visible from the palette menu, then all visible layers are merged and copied to the new layer, as on the right.

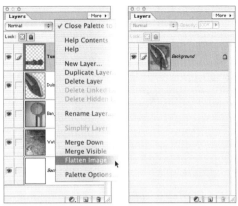

Figure 5.27 Combine all of the layers in a project into a single layer by using the Flatten Image command.

To flatten an image:

Do one of the following:

◆ If the Layers palette is in the palette well, click the triangle at the top of the palette tab.

◆ If the Layers palette is outside the palette well, click the More menu.

◆ Select Flatten Image.

◆ If any layers are invisible, a warning box appears asking if you want to discard the hidden layers. If so, click OK.

The entire layered file is flattened into one layer (**Figure 5.27**).

✔ Tip

■ If there's any chance you may eventually want to make revisions to your layered image, always create a duplicate file before flattening so that the layers are safely preserved in your original. Once you've flattened, saved, and closed a file, there's no way to recover those flattened layers.

Converting and Duplicating Layers

You now know that you can create a new layer using the Layer> New command; in addition, Photoshop Elements creates layers in all sorts of sneaky ways. For example, whenever you copy and paste a selection into an image, it's automatically added to your image on a brand-new layer.

When you start editing an image, you'll often find it convenient to create a selection and convert it to a layer to keep it isolated and editable within your photo. It's also quite easy to duplicate a layer, which is useful when you want to copy an existing layer as is, or use it as a starting point and then make additional changes.

The background layer is unique and by default can't be moved, but sometimes you will need to move it, change its opacity, or apply a blending mode. To do any of those things, you'll need to convert it to a regular layer. And sometimes you'll want to convert an existing layer to the background. While these conversions are not necessary for most simple photo projects, they are quite common when you combine or make composite images.

Figure 5.28 Any selected area can be converted to its own layer.

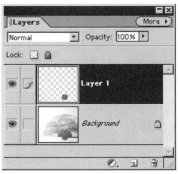

Figure 5.29 Choose Layer > New > Layer via Copy to copy the selection to a new layer.

Figure 5.30 Copying a selection to a new layer leaves the original selection unchanged.

Figure 5.31 The Layer via Cut command cuts the selection to a new layer.

To convert a selection to a layer:

1. Make a selection using any of the selection tools (**Figure 5.28**).

2. From the Layer menu, choose New; *then choose one of the following commands:*

   ▲ To copy the selection, choose Layer via Copy (Ctrl+J/Command+J) (**Figure 5.29**).

   The selection is copied to a new layer, leaving the original selection unchanged (**Figure 5.30**).

   ▲ To cut the selection, choose Layer via Cut (Shift+Ctrl+J/Shift+Command+J)

   The selection is cut to a new layer, leaving a gaping hole in the original layer, with the current background color showing through (**Figure 5.31**).

CONVERTING AND DUPLICATING LAYERS

To duplicate a layer:

1. Select the layer on the Layers palette.

2. Duplicate the layer using *one of the following methods:*

   ▲ If you want to create a new name for the layer, choose Layer > Duplicate Layer.

   The Duplicate Layer dialog box appears, where you can rename the layer (**Figure 5.32**). Note that you can also get to this dialog box from the Layers palette menu.

   ▲ If you're not concerned with renaming the layer right now, just drag the selected layer to the New Layer icon on the Layers palette (**Figure 5.33**).

   The new layer appears right above the previous layer with a "copy" designation added to the layer name (**Figure 5.34**).

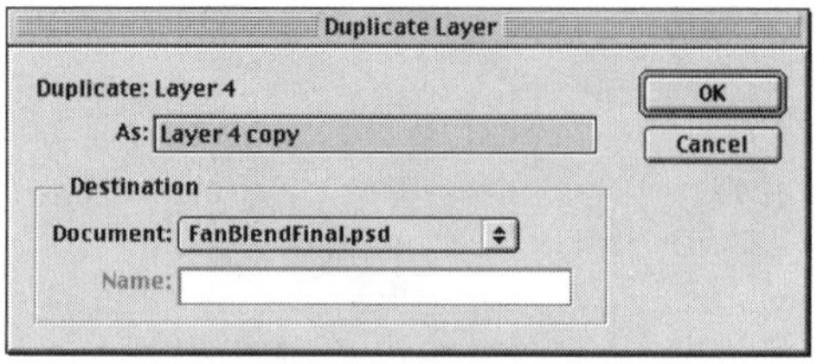

To convert a background to a layer:

1. From the Layer menu, choose New > Layer from Background.

2. If desired, type a new name for the layer and click OK (**Figure 5.35**).

✔ Tip

■ You can also convert the background by double-clicking the background on the Layers palette, which brings up the same New Layer dialog box.

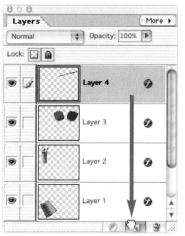

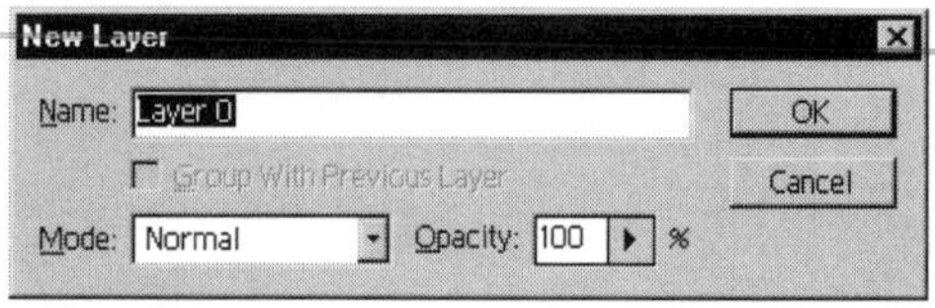

Figure 5.32 Use the Duplicate Layer dialog box to rename your new duplicate layer.

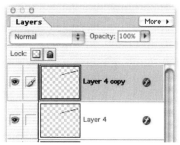

Figure 5.33 You can also duplicate a layer by dragging any existing layer to the New Layer icon on the Layers palette.

Figure 5.34 The new layer appears right above the original layer on the Layers palette.

Figure 5.35 You can convert the background to a layer and rename it during the conversion.

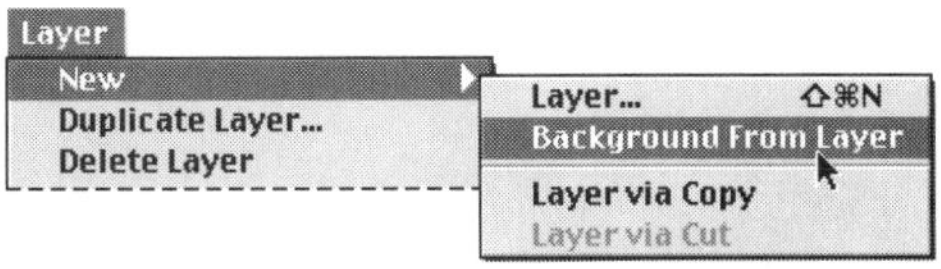

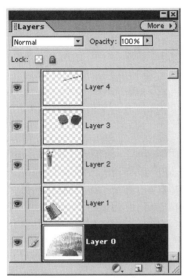

Figure 5.36 You can convert a layer to a background by choosing Layer > New > Background From Layer.

Figure 5.37 The new background appears at the bottom of the Layers palette.

To convert a layer to a background:

1. Select a layer on the Layers palette.

2. From the Layer menu, choose New > Background From Layer (**Figure 5.36**).

   The new background appears at the bottom of the Layers palette (**Figure 5.37**).

✔ Tips

- The Type and Shape tools also each automatically generate a new layer when you use them, keeping those elements isolated on their own unique layers.

- This command won't work if you already have an existing background layer in your Layers palette. Why? Because no image can have two background layers at the same time. To get around this, create a duplicate of the current background layer (you can rename it later). You can then safely delete the background layer, then follow steps 1-2 to convert a regular layer into a background.

CONVERTING AND DUPLICATING LAYERS

Background Layers

When you import a photo from a digital camera or scanner, the photo appears on the *background* (or base) layer in Photoshop Elements. In fact when you open an image file from just about any source, it's very likely that it has been flattened and contains just a background layer. This layer cannot be reordered (that is, its relative position or level cannot be moved), given a blending mode, or assigned a different opacity.

When you create a new image with transparent contents, the bottom layer is called *Layer 1*. This layer can be reordered, and you can change its blending mode or opacity just as with any other layer.

Since a background layer can never be transparent, it works just fine when you want to create an image with no completely transparent areas (which is the vast majority of the time). However, when you want transparent areas (for instance, for a GIF image floating on a Web page), then you'll want to start by creating an image with transparent contents, or by converting an existing background to a regular layer.

Copying Layers Between Images

It's extremely easy to copy layers from one Photoshop Elements document to another. If you're used to the drag-and-drop technique, then you'll be glad to know that this works just fine for copying layers as well as selections. Remember that as you copy and paste selections they end up on their own layers. So layers often contain unique objects that you can easily share between photos.

To drag and drop a layer from the Layers palette:

1. Open the two images you plan to use.

2. In the source image, select the layer you want to copy by clicking it in the Layers palette.

3. Drag the layer's name from the Layers palette into the destination image (**Figure 5.38**).

   The new layer appears both in the image window and on the Layers palette of the destination image (**Figure 5.39**). When you drag a layer from one image into another, the original, source image is not changed. The layer remains intact.

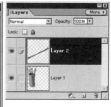

Figure 5.38 To copy a layer, just drag it from the Layers palette and drop it directly onto another image.

Figure 5.39 The new layer appears right above the previously selected (active) layer in the destination image.

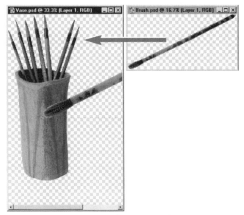

Figure 5.40 The move tool lets you select and duplicate a layer from within the image window.

To drag and drop a layer using the Move tool:

1. Open the two images you plan to use.

2. In the source image, select the layer you want to copy by clicking it, either in the Layers palette, or the image window.

3. Select the Move tool and drag the actual image layer from the source image window to the destination image (**Figure 5.40**).

   The copied layer appears on the Layers palette immediately above the previously active layer.

✔ Tip

■ In some cases, the layer in your source image may be larger than the destination image, in which case not all of the layer will be visible. Just use the Move tool to bring the desired area into view.

To copy and paste a layer between images:

1. In the source image, select the layer you want to copy from by clicking it either in the Layers palette, or the image window.

2. Choose Select > All to select all of the pixels on the layer, or press Ctrl+A/ Command+A.

3. Choose Edit > Copy to copy the layer to the clipboard, or press Ctrl+C/ Command+C.

4. In the destination image, choose Edit > Paste, or press Ctrl+V/Command+V.

   The contents of the copied layer will appear in the center of the destination image.

About Opacity and Blending Modes

One of the most effective and simplest ways to enhance your layered image is to create the illusion of combining one layer's image with another by blending their pixels. This differs from merging layers, as the layers aren't physically merged, but rather appear to mix together. Photoshop Elements provides two easily accessible tools at the top of the Layers palette that can be used alone or in tandem for blending multiple layers together: the Opacity slider and the Blending Modes pop-up menu. The Opacity slider controls the degree of transparency of one layer over another. If a layer's opacity is set at 100 percent, then the layer is totally opaque, and any layers beneath it are hidden. If a layer's opacity is set to 30 percent, then 70 percent of any underlying layers are allowed to show through (**Figure 5.41**).

Blending modes are a little trickier. Whereas Opacity settings strictly control the opaqueness of one layer over another, blending modes act by mixing or blending one layer's color and tonal value with the one below it. The Difference mode, for example, combines one layer's image with a second, and treats the top layer like a sort of negative filter, inverting colors and tonal values where dark areas blend with lighter ones (**Figure 5.42**). For a complete gallery of Photoshop Element's blending modes, see the color plates section of this book.

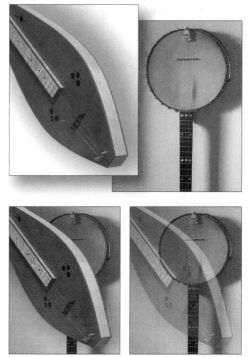

Figure 5.41 Two separate layers (top) compose this simple folk instrument collage. The lower left image displays the top layer with an opacity setting of 100 percent. The lower right image displays the top layer with an opacity setting of 50 percent.

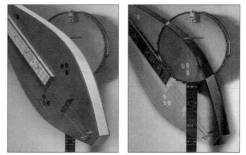

Figure 5.42 The image on the left contains no blending modes; the image on the right displays the top layer with the Difference blending mode applied.

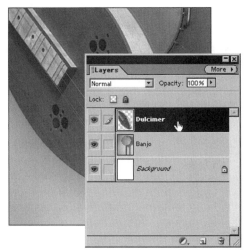

Figure 5.43 The top layer is selected on the Layers palette. Its opacity is set at 100 percent.

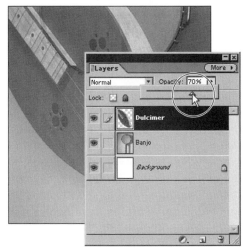

Figure 5.44 You can change a layer's opacity from 0 to 100 percent by dragging the Opacity slider.

To set a layer's opacity:

1. On the Layers palette, select the layer whose opacity you want to change (**Figure 5.43**).

2. To change the opacity, *do one of the following:*

   ▲ Enter a percentage in the Opacity text box, which is located at the top of the Layers palette.

   ▲ Click the arrow to activate the Opacity slider; then drag the slider to the desired opacity (**Figure 5.44**).

✔ Tips

■ You can change the opacity settings in 10 percent increments directly from the keyboard. With a layer selected on the Layers palette, press any number key to change the opacity: 1 for 10 percent, 2 for 20 percent, and so on. Also, as in Photoshop, pressing two number keys in rapid succession will work, i.e. 66%. If this doesn't seem to be working, make sure that you don't have a painting or editing tool selected in the toolbox. Many of the brushes and effects tools can be sized and adjusted with the number keys, and if any of those tools are selected, they take priority over the Layers palette commands.

■ Since a background layer contains no transparency, you can't change its opacity until you first convert it to a regular layer (see "To convert a background to a layer" earlier in this chapter).

ABOUT OPACITY AND BLENDING MODES

To apply a blending mode to a layer:

1. On the Layers palette, select the upper-most layer to which you want to apply the blending mode.

   Remember that blending modes work by mixing (blending) the image pixels of one layer with the layers below it, so your project will need to contain at least two layers in order for a blending mode to have any effect.

2. Select the desired blending mode from the Blending Mode pop-up menu (**Figure 5.45**).

   The image on the layer to which you've applied the blending mode will appear to mix with the image layers below.

✔ Tip

■ You can apply only one blending mode to a layer, but it's still possible to apply more than one blending mode to the same image. After assigning a blending mode to a layer, duplicate the layer and then choose a different blending mode for the duplicate. There are no hard-and-fast rules to follow, and the various blending modes work so differently with one another that getting what you want is largely an exercise of trial and error. But a little experimen-tation with different blending mode combinations (and opacities) can yield some very interesting effects that you can't achieve any other way.

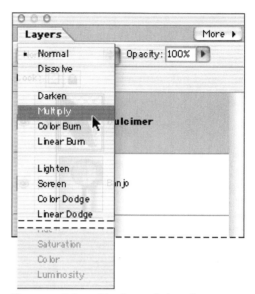

Figure 5.45 Select a blending mode from the Layers palette's Blending Mode menu.

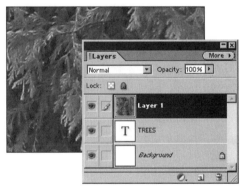

Figure 5.46 This project is composed of two layers: a photograph of cedar branches and the TREE text layer. The branches photo completely covers the text layer in the image on the left, but when grouped with the TREES layer, the branches peek through only where the text is visible.

Creating Masking Effects with Layer Groups

Layer groups provide a simple and quite intuitive way to create a sophisticated masking effect in Photoshop Elements. Any object placed on a layer, including photographic images and lines of editable text, can be used as the basis for masking any number of layer objects above it. Think of the lower, or *base* layer, as a window through which the upper layers are allowed to show through. So, for example, you could have a favorite fishing trip photo framed within the shape of a boat or fish, or a photograph of a forest placed within the word TREES (**Figure 5.46**). Once grouped, any layer within the group can be repositioned independently of the others, or the entire group can be linked and moved as one.

To create a layer group:

1. On the Layers palette, identify the layer that you want to use as your base layer (**Figure 5.47**).

   Your layers must be arranged so that the layer (or layers) you want to group are directly above the base layer.

   continues on next page

Figure 5.47 In this figure, the TREES layer serves as the base layer. It will soon be grouped with the branches layer (Layer 1), which is located directly above it.

2. Still on the Layers palette, select the layer above the base layer; then from the Layer menu choose Group with Previous (**Figure 5.48**), or press Ctrl+G/Command+G.

The two layers are now grouped, and the upper layer is visible only in those areas where the base layer object is present.

On the Layers palette, the base layer's name is underlined, and the grouped layer's name and thumbnail are indented. An icon, placed to the left of the thumbnail, further identifies grouped layers (**Figure 5.49**).

To ungroup layers:

1. On the Layers palette, select the base layer.

2. From the Layer menu, choose Ungroup, or press Shift+Ctrl+G/Shift+Command+G.

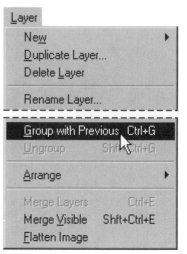

Figure 5.48 Choose Group with Previous to create a layer group.

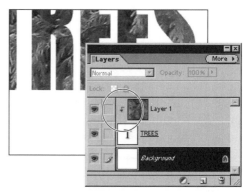

Figure 5.49 A Grouped Layer icon appears after a layer group is created.

Figure 5.50 You must select a layer before you can apply a layer style.

Figure 5.51 Layer styles are divided into different style sets that you can select from the Layer Styles palette menu.

Applying Effects with Layer Styles

With Layer styles, you can add editable effects to individual layer within an image, and you can be as conservative or wild as your heart desires. For example, you can add a subtle drop shadow to an object, or you can go in the opposite direction and set your friend's hair ablaze with the Fire layer style. Beveled edges, glowing borders, and even custom textures can all be applied to any object or text layer. The Layer Styles palette contains a series of style sets, grouped as galleries and accessed from the palette's pop-up menu. Once you've applied a layer style, you can choose to keep it as an active element of a layer and return to and adjust it at any time; or you can choose to merge the layer object and style together to simplify the layer. For a gallery of Photoshop Layer Styles, see the color plates section of this book.

To apply a layer style:

1. On the Layers palette, choose the layer to which you want to apply the layer style (**Figure 5.50**).

2. To open the Layer Styles palette *do one of the following*:

   ▲ From the Window menu, choose Layer Styles.

   ▲ Click the Layer Styles palette in the palette well.

3. On the Layer Styles palette, choose a style set from the palette's pop-up menu (**Figure 5.51**).

   The set you choose presents a gallery from which you can select a specific style.

continues on next page

APPLYING EFFECTS WITH LAYER STYLES

4. In the style gallery, click the style you want to apply to your layer.

The style is instantly applied to the layer object in the image window (**Figure 5.52**), and a Layer Style icon appears next to the layer name on the Layers palette.

To remove a layer style:

◆ To remove a Layer Style, click the Clear Style button in the upper right corner of the palette (**Figure 5.53**).

The Clear Style button will remove all styles from the layer, no matter how many have been applied.

✔ Tips

■ Multiple Layer Styles can be assigned to a single layer, however only one Layer Style from each set can be assigned at a time. In other words, you can assign a drop shadow, bevel, and outer glow style to the same layer all at once, but you can't assign two different bevel styles at the same time.

■ Layer Styles can only be applied to images or text on a regular, transparent layer. If you try and apply a Layer Style to a background, a warning box will ask if you want to first make the background a layer. Click OK and the background will be converted to a layer and your chosen Layer Style will automatically be applied.

■ Elements will allow you apply a Layer Style to a blank layer, but the Layer Style won't have any affect until text or an image is placed on the layer. When you place something on a layer with a previously assigned Layer Style, then it will display with the Layer Style's attribute: drop shadow, beveled edge, and so on.

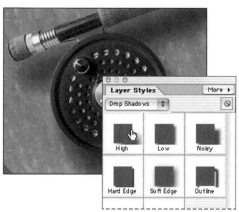

Figure 5.52 Choose a style from the palette gallery to instantly apply the style to a layer.

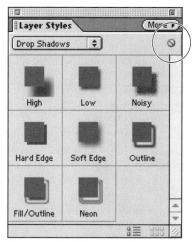

Figure 5.53 Click the Clear Style button to remove all the layer styles from a layer.

APPLYING EFFECTS WITH LAYER STYLES

Figure 5.54 When a layer style is applied, a Layer Style icon appears to the right of the layer name.

Figure 5.55 Use sliders in the Style Settings dialog box to modify the shadow, glow, and bevel styles.

To edit a layer style:

1. On the Layers palette, double-click the Layer Style icon to the right of the layer name (**Figure 5.54**).

   The Style Settings dialog box opens.

2. Make sure that the Preview box is highlighted; then refer to the image window while dragging the active size and distance sliders (**Figure 5.55**).

APPLYING EFFECTS WITH LAYER STYLES

The Style Settings dialog box

Not all of the Layer Styles can be adjusted. But using a series of sliders, a wheel, checkboxes, and radio buttons you *can* make adjustments to drop shadows, inner and outer glows, and bevels styles. Here then is a quick tour of the Style Settings dialog box controls. (The distance and size slider values are all based on units of pixels.)

◆ The Shadow Distance slider quite simply controls the distance that a drop shadow is placed from an object. The larger the number the more shadow is exposed from behind an object. If the distance is set to 0, then the shadow is centered directly under the object and isn't visible.

◆ The Outer Glow Size slider lets you increase or decrease the amount of glow radiating out from the edges of an object.

◆ The Inner Glow Size slider lets you increase or decrease the amount of glow radiating in from the edges of an object.

◆ The Bevel Size slider controls the amount of beveled edge on your object. An inside bevel of 3 will be almost imperceptible, while larger values create an increasingly more pronounced bevel effect.

◆ The Lighting Angle wheel controls the direction of the light source when a bevel or shadow style is applied. Changing the light angle will change which beveled surfaces are in highlight and which are in shadow, and will also control where a drop shadow falls behind an object (**Figure 5.56**).

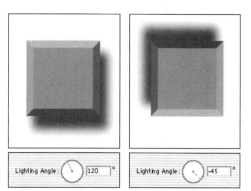

Figure 5.56 The Lighting Angle wheel sets a light source for any bevel or drop shadow styles you apply to a layer, and can be set to any light an object from any angle.

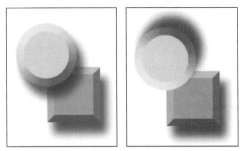

Figure 5.57 When the Global Light checkbox is selected, Layer Styles on multiple layers will all share the same light source (left). When the checkbox is deselected, a different light source can be set for each individual layer (right).

Figure 5.58 When the bevel direction is set to Up, the object bevel appears to come forward (left). When the bevel direction is set to Down, the object bevel appears to recede into the distance (right).

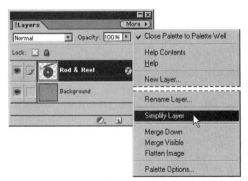

Figure 5.59 Once a style is set the way you like it, you can permanently apply it to a layer object by simplifying the layer.

◆ The Use Global Light checkbox works only if you have bevel or shadow styles applied to more than one layer. If the checkbox is selected, then all the layers will share the same light source, and if the light source is changed on one layer (with the Lighting Angle wheel) the light source on all the layers changes at the same time. If the checkbox is left unselected, then a light source can be set independently for each layer (**Figure 5.57**).

◆ The Bevel Direction Radio buttons control the appearance of a bevel style. If the Up button is selected, the bevel will appear to extrude or come forward, if the down button is selected, the bevel will appear to recede (**Figure 5.58**).

Once you've applied a Layer Style, you can return to it at any time to modify it, but you also have the option of merging the Layer Style with its layer by *simplifying*. In effect, simplifying is like flattening an individual layer. Simplifying a layer, permanently applies a layer style to its layer, and can help to reduce the complexity and file size of your project.

To simplify a layer:

1. On the Layers palette, click to select the layer you want to simplify.

2. From the palette menu on the Layers palette, choose Simplify Layer (**Figure 5.59**).

   The layer style is merged with the layer, and the Layer Style icon disappears from the layer on the Layers palette.

Making Color and Tonal Changes with Adjustment Layers

Adjustment layers let you make color and tonal adjustments to your image (much like the commands we discussed in Chapter 3) without changing the actual pixels in your image. Adjustment layers work like filters, resting above the actual image layers and affecting any image layers below them. They can be especially useful when you want to experiment with different settings or compare the effects of one setting over another. Since you can apply opacity and blending mode changes to adjustment layers (just as you would to any other layer) they offer a level of creative freedom not available from their menu command counterparts. For instance, you can create a Levels adjustment layer above an image, then change the opacity of that adjustment layer to fine-tune the amount of tonal correction applied to the image.

To create an adjustment layer:

1. On the Layers palette, identify the topmost layer to which you want the adjustment layer applied; then select that layer.

    Remember that the adjustment layer affects all layers below it on the Layers palette, not just the one directly below it.

2. At the bottom of the Layers palette, click the Create New Fill or Adjustment Layer button (**Figure 5.60**).

3. From the pop-up menu, choose from the list of adjustment layer options (**Figure 5.61**).

    When you choose an adjustment layer option, its dialog box opens, and a new adjustment layer is created above the selected layer (**Figure 5.62**).

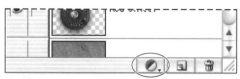

Figure 5.60 Once you've selected a layer, click the Create New Fill or Adjustment Layer button at the bottom of the layer menu.

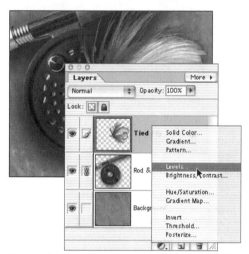

Figure 5.61 Choose an adjustment command from the pop-up menu.

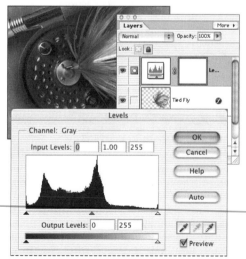

Figure 5.62 Adjustment dialog boxes appear when applicable and mirror the dialog boxes available from the main application menus.

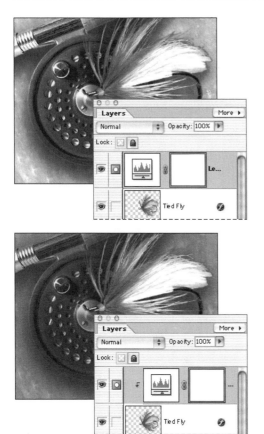

Figure 5.63 In the top image, the Levels adjustment layer is shown applied to every layer in the project. In the bottom image, the adjustment layer has been grouped with the object layer directly below it and so affects only that layer.

4. Use the dialog box sliders to adjust the settings; then click OK to close the dialog box.

   If you want to return to the adjustment layer dialog box later, just double-click its layer thumbnail on the Layers palette.

   By default, an adjustment layer affects all the layers below it in the Layers palette. But if you create a layer group, the effects of the adjustment layer will be limited to one, specific layer.

To apply an adjustment layer to a single layer:

1. In the Layers palette, move the adjustment layer so that it's directly above the layer you want it applied to.

2. With the adjustment layer still selected in the Layers palette, choose Group with Previous from the layer menu, or press Ctrl+G/Command+G.

   The adjustment layer and the one directly below it are grouped, and the effects of the adjustment layer are applied only to that single layer (**Figure 5.63**).

About Fill Layers

By now you may have noticed that the button at the bottom of the palette refers to adjustment and *fill* layers, and that the pop-up menu includes not only tonal correction options such as Levels, but a list of three layer fill options: Solid Color, Gradient, and Pattern. Follow our lead and ignore these. They don't do anything that can't be accomplished by simply creating a new layer and applying a fill or pattern; except that they do it with more overhead, because adjustment layers require more processing power and create larger files than regular layers.

ADJUSTMENT LAYERS

Using the Undo History Palette

The Undo History palette lets you move backward and forward through a work session, allowing you to make multiple undos to any editing changes you've made to your image. Photoshop Elements records every change and then lists it as a separate entry, or *state*, on the palette. With one click, you can navigate to any state and then choose to work forward from there, return again to the previous state, or select a different state from which to work forward.

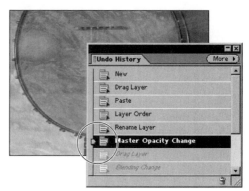

Figure 5.64 Use the palette slider to move to virtually any point in time in the creation of your project.

To navigate through the Undo History palette:

1. To open the Undo History palette, *do one of the following*:
   - ▲ From the Window menu, choose Undo History.
   - ▲ From the palette well, click the Undo History palette tab.

2. To move to a different state in the Undo History palette, *do one of the following*:
   - ▲ Click the name of any state.
   - ▲ Drag the palette slider up or down to a different state (**Figure 5.64**).

✔ Tips

- ■ The default number of states that the Undo History palette saves is 20. After 20, the first state is cleared from the list, and the palette continues to list just the 20 most recent states. The good news is that, at any time, you can bump the number of saved states up to 100, provided that your computer has enough memory. From the Edit menu, choose Preferences > General, then in the Preferences dialog box enter a larger number in the Undo History States field.

- ■ If, on the other hand, memory is at a premium (and you'd rather Photoshop Elements wasn't clogging up your precious RAM by remembering your last 20 selections and brush strokes and filter effects), set the number in the Undo History States field to 1. You can still undo and redo your last action as you work along, but for all practical purposes, the Undo History palette is turned off.

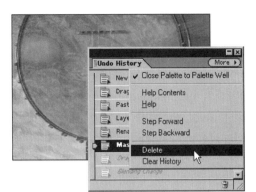

Figure 5.65 Delete any state by selecting it and choosing Delete from the palette menu.

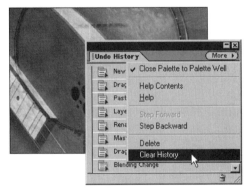

Figure 5.66 If system memory is a concern, you can periodically clear the palette of all states.

To delete a state:

◆ Click the name of any state; then choose Delete from the palette menu (**Figure 5.65**) or click the Trash button.

The selected state and all states following it are deleted.

✔ Tip

■ Deletion of a state can be undone, but only if no changes are applied to the image in the interim. If you make a change to the image that creates a new state on the palette, then all deleted states are permanently lost.

Sometimes—when you're working on an especially complex piece, for instance—the Undo History palette may become filled with states that you no longer need to manage or return to or that begin to take their toll on your system's memory. At any time, you can clear the palette's list of states, without changing the image.

To clear the Undo History palette:

Do one of the following:

◆ From the palette menu, choose Clear History (**Figure 5.66**).

This action can be undone, but it doesn't reduce the amount of memory used by Photoshop Elements.

◆ Hold down Alt/Option; then choose Clear History from the palette menu.

This action *cannot be undone*, but it does purge the list of states from the memory buffer. This can come in handy if a message appears telling you that Photoshop Elements is low on memory.

FIXING AND
RETOUCHING PHOTOS

How often have you thumbed through photo albums and found images you'd wished were better composed or lit more evenly? Or maybe you've sorted through shoeboxes from the attic, disappointed that time and age have taken a toll on those wonderful old photographs of your dad in his high school band uniform and your grandparents honeymooning at the lake. Until recently, there was no simple way to correct or repair photographs, regardless of whether they were out of focus, water damaged, or poorly composed.

All that has changed. Nowadays, armed with little more than an inexpensive scanner and a copy of Photoshop Elements, anyone can retouch and restore old photographs. In this chapter, you learn not only how to straighten and crop a crooked scan, but how to repair a damaged photo, enhance focus and image detail, and even eliminate that troublesome red-eye effect. Though these topics are presented primarily in the context of fixing and correcting older, scanned photographs, most of the techniques presented here can be equally helpful when retouching and enhancing images captured with a digital camera.

Cropping an Image

The one thing that you'll want to do with nearly every image is crop it. In spite of all the wonderful advances in film and digital cameras, rarely is a picture taken with its subjects perfectly composed or its horizon line set at just the proper height. More often than not, subjects are off-center, and unwanted objects intrude into the edge of the picture frame. Take a hint from professional photographers, who almost always use cropping techniques to arrive at that perfect composition. Photoshop Elements offers two simple and quick methods for cropping your images.

Figure 6.1 The Crop tool.

To crop an image using the Crop tool:

1. Select the Crop tool from the toolbox (C) (**Figure 6.1**).

   When you move the pointer over your image, it becomes the Crop tool.

2. In the image window, drag to define the area of the image you want to keep (**Figure 6.2**).

   The image outside the selected area will be dimmed to indicate the portions that will be deleted.

3. If you want to modify your selection, move the pointer over one of the eight handles on the edges of the selection; then drag the handle to resize the selection (**Figure 6.3**).

Figure 6.2 When you crop using the Crop tool, Photoshop Elements gives you visual feedback by highlighting the image that will be preserved and dimming the portions that will be deleted.

Figure 6.3 You can easily move and resize the area you choose to crop by dragging the handles around the perimeter of the cropping selection.

CROPPING AN IMAGE

Figure 6.4 The Cancel and Commit current crop operation buttons are located below the palette well in the options bar.

Figure 6.5 The final, cropped image.

Figure 6.6 Once you make a cropping selection, the Shield display options appear in the options bar.

4. When you're satisfied with your selection, double-click the pointer inside the selection, press Enter/Return, or click the Commit current crop operation button in the options bar (**Figure 6.4**).

If you're just not satisfied with your selection and want to start over, click the Cancel current crop operation button.

The image is cropped to the area you selected (**Figure 6.5**).

The Cropping Shield Display Options

In addition to the Cancel and Commit crop operation buttons, three additional cropping options appear once a selection has been made with the Crop tool, and all allow you to control the display of the dimmed area, or *shield*, around your cropped selection (**Figure 6.6**). Clicking the Shield check box toggles the dimmed area off and on. A single click in the Color box opens the Color Picker, where you can change the color of the dimmed area. The default color is black. Lastly, you can use the Opacity slider to change the strength of the dimmed area from its default of 75%.

CROPPING AN IMAGE

To crop an image using the Rectangular Marquee tool:

1. Select the Rectangular Marquee tool from the toolbox (M) (**Figure 6.7**).

2. In the image window, drag to define the area of the image you want to keep (**Figure 6.8**).

3. From the Image menu, choose Crop (**Figure 6.9**).

   The image is cropped to the area you selected (**Figure 6.10**).

Figure 6.7 The Rectangular Marquee tool.

Figure 6.8 Drag with the Rectangular Marquee tool to define the part of the image you want to crop.

Figure 6.9 You can crop in one, simple action by choosing crop from the Image menu.

Figure 6.10 The final, cropped image.

Straightening an Image

Image

Duplicate Image...	
Rotate ▶	90° Left
Transform ▶	90° Right
Crop	180°
Resize ▶	Custom...
Adjustments ▶	Flip Horizontal
	Flip Vertical
Histogram...	
	Free Rotate Layer
Mode ▶	Layer 90° Left
	Flip Layer Horizontal
	Flip Layer Vertical
	Straighten and Crop Image
	Straighten Image

Figure 6.11 From the Image menu, you can straighten and crop an image in one step.

Figure 6.12 A scanned image (top) can be automatically straightened (center) or straightened and cropped (bottom).

If your experience is anything like ours, you know that it's next-to-impossible to scan a perfectly straight image. Some little gust of wind or seismic anomaly almost always seems to accompany the lowering of the scanner cover. The Straighten Image command works fine for quick fixes, and the Crop tool offers more control for small or subtle adjustments; or in cases where you may want to change the alignment of an image for emphasis or a special effect.

To straighten an image automatically:

From the Image menu, *choose one of the following:*

◆ Rotate > Straighten and Crop Image (**Figure 6.11**).

◆ Rotate > Straighten Image.

The Straighten and Crop Image command will do its best to both straighten the image and delete the extra background surrounding the image. The Straighten Image command simply straightens without cropping (**Figure 6.12**).

Both methods have their own sets of limitations. Rotate and Straighten works best if there is a space of at least 50 extra pixels or so surrounding the image. If this surrounding border is much smaller, Photoshop Elements can have a difficult time distinguishing the actual photograph from the border and may not do a clean job of cropping.

continues on next page

Though you'll still need to manually crop your image after using the Rotate > Straighten Image command, this method is probably a better choice, as you avoid the risk of Photoshop Elements indiscriminately cropping out areas of your image you may want to keep. For the surest control, however, straighten your images using the Crop tool as described in the next procedure.

To straighten an image using the Crop tool:

1. Select the Crop tool from the toolbox.

2. In the image window, drag to select the area of the image you want to crop and straighten.

3. Move the pointer outside the edge of the selection area until it changes to a rotation pointer (**Figure 6.13**).

4. Drag outside of the selection until its edges are aligned with the image border.

5. Drag the selection handles, as necessary, to fine-tune the positioning; then press Enter/Return (**Figure 6.14**).

   The image is cropped and automatically straightened.

Figure 6.13 After you define a preliminary cropping selection (left), you can rotate the selection so that it aligns with your image border (right).

Figure 6.14 Make final adjustments to your cropping selection (left) before Photoshop Elements automatically crops and straightens the image.

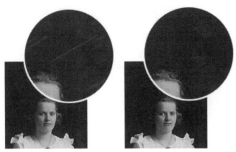

Figure 6.15 After a little practice, you can easily repair a variety of imperfections with the Clone tool. In this photo, the original image is scratched (left), but after cloning and stamping a clear portion of the background, the scratches disappear (right).

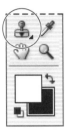

Figure 6.16 The Clone tool.

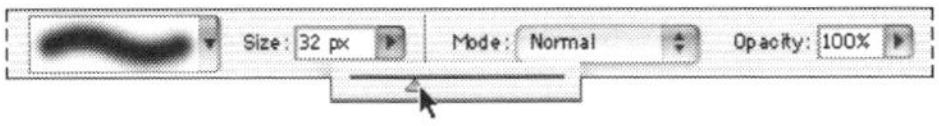

Figure 6.17 Choose any of Photoshop Elements' resizable brushes to apply your cloned repairs.

Using the Clone Stamp Tool

The Clone Stamp tool will quickly become one of your favorite tools, not just for cleaning up and restoring photographs, but for any number of special effects and enhancements. It works on the simple principle of copying and duplicating (cloning) image pixels from one part of an image to another. But rather than creating a hard-edged patch of pixels, the Clone Stamp tool applies the duplicated pixels with a soft-edged, resizable brush. This brush lets you create nearly seamless transitions between your original image and the cloned patch (**Figure 6.15**). The Clone Stamp tool is ideal for repairing tears or scratches in photographs, but can also be used to add or delete objects in your photograph. For example, you can create a hedgerow out of one small bush, or remove telephone lines from an otherwise perfect, blue sky.

To retouch an image with the Clone Stamp tool:

1. Select the Clone Stamp tool from the toolbox (S) (**Figure 6.16**).

2. On the options bar, select a brush size using the Brush Size slider (**Figure 6.17**). The brush size you choose will vary depending on the area you have available to clone from, and the area that you're trying to repair. Larger brush sizes work well for larger open areas like skies or simple, even-toned backdrops, while you may want to use smaller brushes for textured surfaces or areas with a lot of detail.

continues on next page

3. Move the pointer over the area of your image that you want to clone (the pointer becomes a circle, representing the brush size you've specified), then hold down the Alt/Option key.

The pointer becomes a target (**Figure 6.18**).

4. Click once to select the area you want to sample; then release the Alt/Option key and move the pointer to the area to which you want the clone applied (**Figure 6.19**).

5. Hold down the mouse button, and drag to "paint" the cloned portion over the new area.

The original image is replaced with a clone of the sampled image.

Figure 6.18 Once you've found an area of your image that you want to clone, simply hold down Alt/Option and click to select it. Your pointer turns into a bull's-eye target

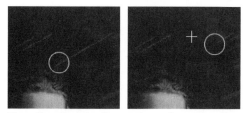

Figure 6.19 Drag the Clone tool over the portion of the image you want to replace (left). As you drag the Clone tool, crosshairs appear, providing a constant reference point as you paint over the image (right).

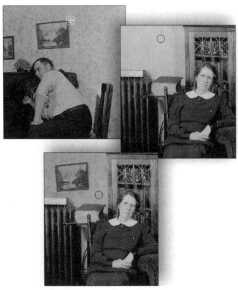

Figure 6.20 The Clone tool provides a controlled method for combining parts of one image with another. Here, with a little cloning from the image on the top left, this woman receives not only a newly papered wall, but a painting to hang from it as well.

To copy images from one picture to another with the Clone Stamp tool:

1. Select the Clone Stamp tool from the toolbox and then select a brush size from the options bar.

2. Holding down Alt/Option, click in the first picture to select the area you want to sample.

3. Click the second picture's image window to make it active, then drag to paint a clone of the sampled image.

4. The original image in the second picture is replaced with a clone of the sampled image from the first (**Figure 6.20**).

✔ Tip

■ Before experimenting with the Clone Tool, it's good practice first to create a new, blank image layer. Creating a separate layer not only protects your original image by leaving it unchanged, but it gives you more creative flexibility. You can apply different cloned areas to different layers and then compare the effect of each by turning the layer visibility settings off and on. And if you apply different cloned areas on separate layers, you can experiment further by applying different blending mode and opacity settings to each clone.

Applying Patterns

Though some of Photoshop Elements' patterns can be a little gimmicky, others, like many of the fabric and rock textures, can be useful when you're trying to repair or retouch a damaged or aged photograph. For example, you might use one of the abstract stone patterns to camouflage a particularly damaged background in an old photo that would be difficult to salvage by any other method. Photoshop Elements provides a default set of patterns plus seven additional sets containing objects as varied as flowers, stone faces, and textured artist's surfaces. Patterns can be applied using two methods. If you have a large area of the same tonal value or color, then you can use the Paint Bucket tool. On the other hand, you have a smaller area made up of varying colors or textures, use the Pattern Stamp tool.

Figure 6.21 The Paint Bucket tool.

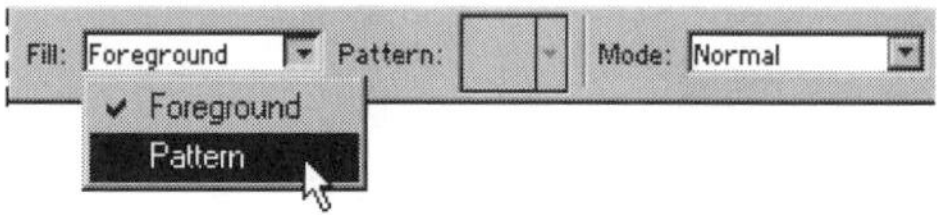

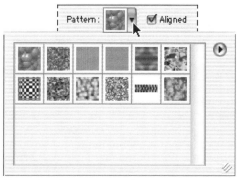

Figure 6.22 Once you've selected the Paint Bucket tool, select Pattern from the options bar.

To apply a pattern to a selected area with the Paint Bucket tool:

1. Select the Paint Bucket tool from the toolbox, or press K (**Figure 6.21**).

2. On the options bar, select Pattern from the Fill pop-up menu (**Figure 6.22**).

3. Still on the options bar, click to open the pattern picker (**Figure 6.23**).

Figure 6.23 Choose a pattern from the aptly named pattern picker on the options bar.

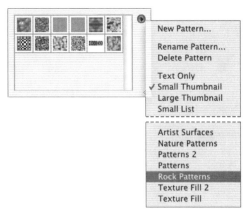

Figure 6.24 You can pick from a default sampler list of patterns or load any one of seven additional pattern sets.

4. Click to choose from the list of default patterns, or click the arrow button to the right of the thumbnail image to open the Pattern palette menu (**Figure 6.24**).

5. Select from the list of pattern sets in the bottom section of the menu.

The pattern picker displays the new pattern library.

6. Return to the image window and click in the area where you want to apply the pattern.

The pattern is painted in the image (**Figure 6.25**).

Figure 6.25 Click the Paint Bucket tool in any large area where you want to apply a pattern. Here, a floral pattern was selected to create brand-new living room wallpaper.

To apply a pattern with the Pattern Stamp tool:

1. In the toolbox, select the Pattern Stamp tool from beneath the Clone Stamp tool (**Figure 6.26**).

   If you hold Alt/Option while clicking on the Clone Stamp tool in the toolbox, you can toggle between the Clone Stamp and Pattern Stamp tools. Or, if the Clone Stamp tool is already selected, you can select the Pattern Stamp tool from the options bar.

2. On the options bar, select a brush size using the Brush Size slider (**Figure 6.27**).

   If you like, you can also make opacity and blending changes, just as you did for the Clone Stamp tool.

3. Pick a pattern by following steps 3 through 5 in the previous procedure.

4. Once you've chosen a pattern, return to the image window, hold down the mouse button, and then drag to paint the pattern in your image (**Figure 6.28**).

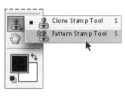

Figure 6.26 The Pattern Stamp tool is hidden underneath the Clone tool. Just hold down Alt/Option and click to access it.

Figure 6.27 Choose a brush size appropriate for your image size and pattern.

Figure 6.28 Position the pattern brush anywhere in your image to paint a pattern.

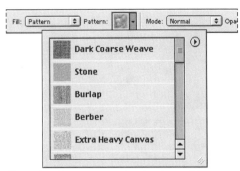

Figure 6.29 You can customize the views of the Patterns palette for easier browsing. The Large List view (shown here) combines easy-to-see thumbnails with descriptive pattern names.

Figure 6.30 Using one of the textured Artist Surfaces patterns, any photo can be made to appear printed or rendered on watercolor paper, canvas, or a variety of other fine art surfaces.

✔ Tips

■ Since the Paint Bucket tool fills areas based on tonal value and color, you'll have the most success filling areas composed of similar values, such as blank walls or clear, cloudless skies. You can adjust the behavior of the Paint Bucket tool by entering different values in the Tolerance text box on the options bar, but the results are a little unpredictable, and the process involves some trial and error.

■ As with Photoshop Elements' new Brushes palette, the Pattern palette offers several viewing options that you can access from the palette menu (**Figure 6.29**). In addition to the default mode of Small Thumbnail, you can view patterns as Text Only (a simple text list of the pattern names); Large Thumbnail (a larger version of the small thumbnails); Small List (tiny thumbnail views accompanied by their pattern names); or our personal favorite, Large List (similar to the Small List, but with nice, large thumbnail views). As a further aid, if Show Tool Tips (the default setting) is selected in the General Preferences dialog box, simply hover over any pattern thumbnail for a second or two to reveal a small pop-up descriptive name of that pattern.

APPLYING PATTERNS

Mount a Photo on an Artist's Canvas

You can create an interesting textured effect for almost any photo by using patterns from the Artist Surfaces set.

1. In the Layers palette, create a new layer above your original photo layer.

2. From the Pattern palette menu, choose the Artists Surfaces pattern set, and then choose from one of the artist surfaces. The Canvas pattern works well.

3. With the pattern layer selected, apply a blend mode (try Multiply) to combine the photo and pattern layers.

4. If you like, adjust the pattern layer's opacity setting.

Your photo will appear to be printed on the textured artist surface (**Figure 6.30**).

Correcting Red Eye

Red eye has long been a source of frustration for the amateur photographer. If you're in an indoor or darkened space, the pupils in your eyes grow larger to let in more light, and can't shrink (dilate) quickly enough to compensate for the sudden surprise of a camera flash. That light, reflecting off the back of the eye and into the camera lens, causes red eye. Many newer cameras have flashes that flicker before the picture is actually snapped, giving the subject's pupils a chance to dilate and greatly reducing the effects of red eye. But chances are that you still have some older photos lying around that you'd like to repair. The Red Eye Brush tool offers an effective way to remove red eye, simply by changing pixels from one color to another.

To remove red eye from a photograph:

1. Select the Red Eye Brush tool from the toolbox, or Press Y (**Figure 6.31**).

2. Click the Default Colors button (**Figure 6.32**) to reset the Current and Replacement colors on the options bar; then check that the sampling method is set to First Click (**Figure 6.33**).

   Selecting First Click changes the color beneath the Red Eye brush crosshairs (in this case, the red portion of the eye) to the replacement color as soon as you first click the mouse button, and continues to change the red color as long as you hold down the mouse button and drag over the image.

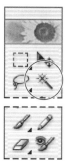

Figure 6.31 The Red Eye Brush tool.

Figure 6.32 Click on the Default Color button to replace the red in the eye with the default neutral gray color.

Figure 6.33 If it's not already selected, make sure the Sampling method is set to First Click.

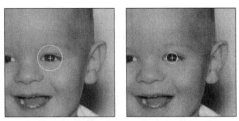

Figure 6.34 Place the brush pointer directly over the pupil, then simply resize the brush and click to remove the red eye effect.

Figure 6.35 Set a higher tolerance value if the red eye isn't completely removed with one mouse click.

The Red Eye Brush's Current Color Setting

Current Color, the other Red Eye brush setting on the options bar, changes a specified color in your image to the replacement color, just as the First Click setting does. But rather than sampling the color directly from your image as you would with the First Click setting, Current Color asks you to use the Color Picker to choose (or, more precisely, *guess*) the color you want to change, and *then* use the Red Eye brush to apply the change. If all of that sounds a little confusing, we couldn't agree more. When used with the First Click option, the Red Eye brush is an elegant, powerful, and simple tool. The Current Color setting adds a level of complexity to the process with little or no discernable reward for removing red eye from a photo.

3. If necessary, zoom in on the area you want to correct, then position the brush pointer (the circle and crosshair) over the red eye in the photo.

Notice that the color in the Current box changes to the red eye color, while the color in the Replacement box remains black.

4. With the crosshair centered over the eye, click the "[" and "]" keys to resize the brush until it just covers the red in the pupil (**Figure 6.34**).

With this keyboard shortcut, the brush is resized, up or down, in 10 pixel increments and is a handy way to surround just the area you want to correct. Don't worry if the brush size extends slightly into the true color of the pupil or the white of the eye. Because you chose First Click in step 2, only the red in the eye will be affected.

5. With the brush pointer still centered over the eye, click the mouse button once.

The Red Eye brush works by replacing the current color directly beneath (red) to a tint of the replacement color. Since the replacement color is black, the red in the eye changes to a muted gray, removing the red eye.

✔ Tip

■ If you find that you need to click more than once to remove the red eye from your image, the tolerance value on the options bar may be set too low. Photoshop Elements' default tolerance value of 30% works well for most images, but if it's set much below that, you may be left with residual red pixels in your subject's eye. If all the red isn't removed on that first mouse click, it's easy to fix. Undo the action, use the tolerance slider to set a higher value, and then click in your subject's eye again (**Figure 6.35**). If the tolerance is set properly, all the red should be removed with one click.

Sharpening Image Detail

Although most scanners do a pretty good job of capturing images, a little sharpness or crispness of detail seems to almost always get lost in the conversion process. If an original photo is even just slightly fuzzy, the act of converting it to pure, digital information may accentuate the detail enough to make the fuzziness even more noticeable when viewed on your computer screen. Even photos you've captured directly from a digital camera may not quite "pop" the way you'd like them to. In addition, any time you resize an image by resampling, pixels may be lost in the process, and so you also lose some degree of image detail.

Photoshop Elements offers several automatic sharpening options (Sharpen, Sharpen Edges, and Sharpen More), but all offer so little control that you may prefer not to use them. Instead, you may prefer the Unsharp Mask command, which offers plenty of control through an interactive, intuitive dialog box. The Unsharp Mask command works by finding pixels with different tonal values and then slightly increasing the contrast between those adjoining pixels and so creating a sharper edge. The resulting correction can help to enhance detail and bring blurred or fuzzy areas throughout an image into clearer focus.

To sharpen an image:

1. From the Filter menu, choose Sharpen > Unsharp Mask to open the Unsharp Mask dialog box (**Figure 6.36**).

2. Make sure that the Preview box is checked; then drag the sliders to adjust the image's sharpness.

   ▲ The Amount slider sets the percentage of contrast that is applied to the pixels and so determines the degree of sharpness you apply. For high-resolution images (those above around 150 pixels

Figure 6.36 The Unsharp Mask dialog box contains sliders to adjust the degree of sharpening you apply to your image.

Figure 6.37 The Amount slider controls the percentage of sharpness applied to your image. The image on the left was corrected at 80 percent, and the one on the right was corrected at 150 percent.

Figure 6.38 The Radius slider controls the number of pixels that Photoshop Elements includes in any sharpened edge. Smaller numbers include fewer pixels, and larger numbers include more pixels. The image on the left was set to 1, and the image on the right was set to 6.

Figure 6.39 The preview area of the dialog box lets you view a specific area of your image so that you can see what affect your settings are having. Drag to move the preview to a different portion of your image.

per inch), set the Amount slider to between 150 and 200 percent. For lower-resolution images, use settings somewhere around 30 to 80 percent (**Figure 6.37**).

▲ The Radius slider determines the number of pixels surrounding the contrasting edge pixels that will also be sharpened. Though the radius can be set all the way to 250, you should never have to enter a value higher than around 2, unless you're trying to achieve a strong, high-contrast special effect (**Figure 6.38**).

▲ The Threshold slider tells Photoshop Elements how different the contrasting pixels need to be before it should apply sharpening to them. A value of 0 sharpens the whole image; entering increasingly larger numbers sharpens only areas of higher contrast. For most purposes, you should leave the Threshold value set to 0.

Use the preview area to see a detailed view of your image as you apply the changes. You can move to a different area of an image by holding down the mouse button and dragging with the hand pointer in the preview screen (**Figure 6.39**). You can also zoom in or out of an area using the minus and plus buttons below the lower corners of the window.

3. When you're satisfied with the results, click OK to close the dialog box and apply the changes.

SHARPENING IMAGE DETAIL

Enhancing Image Detail

Whereas the Unsharp Mask command works best on entire images or large portions of images, a couple of tools are better suited for making sharpening and focus adjustments in smaller, more specific areas of an image. Not surprisingly, the Blur tool softens the focus in an image by reducing the detail, and the Sharpen tool helps bring areas into focus. Both tools can be further fine-tuned using controls on the options bar. You use both the Blur and Sharpen tools by dragging a resizable brush through the area that you want to affect. Since the brushes offer you precise control over where the blur or sharpness is applied, the tools are ideal for subtle, special effects. For instance, you can create a sense of depth by blurring selected background areas while keeping foreground subjects in focus, or enhance the focus of a specific foreground subject so that it better stands out from others.

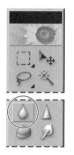

Figure 6.40 The Blur tool.

To blur a specific area or object:

1. Select the Blur tool from the toolbox, or press R (**Figure 6.40**).

2. On the options bar, select a brush size using the Brush Size slider.

   If you want, you can also select a blend mode and enter a Strength percentage. The higher the percentage, the more the affected area is blurred.

3. Move the brush pointer to the area of your image that you want to blur; then hold down the mouse button and drag through the area (**Figure 6.41**).

   As you drag, the area is blurred.

Figure 6.41 Drag the brush through the area you want to blur. You can resize the brush as you work on larger and smaller areas.

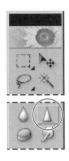

Figure 6.42 The Sharpen tool.

Figure 6.43 The gentleman's face in the original photo (left) is blurred, and lacks definition and detail. After dragging the brush pointer through his face and collar, the sharpness and focus in those areas is greatly improved (right).

To sharpen a specific area or object:

1. Select the Sharpen tool from the toolbox, or press P (**Figure 6.42**).

2. On the options bar, select a brush size. If you prefer, choose a blend mode and enter a Strength percentage. The higher the percentage, the more the affected area is sharpened.

3. Move the brush pointer to the area of your image that you want to sharpen; then hold down the mouse button and drag through the area (**Figure 6.43**).

   As you drag, the area is sharpened.

✔ Tip

■ You can use the Blur and Sharpen tools together when you want to draw attention to a particular person or object. First, use the Blur tool to soften the focus and detail of the subjects that you want to appear to recede into the background. Then use the Sharpen tool to bring the subject of primary interest into even sharper focus.

ENHANCING IMAGE DETAIL

Blending Image Elements with the Smudge Tool

The Smudge tool is one of those specialty tools that's a little hard to classify. Traditionally, it's grouped with the Blur and Sharpen tools in Photoshop's toolbox and is often used for retouching tasks. The Smudge tool's closest cousin may be the Blur tool, as it can also be used to soften edges and transitions in an image. Its real strength though, lies in its ability to push and pull image pixels around in your picture. Drag the tool through an area, and its pixels smear and blend with the adjacent pixels as if you were pulling a brush through freshly applied paint. Use the Smudge tool in backgrounds and other areas where you may need to smooth flaws or imperfections and retaining detail isn't critical. With a little practice, you can also create some convincing painterly effects by varying the length and direction of the brushstrokes. As with the Blur and Sharpen tools, the Smudge tool's effects can be adjusted with controls on the options bar.

To use the Smudge tool:

1. Select the Smudge tool from the toolbox, or press F (**Figure 6.44**).

2. On the options bar, select a brush size using the Brush Size slider.

   Just as with the Blur and Sharpen tools, you can select a blend mode and enter a Strength percentage. The higher the percentage, the more the affected area is smudged.

3. Move the brush pointer to the area of your image that you want to smudge; then hold down the mouse button and drag through the area (**Figure 6.45**).

   As you drag, the area is softened and blended.

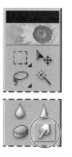

Figure 6.44 Photoshop Elements' Smudge tool.

Figure 6.45 Images with a lot of dust specks and other small imperfections (like this man's suit, left) are good candidates for retouching with the Smudge tool. Work on one small area at a time to blend away and soften the dust and scratches (right).

✔ Tip

- The Smudge tool tends to produce a more artificial effect than the other retouching tools, so use it with moderation. Unless your intent is to create a wet paint effect in a large portion of your image, limit use of the Smudge tool to repairing or smoothing small, unobtrusive areas. You don't want a small repair to become the focus of attention.

Figure 6.46 The Dodge tool.

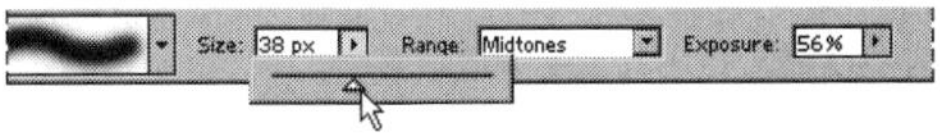

Size: 38 px ▸ Range: Midtones ▾ Exposure: 56% ▸

Figure 6.47 Choose a brush size from the Options bar.

Using the Tonal Adjustment Tools

In traditional photography, technicians can control darkness and lightness values on specific parts of an image by masking off one area of film while exposing another. In the process, selected areas are either *burned in* (darkened) or *dodged* (lightened). Photoshop Element's Burn and Dodge tools replicate this effect without the bother of creating masks. Instead, you simply drag an adjustable tool's brush pointer through the area you want to affect, leaving the rest of the image unchanged. If one portion of an image is dramatically overexposed or washed out, while another portion is underexposed, the Dodge and Burn tools can be used to target and correct just those specific problem areas. The Sponge tool, which works in much the same way as the Dodge and Burn tools, increases or decreases the intensity of the color, rather than the lightness and darkness values. You can use the Sponge tool to bring colors back to life in badly faded, older photographs, or work in the opposite direction, pulling the color out of a newer photo and creating an antique, faded, or color-tinted effect.

To lighten a portion of an image with the Dodge tool:

1. Select the Dodge tool from the toolbox (O) (**Figure 6.46**).

2. On the options bar, select a brush size using the Brush Size slider (**Figure 6.47**). Pick a brush size appropriate to your image. For most images, a brush size betwen 20-40 pixels is a good place to start.

continues on next page

You can also select a specific tonal range to lighten (shadows, midtones, or highlights) and control the amount of lightness applied, with the Exposure setting (**Figure 6.48**).

3. Move the brush pointer to the area of your image that you want to lighten; then hold down the mouse button and drag through the area (**Figure 6.49**).

To darken a portion of an image with the Burn tool:

1. Select the Burn tool from the toolbox (J) (**Figure 6.50**).

2. In the options bar, select a brush size using the brush size slider.

   If you'd like, you can also select a specific tonal range to darken (shadows, midtones, or highlights) and control the amount of darkness applied with the exposure setting.

3. Move the brush pointer to the area of your image that you want to darken, then hold down the mouse button and drag through the area (**Figure 6.51**).

Figure 6.48 Select the part of the tonal range you most want to affect with Photoshop Element's tonal adjustment tools. With both the Dodge and Burn tools, you can choose to limit your changes to just the shadow, midtone, or highlight areas.

Figure 6.49 Drag the Dodge or Burn brush through any area to lighten or darken the pixels while preserving image detail. Here, we've used the Dodge tool to lighten the radio in the original picture (left), making it much easier to see (right).

Figure 6.50 The Burn tool.

Figure 6.51 In this image, the children in the wagon were badly washed out, while the rest of the image wasn't in bad shape (left). The Burn tool was used to restore lost detail and add some much needed form and dimension by darkening the pixels in the shadow and midtone areas (right).

Figure 6.52 Photoshop Elements' Sponge tool.

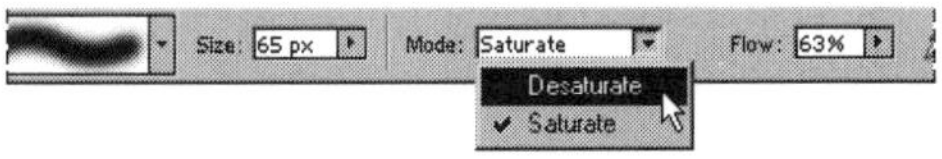

Size: 65 px | Mode: Saturate | Flow: 63%
Desaturate
✓ Saturate

Figure 6.53 On the options bar, you can choose whether you want the Sponge tool to add or subtract color.

To adjust the color saturation with the Sponge tool:

1. Select the Sponge tool from the toolbox (**Figure 6.52**).

2. On the options bar, select a brush size using the Brush Size slider.

3. From the Mode pop-up menu on the options bar, select whether you want to saturate (add) or desaturate (subtract) color (**Figure 6.53**).

   You can also adjust the amount of color to be added or subtracted using the Flow Percentage slider.

4. Move the brush pointer to the area of your image where you want to change the color's intensity; then hold down the mouse button and drag through the area.

USING THE TONAL ADJUSTMENT TOOLS

Removing Color

Photoshop Elements offers two distinct ways to remove color from an image: converting to grayscale mode, and using the Remove Color command. The differences may seem subtle at first, but the changes they make to your files are really quite significant.

As we mentioned in Chapter 3, an RGB image is constructed of three different color channels (red, green, and blue) which combine in different percentages to produce a full-color image, and that a grayscale image is constructed of just one grayscale channel.

Rather than compressing the color information into one channel, the Remove Color command creates an image that *appears* to be in grayscale, but remains in RGB. The gray tones are actually created by combining equal parts of RGB values in each pixel. Since it's still technically an RGB image, and still composed of three channels, there's no saving of file size. So why use it? Unlike converting to grayscale (which removes all color information from an image) you can use the Remove Color command to remove color from just a portion of an image. This can be used to great effect for highlighting or dimming specific areas, creating neutral fields to place type, or as a first step before applying a colorization or color tinting effect.

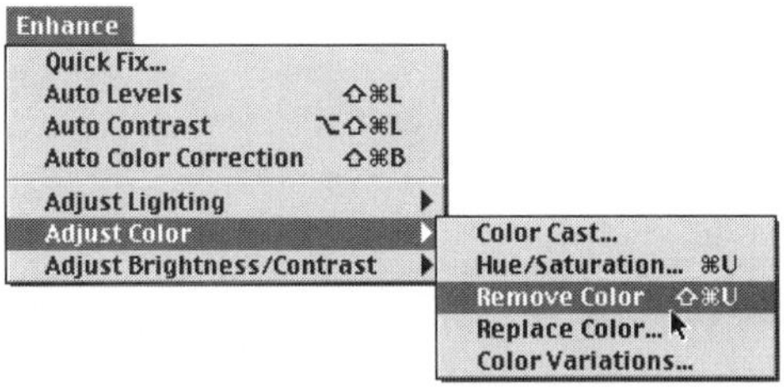

Figure 6.54 You can remove the color from all, or just a portion of an image, by using the Remove Color command.

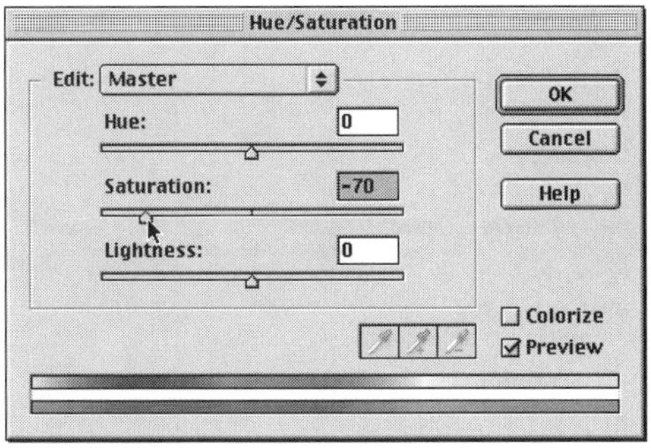

Figure 6.55 Use the Saturation slider in the Hue/Saturation dialog box to control the amount of color you remove from an image.

To apply the Remove Color command:

1. Using any of the selection or marquee tools, select the area of your image you want to remove the color from.

   If you want to apply the Remove Color command to an entire image, it's not necessary to make a selection.

2. From the Enhance menu, choose Adjust Color > Remove Color, or press Shift+Ctrl+U/Shift+Command+U (**Figure 6.54**).

   All color is removed from your image, and is replaced by varying levels of gray.

✔ Tip

- You can actually control how much color to remove from an image or selection by using the Saturation slider in the Hue/Saturation dialog box. From the Enhance menu, choose Adjust Color > Hue/Saturation, or press Ctrl+U/ Command+U to open the dialog box, then move the Saturation slider to the left until you achieve the desired effect (**Figure 6.55**). 0 on the saturation scale represents normal color saturation, while -100 (all the way to the left) represents completely desaturated color, or grayscale.

Adding a Color Tint to an Image

Using a technique called *colorization,* you can add a single color tint to your images, simulating the look of a hand-applied color wash, or the warm, antique glow of an old sepia-toned photograph. You can apply the effect to any image, even if it was originally saved as grayscale, as long as you first convert it to RGB. In addition to colorizing an entire image, you can use any of the selection tools to isolate and tint just a specific area or object. Since the different shades of color applied are determined by the image's original tonal values, photographs with good brightness and contrast levels make the best candidates for colorizing. (For information on tonal values and levels, see "About Tonal Correction" in Chapter 3).

To colorize an image:

1. Using any of the selection or marquee tools, select the area of your image you want to colorize.

   If you want to colorize an entire image, it's not necessary to make a selection.

2. From the Enhance menu, choose Adjust Color > Hue/Saturation, or press Ctrl+U/Command+U to open the Hue/Saturation dialog box (**Figure 6.56**).

3. See that the Preview checkbox selected, then click the Colorize check box (**Figure 6.57**).

   Clicking the Colorize check box converts all the color in the image to a single hue.

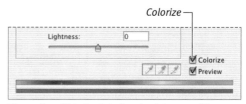

Figure 6.56 Open the Hue/Saturation dialog box to access the Colorize option.

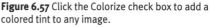

Figure 6.57 Click the Colorize check box to add a colored tint to any image.

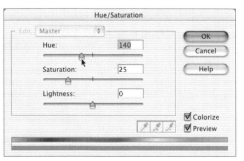

Figure 6.58 The position of the Hue slider determines the color your tinted image will be.

4. Drag the Hue slider right or left until you arrive at the color you like (**Figure 6.58**).

5. Drag the Saturation slider to adjust its values.

   Dragging the slider to the left moves the color's saturation value closer to gray, while dragging it to the right moves its value closer to a pure, fully saturated color.

6. Drag the Lightness slider to adjust the color's brightness values.

   Dragging to the left dims the color's brightness value, shifting it closer to black, while dragging to the right brightens its value, shifting it closer to white.

7. Click OK to close the Hue/Saturation dialog box.

   Your image is now composed of different values of the single color hue you selected.

7

FILTERS AND EFFECTS

For decades, photographers have used lens filters to improve and alter the look of their photographs. Filters are frequently used to change the intensity of color values and to lighten certain tones and darken others. In addition to using filters, photographers also rely on darkroom and printing techniques to create wonderfully creative effects.

But thanks to the advancements of digital technology, users don't have to fiddle with chemicals or additional camera equipment to enhance their photographs. The filters and effects included in Photoshop Elements go way beyond what's been possible in traditional photography. Many of these filters (such as the Sharpen filters) allow you to make subtle corrections and improvements to your photos, while other filters, such as Artistic, Stylize, and Sketch, can transform an image into a completely new piece of artwork. Photoshop Elements also provides effects you can add to your photos, including striking image effects (lizard skin, anyone?) as well as type effects and unique textures.

In this chapter, we explore the many ways you can use filters and effects to take your work to a whole new level, and the filter and effects galleries will help you visualize some of the creative ways you can apply these techniques to your own photos.

Using the Filters and Effects Palettes

Photoshop Elements includes over 100 filters and over 50 effects, offering you almost unlimited possibilities for tweaking and enhancing your images. Most filters include a dialog box where you can preview any changes and adjust the settings for either a subtle or dramatic effect. And some of the filters (such as the Liquify filter) are so complex that they seem like separate little applications within Photoshop Elements.

Effects work a bit differently than filters. When you apply an effect, Photoshop Elements actually runs through a series of automatic actions in which a number of filters and layer styles are applied to your image. Effects are a bit more complex than filters. If you want to add a drop shadow, picture frame, or brushed-metal type to a photo, browse through the Effects palette to see what's available.

To view the Filter or Effects palette:

Do one of the following:

◆ Choose Window > Filters or Window > Effects.

◆ Click the Filters palette tab or Effects palette tab in the palette well.

 You can choose to work with either of these palettes open in the well, or you can drag them into your work area for easier access.

To change the number of filters or effects displayed in the palette:

Do one of the following:

◆ If it's not already selected, choose All from the pop-up menu at the top of either palette to see all filters or effects (**Figure 7.1**).

◆ Select a set of filters or effects from the list at the top of either palette to see just the ones in that set (**Figure 7.2**).

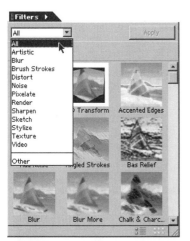

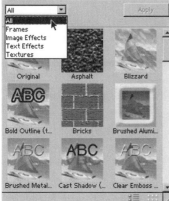

Figure 7.1 If it's not already selected, choose All on the Filters and Effects palettes to see all filters and effects displayed at the same time.

Figure 7.2 To scan your choices more quickly, select a specific group of filters or effects.

To change the palette view:

Do one of the following:

◆ Click the Thumbnail View button to view filters or effects as thumbnails (this is the default) (**Figure 7.3**).

◆ Click the List View button to view filters or effects as a list of effects or filter names. (**Figure 7.4**).

When you select a name in List view, the thumbnail for that specific filter or effect appears under the sample image at the left side of the palette (**Figure 7.5**).

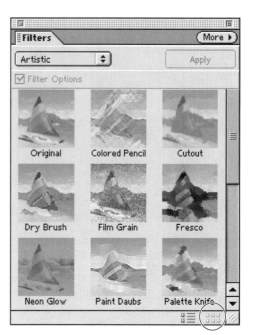

Figure 7.3 Thumbnail view is the default option for viewing filters and effects.

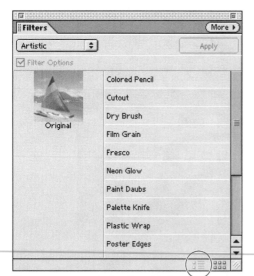

Figure 7.4 Once you're familiar with the Filters palette, you may find it easier to work in List view, as it's faster to navigate than the default Thumbnail view.

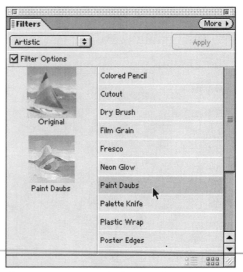

Figure 7.5 In List view, the thumbnail for the selected filter or effect appears in the first column of the palette.

USING THE FILTERS AND EFFECTS PALETTES

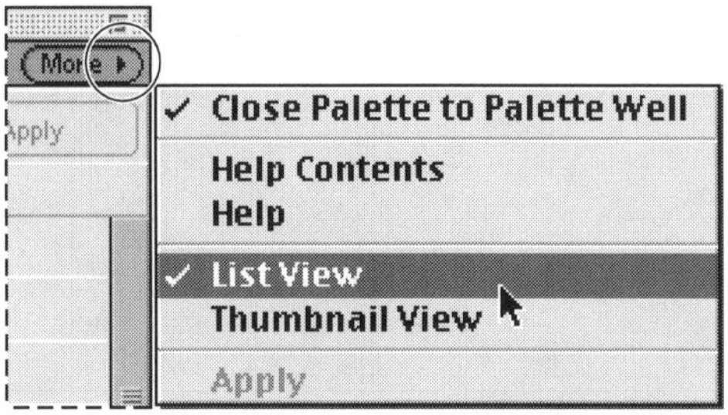

Figure 7.6 Preferences for the Thumbnail and List views are also available from the Filters palette menu.

✔ Tips

- If you want to scroll through the different filters and effects more quickly, choose Thumbnail View or List View from the Filters or Effects palette menu (**Figure 7.6**).

- You can also install and use filter plug-ins created by third-party developers. When installed, these will usually appear at the bottom of the Filters palette menu.

Filter and Effect Plug-ins

Plug-ins provide a nifty way to extend your Photoshop Elements experience. Want to add some sophisticated 3D shadows or translucent effects to your photos? If you can't find the effect or filter you want in Photoshop Elements, chances are good that a plug-in might do the trick. You're in luck—most of the plug-ins designed for Photoshop will work just as well in Photoshop Elements, since both applications use the same file format (PSD). Some plug-in packages, clearly meant for professionals and creative types, don't come cheap—they can cost a few hundred dollars. But many plug-ins are available free of charge. One of the best places to start looking for filter and effect plug-ins is at the Adobe Xchange site (`http://xchange.studio.adobe.com/`), where you can download and share filters, effects, and other plug-in goodies with other Photoshop and Photoshop Elements users.

USING THE FILTERS AND EFFECTS PALETTES

Applying Filters and Effects

Depending on the filter or effect you choose and the size of your image, your computer can take a while to apply and display these changes. Of course, computing power increases dramatically every year, along with the typical amount of RAM installed in most new machines. Both the speed of your processor and amount of RAM contribute to faster processing of these transformations. Fortunately, almost all of the filters include a preview window, which allows you to see the result of the filter before you decide to apply it to your image.

Effects don't include a preview window, but you'll find useful examples of each effect on the Effects palette, as well as in the effects gallery later in this chapter. For many filters and effects, a good approach is to select a small area of your image and apply the change to see the results—that way, you don't waste a lot of time waiting for your computer to process changes to the entire image. The exceptions are effects like Frames or Photo Corners, where the effect is designed to be applied to your entire image. A few effects (such as the Cutout and Recessed frame effects) require you to make a selection before you can apply the effect.

To apply a filter:

1. To apply a filter to an entire layer, select the layer on the Layers palette to make the layer active. To apply a filter to just a portion of your image, select an area with one of the selection tools (**Figure 7.7**).

2. *Do one of the following:*
   ▲ Double-click the filter on the Filters palette (**Figure 7.8**).

Figure 7.7 Filters and effects can be applied to an entire layer or to a selection.

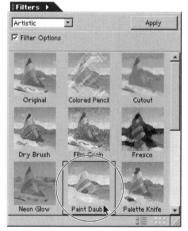

Figure 7.8 To select a filter on the Filters palette, just double-click the filter.

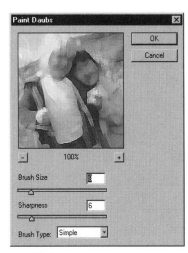

Figure 7.9 Most filters include a dialog box with options that change the way the filter looks when applied to your image.

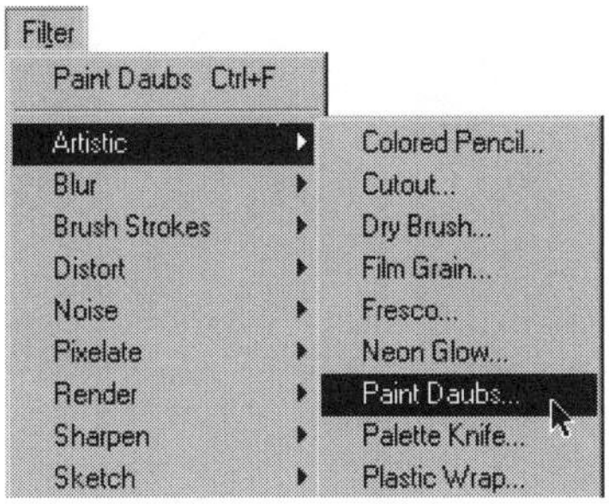

Figure 7.10 To see which filters include dialog box options, refer to the Filter menu. Filters with options include an ellipsis (...) after their names.

If no options are available, then the filter will automatically be applied to your image. If the filter includes options, the filter's dialog box will appear (**Figure 7.9**).

▲ Choose a filter from the submenus of the Filter menu.

   If you look at the Filter menu, you'll see that filters with additional options (and their own unique dialog box) include ellipses (...) after their names (**Figure 7.10**).

▲ Drag any filter from the Filters palette onto your image.

3. If the filter includes a dialog box with options, experiment with the available values and options until you get the look you want.

continues on next page

APPLYING FILTERS AND EFFECTS

4. If the dialog box includes a preview window, you can change the view; *do one of the following:*

  ▲ To zoom in or out, click either the Zoom In (plus sign) or Zoom Out (minus sign) (**Figure 7.11**).

  ▲ Drag your image within the preview window to see a specific area of your image (**Figure 7.12**).

5. Click OK to apply the filter.

The filter is applied to your image (**Figure 7.13**).

If you're not happy with the result, choose Edit > Undo or select the previous state from the Undo History palette.

If you want to instantly apply a filter from the palette menu without previewing it or choosing additional options from the dialog box, uncheck the Filter Options box at the top of the Filters palette.

✔ Tip

■ To view a collection of filter "recipes" you can apply to your own images, see the color plate section of this book.

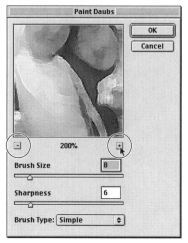

Figure 7.11 Filter dialog box previews include Zoom buttons to change the magnification of the preview image.

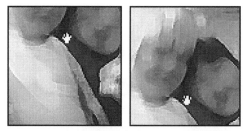

Figure 7.12 To move around (or pan) the preview image, just move your pointer over the preview window until the pointer changes to the Hand tool. Then click and drag to move the image.

Figure 7.13 Click OK to see the filter applied to your image.

APPLYING FILTERS AND EFFECTS

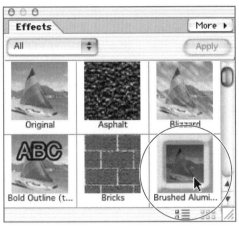

Figure 7.14 To choose an effect on the Effects palette, select the effect and then click Apply, or just double-click the effect. You can also drag an effect or filter directly onto your image.

To apply effects:

1. To apply an effect to an entire layer, select the layer to make it active. To apply an effect to just a portion of your image, select an area with one of the selection tools.

2. Select an effect from the Effects palette and click Apply, or just double-click an effect on the palette (**Figure 7.14**).

   If you prefer, you can also drag any effect from the Effects palette directly onto your image.

   When you apply an effect, it creates one or more new layers immediately above the selected layer (**Figure 7.15**).

continues on next page

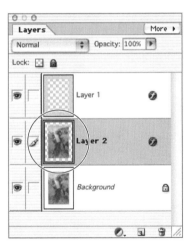

Figure 7.15 When you apply an effect, it generates one or more layers above the selected layers. The number of new layers depends on the series of actions required to create the specific effect.

APPLYING FILTERS AND EFFECTS

187

✔ Tips

- To reduce the visible impact of an effect, change the opacity with the slider on the Layers palette.

- Sometimes the filter or effect name and/or thumbnail representation doesn't tell the whole story. Experiment by pushing the filter and effect options to extreme limits. You'll often been surprised by the results. Print a copy of your image for future reference and use on other photos. It's also a good idea to rename the layer with a descriptive name related to the effect you used: for instance, Blizzard 30%.

- To change the look of an effect, experiment with the various blend modes on the Layers palette.

The Filter Dialog Boxes

Given the sheer number of filters in Photoshop Elements, there's no way we can cover the specific steps for each individual filter in the space of this book. Fortunately, the vast majority of these filters work in the same way, so once you've used a couple of them, you can figure out the rest pretty easily. Almost every filter's dialog box contains a preview window and slider bars that allow you to control the level and intensity of the filter. When using a filter for the first time, you should check it out by previewing the default filter setting and applying it by clicking OK. Not what you wanted? Just press Ctrl+Z/Command+Z to undo your changes and start over. Once you're back in the filter's dialog box, you can experiment by adjusting the sliders to preview more dramatic results in your photo.

Filter Gallery

Artistic filters

Original image

Colored Pencil

Cutout

Dry Brush

Film Grain

Fresco

Neon Glow

Paint Daubs

Palette Knife

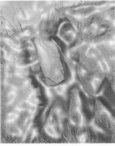

Plastic Wrap

Poster Edge

Rough Pastels

Smudge Stick

Sponge

Underpainting

Watercolor

Blur filters

Original image

Blur

Blur More

Gaussian Blur

Motion Blur

Radial Blur

Smart Blur (Normal)

Smart Blur (Overlay Edge)

Brush Strokes filters

Original image

Accented Edges

Angled Strokes

Crosshatch

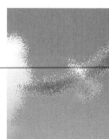

Spray Strokes

Dark Strokes

Ink Outlines

Spatter

Sumi-e

Distort filters

Original image

Diffuse Glow

Glass

Liquify

Ocean Ripple

Pinch

Polar Coordinates

Ripple

Shear

Spherize

Twirl

Wave

ZigZag

Noise filters

Original image

Add Noise

Despeckle

Dust & Scratches

Median

FILTER GALLERY

191

Pixelate filters

Original image

Color Halftone

Crystallize

Facet

Fragment

Mezzotint

Mosaic

Pointillize

Render filters

Original image

Clouds

Difference Clouds

Lens Flare

Lighting Effects

FILTER GALLERY

Sharpen filters

Original image

Sharpen Edges

Sharpen More

Unsharp Mask

Sketch filters

Original image

Bas Relief

Chalk & Charcoal

Charcoal

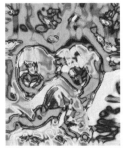

Chrome

Conte Crayon

Graphic Pen

Halftone Pattern

Note Paper

Photocopy

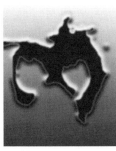

Plaster

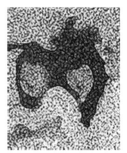

Reticulation

FILTER GALLERY

Sketch filters *continued*

Stamp

Torn Edges

Water Paper

Stylize filters

Original Image

Diffuse

Emboss

Extrude

Find Edges

Glowing Edges

Solarize

Tiles

Trace Contour

Wind

Texture filters

Original Image

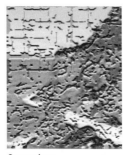

Craquelure

Grain

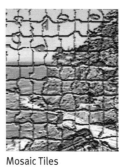

Mosaic Tiles

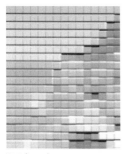

Patchwork

Stained Glass

Texturizer

FILTER GALLERY

Effects Gallery

Frames effects

Original Image

Brushed Aluminum

Cut Out

Drop Shadow

Foreground Color

Photo Corners

Recessed Frame

Ripple Frame

Spatter Frame

Strokes Frame

Text Panel

Vignette

Waves

Wild Frame

Wood Frame

Image effects

Original Image

Blizzard

Flourescent Chalk

Lizard Skin

Neon Nights

Oil Pastel

Soft Flat Color

Soft Focus

Text effects

Original Image

Bold Outline

Brushed Metal

Cast Shadow

Clear Emboss

Confetti

Soft Flat Color

Soft Focus

Text effects *continued*

Sprayed Stencil

Thin Outline

Water Reflection

Wood Paneling

Texture effects

Original Image

Asphalt

Bricks

Cold Lava

Gold Spinkles

Green Slime

Marbled Glass (layer only)

Molten Lead

Rosewood

Rusted Metal

Sandpaper

Sunset (layer only)

EFFECTS GALLERY

Figure 7.16 You can apply the Motion Blur filter to an entire layer or to only a selection. In some cases, such as this photo of the two girls on the beach, you can just select a general area around the object you want to blur.

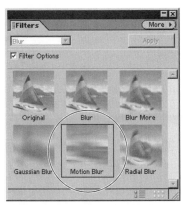

Figure 7.17 Once you've chosen a layer or selection, double-click Motion Blur thumbnail on the Filters palette.

Simulating Action with the Blur Filters

Did you ever try to get kids to stand still so you could take their picture, only to find yourself with a ho-hum batch of static pictures where everyone looks frozen in their tracks? Photoshop Elements includes a couple of blur filters that can create a sense of motion where none exists. In many cases, you'll want to select a specific area in your photo when using these filters, so that the motion or movement is applied to one object, such as a person, your dog, or a pair of shoes.

The Motion Blur filter blurs a layer or selection in a specific direction and intensity. The result can simulate the look of taking a picture of a moving object with a fixed exposure or of panning a camera across a still scene.

The Radial Blur filter can create the impression of a camera zoom or of an object moving toward or away from you. You can also create the impression of an object spinning at variable rates of speed. In either case, the Radial Blur filter lets you control the center of the effect and the amount of blurring or motion.

To add a motion blur to an image:

1. Select the desired layer to make it active. To create a feeling of motion in just a portion of your image, select an area with one of the selection tools (**Figure 7.16**).

2. *Do one of the following:*
   - ▲ Double-click the Motion Blur filter on the Filters palette (**Figure 7.17**).
   - ▲ Choose Filter > Blur > Motion Blur from the main menu.

continues on next page

The Motion Blur dialog box appears with options for the motion angle and distance (**Figure 7.18**).

3. Set the Angle and Distance options to get the look you want. You can refer to the preview window in the dialog box, and if the Preview option is checked, you can also see the results in the main image window.

   By default, the Angle option is set to 0°, meaning that the pixels will be blurred along the horizontal axis as shown next to the Angle text box. So the impression of motion will be right to left (or left to right) across your screen. You can change the angle by dragging the line on the Angle icon or by entering a number of degrees in the Angle text box.

   The Distance option determines the number of pixels included in the linear blur, with the default set to 30 pixels (a moderate amount of blurring). When you reach the upper limits of this option (999 pixels), the objects in your photo may be barely recognizable.

4. When you are satisfied with the effect, click OK to apply it to your image (**Figure 7.19**).

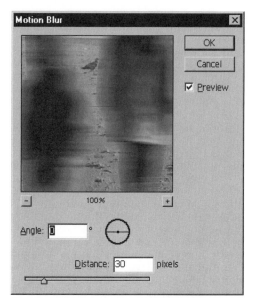

Figure 7.18 The Motion Blur dialog box includes options for the angle and distance of the effect.

Figure 7.19 Click OK to see the Motion Blur filter applied to your image. If you want to back up and try again, just choose Edit > Undo and experiment with different settings.

Figure 7.20 A circular selection, like this windmill, works particularly well with the Radial Blur filter.

To add a circular blur to an image:

1. Select the desired layer to make it active. To create a feeling of radial motion in just a portion of your image, select an area with one of the selection tools.

   A circular (elliptical) selection works especially well when you want to create a circular effect (**Figure 7.20**).

2. Select the Radial Blur by *doing one of the following*:

   ▲ Double-click the Radial Blur filter on the Filters palette (**Figure 7.21**).

   ▲ Choose Filter > Blur > Radial Blur from the main menu.

   The Radial Blur dialog box appears, with options for amount of blur, blur center, blur method, and effect quality (**Figure 7.22**).

   continues on next page

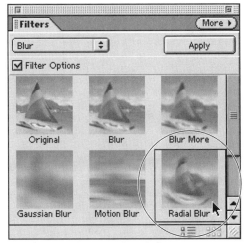

Figure 7.21 The Radial Blur filter is located next to the Motion Blur filter on the Filters palette.

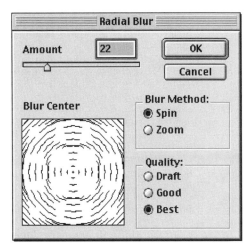

Figure 7.22 The Radial Blur dialog box includes options for the amount and method of blur. This filter does not include a preview, but the Quality options include Draft, which you can use to quickly apply and view the effects of the filter on your image.

3. Set the Amount and Blur Center values for the Radial Blur effect.

The two Blur Method options are Spin and Zoom. Choose Spin to blur along circular lines (**Figure 7.23**) or Zoom to blur along lines radiating from the center, as if you were zooming in or out of an image (**Figure 7.24**).

4. Select a Quality option for the filter.

Draft quality results in quicker completion of the filter, but with slightly coarse results. The **Good** and **Best** options both take a bit longer to complete and provide a smoother look; there's not a big difference between these two options.

5. When you are satisfied with the effect, click OK to apply it to your image.

✔ Tip

- The Radial Blur filter doesn't include a preview window, so if you aren't happy with your results and want to try different settings, just click the Step Backward button (or press Ctrl+Z/Command+Z) to try again.

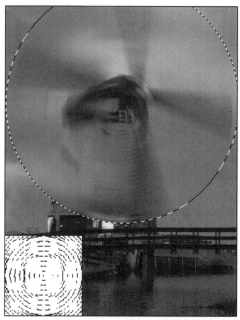

Figure 7.23 The Spin method creates the impression of an object spinning around a center point. To change the center point, drag the preview in the Blur Center window.

Figure 7.24 The Zoom method creates the sense of an object moving toward or away from you.

SIMULATING ACTION WITH THE BLUR FILTERS

The Blur Filters

We've covered the steps for using a couple of our favorite blur filters, but the others are just as powerful and fun to use. Here's a summary of how they work and when you might want to use them.

Blur softens the look of an image or selected area and is great for retouching photos where there's a harsh edge or transition. The results are similar to what you get with the Blur tool.

Blur More works like the Blur filter, but with much greater intensity— it's like using the Blur filter three times on the same image. The results are often too dramatic for minor photo retouching, but are great for blurring one particular area of an image (like the border), thereby emphasizing the untouched areas. Keep in mind that the Blur and Blur More filters don't include a dialog box or preview window. Just select a layer or area and apply the filter to see the results.

Gaussian Blur allows you a greater amount of control, and you can use this filter to make anything from minor to major adjustments to your image. For most simple photo retouching, the Blur command works well, but if you're not happy with your results and want to tweak a bit, try Gaussian Blur.

Motion Blur can be used to simulate a moving object or the panning of a camera.

Radial Blur results in either a zooming or spinning motion, depending on the option you choose.

Smart Blur lets you build customized blurs, with complete control over the blur radius (the distance of the blur effect) and threshold (pixels below the threshold value aren't blurred). Smart Blur is useful for softening an image, or for times when you want a more subtle blur effect.

SIMULATING ACTION WITH THE BLUR FILTERS

Distorting Images

The Distort filters include an amazing array of options that let you ripple, pinch, shear, and twist your images. Experiment with all of the Distort filters to get a feel for the different effects you can add to your images. But one filter stands above all the others in its power, flexibility, and fun factor: the Liquify filter.

The Liquify filter creates amazing effects by letting you warp, twirl, stretch, and twist pixels beyond the normal laws of physics You've probably seen plenty of examples of this filter, where someone's face is wildly distorted with bulging eyes and a puckered mouth. However, you can also use the Liquify filter to create more subtle changes and achieve effects that would be impossible with any other tool.

The Liquefy filter is unique in that it includes a dialog box with its own complete set of image-manipulation tools. And because the Liquify filter works within its own dialog box, you can't undo specific changes with the Edit > Undo command or Undo History palette. Fortunately, the Liquify filter offers its own Reconstruct tool to restore any area to its original (or less contorted) state. The Reconstruct tool allows you to "paint" over your image and gradually return to the original version, or stop at any state along the way. If you just want to go back and start over, then clicking the Revert button is the quickest method.

Figure 7.25 The Liquify filter appears in the Distort category in the Filters palette menu.

Liquify Tools   *Liquify Tool Options*

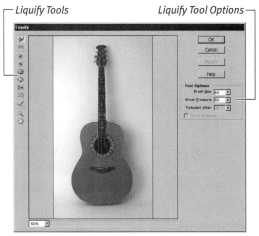

Figure 7.26 The Liquify dialog box includes its own set of distortion tools and includes options for changing the brush size and pressure.

To distort an image with the Liquify filter:

1. Select an entire layer, or make a selection of the area you want to change.

2. Choose Filter > Distort > Liquify from the main menu, or click the Liquify filter on the Filters palette (**Figure 7.25**).

    If your image includes a type layer, you will be prompted to simplify the type to continue. This means that the type layer will be flattened into the rest of your image's layers. Be aware that if you click OK, then the type will no longer be editable.

    The Liquify dialog box appears, with a preview of the layer or selection area. The Warp tool is selected by default, with a brush size of 64 and a pressure of 50 (**Figure 7.26**).

    You'll probably find that you will want to change both the brush size and pressure during the course of your work.

3. To change the brush settings, *do one of the following:*

    ▲ To change the brush size, drag the slider or enter a value in the option box. The brush size can range from 1 to 600 pixels.

    ▲ To change the brush pressure, drag the slider or enter a value in the option box. The brush pressure can range from 1 to 100 percent.

    continues on next page

4. Distort your image with any of the Liquify tools, located on the left side of the Liquify dialog box (**Figure 7.27**) to achieve the look you want. To use any tool, simply select it (just as you do tools on the main toolbar) and then move your pointer into the image (**Figure 7.28**).

To undo changes:

◆ Still in the Liquify dialog box, click the Reconstruct tool, then, while holding down your mouse button, "brush" over your image to gradually undo each change you've made.

To undo all Liquify changes:

◆ Still in the Liquify dialog box, click the Revert button to return the image to its original state.

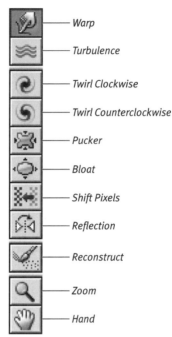

Warp

Turbulence

Twirl Clockwise

Twirl Counterclockwise

Pucker

Bloat

Shift Pixels

Reflection

Reconstruct

Zoom

Hand

Figure 7.27 Use the Reconstruct tool to gradually remove distortion from any portion of your image.

The Liquify Tools

Warp lets you push pixels around as you drag with the mouse.

Turbulence works in a manner similar to the Warp tool, but it incorporates some actions of the other Liquify tools to create random variations, or turbulence. You can change the amount of turbulence with the Turbulence Jitter slider in the tool options.

Twirl Clockwise and **Twirl Counterclockwise** rotate pixels in either direction.

Pucker moves pixels toward the center of the brush area.

Bloat moves pixels away from the brush center and toward the edges of your brush.

Shift Pixels moves pixels perpendicular to the direction of your brush stroke.

Reflection copies pixels to the brush area, allowing you to create effects similar to a reflection in water.

Reconstruct restores distorted areas to their original state. As you brush over areas with this tool, your image gradually returns to its original state, undoing each change you've made with the Liquify tools. You can stop the reconstruction at any point and continue from there.

The **Zoom** and **Hand** tools work just like the ones on the Photoshop Elements toolbar.

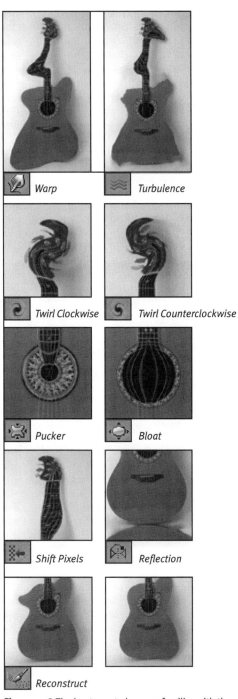

Warp

Turbulence

Twirl Clockwise

Twirl Counterclockwise

Pucker

Bloat

Shift Pixels

Reflection

Reconstruct

Figure 7.28 The best way to become familiar with the Liquify distortion tools is to play with them on a variety of images, as in this series of guitar images.

✔ Tip

■ Here's another way to undo changes to your image: Still in the Liquify dialog box, hold down the Alt/Option key. The Cancel button changes to Reset. Click the Reset button to undo any changes you've made with the Liquify tools. The Revert and Reset buttons work the same way, but the Reset button, true to its name, also resets the Liquify tools to their original settings.

Creating Lights and Shadows

Lights and shadows add drama to almost any photograph. There's still no better way to implement lighting effects than by planning for your lighting before you take your picture. However, there are many times when you just can't control these factors—but Photoshop Elements includes some nifty filters to help you enhance the lighting after the fact.

The Lighting Effects filter lets you create a seemingly infinite number of effects through the combination of light styles, properties, and even a texture channel. It's almost like having your own little lighting studio right on your desktop. The Lens Flare filter simulates the refraction of light shining inside a camera lens. This filter works really well if you've created an image with Photoshop Element's painting and drawing tools and want to make it look like it was shot with a camera. You'll see this technique used quite a bit in computer-animated movies, to give them a more realistic look. Keep in mind, however, that your image must be in RGB mode to use these lighting filters.

To add lighting effects to an image:

1. Select the desired layer to make it active. To confine the lighting effect to just a portion of your image, select an area with one of the selection tools.

2. Select the Lighting Effect filter by *doing one of the following:*
   ▲ Double-click the Lighting Effect filter on the Filters palette (**Figure 7.29**).
   ▲ Choose Filter > Render > Lighting Effects from the main menu.
   The Lighting Effects dialog box appears (**Figure 7.30**).

3. Choose a Style (**Figure 7.31**).

Figure 7.29 The Lighting Effects filter appears in the Render category on the Filters palette menu.

Figure 7.30 When you first open the Lighting Effects dialog box, it may seem a bit intimidating. Worry not. Just experiment with the settings to see the range of effects possible with this filter.

```
2 O'clock spotlight
2 O'clock spotlight
Blue Omni
Circle of Light
Crossing
Crossing Down
Default
Five Lights Down
Five Lights Up
Flashlight
Flood Light
Parallel Directional
RGB Lights
Soft Direct Lights
Soft Omni
Soft Spotlight
Three Down
Triple Spotlight
```

Figure 7.31 The Style pop-up menu reveals 17 unique lighting styles.

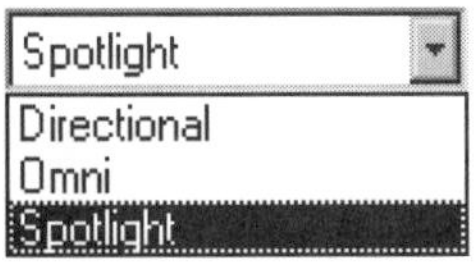

4. Choose a Light Type (**Figure 7.32**).

5. Set light properties (**Figure 7.33**).

6. When you are satisfied with the effect, click OK to apply it to your image (**Figure 7.34**).

Spotlight ▾

Directional
Omni
Spotlight

Figure 7.32 The Light Type pop-up menu includes Directional, Omni, and Spotlight options. Each lighting style is based on one of these three light types.

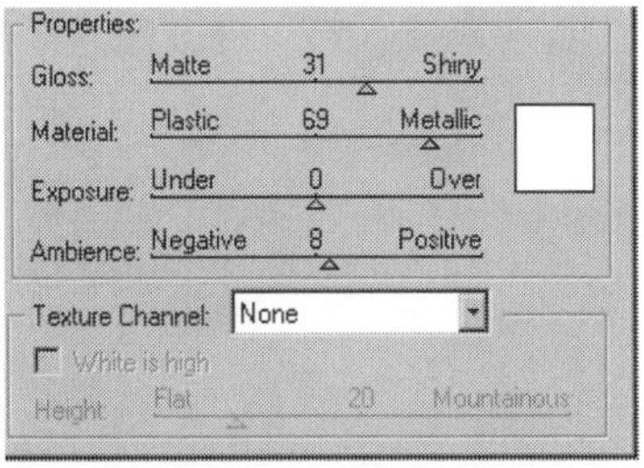

Properties:
Gloss: Matte   31   Shiny
Material: Plastic   69   Metallic
Exposure: Under   0   Over
Ambience: Negative 8   Positive
Texture Channel: None ▾
☐ White is high
Height   Flat   20   Mountainous

Figure 7.33 The Properties area of the Lighting Effects dialog box offers an almost infinite combination of settings that you can use to change the appearance and intensity of the lighting.

Figure 7.34 After selecting the lighting options you want, click OK to apply them to your image. This image combines the Lighting Effects filter with the Solarize filter for a futuristic look.

Light styles and types

The Lighting Effects dialog box offers a mind-boggling number of properties, light types, and styles, making it more than a little difficult to figure out where to start. Here's a list of some of the most useful lighting styles and types, along with some pointers on how styles work with light types and properties.

Lighting styles

2 o'Clock Spotlight adds a soft-focus yellow light to the center of your image.

Flashlight focuses a direct spotlight on the center of the image, with the rest of the image darkened. It's set at a medium intensity with a slightly yellow cast.

Floodlight has a wider focus and casts a white light on your image.

Soft Omni and **Soft Spotlight** provide gentle lightbulb and spotlight effects respectively, and work well for many different kinds of images.

Blue Omni adds a blue overhead light to your image, and offers insight into how lighting styles and types work together. If you select this light type, you'll see a blue color box in the Light Type area of the dialog box (**Figure 7.35**). If you click on this box, the Color Picker appears, letting you change the color to anything you want. Once you've chosen a new color, click Save to apply your custom lighting style to your photo.

This is not a comprehensive list of all the lighting styles in the Lighting Effects dialog box, but an overview of the ones we think you'll find most useful. Most of the remaining lighting styles create more dramatic and specialized effects (for example, RGB Lights consists of red, yellow, and blue spotlights), but are worth exploring if you want to add more creative effects to your image.

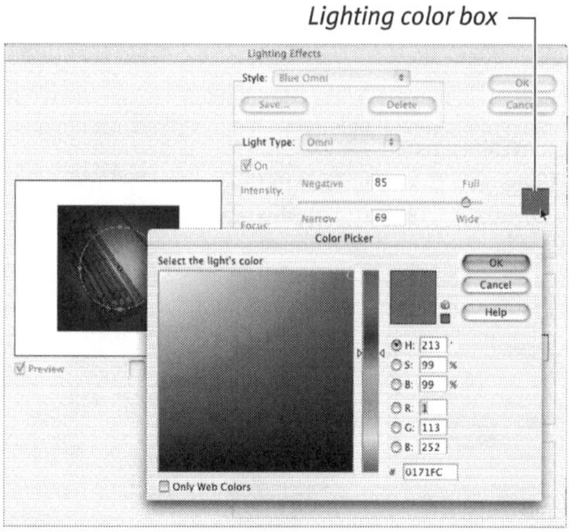

Lighting color box

Figure 7.35 Some lighting styles, such as Blue Omni, include colored lights. Feel free to change the color by clicking the lighting color box, which opens the color picker.

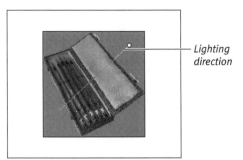

Figure 7.36 The Directional light produces a light source that shines in one direction across your photo, as indicated by the line in the image preview window.

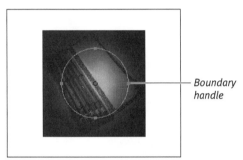

Figure 7.37 The Omni light creates the impression of a light shining directly onto your photo, To change the size of the lit area, just drag one of the boundary handles.

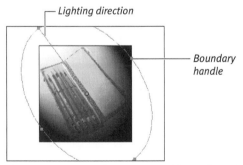

Figure 7.38 The Spotlight is represented by an elliptical boundary in the preview. Drag a handle to change the area being lit, and drag the lighting direction line to change the direction of the light source.

Light types

Directional creates an angled light that shines from one direction across your photo (**Figure 7.36**).

Omni produces a light that shines down on your image from above (**Figure 7.37**).

Spotlight creates a round spotlight in the center of your image. In the preview mode, you'll see that the boundaries of the light look like an ellipse. You can change the size of the ellipse by dragging any of the handles. To change the direction of the light, just drag to move the line (**Figure 7.38**).

When you select a light style, it automatically defaults to whichever light type best supports that look—so, for example, the Floodlight style uses the Spotlight type.

Light properties

Once you've picked a light style and type, you have complete control over four different lighting properties. To change these, just move the sliders to the left or right.

Gloss establishes how much light reflects off your image and can be set from Matte (less reflection) to Shiny (more reflection).

Material determines how much light reflects off your image. It can be set from Plastic to Metallic (and quite frankly, we find these descriptive terms less than helpful). As you move the setting toward Plastic, the color of your light grows stronger, and if you choose Metallic, the color of your image shows through more.

continues on next page

Exposure increases or decreases the light. If you click through the light types, you'll notice that most of them leave this setting at 0, or very close. This is one setting you may just want to leave as is or make only subtle changes to since it has such a pronounced impact on the light.

Ambience refers to ambient lighting, or how much you combine the particular lighting effect with the existing light in your photo). Positive values allow in more ambient light, and negative values allow less.

To add a lens flare:

1. Select the desired layer to make it active. To confine the lighting effect to just a portion of your image, select an area with one of the selection tools.

2. Select the Lens Flare filter by *doing one of the following*:

   ▲ Double-click the Lens Flare filter on the Filters palette (**Figure 7.39**).

   ▲ Choose Filter > Render > Lens Flare from the main menu.

   The Lens Flare dialog box appears, with options for the Brightness, Flare Center, and Lens Type (**Figure 7.40**).

3. Set the brightness option by dragging the slider to the right to increase or to the left to decrease the brightness.

4. To move the flare center, just click the image preview to move the crosshairs to another location.

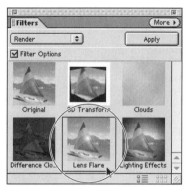

Figure 7.39 The Lens Flare filter is located next to the Lighting Effects filter on the Filters palette.

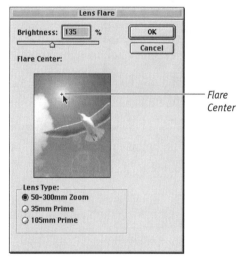

Flare Center

Figure 7.40 The Lens Flare dialog box is much simpler than the one used for Lighting Effects. Use this dialog box to adjust the brightness, flare center, and lens type.

Before   After

Figure 7.41 To add more atmosphere to this photo, we applied the Lens Flare filter with the default brightness of 135 percent and the 50–300mm Zoom lens option.

50–300mm Zoom   35mm Prime   105mm Prime

Figure 7.42 The subtle differences among the three lens options are shown here.

5. Set the Lens Type options as desired; when you're happy with what you see, click OK to apply the filter to your image (**Figure 7.41**).

The options include settings for three common camera lenses (50–300mm Zoom, 35mm, and 105mm), and the filter creates a look similar to the refraction or lens flare you'd get with each (**Figure 7.42**).

Using Textures

You can use Photoshop Elements' many textures to add special effects and virtual "frames" to your photos. For example, you might add the Sunset texture to a portion of your favorite beach photo, or add the Wood Frame texture to a photo before printing it. The Effects palette offers 15 textures that can be applied to either a selected area or your entire image. Keep in mind, however, that textures that include *(layer)* after their name can be applied only to an entire layer, not a selection. These include the Ink Blots, Marbled Glass, Sunset, and Wood - Pine textures.

The Filters palette includes a smaller, more subdued assortment of textures. These tend to be a little less dramatic than the ones you'll find on the Effects palette.

There's also an important distinction to keep in mind when choosing textures from these different palettes: textures from the Effects palette are applied to your image on a separate layer, whereas textures from the Filters palette are applied to the current layer.

If you still can't find the texture you're looking for, you're welcome to load a few additional textures. Photoshop Elements keeps a stash of secret textures in the Textures folder in the Adobe Photoshop Elements folder.

Figure 7.43 To apply a texture to just a portion of your image, make a selection with the Marquee or Lasso tool. We used the Polygonal Lasso to create this selection.

To apply texture to an image:

1. *Do one of the following:*
   - ▲ To apply a texture to a specific area, first make a selection with one of the marquee or lasso tools (**Figure 7.43**).
   - ▲ To apply a texture to the entire image, no selection is necessary.

Figure 7.44 Double-click any texture to instantly apply it to your image.

2. From either the Effects or Filters palette, select the Texture pop-up menu; then double-click the desired texture (**Figure 7.44**).

The texture is applied to either the selection or your entire image (**Figure 7.45**). If you've chosen a texture from the Effects palette, the texture also appears as its own unique layer on the Layers palette (**Figure 7.46**).

continues on next page

Figure 7.45 After you apply the texture, it will appear in the selected area at 100% opacity. Here, we added the Asphalt texture to the beach to create a faux "road."

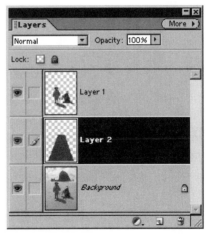

Figure 7.46 Textures selected from the Effects palette appear on their own layer on the Layers palette. In this example, the texture layer has already been moved below Layer 1, which contains the children.

USING TEXTURES

3. If necessary, adjust the blending mode and opacity on the Layers palette (**Figure 7.47**).

You can't adjust the blending mode or opacity of a background layer (it's locked by default), so it's a good idea to create a duplicate or adjustment layer *before* applying textures to your image.

✔ Tip

- After you've selected and applied a texture to your image, you can adjust the intensity of the texture by using the opacity control slider on the Layers palette. (Make sure you haven't applied the texture to a background layer, which is locked.) Since many Photoshop Elements textures are opaque, reducing the opacity level of the texture layer lets your original image peek through, creating a wonderfully unique effect. For example, if you apply the Gold Sprinkles texture to a self-portrait and then reduce the opacity of the texture layer, you'll find you've turned yourself into Goldfinger.

Figure 7.47 In this example, the opacity has been changed to 50 percent to make the new "road" blend in better with the beach.

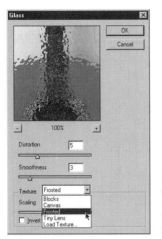

Figure 7.48 The Glass filter is one of many that includes a Texture pop-up menu.

Figure 7.49 You can apply an existing texture, load one of your own, or import one from another application as long as it's in the Photoshop file format.

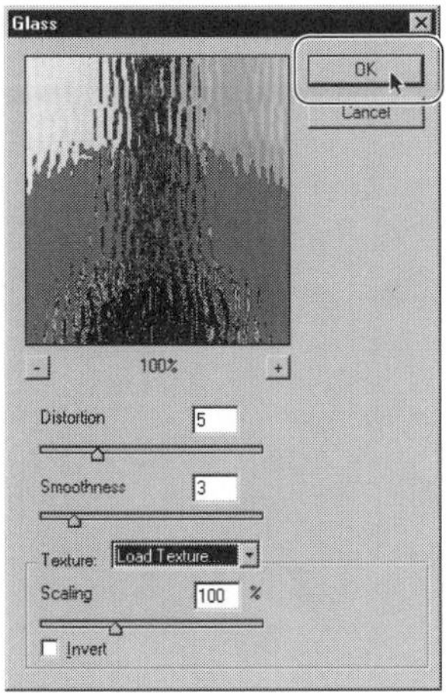

Figure 7.50
After you load a texture, the result is shown in the preview window.

To load additional textures:

1. On the Filters palette menu, select the All pop-up menu if it isn't already selected and make sure that the Filter Options button below it is checked.

2. Choose the Conté Crayon, Glass, Rough Pastels, Texturizer, or Underpainting filter from the Filters palette.

   The filter's dialog box appears with a Texture pop-up menu as one of the setting options (**Figure 7.48**).

3. Select from the list of available textures, or choose Load Texture and then choose the desired texture file (**Figure 7.49**).

   Photoshop Elements includes a premade set of textures that you'll see in the pop-up menu.

4. Click OK to apply the texture (**Figure 7.50**).

✔ Tip

■ If you have a scanner or digital camera, you can use it to create your own textures. Try scanning or photographing any object with an unusual or patterned surface, such as a piece of cloth, gift wrap, your dog, even a slab of slate (as long as it doesn't crush your scanner). Import the texture into your computer; then load the texture into the Presets > Textures folder in the Photoshop Elements folder on your computer's hard drive. Be sure to save your texture in the Photoshop (PSD) file format.

USING TEXTURES

Creating Your Own Filters

If all the existing filters aren't enough, you can create your own filters through a rather arcane feature called the Custom dialog box. (Warning! We're now entering territory that's a bit on the advanced side, even for seasoned Photoshop users.)

The Custom filter allows you to control the brightness value of each pixel, influencing the neighboring pixels through a process called convolution (a mathematical operation). The first time you try this, it very likely *will* seem *convoluted,* but hang in there. With patience and creativity, you can craft filters that would be impossible to create using any other approach.

To create your own filter:

1. Choose Filter > Other > Custom, or select the Custom filter from the Filter palette.

   The Custom dialog box appears. You can change the brightness of each pixel in the image. As you make changes, each pixel is given a new value based on surrounding pixels (**Figure 7.51**).

2. Select the center text box, which controls the initial brightness value for the filter. Enter a value from −999 to +999 (**Figure 7.52**).

   The higher the number, the brighter the filter result becomes.

3. Select a text box next to the first pixel box to change the value of the adjacent pixels.

   You don't need to enter values in all of the boxes. Just let the visible results be your guide. (**Figure 7.53**).

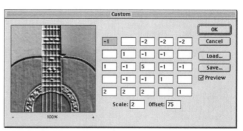

Figure 7.51 The Custom dialog box lets you change the brightness of each pixel.

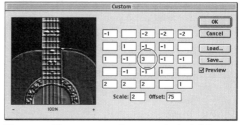

Figure 7.52 The center text box controls the brightness of the selected pixels. The higher the number you enter, the brighter the pixels become.

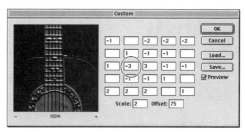

Figure 7.53 Text boxes next to the center box control the brightness of the surrounding pixels.

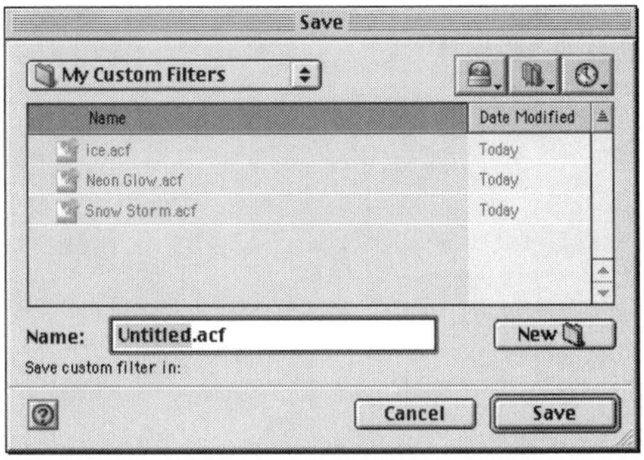

Figure 7.54 You can name and save your own custom filters and then apply them to other images.

4. Change the Scale value to adjust the intensity of the effect.

    The filter takes the total of the values you've entered, and divides them by the value you've entered here. If the overall effect is too strong, try increasing the Scale value to tone down the intensity of the filter.

5. Change the Offset value.

    If you like the look of the filter so far, but think it's too dark, try entering a positive value. If it's too light, enter a negative value.

6. Click OK to apply the custom filter.

    The Load and Save buttons allow you to save and reapply custom filters (**Figure 7.54**).

Using a Custom Filter Example

If you can't create a suitable filter through your experimentation with the Custom filter settings, give this a try. Open an image within Photoshop Elements and then open the Custom dialog box. Enter the settings shown in **Figure 7.55** and click Apply. The results should resemble something like a very subtle crayon drawing (**Figure 7.56**). If you like the results, be sure to save your filter so you can use it again. Then load and reapply this filter a second time to create a very distinct crayon effect (**Figure 7.57**). Incidentally, when you load this filter, you'll notice that any box where you entered a 0 is now empty. That's normal, and is just the way the filter should look.

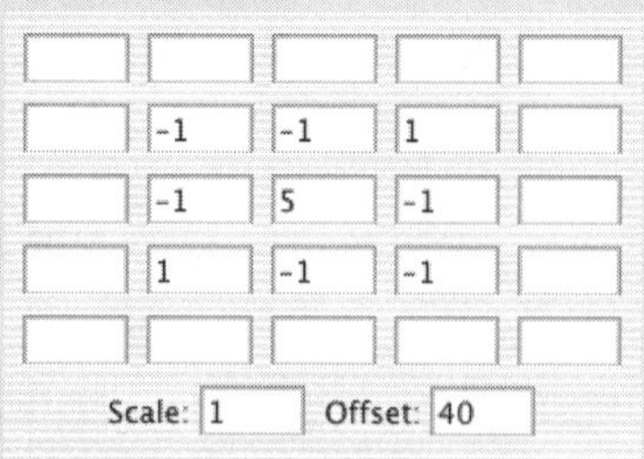

	-1	-1	1	
	-1	5	-1	
	1	-1	-1	

Scale: 1   Offset: 40

Figure 7.55 Try entering the options shown here to produce an artistic, crayonlike filter.

Figure 7.56 When you apply this custom filter the first time, the results are very subtle.

Figure 7.57 Apply the filter a second (or even third) time to the same image to see a more dramatic change.

Working with Color

Most images imported from a digital camera or scanner will open in RGB mode. RGB is shorthand for red, green, and blue, the only three colors that your computer monitor actually displays. RGB combines the three colors in different proportions and intensities to create the thousands or milions of colors you see onscreen. RGB is Photoshop Elements' default color mode, and is the best mode to work in when making color and tonal corrections.

Color cast refers to a shift of color to one extreme or another, and is sometimes introduced into digital photos or scanned images. The image at top left has an unfortunate pinkish cast, which we removed by applying the Auto Color Correction command (below right).

Use the Replace Color command to select a specific color, even if it appears in different areas of the same image, and then replace that color universally. Here, we changed the girls' coats from pink to a sunny yellow.

When you convert an image to grayscale, the three RGB color channels are reduced to just one one grayscale channel. Although the color is removed, a grayscale image still retains all the subtle gradients and tonal value in the original color version.

Blending Modes
A complete gallery of the blending modes you can apply from the Layers palette.

Layer 1 and Background

Normal

Dissolve

Darken

Multiply

Color Burn

Linear Burn

Lighten

Screen

Color Dodge

Linear Dodge

Overlay

Soft Light

Hard Light

Vivid Light

Linear Light

Pin Light

Difference

Exclusion

Hue

Saturation

Color

Luminosity

Layer Styles Sampler
A sample gallery of the styles you can apply from the Layer Styles palette.

Layer 1 and Background

Normal

Simple Inner
Bevel style

Hard Edge
Drop Shadow style

Soft Edtge
Drop Shadow style

Small Border
Inner Glow style

Low
Inner Shadow style

Noisy Stripes
Inner Shadow style

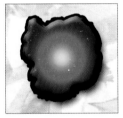

Color Target
Complex style

White Grid on Orange
Complex style

Rose Impressions
Complex style

Orange Translucent
Glass Button style

Tile Mosaic
Image Effects style

Satin Sheets
Patterns style

Waves
Patterns style

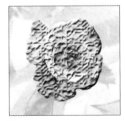

Bumpy
Patterns style

Blue/Gray Swirl
Wow Chrome style

Shiny Round Bevel
Wow Chrome style

Yellow Neon
Wow Neon style

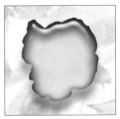

Aqua Blue Plastic
Wow Plastic style

Filters
Add artistic effects to your photos by applying these filters from the Filters menu or palette.

Artistic > Cutout
No. of Levels: 8
Edge Simplicity: 2
Edge Fidelity: 2

Stylize > Wind
Method: Blast
Direction: From the
Right

Distort > Zig Zag
Amount: 35%
Ridges: 11
Style: Pond Ripple

Brush Strokes > Spatter
Spray Radius: 12
Smoothness: 5

Artistic > Dry Brush
Brush Size: 4
Brush Detail: 10
Texture: 2

Filters Add artistic effects to your photos by applying these filters from the Filters menu or palette.

Pixelate > Crystallize
Cell Size: 12

Stylize > Emboss
Angle: 135 °
Height: 8 pixels
Amount: 110%

Artistic > Cutout (layer 1)   **Sketch > Stamp** (layer 2)
No. of Levels: 3   Light/Dark Balance: 25
Edge Simplicity &Fidelity: 4   Smoothness: 5

Combine both layers using the Soft Light blending mode.

Render > Lens Flare
Brightness: 135
Lens Type: 105mm Prime

Creative Techniques

Create a panorama with Photomerge

Step 1 Collect all the photos together that you want to assemble into your panorama.

Step 2 Photomerge does its best to assemble your photos together, but you can always adjust their arrangement or position by hand.

Step 3 Once all the images have been merged, you can apply special lighting and perspective effects, and can change the location of the panorama's vanishing point, if you like. When you're finished making your adjustments, Photoshop Elements saves your panorama as a separate file, where you can then crop it and make any final color and tonal adjustments.

Web Photo Gallery

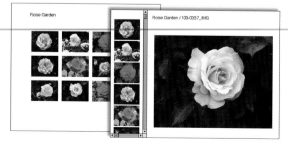

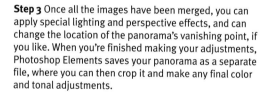

You can create an interactive gallery of your photos with the Web Photo Gallery feature. Using the Web Photo Gallery dialog box, you can organize your images and choose from a variety of Web page backgrounds and interfaces. When you're ready, Photoshop Elements automatically formats and copies your selected images to a single folder, and even generates the required HTML code for you.

Creative Techniques

Creating Animated GIFs

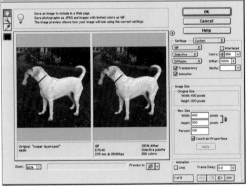

Step 1 Open all the images that you want to use as frames within your animation, then decide on the order that you want them to appear. If you download frames from a video camera, Photoshop Elements gives you several options for naming them in sequence, which can make this task a lot easier.

Step 2 Open a new file, sizing it to the dimensions you want your final animation to be, then drag the individual frames, in order, into the new file. A new layer is created with each image you add to the file. The first frame of your animation will become Layer 1, the second frame will become Layer 2, and so on.

Step 3 With your new layered file still open, choose File > Save for Web to open the Save For Web dialog box. The dialog box opens, with a preview of a sample frame of your animation, and displays according to the optimization settings you choose in the dialog box. Select a GIF setting, then click to select the Animate check box. Photoshop Elements automatically optimizes all the frames of your animation. You can then click the controls at the bottom of the window to preview and set timing and looping options before you click OK to complete your animation.

You can also create animation from a still image by duplicating the image and placing the copies onto a series of layers. By slightly shifting the position of each layer either horizontally or vertically, the saved animation will create the illusion of a camera panning through your photograph.

Creative Techniques

Compositing Images

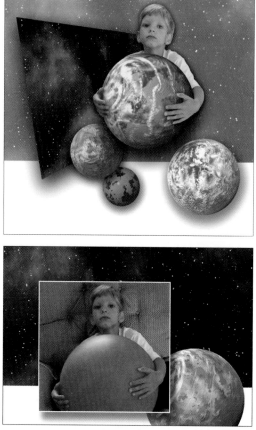

When you combine multiple images together to create a totally new image, that's called compositing. With the help of Photoshop Elements' flexible selection tools and powerful Layers palette, you can combine almost any number of images together to create fun effects.

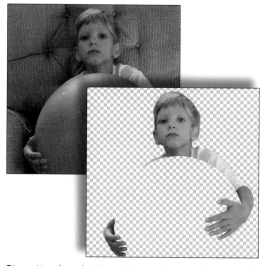

Step 1 Open all the images that you want to include in your new composite image.

Step 2 Use the selection and eraser tools to clean up and remove portions of your images that you don't need.

Step 3 Begin your composite by copying and pasting the first file into the background file.

Step 4 Continue to add other image elements until you're satisfied with your composition. Add Layer styles to enhance the image, if appropriate. In this example, we applied the Low Drop Shadow to the boy so that his hands and arm cast a subtle shadow on the planet he's holding.

PAINTING AND DRAWING

Back in 1984, a fast-growing company just south of San Francisco introduced a little beige box with a tiny 9-inch monitor that could display and print only black-and-white images and that was incapable of reproducing even remotely convincing photographic images. What it could reproduce was strictly limited to a resolution of 72 pixels per inch. Yet the graphic arts world went nuts over this new computer—Apple's earliest Macintosh—because bundled in its modest software suite, alongside its stunted word processor, was MacPaint.

Painting and drawing programs have progressed by leaps and bounds since taking those first baby steps, but one feature remains common: they're still so much fun to use! In this chapter, you'll learn how to use Photoshop Element's built-in drawing and painting tools to create original artwork or to enhance your digital photos, whether you're filling parts of your image with color, creating a blended gradient, adding a decorative stroked border to a logo or design element, or "painting" a photo with Impressionist-style brushstrokes.

About Bitmap Images and Vector Graphics

Photoshop Elements' painting and drawing tools render artwork in two fundamentally different ways: they're designed to manipulate and create two different kinds of graphics.

The painting tools, including all the varied fills, gradients, brushes, and erasers, work by making changes to pixels—adding them, removing them, or changing their color. They're all about the manipulation and alteration of *bitmap images,* or bitmaps. A bitmap image is composed entirely of tiny pixels. Digital photos, the mainstay of Photoshop Elements, are bitmap images. While you can apply paintbrushes, color fills, special effects, and filters to bitmaps, they simply don't resize well. If you try to enlarge a digital photo, for example, you'll see that its image quality suffers as the pixels get bigger, resulting in a blurry mess.

The drawing tools (shape creation tools, really) form images not by manipulating pixels but by constructing geometric paths based on precise mathematical coordinates, or *vectors.* Images created with these drawing tools, known as *vector graphics,* hold one decided advantage over their bitmap cousins: they can be scaled up or down, virtually infinitely, with no loss of detail or resolution (**Figure 8.1**). Photoshop Elements' scalable fonts, for example, are based on vector shapes, so they can be stretched, warped, and resized to your heart's content. Vector graphics also tend to be smaller than comparable bitmap images, since a path shape requires less information for your computer to process and render than a similar shape constructed of pixels.

Although they're designed to work with different kinds of graphics, Photoshop Elements' painting and drawing tools are equally easy to use, and work well together if you want to combine vector and bitmap graphics—such as adding type or custom shapes to a favorite photo.

Figure 8.1 A photographic bitmap image (top) is constructed of pixels. Any attempt to zoom in on or enlarge a portion of the image can make the pixels more pronounced and the image more pixelated. A vector image (bottom) is drawn with a series of geometric paths, rather than pixels. Vector graphics can be enlarged or reduced with no loss of detail or resolution.

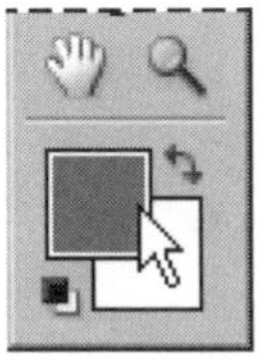

Figure 8.2 Clicking the foreground or background color swatch in the toolbox opens the Color Picker.

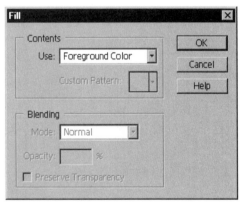

Figure 8.3 The Fill dialog box offers several options for filling a layer or selection with color.

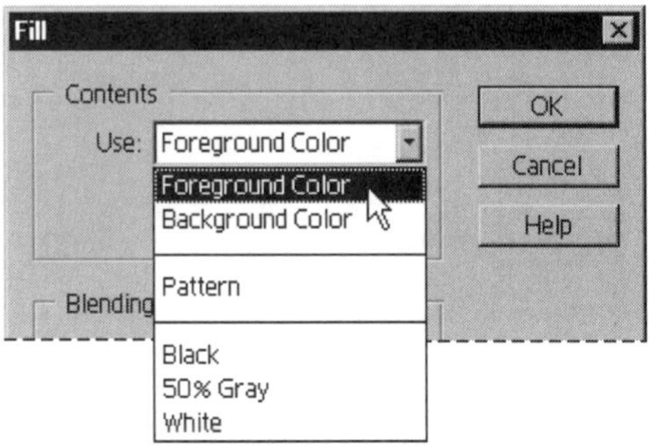

Figure 8.4 The Use pop-up menu contains various sources from which to choose a fill color. Choose the Foreground Color option to apply a specific color chosen from the Color Picker or Swatches palette.

Filling Areas with Color

You have two primary ways of filling areas with a pure, solid color. With the Fill dialog box, you can quickly blanket an entire layer, or a selected area of a layer, with color. The Paint Bucket tool operates in a more controlled manner, filling only portions of areas based on properties that you set on the options bar. Either method works especially well for those times when you want to cover large, expansive areas with a single color.

To fill a selection or layer with color:

1. Using any of the selection or marquee tools, select the area of your image you want to fill with color.

    If you want to fill an entire layer, it's not necessary to make a selection.

2. To select a fill color, *do one of the following:*

    ▲ Click either the current foreground or background color swatch at the bottom of the toolbox (**Figure 8.2**) to open the Color Picker; then select a color.

    ▲ From the Swatches palette, click any color to select it.

3. From the Edit menu, choose Fill, or press Shift+Backspace/Shift+Delete.

    The Fill dialog box opens (**Figure 8.3**).

4. From the Use pop-up menu, choose a source for your fill color (**Figure 8.4**).

    In addition to the foreground and background colors, you can use the Fill command to fill a selection or area with a pattern or with black, white, and 50 percent gray.

5. From the Blending area of the dialog box, select a blending mode and opacity for your fill. (For more information on blending modes, see "About Opacity and Blending Modes" in Chapter 5.)

continues on next page

FILLING AREAS WITH COLOR

6. Click the Preserve Transparency check box if you want to preserve a layer's transparency when you apply the fill.

7. Click OK to close the dialog box.

The selection or layer is filled with the color and properties you specified (**Figure 8.5**).

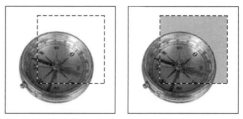

Figure 8.5 In this example, an area of the Background layer is selected (left), then filled with a color using the Fill dialog box (right).

✔ Tips

- To save time, you can use simple keyboard shortcuts to fill a selection or layer with either the current foreground or background color. Alt+Backspace/ Option+Delete will fill a selection or layer with the current foreground color, and Ctrl+Backspace/Command+Delete applies the current background color.

- To swap the foreground and background colors, press X.

- To convert the foreground and background color to black and white, press D.

About Preserving Transparency

The Preserve Transparency check box works just like the Lock Transparent Pixels button on the Layers palette. If the check box is highlighted and you fill a layer that has both opaque and transparent pixels, the transparent areas will be locked (or protected), and only the opaque areas of the layer will be filled (**Figure 8.6**). If you check Preserve Transparency and then try to fill an empty layer (one containing only transparent pixels), the layer will remain unfilled. That's because the whole layer, being transparent, is locked. If you fill a flattened layer, like Photoshop Elements' default Background layer, the check box is dimmed and the option isn't available because a Background layer contains no transparency.

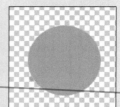

Figure 8.6 When a layer (left) is filled using the Preserve Transparency option, the transparent areas of the layer will remain protected and untouched, and only the layer object will accept the fill color (right).

FILLING AREAS WITH COLOR

Figure 8.7 The Paint Bucket tool.

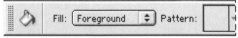

Figure 8.8 To fill an area with a color, Foreground must be selected on the option bar's Fill pop-up menu.

Figure 8.9 The Paint Bucket tool takes advantage of all of Photoshop Elements' blending modes and opacity options.

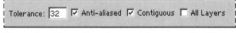

Figure 8.10 The options bar contains several settings you can use to fine-tune the Paint Bucket's fill properties.

To apply fill color with the Paint Bucket tool:

1. Select the Paint Bucket tool from the toolbox (K) (**Figure 8.7**).

2. Select a foreground color from either the Color Picker or the Swatches palette.

3. On the options bar, check that Foreground is selected in the Fill pop-up menu (**Figure 8.8**).

   The Paint Bucket tool can also be used to fill an area with a pattern.

4. Again on the options bar, select a blending mode and opacity setting, if desired (**Figure 8.9**).

5. Still on the options bar, set a Tolerance value; then specify whether you want the colored fill to be anti-aliased, to fill only contiguous pixels, or to affect all layers (**Figure 8.10**).

   For more information on these options, see the Paint Bucket sidebar on the following page.

6. Click the area of your image where you want to apply the colored fill.

   The selected color is painted into your image (**Figure 8.11**).

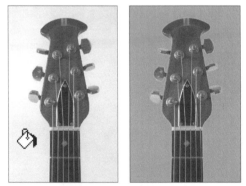

Figure 8.11 The Paint Bucket tool fills areas based on their tonal values. Here it automatically selects and fills just the light-colored background area.

FILLING AREAS WITH COLOR

How Does That Paint Bucket Tool Work, Anyway?

If you're familiar with other painting and drawing programs, Photoshop Elements' Paint Bucket tool may leave you scratching your head. In many paint programs, the Paint Bucket tool does little more than indiscriminately dump color across large areas of an image. But Photoshop Elements' Paint Bucket tool is much more intelligent and selective about where it applies color. Depending on the parameters you set in the options bar, it fills areas based on the tonal values of their pixels.

The **Tolerance** slider determines the range of pixels the Paint Bucket fills. The greater the value, the larger the range of pixels is filled.

Click **Anti-aliased** to add a smooth, soft transition to the edges of your color fill.

Click **Contiguous** to limit the fill to pixels similar in color or tonal value that touch, or are *contiguous* with, one another. If you're using the Paint Bucket tool to switch your car's color from green to blue, this ensures that only the *car's* green pixels are turned blue—not all the green pixels within the entire image.

If you select the **All Layers** checkbox, Photoshop Elements recognizes and considers pixel colors and values across all layers, but the fill is applied only to the active layer. This means that if you click the Paint Bucket tool in an area of any *inactive* layer, the fill will be applied to the current *active* layer (**Figure 8.12**).

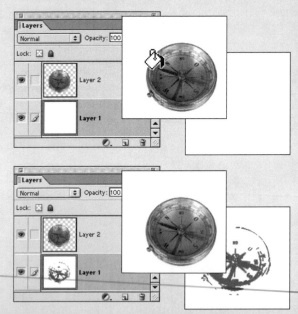

Figure 8.12 If the All Layers checkbox is selected and you click the Paint Bucket tool in an inactive layer (top), the fill for that specific area is applied to the active layer (bottom).

Figure 8.13 The Gradient tool.

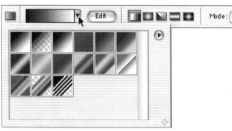

Figure 8.14 Open the gradient picker to select from sets of gradient thumbnails.

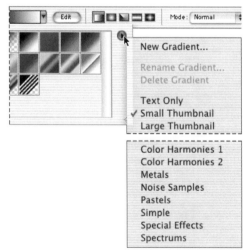

Figure 8.15 The gradient picker's menu offers several picker display options plus access to a variety of gradient sets.

Filling Areas with a Gradient

The Gradient tool fills any layer or selection with smooth transitions of color, one blending gradually into the next. They can be rendered as opaque fills or seamlessly incorporated into a layered project using any of Photoshop Elements' blending modes and opacity settings. You can use a gradient to create an effective background image for a photo; to screen back just a portion of an image; to create an area on which to place type; or you can apply it to any shape or object to simulate the surface texture of metal or glass.

To apply a gradient fill:

1. Using any of the selection or marquee tools, select the area of your image where you want to apply the gradient.

   If you want to fill an entire layer, you don't need to make a selection.

2. Select the Gradient tool from the toolbox (G) (**Figure 8.13**).

3. On the options bar, click to open the gradient picker (**Figure 8.14**).

4. Click to choose from the list of default gradients, or if you want to view additional gradient sets, click the More button (the triangle to the right of the thumbnail images) to open the Gradient palette menu (**Figure 8.15**).

5. Select from the list of gradient sets in the bottom section of the menu.

   The gradient picker displays the new gradient set.

   continues on next page

6. On the options bar, click to choose a gradient type (**Figure 8.16**).

You can choose from among five gradient types: Linear, Radial, Angle, Reflected, and Diamond

7. In the image window, click and drag in the area where you want to apply the gradient (**Figure 8.17**).

The selection or layer is filled with the gradient.

✔ Tip

■ Hold down the Shift key to constrain a gradient horizontally, vertically, or at a 45-degree angle.

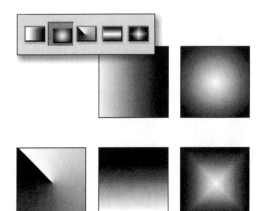

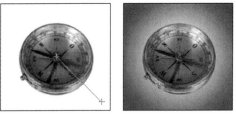

Figure 8.16 Click a gradient type button on the options bar to draw one of five gradient types.

Figure 8.17 Drag from the center to the edge to create a halo effect with the Radial gradient.

FILLING AREAS WITH A GRADIENT

Figure 8.18 The Edit button on the options bar opens the Gradient Editor.

Gradient thumbnails   *Gradient preview bar*

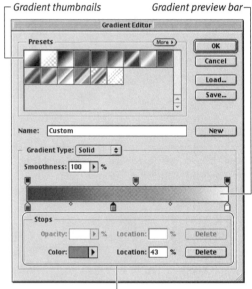

Gradient stop settings

Figure 8.19 The Gradient Editor dialog box.

Creating and Saving Custom Gradients

Although Photoshop Elements ships with a wide variety of gradients and gradient sets, at some point, you may want to create your own customized gradient effects. All of the tools you'll need are provided in one powerful package. With the Gradient Editor, you can not only create new gradients—you can create and save new gradient sets, which you can then access and load from the gradient picker. In addition, you can use Photoshop Elements' Preset Manager to organize and edit your new gradient sets.

To create a new gradient:

1. Select the Gradient tool from the toolbox.

2. On the options bar, click the Edit button to the right of the gradient picker (**Figure 8.18**).

   The Gradient Editor dialog box opens (**Figure 8.19**).

3. From among the gradient thumbnails in the Presets area, click to select a gradient similar to the one you want to create.

   Keep in mind that any new gradient you create must be based on an *existing* gradient, so you can save yourself a little time by starting with a gradient that has properties (numbers of bands of color, opacity settings, and so on) similar to the new gradient that you have in mind.

   You create and modify gradients primarily by editing the gradient preview in the lower portion of the dialog box. Color stops on the bottom side of the gradient preview define which colors a gradient contains, while opacity stops along the top allow you to add levels of transparency to different sections of the gradient.

   continues on next page

4. Click a color stop to select it
(**Figure 8.20**).

5. To assign a new color to the color stop,
do one of the following:

▲ Click directly in the Color box to
open the Color Picker; then select a
new color from there.

▲ Click the arrow next to the color box
to open the color pop-up menu. From
the pop-up menu, choose either the
current foreground or background
color (**Figure 8.21**).

Be aware that this option doesn't assign
a specific color to the color stop, but creates a kind of link to the foreground or
background color swatch in the toolbox.
This means that if you change the foreground or background color, the color stop
(and the section of gradient it defines)
will change color too.

If you want to permanently assign a current foreground or background color to a
color stop, first select either option from
the pop-up menu, then choose User Color
from the same menu. Selecting User color
will break the link to the toolbox swatches
and lock that color into the color stop
(**Figure 8.22**).

The gradient preview changes to reflect
the color change.

Assign colors to the remaining color
stops in the same fashion.

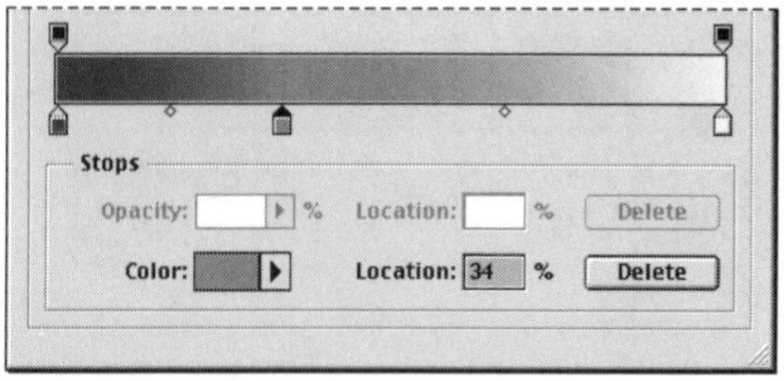

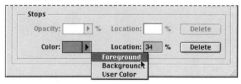

Figure 8.20 You can position the Gradient Editor's
color stops anywhere on the gradient preview bar.

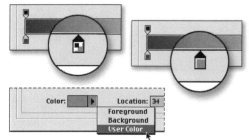

Figure 8.21 Assign a foreground or background color
to a color stop from the Color pop-up menu.

Figure 8.22 Select User Color from the Color pop-up
menu to change a linked foreground or background
color stop (left) to an unlinked, self-contained color
stop (right).

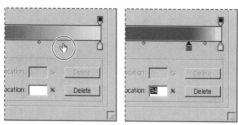

Figure 8.23 You can add and modify any number of new color stops.

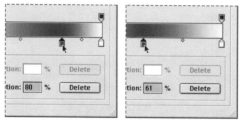

Figure 8.24 Move a color stop to change a color's location in the gradient.

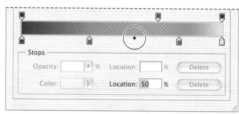

Figure 8.25 A gradient midpoint at its default location halfway between two color stops.

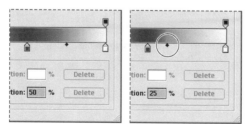

Figure 8.26 As you move a gradient midpoint, you change the position of the transition area where two colors in the gradient mix together.

6. To add a new color stop, move the pointer to any spot directly below the gradient preview; then click once (**Figure 8.23**).

   A new color stop appears, which in turn adds a new color to the gradient in the gradient preview.

   The color of the new color stop is determined by the current color displayed in the Color box. If the Color box is grayed-back and inactive, then the last color that appeared in the Color box will be applied to the new color stop.

7. To move a color stop, *do one of the following:*

   ▲ Click and drag the stop to a new location below the gradient preview (**Figure 8.24**).

   ▲ Enter a percentage value in its Location text box, below the gradient preview.

   As the color stop moves, the color associated with it in the gradient preview will shift accordingly.

   Between each set of color stops is a gradient midpoint—the point where two gradient colors meet and mix. The default midpoint location is 50%, or exactly half way between color stops (**Figure 8.25**).

8. To move a gradient midpoint, *do one of the following:*

   ▲ Click and drag the midpoint to anywhere between its two color stops.

   ▲ Enter a percentage value in its Location text box, below the gradient preview (**Figure 8.26**).

   As the midpoint moves, the area where the two colors mix in the gradient preview will shift accordingly.

continues on next page

CREATING AND SAVING CUSTOM GRADIENTS

9. Drag the Smoothness slider above the gradient preview, to decrease or increase the smoothness of the transitions between the new gradient color and those surrounding it (**Figure 8.27**).

10. To remove a color stop, drag the stop straight down, away from the gradient preview.

    The color stop disappears, as does its associated color in the gradient preview.

11. To change a gradient's opacity, click to select an opacity stop, located above the gradient preview; then move the Opacity slider in the lower portion of the dialog box (**Figure 8.28**).

    Additional opacity stops can be added just like color stops, by clicking directly *above* the gradient preview.

12. Name your gradient, if you like; then click the New button.

    Your new gradient appears with the other thumbnail views in the Presets portion of the dialog box (**Figure 8.29**).

13. Click OK to close the dialog box.

    Your new gradient is displayed in the gradient picker preview, on the options bar.

    When you create a new gradient, it's saved (at least temporarily) in Photoshop Elements' preset file. But once you reset the gradients in the gradient picker or select a different gradient set, any new gradients you've created will be lost. Fortunately, you can use the Gradient Editor and gradient picker to save your own gradient sets.

✔ Tip

■ If you open the Swatches palette prior to opening the Gradient Editor, you can assign colors to color stops by clicking on the swatches in the palette. Remember, you'll need to have the palette open on your desktop, outside of the palette well, in order to access it once the Gradient Editor is open.

Figure 8.27 With the Smoothness slider set at 100% the transitions between colors are subtle and gradual (top). As the slider moves closer to 0, the transitions become a bit more harsh (bottom).

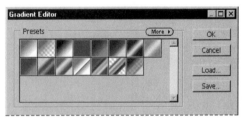

Figure 8.28 Opacity stops, in tandem with the Opacity slider, allow you to change the opacity of areas within a gradient.

Figure 8.29 When you create a new gradient, it's automatically displayed with the other gradients in the Presets thumbnail window.

CREATING AND SAVING CUSTOM GRADIENTS

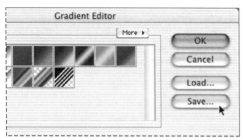

Figure 8.30 Click the Gradient Editor's Save button to open the Save dialog box.

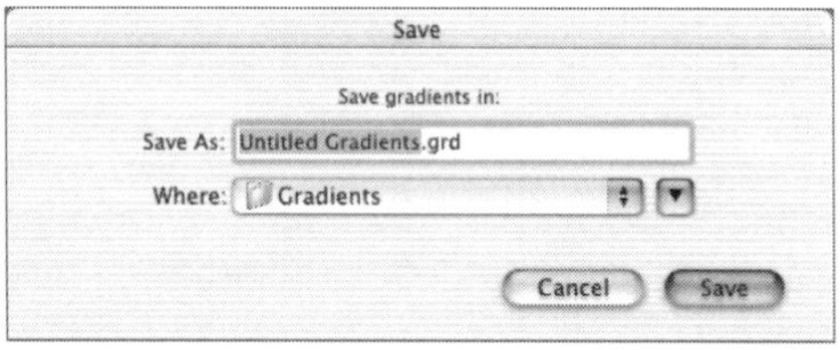

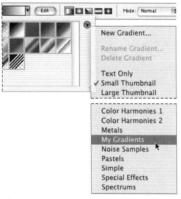

Figure 8.31 Enter a name for your new gradient set in the Save As text box.

Figure 8.32 The next time you start Photoshop Elements, your new gradient set appears with the others on the gradient picker menu.

Figure 8.33 The Preset Manager is actually four different preset managers in one.

To create a new gradient set:

1. Create as many new custom gradients as you like, as described in the previous procedure.

2. In the Gradient Editor dialog box, click the Save button (**Figure 8.30**).

   The Save dialog box opens with the Gradients presets folder automatically selected as the destination to which your new gradient set will be saved (**Figure 8.31**).

3. Enter a new name for your gradient set; then click Save.

   Your new gradient set will be saved with the others (**Figure 8.32**), but it won't appear on either the More menu in the Gradient Editor or the pop-up menu in the gradient picker until after you quit and then restart Photoshop Elements.

   Once you've created a new gradient set, particularly if you've based it on an existing set, you may want to do a little house-keeping by saving some gradients and throwing others away. You can use the Photoshop Elements Preset Manager to clean up your new gradient sets.

To edit a gradient set:

1. From the Edit menu, choose Preset Manager to open the Preset Manager dialog box.

2. From the Preset Type pop-up menu, choose Gradients (**Figure 8.33**), or press Ctrl+3/Command+3.

continues on next page

3. From the Preset Manager's More menu, choose the gradient set that you want to edit.

Remember that if you've created a new gradient set, you'll need to quit and then restart Photoshop Elements before your new set will appear in any of the pop-up menus.

4. In the thumbnail area, Shift+click to select only the gradients that you want to keep in your gradient set (**Figure 8.34**).

If you select a gradient by mistake, deselect it by holding down Shift and clicking it a second time.

5. Click the Save Set button to open the Save dialog box.

6. Check that the name in the File Name text box is the same as the one that you've been editing; then click Save.

Your gradient set will be resaved, this time containing only those gradients that you selected in step 4.

Alternatively, you can enter a different name in the File Name text box to create a brand-new gradient set.

Figure 8.34 Every gradient thumbnail you select will be included in your new gradient set when you click Save Set.

Gradient Types

You can create two gradient types from the Gradient Editor: Solid and Noise.

Solid is the default gradient type. When creating or editing a gradient in Solid mode, you can add color and opacity stops and adjust the smoothness of the transition between colors with a percentage slider. You can also change the location of the Color and Opacity stops and their midpoints.

Noise is, well, largely useless. Noise creates random bands of color based on either the RGB or HSB color model, and although there must be some good application for it somewhere, we have yet to stumble on what it might be. Feel free to experiment with this gradient, but you probably won't end up using it much.

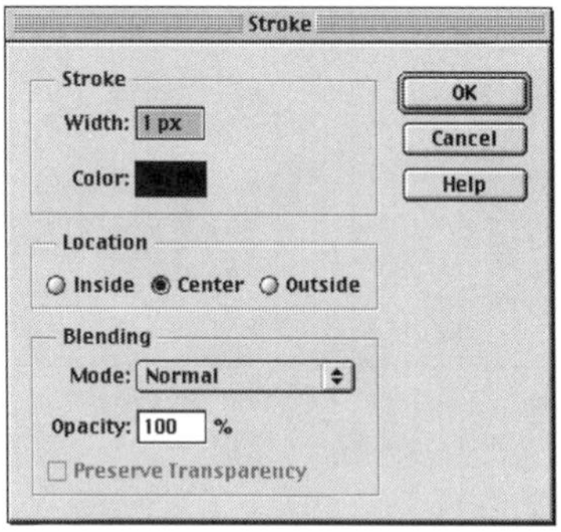

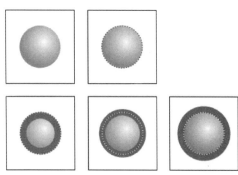

Figure 8.35 The Stroke dialog box.

Figure 8.36 Once an object is selected (top row), you can stroke it either inside, centered on, or outside of the selection (bottom row).

Adding a Stroke to a Selection or Layer

Photoshop Elements' Stroke command adds a colored rule or border around any selected object or layer. With the Stroke command, you can easily trace around almost anything, from simple rectangle or ellipse selections to complex typographic characters. Since you can control both the stroke's thickness and where the stroke is drawn in relation to a selection (inside, outside, or centered), you can create everything from delicate, single-ruled outlines to decorative, multiple-stroked borders and frames.

To apply a stroke:

1. Using any of the selection or marquee tools, select the area of your image to which you want to add a stroke.

   If you're adding a stroke to an object on its own transparent layer, there's no need to make a selection. Instead, just check that the layer is active on the Layers palette.

2. From the Edit menu, choose Stroke to open the Stroke dialog box (**Figure 8.35**).

3. In the Width text box, enter the stroke width, in pixels.

   There's no need to enter the pixel abbreviation (px) following the number value.

4. Change the stroke color by clicking the color box and opening the Color Picker.

5. Select the location of the stroke.

   The location determines where the stroke is drawn: inside, outside, or centered directly on the selection (**Figure 8.36**).

continues on next page

6. Ignore the Blending portion of the dialog box for now.

7. Click OK to apply the stroke to your selection or layer (**Figure 8.37**).

✔ Tip

■ Photoshop Elements uses the foreground color for the stroke color unless you change it in the Stroke dialog box. So if you want to pick a stroke color from the Swatches palette, *first* click the Swatches palette to assign the foreground color before anything else; *then* choose Stroke from the Edit menu. The color you chose from the Swatches palette will appear as the stroke color in the dialog box.

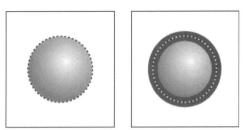

Figure 8.37 Select an object (left), then choose the Stroke command to apply a stroke (right).

Creating a Stroke Layer

It's a good habit to create a new layer before applying strokes to your image. That way, you can control attributes such as opacity and blending modes right on the Layers palette. You can even turn strokes off and on by clicking the stroke layer's visibility icon. If you're adding a stroke to a selection, simply create a new layer and then follow the steps in the previous task, "To apply a stroke." If you're stroking an object on a transparent layer and want its stroke on a separate layer, you need to perform a couple of additional steps:

1. Identify the object to which you want to add a stroke; then press Ctrl/Command and click once on the layer on the Layers palette.

   The object is automatically selected in the image window (**Figure 8.38**).

2. Create a new layer by clicking the New Layer button at the bottom of the Layers palette.

3. With the new layer selected on the Layers palette, choose Stroke from the Edit menu; then follow steps 3 through 7 of the previous procedure.

   A stroke will be created for the object, but placed on its own layer.

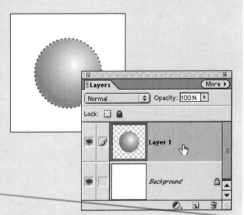

Figure 8.38 Ctrl+click/Command+click the Layers palette to create a selection around a layer object.

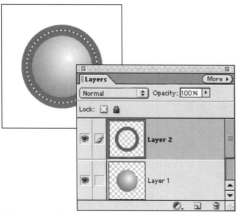

Figure 8.39 The first step in creating a multi-ruled border is to create a thick stroke. Here, we used a stroke of 6 pixels.

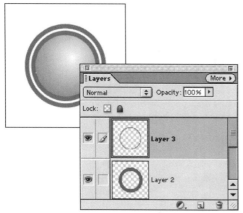

Figure 8.40 Placing a narrow stroke of a different color over the broad first stroke creates an attractive three-ruled border.

To create a decorative border:

1. Make a selection, either by using one of the selection or marquee tools, or by selecting an object on a transparent layer as described in the "Creating a Stroke Layer" sidebar on the previous page.

2. Create a new layer; then apply a wide stroke to the selection (**Figure 8.39**). Try using a stroke of 4-6 pixels to start.

3. With the selection still active, create a new layer above the first.

4. Apply a stroke narrower than the first and in a contrasting color or value (**Figure 8.40**).

5. Continue to add stroke layers until you achieve the desired result.

✔ Tip

- You can create different effects by adding inside and outside strokes.

Using the Brush Tool

The Brush tool is a near limitless reservoir of hundreds of different and unique brushes. You can apply painted brush strokes directly to the surface of any photograph, or open a new file to serve as a blank canvas upon which you can create an original work of fine art. The dozen preset brush libraries offer selections as varied as Calligraphic, Wet Media, and Special Effects, and any brush can be resized from 1 pixel to a staggering 2500 pixels in diameter. You can paint using any of Photoshop Elements' blending modes and opacity settings, and you can turn any brush into an airbrush with a single click of a button. So whether you're a budding Van Gogh, would like to add a color-tint effect to an antique black and white photograph, or just enjoy doodling while talking on the phone, Photoshop Elements' brushes can help to bring out your inner artist.

Figure 8.41 The Brush tool.

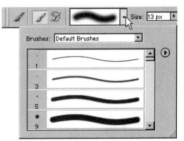

Figure 8.42 Open the Brush Presets palette to select from sets of different brushes.

To paint with the Brush tool:

1. To select a paint color, *do one of following:*
   - ▲ Click the current foreground color swatch at the bottom of the toolbox to open the Color Picker.
   - ▲ Choose a color from the Swatches palette.

2. Select the Brush tool in the toolbox (B) (**Figure 8.41**).

3. On the options bar, click to open the Brush Presets palette (**Figure 8.42**).

   For more information on customizing this view, see the sidebar "Brush Display Options" on the next page.

4. Click to choose from the list of default brushes, or select a different brush set from the Brushes pop-up menu (**Figure 8.43**).

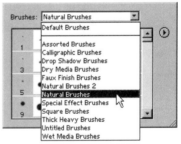

Figure 8.43 The Brushes pop-up menu gives you access to a variety of brush sets.

Figure 8.44 Use the brush size slider to resize your brush.

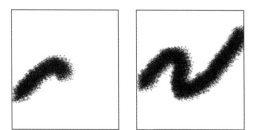

Figure 8.45 Create realistic brush effects simply by dragging through the image window.

Once you've selected a brush, you can use it at its predefined size, or you can resize it using the brush Size slider on the options bar (**Figure 8.44**).

5. Again on the options bar, select a blend mode and opacity setting.

6. In the image window, drag to paint a brush stroke (**Figure 8.45**).

Brush Display Options

The Brush Presets palette offers several viewing options that you can access from the palette menu.

Stroke Thumbnail: Default option; shows a sample brush stroke and a dab of the selected brush.

Text Only: Provides a simple text list of all of the brush names; very helpful if you're looking for a specific brush.

Small Thumbnail: Displays small pictorial views of a single dab of a brush.

Large Thumbnail: Shows a larger version of the Small Thumbnail display.

Small List: Displays tiny thumbnail views accompanied by their brush names.

Large List: Similar to the Small List view, but with nice, big thumbnail views.

Additionally, you can hover the mouse over any brush thumbnail for a second or two to display a descriptive name of that brush. (If nothing appears when you hover over the thumbnails, choose Edit > Preferences > General and click the Show Tool Tips option to select it.)

✔ Tips

- You can easily resize brushes on the fly using simple keyboard shortcuts. Once a brush of any size is selected, press the] or [key to increase or decrease the current brush size to the nearest unit of 10 pixels. Thus, if you're painting with a brush size of 23 pixels and press the] key, the brush size increases to 30 pixels and then grows in increments of 10 each subsequent time you press]. Conversely, a brush size of 56 pixels is reduced to 50 pixels when you press the [key, and the brush continues to shrink by 10 pixels each time thereafter that you press [.

- When any tool that uses a brush-type pointer is selected (the Eraser, Blur, Sharpen, and Clone tools, for instance), the same keyboard shortcuts as described in the preceding tip apply.

- Almost any brush can be made to behave like an airbrush simply by clicking the Airbrush button on the options bar (**Figure 8.46**). With the Airbrush selection activated, paint flows more slowly from the brush and gradually builds denser tones of color. The Airbrush option is most effective when applied to soft, round brushes or to brushes with scatter and spacing properties. (For more information on scatter and spacing properties, see the sidebar "Understanding the Brush Dynamics Palette" later in this chapter.)

Figure 8.46 Click the Airbrush button on the options bar to give a brush the characteristics of an airbrush.

USING THE BRUSH TOOL

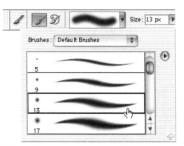

Figure 8.47 To create a new brush, select an existing brush and then customize its properties.

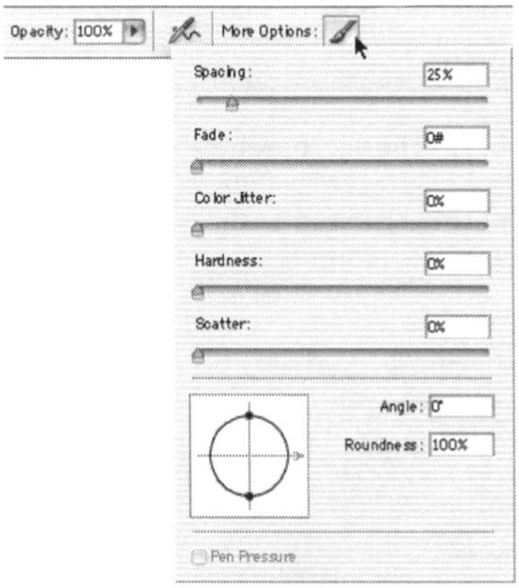

Figure 8.48 The Brush Dynamics palette contains slider controls to modify a brush shape.

Creating and Saving Custom Brushes

With so many different brushes and brush sets at your disposal, you may be surprised to discover that you can change not only the *size* of brushes, but other characteristics such as flow, shape, and color. Photoshop Elements provides you with all of the tools you need both to modify existing brushes and to create your own from photographs or scanned objects, such as leaves or flower petals. Once you've created a new brush, you can store it temporarily in an existing brush set or save and organize it into a new brush set of your own. Any new brush sets you create can then be accessed and loaded from the Brushes pop-up menu on the Brush Presets palette.

To create a custom brush:

1. Select the Brush tool from the toolbox (B).

2. From the list of preset brushes on the options bar, click to select a brush you want to customize (**Figure 8.47**).

3. On the options bar, click the More Options button to open the Brush Dynamics palette (**Figure 8.48**).

4. Use the sliders on the palette to modify the Spacing, Fade, Color Jitter, Hardness, and Scatter properties of the brush.

   For more information on these slider controls, see the "Understanding the Brush Dynamics Palette" sidebar later in this chapter.

continues on next page

5. If you want, you can adjust the angle and roundness of the brush, and if you have a pressure-sensitive digital tablet connected to your computer, you can make your brush pressure sensitive (**Figure 8.49**).

As you move the sliders, or enter angle and roundness values, you can refer to the brush presets preview on the option bar to see the effects of your changes. All but the Color Jitter property will be reflected in the preview on the options bar (**Figure 8.50**).

6. When you're satisfied with your changes, click anywhere on the options bar to close the palette.

7. On the options bar, use the brush Size slider to size your brush.

8. Still on the options bar, open the Brush Presets palette; then select New Brush from the palette options menu (**Figure 8.51**).

The Brush Name dialog box opens.

9. Type a name for your new brush; then click OK.

Your new brush appears at the bottom of the current brush presets list, on the Brush Presets palette (**Figure 8.52**).

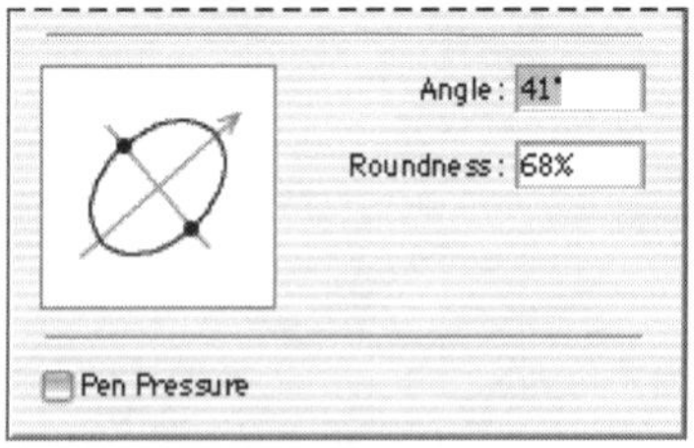

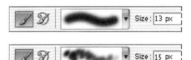

Figure 8.49 The lower portion of the Brush Dynamics palette offers controls for angle, roundness, and pressure sensitivity.

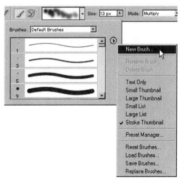

Figure 8.50 The Brush Presets preview area displaying an original brush (top) and the same brush customized on the Brush Dynamics palette (bottom).

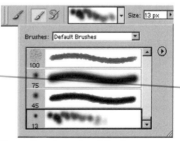

Figure 8.51 Save your customized brushes on the Brush Presets palette menu.

Figure 8.52 A new brush is always displayed at the bottom of the palette list.

Understanding the Brush Dynamics Palette

With a little bit of exploration, you'll find Photoshop Elements' Brush Dynamics palette to be useful tool for creating new brushes and modifying the attributes of existing ones.

The **Spacing** slider controls the spacing of the brush shape and is based on a percentage of the brush's current size (**Figure 8.53**). The default for most round brushes is 25 percent; 5 percent seems to be the optimum for most of the fine-art brushes such as the Chalks, Pastels, and Loaded Watercolor brushes.

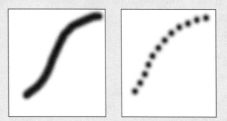

Figure 8.53 A brush spacing value of 25 percent (left) and 75 percent (right).

The **Fade** slider sets the number of steps a brush takes to fade to transparent and can simulate the effect of a brush running out of paint as it draws across a surface. One step is equal to a brush width, so the fade effect is somewhat dependent on the Spacing attribute (**Figure 8.54**).

Figure 8.54 A brush fade value of 0 (left) and 15 (right).

The **Color Jitter** slider determines how randomly the brush renders color, based on the foreground and background colors. The lower the jitter percentage, the more the foreground color is favored. If the percentage is set to the maximum of 100 percent, then the foreground and background colors (and mixtures of the two colors combined) are represented in equal measure throughout the brushstroke.

The **Hardness** slider controls the hardness or softness of a brushstroke's edges. A Hardness value of 100 percent creates a solid brushstroke with no soft edges (**Figure 8.55**).

Figure 8.55 A brush hardness value of 0 percent (left) and 100 percent (right).

The **Scatter** slider determines how much a brush shape is spread around with each stroke. The higher the percentage value, the more brush shapes are scattered and spread across an area. Lower percentage values create almost no scatter at all (**Figure 8.56**).

The **Angle** value allows you to rotate a brush shape to any angle, and the **Roundness** value can be used to flatten out or squish a brush shape.

Figure 8.56 A brush scatter value of 0 percent (left) and 30 percent (right).

To create a brush from a photographic object:

1. Open an image that contains an object or area from which you want to create a new brush.

2. To select an object from the image, *do one of the following:*

   ▲ Using one of the selection tools, select the object or portion of a photograph you want to make into a brush. The Selection Brush and Magnetic Lasso tools both work well for this kind of selection (**Figure 8.57**).

   ▲ If you already have an object on its own transparent layer, hold down Ctrl/Command and click.

3. From the Edit menu, choose Define Brush. The Brush Name dialog box opens with a representation of your new brush in its preview box (**Figure 8.58**).

4. Enter a name for the brush; then click OK to close the dialog box.

5. Select the Brush tool from the toolbox; then from the options bar, open the Brush Presets palette.

   Your new brush appears at the bottom of the current brush presets list (**Figure 8.59**).

6. Click to select the new brush; then on the options bar, click the More Options button to open the Brush Dynamics palette.

7. Use the sliders on the palette to modify the brush attributes; then click anywhere on the options bar to close the palette.

Figure 8.57 A custom brush can be made out of virtually any selected object. Here, a group of painted flowers on a vase has been selected.

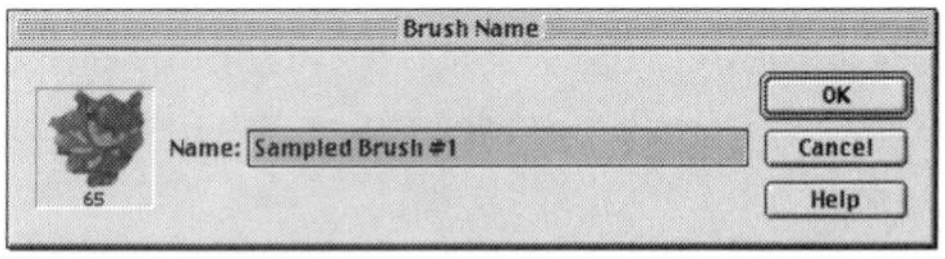

Figure 8.58 The selection appears in the brush preview of the Brush Name dialog box.

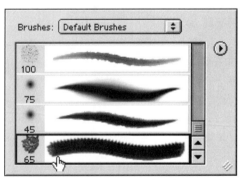

Figure 8.59 Once saved, your new brush appears in the brush presets list.

✔ Tips

- You can use these kinds of brushes to great effect as background textures, type borders, or homemade "rubber stamps" for greeting cards and invitations.

- Images with high contrast generally work best as brush shapes. Remember that you're not saving any color information—just the object's shape and its tonal values—so you'll want to use shapes with as much defined detail as possible.

- Don't be discouraged if you can't seem to duplicate the color and scatter effects of preset brushes such as Maple Leaves. A good number of the built-in brushes weren't created in Photoshop Elements at all, but in Adobe Photoshop. Photoshop offers a host of additional controls, including jitter properties for scatter, angle, hue, and size. For now, while you're working in Photoshop Elements, any blowing leaves or dune grass you create will all have to face the same direction.

CREATING AND SAVING CUSTOM BRUSHES

Managing Brush Sets

Managing Photoshop Elements' brushes is no different than managing its other presets (such as gradients and patterns). When you create a new brush, it's saved in the presets file. But once you reset the brushes on the Brush Presets palette or select a different brush set, any new brushes you've created will be lost. You can use the Preset Manager to create and save your new brush sets.

To create a new brush set:

1. Create as many new brushes as you like, as described in the previous procedures.

2. From the Brush Presets palette menu, choose Preset Manager (**Figure 8.60**).

   The Preset Manager dialog box opens to the current brush set displayed on the Brush Presets palette (**Figure 8.61**).

3. Scroll through the thumbnail views until you find the brushes you want to include in your new set.

4. In the thumbnail area, Shift+click to select all of the brushes that you want to include (**Figure 8.62**).

   If you select a brush by mistake, you can deselect it by holding down Shift and clicking the thumbnail a second time.

5. Click the Save Set button to open the Save dialog box.

6. In the File Name text box, enter a new name to describe your brush set; then click Save (**Figure 8.63**).

   Your brush set will be saved with the brushes you selected in step 4.

   Your new brush set will be saved with the others, but it won't appear on either the More menu in the Preset Manager or the Brushes pop-up menu on the Brush Presets palette until after you quit and then restart Photoshop Elements.

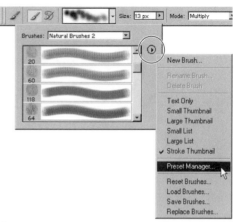

Figure 8.60 You can open the Preset Manager directly from the Brush Presets palette.

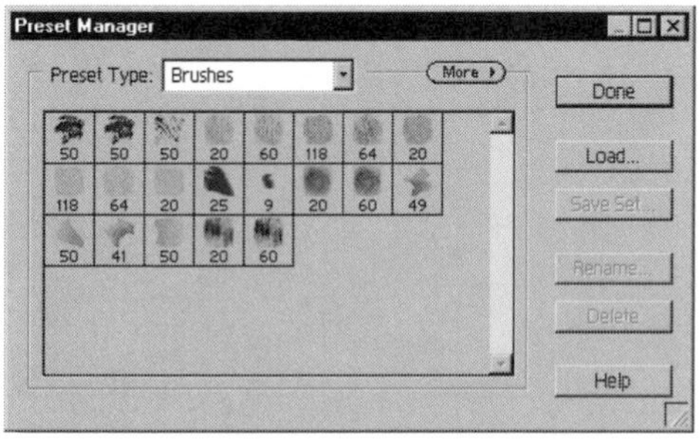

Figure 8.61 The Brushes Preset Manager.

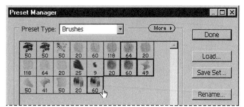

Figure 8.62 Select brushes you want included in your new brush set.

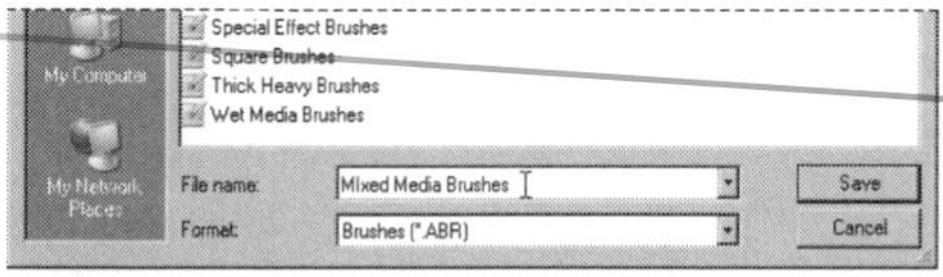

Figure 8.63 Name your new brush set in the Save dialog box.

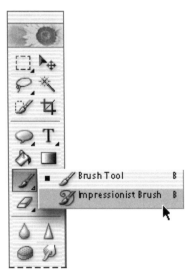

Figure 8.64 The Impressionist Brush tool.

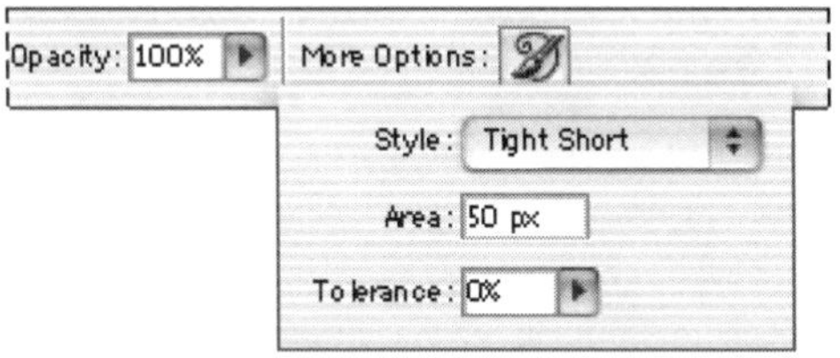

Figure 8.65 The Impressionist Brush Options palette has controls for different brush styles and the amount of image area they affect with each brush stroke.

Creating Special Painting Effects

The Impressionist Brush tool adds a painterly look to any photographic image. Though similar in effect to some of the Artistic and Brush Stroke filters, the Impressionist Brush tool allows you to be much more selective about which areas of an image it's applied to. That's because it uses the same scaleable, editable brushes as the Brush tool. You can use the Impressionist Brush tool to create compelling works of art from even the most mundane of photographs.

To paint with the Impressionist Brush tool:

1. Open the image to which you want to apply the Impressionist Brush effect.

2. Select the Impressionist Brush tool from beneath the Brush tool in the toolbox (**Figure 8.64**).

   Alternatively, you can press B to select the Brush tool and then press Shift+B to toggle to the Impressionist Brush tool.

3. On the options bar, select a brush from the Brush Presets palette.

   You can, of course, use any brush with the Impressionist Brush tool, but the round, soft-sided brush that Photoshop Elements picks as the default works especially well.

4. Again on the options bar, select a size with the brush Size slider.

   You can also select a mode and an opacity option, though in most cases the defaults of Normal and 100 percent are fine.

5. Still on the options bar, click the More Options button to open the Impressionist Brush Options palette (**Figure 8.65**).

continues on next page

CREATING SPECIAL PAINTING EFFECTS

6. From the Style pop-up menu, select a brush style (**Figure 8.66**).

We tend not to stray much beyond the top three Styles (Tight Short, Medium, and Long), though the Dab style also creates some pretty effects.

7. In the Area text box, enter a value, in pixels, for the amount of area you want to affect with each stroke of the brush.

For example, let's say you start with a brush that makes a single brush mark 10 pixels wide, and then select an Area value of 80 pixels. As you move the brush through the image—and depending on the brush style you chose—it will swoosh around an area of 80 x 80 pixels, distributing the paint in 10-pixel dollops (**Figure 8.67**).

8. If desired, select a Tolerance setting to determine the range of pixels affected.

You may want to keep the **Tolerance** slider set at 0 percent, just leaving it alone. In use with the Impressionist brush, this tool seems wildly erratic and not worth the trouble.

9. In the image window, drag the brush through your image.

The image takes on a painterly look wherever the Impressionist Brush tool is drawn through it (**Figure 8.68**).

✔ Tips

■ Images with resolutions of 150 pixels per inch and higher make the best candidates for the Impressionist Brush tool, as the higher resolution helps to preserve detail that can be lost when you apply this effect to lower-resolution images.

■ Stick to using smaller brush sizes, particularly on low-resolution images. Although any rules of thumb vary from image to image and are somewhat dependent on the subject matter, a good starting place is a brush size between 6 and 10 pixels and an Area setting of between 30 and 50.

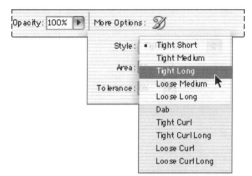

Figure 8.66 Brush styles vary from subtle (Dab) to extravagant (Loose Curl Long).

Figure 8.67 The Area setting can have quite an impact on the way the Impressionist Brush tool affects your photograph. In both of these photos, a single brush stroke with a brush size of 10 pixels was drawn through each photo. The image on the left was painted with an Area value of 20 pixels, and the image on the right was painted with an Area value of 80 pixels.

Figure 8.68 Simply drag the brush through your photo to create a work of art.

CREATING SPECIAL PAINTING EFFECTS

Figure 8.69 The Eraser tool.

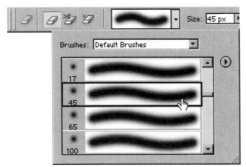

Figure 8.70 The same brush presets are available for the Eraser tool as for the Brush tool.

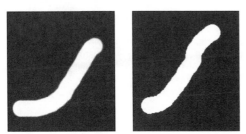

Figure 8.71 An eraser in Brush mode (left) and in Pencil mode (right).

Erasing with Customizable Brush Shapes

The images or brushstrokes you choose to remove from a photograph are often as important as those you decide to add or leave behind. The basic Eraser feature is a powerful tool for cleaning up and fine-tuning your images, taking full advantage of every brush style and size that Photoshop Elements has to offer. Not only can you perform routine erasing tasks such as rubbing away stray pixels, but you can customize an eraser's brush and opacity settings to create unique texture, color, and pattern effects. Three modes allow you to customize your erasers even further, so that you can erase with soft-edged brush shapes, hard-edged pencil shapes, or a simple hard-edged square block.

To use the Eraser tool:

1. Select the Eraser tool from the toolbox (E) (**Figure 8.69**).

2. On the options bar, select a brush from the Brush Presets palette (**Figure 8.70**).

3. Again on the options bar, select a size using the brush Size slider.

4. From the Mode pop-up menu, select one of the three eraser modes.

   If you select a soft, anti-aliased brush and then choose Pencil from the mode menu, the eraser will become coarse and aliased (**Figure 8.71**).

5. Still on the options bar, select an opacity using the Opacity slider.

6. In the image window, drag the eraser through your image.

   The image is erased according to the attributes you've applied to the eraser.

Erasing on Flattened versus Layered Images

The Eraser tool functions in a fundamentally different way, depending on whether it's erasing on a flattened image, such as Photoshop Elements' default background, or on a layer of a multilayered file. When erasing on a flattened image, the Eraser tool doesn't really erase at all. Instead, it *replaces* the image with the current background color displayed in the toolbox. In other words, it simply *paints over* the image with the background color (**Figure 8.72**).

Figure 8.72 On a flattened image layer, the Eraser tool paints with the current background color wherever the eraser is dragged.

On the other hand, when erasing a portion of an image from a layer, the Eraser tool actually *removes* the pixels from the layer, creating a transparent hole and exposing the image on the layer directly below it (**Figure 8.73**).

✔ Tip

■ You're not limited to round or square brush shapes for your erasers. Any brush, even pictorial ones (for instance, Maple Leaves and Dune Grass) or photographic ones (like Scattered Leaves) can be used as erasers. Try experimenting with different brush shapes and opacity settings to create unusual textures and patterns in your photographs.

Figure 8.73 When erasing on a layer with transparency, the Eraser tool actually removes image pixels (here, the tip of the paintbrush) and exposes the image on the layer below (the paint cup).

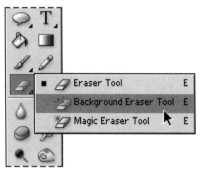

Figure 8.74 The Background Eraser tool.

Erasing Backgrounds and Other Large Areas

The Background Eraser tool is an intelligent (and really quite amazing) little feature. Not only does it remove the background from around very complex shapes, but it does so in a way that leaves a natural, softened, anti-aliased edge around the foreground object left behind. This technique would be impossible to pull off with the regular eraser tool, as it indiscriminately removes whatever pixels it touches. Because it erases pixels based on colors and tonal values that you control and modify, there is rarely much additional cleanup required once the background has been removed. Additionally, since the Background Eraser tool always erases to transparency, if you use it to remove the background from even a flattened layer, it automatically converts that layer to a floating, transparent one. This allows you to easily place a new background behind the foreground image, or to move it to a different image altogether.

To use the Background Eraser tool:

1. Select the Background Eraser tool from beneath the Eraser tool in the toolbox (**Figure 8.74**).

   Alternatively, you can press E to select the Eraser tool and then press Shift+E to toggle to the Background Eraser tool.

2. On the options bar, select a size using the brush Size slider.

   continues on next page

3. From the Limits pop-up menu, select one of the two limit modes (**Figure 8.75**).

Contiguous mode erases any pixels within the brush area that are the same as those currently beneath the crosshairs, as long as they're touching one another.

Discontiguous mode erases all pixels within the brush area that are the same as those beneath the crosshairs, even if they're not touching one another.

4. Select a Tolerance value, using the Tolerance slider (**Figure 8.76**).

The Tolerance value controls which pixels are erased according to how similar they are to the pixels beneath the eraser crosshairs. Higher Tolerance values increase the range of colors that are erased, and lower values limit the range of colors erased.

5. In the image window, position the eraser pointer on the edge where the background and foreground images meet and then drag along the edge.

The background portion of the image is erased, leaving behind the foreground image on a transparent background (**Figure 8.77**). Since the brush erases only pixels similar to the ones directly below the crosshairs, the entire background can be completely erased while leaving the foreground image intact.

Figure 8.75 The Limits pop-up menu controls which pixels beneath the brush are sampled and erased.

Figure 8.76 You use the Tolerance slider to increase or decrease the number of pixels sampled based on their similarity to one another.

Figure 8.77 Begin by placing the crosshairs of the brush in the background portion of the image (left), then drag the brush along the outside edge of the foreground object to erase the background (right). Continue around the edge of the foreground object until it's completely separated from the background.

✔ Tips

- It's okay if the circle (indicating the brush size) overlaps onto the foreground image, but be sure to keep the crosshairs over just the background area. The Background Eraser tool, of course, doesn't really know the difference between background and foreground images, and is simply erasing based on the colors selected, or *sampled*, beneath the crosshairs. If the crosshairs stray into the foreground image, that part of the image will be erased, too.

- There's a third eraser tool—the Magic Eraser tool—that we've chosen not to cover here because, frankly, it doesn't work very well. It operates on the same principle as the Magic Wand tool (and, to some extent, the crosshairs on the Background Eraser tool): by deleting like pixels based on color or tonal value. That's all well and good, but you're not given any feedback or any opportunity at all to modify your selection. You just click, and poof—a large area of color is gone. Since the erasure typically is either not quite enough or a little too much, you undo, reset the tolerance, try again, undo—well, you get the idea. The other two erasers work fabulously well, so we suggest just keeping the Magic Eraser tool in the toolbox.

Understanding Shapes

In Photoshop Elements, you create shapes not by rendering them with pixels, but by constructing them from vector paths. In Photoshop Elements, those vector paths are actually vector *masks*. We'll use some simple circle and square shapes to illustrate what that means.

Each time you draw a shape with one of the shape tools, Photoshop Elements is performing a little behind-the-scenes sleight of hand. Although it may appear that you're drawing a solid, filled circle, for instance, what you're really creating is a new layer containing both a colored fill and a mask with a circle-shaped cutout (**Figure 8.78**). When you move, reshape, or resize a shape, you're actually just moving or reshaping the cutout and revealing a different area of the colored fill below it (**Figure 8.79**). When you add to or subtract from a shape by drawing additional shapes, you're simply revealing or hiding more of the same colored layer (**Figure 8.80**).

Every time you create a new shape, a new shape *layer* is added to the Layers palette. A shape layer is represented in the palette thumbnails by a gray background (the mask) and a white shape (the mask cutout, or path). Since a shape's outline isn't always visible in the image window—if you deselect it, for instance—the Layers palette provides a handy, visual reference for every shape in your project (**Figure 8.81**). And as with any other layered image, you can use the Layers palette to hide a shape's visibility and even change its opacity and its blending mode.

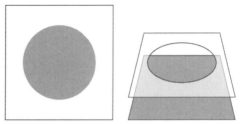

Figure 8.78 When you draw a shape, you're actually drawing a shape *mask*.

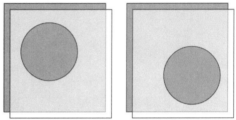

Figure 8.79 Moving a circle shape really means moving the circle cutout portion of the mask.

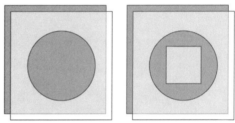

Figure 8.80 Adding a shape to a layer masks off another portion of the colored fill below it, in this case giving the illusion that the circle has a square hole in its center.

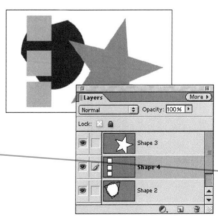

Figure 8.81 Every shape or combination of shapes appears on its own layer on the Layers palette.

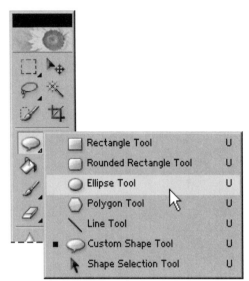

Figure 8.82 The Ellipse shape tool.

Figure 8.83 All of the shape tools are accessible from both the toolbox and the options bar.

Drawing Basic Shapes

In Photoshop Elements, you can draw five basic geometric shapes (a shape selection tool and a tool for creating custom shapes are discussed in detail later in this chapter). Shapes can be drawn freely simply by clicking and dragging, or they can be constrained according to your specification of size, proportion, and special characteristics. You can use the shape tools to create logos or geometric designs, or, because a new layer is created with every shape you draw, you can draw shapes directly over any photograph or scanned image without fear of damaging the image itself.

To draw a shape:

1. Select a shape tool from the toolbox (U) (**Figure 8.82**).

   To cycle through the shape tools, press Shift+U until you arrive at the shape you want.

   Alternatively, once you've selected a shape tool in the toolbox, you can select a different shape from the options bar (**Figure 8.83**).

2. To select a shape color, *do one of following:*

   ▲ Click the current foreground color swatch at the bottom of the toolbox, or click the color box on the options bar, to open the Color Picker.

   ▲ Choose a color from the Swatches palette.

   continues on next page

3. If they're available for the tool you've selected, you can set special properties for your shape before you draw. On the options bar, enter values specific to the shape you've chosen (**Figure 8.84**).

For the Rounded Rectangle tool, you can enter a corner radius. For the Polygon tool, you can enter the number of sides. For the Line tool, you can enter a pixel weight.

4. On the options bar, click the arrow next to the shape buttons to open the Geometry Options palette (**Figure 8.85**).

In the Geometry Options palette, select from the available options for that particular shape or leave the options set to the default of Unconstrained.

5. In the image window, click and drag to draw the shape (**Figure 8.86**).

If you like, you can add a style to your shape from the Custom Shape tool's built-in style picker.

6. On the options bar, click the icon or arrow to open the style picker (**Figure 8.87**).

7. Choose from the list of available styles or click the arrow button to the right of the thumbnail images to open the Style palette menu **Figure 8.88**).

The style picker displays the new style set.

Figure 8.84 Some shape tools, such as the Polygon tool, have properties you can set on the options bar.

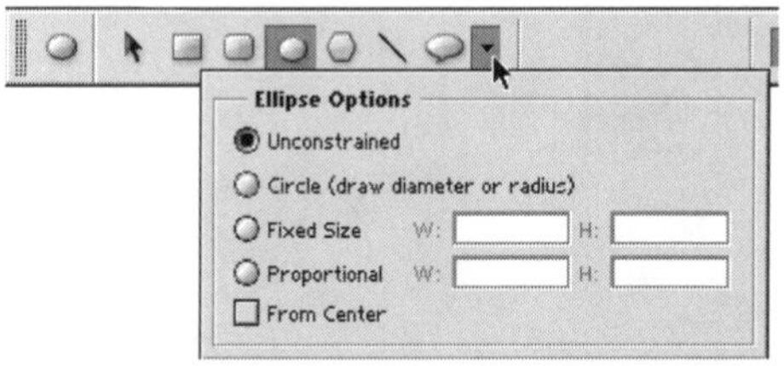

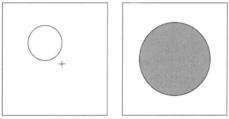

Figure 8.85 Every shape tool has its own particular set of geometry options.

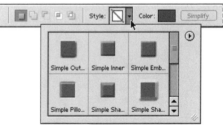

Figure 8.86 Drawing a shape is as simple as clicking and dragging.

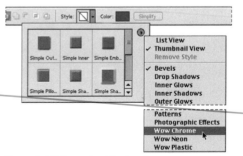

Figure 8.87 Whenever any of the custom shape tools are selected, the shape tool style picker appears on the options bar.

Figure 8.88 The style picker's palette menu contains a variety of fun and interesting style sets.

Figure 8.89 A simple circle drawn with the ellipse shape tool (left) is transformed into a shiny, chrome button (right) using just one of the many styles from the style picker.

8. Click a style in the style picker to apply it to your shape (**Figure 8.89**).

9. To deselect the shape and hide the path outline, press Enter/Return.

About the Shape Geometry Options Palettes

Each shape tool (with the exception of the Shape Selection tool) has its own unique Geometry Options palette. The two rectangle tools and the Ellipse and Custom Shape tools all offer similar options for defining size, proportions, and constraint properties, and the Polygon and Line tools each have their own unique sets of options (**Figure 8.90**). The Polygon tool's most distinctive option is the Star check box. When Star is selected, you're presented with a couple of indent properties that fold the polygon in on itself, so that the points of its angles become the tips of a star shape (**Figure 8.91**). When the Line tool is selected, you can choose from a small set of Arrowhead options based on the pixel weight of the line.

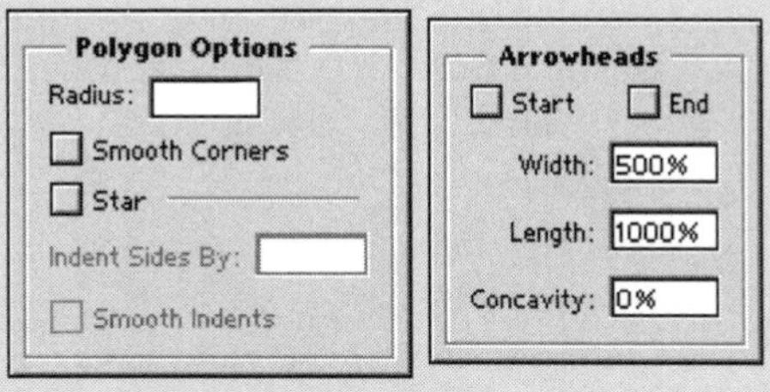

✔ Tip

■ To constrain the proportions of any shape (to make a rectangle a perfect square or an ellipse a perfect circle, for example) without the aid of the Geometry Options palette, hold down the Shift key as you drag.

Figure 8.90 The Polygon tool's geometry options and the Line tool's arrowhead options.

Figure 8.91 Using the Polygon tool's Star option, a six-sided polygon (left) can be changed into a six-sided star (right).

Transforming Shapes

You're not limited to creating shapes in Photoshop Elements. You can also scale (resize), rotate, and distort them to your liking. Shapes can be altered either numerically, by entering specific values on the options bar, or manually, by dragging their control handles in the image window. Constraint options, such as proportional scaling, are available for most transformations, and a set of keyboard shortcuts helps to simplify the process of adding distortion and perspective.

To scale a shape:

1. Select the Shape Selection tool *by doing any of the following*:
   - ▲ Choose the Shape Selection tool from beneath the current shape tool in the toolbox (**Figure 8.92**).
   - ▲ Press U to select any shape tool and then press Shift+U to toggle to the Shape Selection tool.
   - ▲ Select any shape tool in the toolbox, then choose the Shape Selection tool from the options bar (it looks like an arrow).

2. In the image window, select the shape with the Shape Selection tool.

3. From the Image menu, choose Transform Shape > Free Transform Shape, or press Ctrl+T/Command+T.

   The options bar changes to show the scale and rotation text boxes and the reference point locator (**Figure 8.93**).

4. On the options bar, click to set a reference point location.

   The reference point determines what point your shape will be scaled to: toward the center, toward a corner, and so on (**Figure 8.94**).

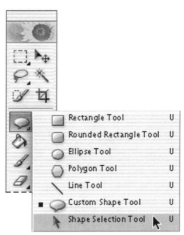

Figure 8.92 The Shape Selection tool.

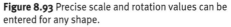

Figure 8.93 Precise scale and rotation values can be entered for any shape.

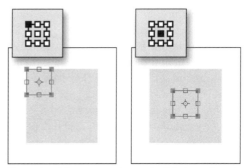

Figure 8.94 These rectangles are both being reduced in size by about half. The one on the left is scaled toward its upper left corner, and the one on the right is scaled toward its center.

Figure 8.95 The Commit Transform button scales the shape to the size you define.

5. If you want to scale your shape proportionately, click the lock icon between the width and height text boxes.

6. Enter a value in either the height or width text box.

   The shape is scaled accordingly.

7. On the options bar, click the Commit Transform button (**Figure 8.95**), or press Enter/Return.

8. Click the Commit Transform button a second time (or press Enter/Return) to deselect the shape and hide the path outline.

✔ Tips

- You can scale a shape manually by selecting it with the Shape Selection tool and then dragging any one of the eight handles on the selection border. Constrain the scaling by holding down the Shift key while dragging one of the four corner handles.

- If you want to simply reposition a shape in the image window, click anywhere inside the shape with the Shape Selection tool and then drag the shape to its new position.

TRANSFORMING SHAPES

To rotate a shape:

1. Select the Shape Selection tool from the toolbox or options bar.

2. In the image window, select the shape with the Shape Selection tool.

3. From the Image menu, choose Rotate > Free Rotate Layer (**Figure 8.96**).

   The options bar changes to show the scale and rotation text boxes and the reference point locator.

4. On the options bar, click to set a reference point location.

   The reference point determines the point that your shape will be rotated around (**Figure 8.97**).

5. Enter a value in the rotate text box.

   The shape will rotate accordingly.

6. On the options bar, click the Commit Transform button, or press Enter/Return.

7. Click the Commit Transform button a second time (or press Enter/Return) to deselect the shape and hide the path outline.

✔ Tips

- To rotate your shape in 90- or 180-degree increments or to flip it horizontally or vertically, choose Image > Rotate; then pick from the list of five menu commands below the Free Rotate Layer command.

- You can rotate a shape manually by selecting it with the Shape Selection tool and then moving the pointer outside of the selection border until it becomes a rotation cursor (**Figure 8.98**). Drag around the outside of the selection border to rotate the shape. In addition, you can constrain the rotation to 15-degree increments by holding down the Shift key while dragging the rotation cursor.

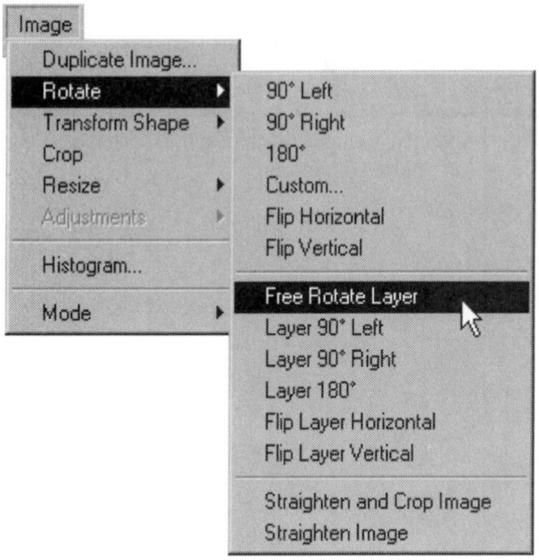

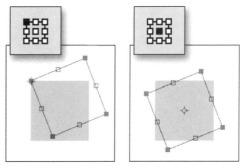

Figure 8.96 You can apply any of the layer rotation menu commands to your shapes.

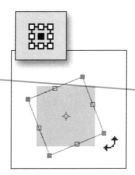

Figure 8.97 These rectangles are both being rotated about 20 degrees. The one on the left is rotated around its upper left corner, and the one on the right is rotated around its center.

Figure 8.98 Rotate any shape manually by dragging it around its reference point with the rotation pointer.

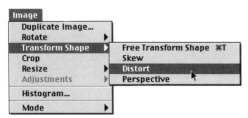

Figure 8.99 Choose one of the three specific transformation commands.

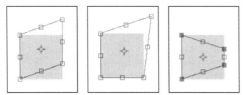

Figure 8.100 The same square shape transformed using Skew (left), Distort (center), and Perspective (right).

To distort a shape:

1. Select the Shape Selection from the toolbox or options bar.

2. In the image window, select the shape with the Shape Selection tool.

3. From the Image menu, choose Transform Shape; then choose Skew, Distort, or Perspective (**Figure 8.99**).

4. On the options bar, check that the reference point location is set to the center.

    The reference point can, of course, be set to any location, but the center seems to work best when applying any of the three distortions.

5. Drag any of the shape's control handles to distort the shape.

    Dragging the control handles will yield different results depending on the distort option you choose (**Figure 8.100**).

6. On the options bar, click the Commit Transform button, or press Enter/Return

7. Click the Commit Transform button a second time (or press Enter/Return) to deselect the shape and hide the path outline.

TRANSFORMING SHAPES

Distortion Shortcuts

With a few keyboard shortcuts, you can avoid having to return to the Image menu each time you want to apply a different distortion.

From the Image menu, choose Transform Shape > Free Transform Shape; then use the following shortcuts while dragging the shape handles in the image window:

To Distort: Ctrl/Command

To Skew: Ctrl+Alt/Command+Option

To create Perspective: Ctrl+Alt+Shift/Command+Option+Shift

Creating Custom Shapes

Once you've gained a basic understanding of working with Photoshop Elements' geometric shapes, you can begin adding those shapes together to create even more interesting and intricate shapes. Shape option buttons allow you to perform a little vector path magic by creating brand-new shapes out of the intersections and overlapping portions of the simple rectangle, ellipse, and polygon shapes.

The Custom Shape tool is in a world unto itself, working from a library of nearly 400 complex vector graphics grouped into categories as diverse as ornaments, music, fruit, symbols, and nature—far beyond the relatively simple icons and graphics you can build with the basic geometric shape tools.

To add a shape to an existing shape:

1. Follow steps 1 through 5 in the task "To draw a shape" earlier in this chapter. Make sure that this first shape's path remains selected (**Figure 8.101**).

2. From either the toolbox or the options bar, select the shape tool for the next shape you want to add.

   You can use the same shape more than once, if you wish.

3. On the options bar, set color, value, and geometry options as desired.

4. Still on the options bar, click to select one of the shape area options (**Figure 8.102**).

5. In the image window, click and drag to draw the new shape (**Figure 8.103**).

6. To deselect the shapes and hide their path outlines, press Enter/Return.

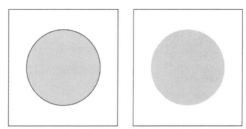

Figure 8.101 When a shape is selected, its path outline is visible (left). The path disappears when the shape is deselected (right).

Figure 8.102 The shape area options define how one shape reacts with another.

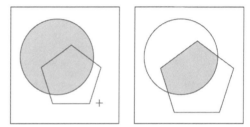

Figure 8.103 As the new shape is drawn, only its outline is visible (left). When the new shape is completed, it's filled according to the preset shape area option (right). In this case, the option was set to Intersect Shape.

✔ Tip

- The Layers palette can be a useful tool when working with the shape tools. Its layer thumbnails provide good visual feedback, particularly when you're building complex shapes and want to verify that the new shapes you create are being placed on the correct layers.

CREATING CUSTOM SHAPES

About the Shape Area Options Buttons

Photoshop Elements gives you five options to pick from when creating a new shape or modifying an existing one (**Figure 8.104**).

Create New Shape Layer does just that, drawing a new shape on its own, separate layer.

Add to Shape Area draws a new shape on the same layer as the existing shape.

Subtract from Shape Area adds a shape to the same layer as the existing shape, creating a cutout or hole.

Intersect Shape Areas adds a shape to the same layer as the existing shape and causes only those areas where the two shapes overlap to be visible.

Exclude Overlapping Shape Areas does just the opposite of Intersect Shape Areas, creating a cutout or hole where the two shapes overlap.

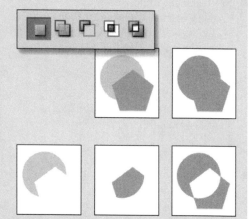

Figure 8.104 On the options bar, click to select one of five shape area options.

To combine multiple shapes:

1. Select the Shape Selection tool from the toolbox or from the options bar.

2. In the image window, click to select the first shape; then Shift+click to select the additional shapes you want to group (**Figure 8.105**).

3. On the options bar, click the Combine button (**Figure 8.106**).

   The shapes are now combined into a single, complex shape.

✔ Tips

- When selecting multiple shapes, work from the inside out. In other words, if you have a large shape with a smaller cutout or intersecting shape inside of it, select the smaller, inside shape first. Photoshop Elements doesn't assign any stacking order per se to multiple shapes on a layer, but if a larger, outside shape is selected first, the selection sort of covers up any smaller shapes inside, making them next to impossible to select.

- Up until the moment that multiple shapes are grouped together with the Combine button, they can be selected individually and then scaled, rotated, and distorted and even duplicated with the Copy and Paste commands.

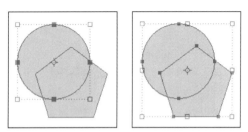

Figure 8.105 Shift+click to select the shapes you want to combine.

Figure 8.106 The Combine button groups multiple shapes together.

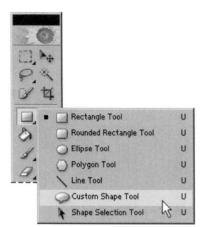

Figure 8.107 The Custom Shape tool.

Figure 8.108 The Custom Shape tool has geometry options similar to those for the Ellipse and Rectangle tools.

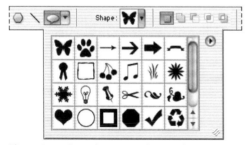

Figure 8.109 Open the custom shape picker to select from sets of complex shape thumbnails.

To draw a custom shape:

1. Select the Custom Shape tool *by doing one of the following:*

   ▲ Select the Custom Shape tool from beneath the current shape tool in the toolbox (**Figure 8.107**).

   ▲ Press U to select any shape tool; then press Shift+U to toggle to the Custom Shape tool.

   ▲ Select any shape tool in the toolbox; then select the Custom Shape tool from the options bar.

2. To select a shape color, *do one of following:*

   ▲ Click the current foreground color swatch at the bottom of the toolbox, or click the color box on the options bar, to open the Color Picker.

   ▲ Choose a color from the Swatches palette.

3. On the options bar, click the arrow next to the Custom Shape button to open the Geometry Options palette (**Figure 8.108**). Select from the available options or leave the options set to Unconstrained.

4. Still on the options bar, click to open the custom shape picker (**Figure 8.109**).

continues on next page

5. Click to choose from the list of default shapes, or select a different shape set from the Custom Shapes pop-up menu (**Figure 8.110**).

6. In the image window, click and drag to draw the selected shape (**Figure 8.111**).

7. To deselect the shape and hide the path outline, press Enter/Return.

✔ Tip

■ Custom shapes can be used in combination with other shapes and with the shape area options just like any of the basic geometric shapes.

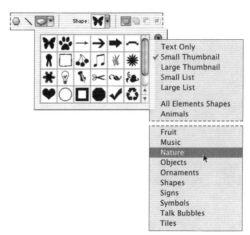

Figure 8.110 The custom shape picker's palette menu offers access to a variety of custom shape sets.

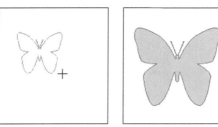

Figure 8.111 You draw a custom shape just as you would any other shape: simply by clicking and dragging. Here, we clicked to apply the butterfly shape (left) and then dragged with the mouse to enlarge it (right).

CREATING CUSTOM SHAPES

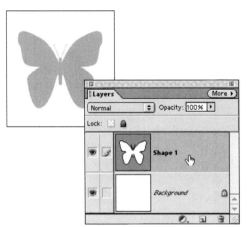

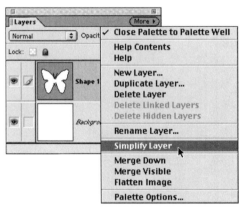

Figure 8.112 Use the Layers palette to select a custom shape's layer.

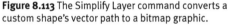

Figure 8.113 The Simplify Layer command converts a custom shape's vector path to a bitmap graphic.

Figure 8.114 The vector path layer thumbnail (left) and the converted bitmap thumbnail (right).

If you ever want to paint on a shape or apply any filter effects to it, you'll first need to convert the shape from a vector path to a bitmap.

To convert a vector shape to a bitmap:

1. To open the Layers palette, *do one of the following:*

   ▲ From the Window menu, choose Layers.

   ▲ Click the Layers tab in the palette well.

2. On the Layers palette, click to select the layer containing the shape (or shapes) you want to convert to bitmaps (**Figure 8.112**).

3. On the Layers palette, click the More button and select Simplify Layer (**Figure 8.113**).

   If the Layers palette is on your desktop rather than in the palette well, select Simplify Layer from the palette's More menu.

   The vector shape is converted to a bitmap, and instead of showing the shape's path, the layer thumbnail displays the shape's image on a transparent background (**Figure 8.114**).

CREATING CUSTOM SHAPES

267

WORKING WITH TYPE

When you think about all of the sophisticated photo retouching, painting, and drawing you can do in Photoshop Elements, manipulating type may fall pretty far down on your to-do list. However, you can do some amazing things with the type tools, including using them to create projects such as greeting cards, posters, announcements, and invitations—and you don't even have to fire up another software application.

This chapter covers the text formatting options and special type effects you can create with Photoshop Elements. If you've had any experience at all with word processing programs, then the basic text formatting options will seem very familiar to you. Unlike a word processor, however, Photoshop Elements lets you create myriad special effects, using the type warping and masking tools and layer styles.

Creating and Editing Text

When you use the type tools, your text is automatically placed on a new, unique layer. Since the text exists on its own layer, you can do all the things to your text that layers allow, including moving, applying blending modes, and changing the opacity. Also, having text on its own layer allows you to go back and edit the text whenever you want, with a minimum of fuss.

Editing text is very simple—pretty much the same as in any word processor. One difference is the way you make a final confirmation of the changes you have entered. This is done with the Commit Current Edits button and with its partner, the Cancel Any Current Edits button, which together allow you to change your mind as often as you want.

It's very common that you'll want to adjust to location of your text, and this is done just as easily as on any other layer. If you want to paint on your text or apply filters or effects to it, you'll need to simplify the layer to convert it to a standard bitmap. But remember: after a type layer has been simplified, it becomes part of the image, which means that you can no longer edit the text. Fortunately, during any work session (that is, until you close the file) the Undo History palette will always let you go back to an earlier version of your project, returning to the state before your type was simplified. And you can always save a separate version of your file prior to simplifying the type layer.

To add text to an image:

1. With an image open, click the horizontal or vertical type tool on the toolbar (**Figure 9.1**).

   Your pointer changes to look like an I-beam, as in many other text editing programs (**Figure 9.2**).

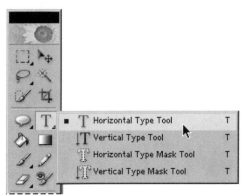

Figure 9.1 Click the type tool icon to choose from four different type tools.

Figure 9.2 When using one of the type tools, your pointer changes appearance to look like an I-beam. The text entry point is indicated by a vertical line whose height is based on the type size.

Figure 9.3 After you click once to establish the insertion point of your type, just start entering text. You'll need to press the Return/Enter key to move to a new line.

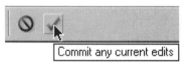

Commit any current edits

Figure 9.4 To confirm the text you've just entered or any changes you've made, click the Commit Current Edits check mark on the options bar.

Figure 9.5 Using the type tools automatically creates a new layer on the Layers palette. The layer name is the text you entered.

2. In the image window, move the pointer to the area where you want to insert your text.

3. Type your text on the image (**Figure 9.3**). If you want to start a new line, press Enter (Windows) or Return (Mac OS).

4. To confirm the text you've entered, *do one of the following:*

   ▲ Click the Check Mark (OK) button on the options bar (**Figure 9.4**).

   ▲ Press the Enter key on the numeric keypad.

   ▲ Click anywhere in your image, click a palette, or click a tool on the toolbar.

   A new type layer is automatically created and is visible on the Layers palette. The layer name is the text you entered (**Figure 9.5**).

✔ Tips

- If you want to add more text to a separate part of your image, simply repeat steps 1 through 4. The new text will be added to its own separate type layer.

- Your image must be in grayscale or RGB mode if you want to add type to it. Photoshop Elements' two other image modes, bitmap and index, don't support type layers.

CREATING AND EDITING TEXT

271

To edit text:

1. Click the appropriate type layer on the Layers palette (**Figure 9.6**).

2. In the image window, click in the text and edit as you would with any basic word processor, pressing the backspace key to delete individual characters, or double-clicking directly on the text to select all the text at once (**Figure 9.7**).

3. Confirm your edits by clicking anywhere in your image.

   If you change your mind, you can click Cancel to return to your last edit (**Figure 9.8**).

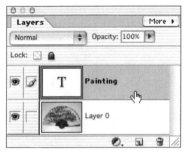

Figure 9.6 To make changes to existing text, click the appropriate layer on the Layers palette.

Figure 9.7 You can delete or make other changes to your text by pressing the delete key and entering new text.

Figure 9.8 If you decide you want to abandon any edits and return to the original text, just click the Cancel Any Current Edits button on the options bar.

Point Type versus Paragraph Type

Photoshop Elements uses what's known as *point* type. This means that when you enter text, the line of text will continue until you press the Return key to create a second line. The full-fledged version of Adobe Photoshop also includes what's called *paragraph* type. With paragraph type, you can create a text area, and the type will automatically wrap to a new line when you reach the edge of the boundary box. Photoshop Elements is great for doing small (but still creative) projects, but if your work involves working with a lot of type (like advertisements or professional brochures) then you might want to move up to the full version of Adobe Photoshop.

Figure 9.9 Since your text exists on its own separate layer, you can move your text to different areas in your image by using the Move tool.

To move text:

1. On the Layers palette, click the type layer that you want to move.

2. Click the Move tool on the toolbar.

   When you click the Move tool, your type is surrounded by a selection bounding box, allowing you to move the type as a single object anywhere on your image.

3. In the image window, drag your text to a new location (**Figure 9.9**).

To simplify a type layer:

1. Choose a type layer on the Layers palette by clicking on it.

2. From the main menu, select Layer > Simplify Layer (**Figure 9.10**).

   The layer representation changes from the T icon to a thumbnail of the simplified text (**Figure 9.11**).

Figure 9.10 To merge your type layer with the rest of your image, choose Layer > Simplify Layer. Once you do this, the type becomes part of the image and can't be edited with the type tools.

Figure 9.11 After you simplify a type layer, the icon changes to show a thumbnail view of the type.

Changing the Look of Your Type

You'll probably be pretty comfortable using the type formatting tools in Photoshop Elements since they consist of the standard array of text formatting options, including the font family, font style, and font size. The first thing you'll probably want to do is change the font size, as Photoshop Elements' type tool is automatically set to 12 or 14 points, which in many cases will be too small. Making the type bigger makes it *much* easier for you to see how the type looks in your image. You can also change the text alignment and text color. All of these options are available on the text options bar (**Figure 9.12**).

To change any of these attributes, you first need to select the text characters you want to change. Most of the time, you'll want to select and apply changes to an entire line of text, but you can also select individual words or even individual characters.

To select text:

1. Click the appropriate type layer on the Layers palette, or click on the type itself with the Move tool to select it.

2. Select a type tool.

3. To select the text, drag across the characters to highlight them (**Figure 9.13**), *or do one of the following*:

   ▲ Double-click within its text to select one word (**Figure 9.14**).

   ▲ Triple-click to select the entire line of text (**Figure 9.15**).

✔ Tip

■ You can select all of the text on a layer without even touching the text with your pointer. Just select the type layer on the Layers palette and double-click the T icon.

Figure 9.12 The type formatting tools are all available on the type options bar.

Figure 9.13 To select your text, drag across it with the text pointer.

Figure 9.14 Double-click within a word to select it.

Figure 9.15 Triple-click anywhere in a line of type to select the entire line.

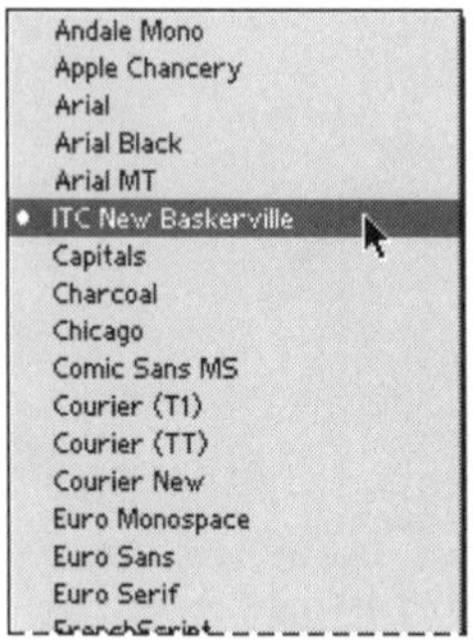

Andale Mono
Apple Chancery
Arial
Arial Black
Arial MT
● ITC New Baskerville
Capitals
Charcoal
Chicago
Comic Sans MS
Courier (T1)
Courier (TT)
Courier New
Euro Monospace
Euro Sans
Euro Serif
FrenchScript

Figure 9.16 All available fonts are listed on the font family menu.

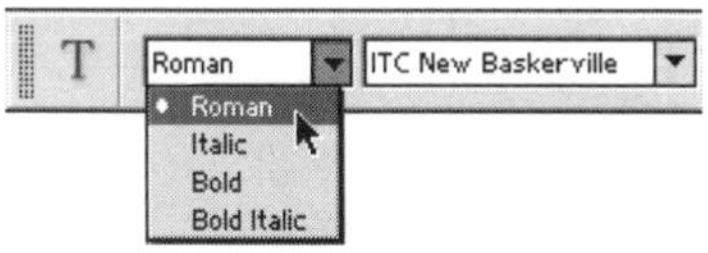

T   Roman ▾   ITC New Baskerville ▾
      ● Roman
        Italic
        Bold
        Bold Italic

Figure 9.17 Many fonts allow you to select a style from the font style menu.

a_a   T T T T

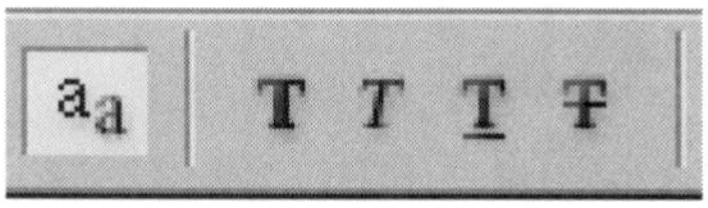

Figure 9.18 If a font doesn't include style options, you can apply a bold or italic format with the buttons on the options bar.

To choose the font family and style:

1. Select the text you want to change.

2. From the options bar, choose a font from the font family menu (**Figure 9.16**).

3. Still on the options bar, choose a style from the font style menu (**Figure 9.17**).
   If the font family you selected doesn't happen to include a particular style, you can click the Faux Bold or Faux Italic button to change the look of your text (**Figure 9.18**).

✔ Tip

■ If you haven't memorized the look of each and every font on your computer (and who has?), there's an easy way to view examples and choose the font. First select your text; then, on the options bar, click directly in the font family box. The current font name will appear highlighted. Now you can use Up and Down Arrow keys on your keyboard to scroll through all of the fonts. As you scroll through the list, your text automatically changes to the selected font (this little technique works with styles and sizes, too) (**Figure 9.19**).

Figure 9.19 Press the Up and Down Arrow keys on your keyboard to scroll through all of the fonts on the menu. Your type will change appearance as the font list scrolls.

CHANGING THE LOOK OF YOUR TYPE

275

To change the font size:

1. Select the text you want to change.

2. Choose a size from the type size menu on the options bar (**Figure 9.20**).

   To change to a type size not listed on the menu, just enter a new value in the type size text box. The default type measurement is set to points, but you can also use other units of measure (in, cm, px, or pica).

✔ Tips

- You can quickly adjust the type size up and down with keyboard shortcuts. Just select your text and then press Ctrl+Shift+. (period)/ Command+Shift+. (period) to increase the size in 2-point increments. To reduce the size of the text, press Ctrl+Shift+, (comma)/ Command+Shift+, (comma) (**Figure 9.21**).

- To change the default unit of measurement for type, select Edit > Preferences > Units and Rulers (Windows and Mac OS 9) or Photoshop Elements > Preferences > Units and Rulers (Mac OS X) (**Figure 9.22**). Here you can select among pixels, points, and millimeters (mm) (**Figure 9.23**).

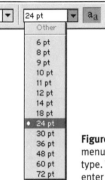

Figure 9.20 Use the type size menu to adjust the size of your type. To use a size not listed, just enter it in the text box.

48 pt

50 pt

52 pt

Figure 9.21 To fine-tune your type size, press Ctrl+Shift+. (period)/Command+Shift+. (period) to increase the size in 2-point increments. Press Ctrl+Shift+, (comma)/Command+Shift+, (comma) to reduce the font size by 2 points.

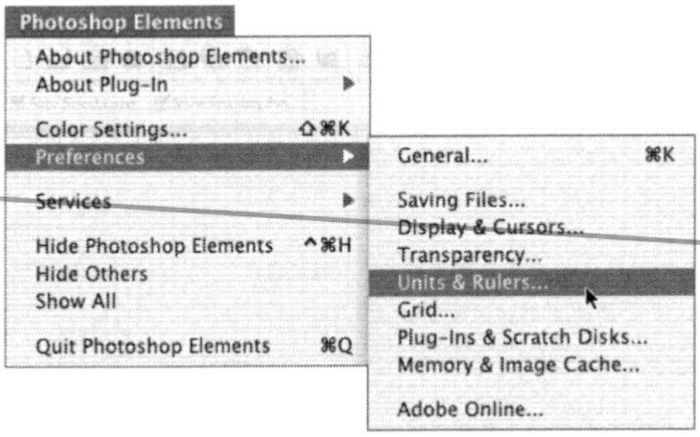

Figure 9.22 In Mac OS X, Preferences is found on the Photoshop Elements menu on the main menu bar.

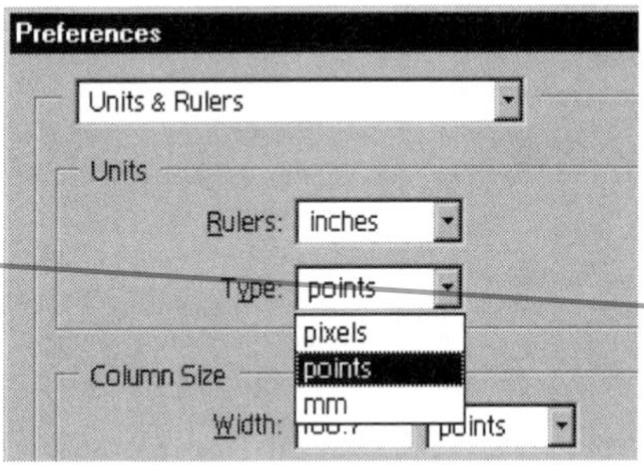

Figure 9.23 You can set type unit preferences to pixels, points, or millimeters.

Figure 9.24 You can apply the underline and strikethrough styles from the options bar.

Figure 9.25 When you apply an underline to vertical text, it appears on the left side of the text.

Left Align

Center Align

Right Align

Figure 9.26 When you realign type, it shifts around the origin, or the first point you clicked when entering the type.

To apply underline or strikethrough:

1. Select the text you want to change.

2. Click either the Underline or Strikethrough button on the options bar to apply that style to your text (**Figure 9.24**). If your type layer is set to a vertical orientation, the line will appear on the left side of the type (**Figure 9.25**).

To change the alignment:

1. Select the text you want to change.

2. From the options bar, choose an alignment option (**Figure 9.26**).

   The type will shift in relationship to the origin of the line of text. The origin is the place in your image where you first clicked before entering the type.

   ▲ **Left Align** positions the left edge of each line of type at the origin.

   ▲ **Center Align** positions the center of each line of type at the origin.

   ▲ **Right Align** positions the right edge of each line of type at the origin.

CHANGING THE LOOK OF YOUR TYPE

To change the text color:

1. Select the text you want to change.

2. Click the color selection box on the options bar (**Figure 9.27**).

   The Color Picker appears. Choose a new type color from the Color Picker (**Figure 9.28**), then click OK to apply the new color to your text.

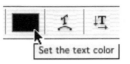

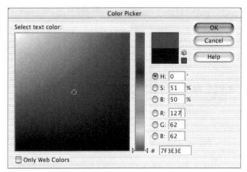

Figure 9.27 You can change the text color by clicking the color selection box.

Figure 9.28 Use the Color Picker to select a new text color.

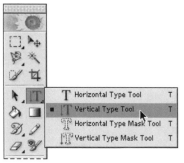

Figure 9.29 The Vertical Type tool is located right under the Horizontal Type tool.

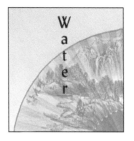

Figure 9.30 When you use the Vertical Type tool, your text appears in descending order (from the top down) on your image.

Figure 9.31 When you press Return/Enter, another line of vertical type is entered to the left of the first.

Working with Vertical Text

Most of the time, you'll be using the standard, Horizontal Type tool. But you can also change your type to a vertical orientation whenever you want. One of the reasons that Photoshop Elements includes both horizontal and vertical type is to accommodate the needs of the Asian-language versions of the product, such as Korean, Japanese, and Chinese.

To create vertical text:

1. With the image window open, click the Vertical Type tool on the toolbar (**Figure 9.29**).

    The pointer changes to an I-beam.

2. Move the pointer to the area where you want to insert your text.

3. Type your text on the image (**Figure 9.30**). The characters appear in descending order on your image.

4. To start a new line that will appear to the left of the first line, press Enter/Return (**Figure 9.31**).

    To create and control the location of another line of vertical text, simply reselect the Vertical Type tool and create a separate, independent vertical type layer.

To change the orientation of the text:

1. Select a type layer on the Layers palette.

2. Select the type tool on the toolbar and then click the Flip Orientation button on the options bar (**Figure 9.32**).

   The text changes to the opposite orientation. If your text is horizontal, it flips to vertical orientation—and vice versa.

✔ Tip

■ If you have Asian language fonts installed in your computer and you want to use the Asian type formatting options, choose Edit > Preferences > General (Windows and Mac OS) or Photoshop Elements > Preferences > General (Mac OS X) and select Show Asian Text Options (**Figure 9.33**).

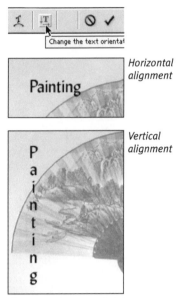

Figure 9.32 You can switch between horizontal and vertical type by clicking the Flip Orientation button on the options bar.

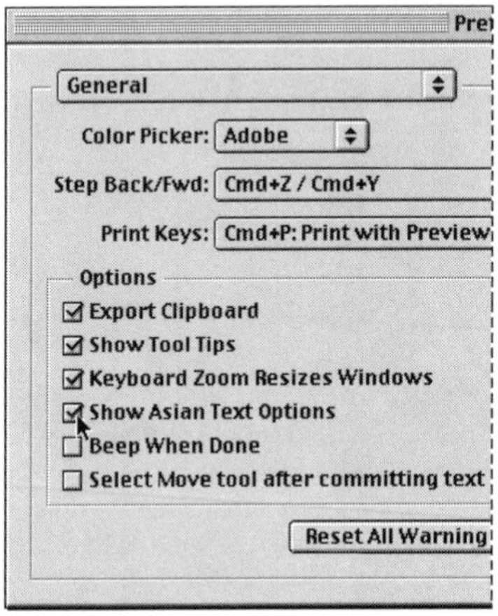

Figure 9.33 If your system supports Asian text options, you can work with them by selecting this feature in the Preferences > General dialog box.

Anti-aliasing on

Anti-aliasing off

Figure 9.34 You'll usually want to anti-alias your type, especially when using larger type sizes. This example shows 60-point type viewed at 200 percent.

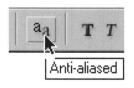

Figure 9.35 When using type sizes of about 14 points or less, you may want to turn off anti-aliasing so that your text doesn't become blurry. This example shows 10-point type viewed at 200 percent.

Figure 9.36 You can turn anti-aliasing off and on with the button on the options bar.

Figure 9.37 Anti-aliasing can also be controlled from the main menu by choosing Layer > Type > Anti-Alias On or Off.

Anti-aliasing Type

You can choose to smooth the edges of, or *anti-alias*, your type, just as you can with image selections as discussed in Chapter 4. In most cases, you'll be using Photoshop Elements to create fairly large, display-size text. For this reason, you'll normally want to anti-alias your text so that it doesn't appear to be jagged (**Figure 9.34**).

The exception is in cases where you are using smaller font sizes, such as 14 points or less, and are planning to use the image for on-screen viewing on the Web. At smaller sizes, anti-aliasing actually makes your text less readable, and the smoothing effect looks more like blurring (**Figure 9.35**). Also, in the process of anti-aliasing, many more colors are generated, and not all Web browsers support all of these colors, so some unwanted color artifacts may appear around the edges of your type.

To turn anti-aliasing on and off:

1. Select a type layer on the Layers palette.

2. *Do one of the following:*
   ▲ Click the Anti-aliased button on the options bar. To deselect anti-aliasing, click the button again (**Figure 9.36**).
   ▲ From the main menu, choose Layer > Type > Anti-Alias On or Layer > Type > Anti-Alias Off (**Figure 9.37**).

ANTI-ALIASING TYPE

281

Warping Text

Photoshop Elements lets you distort text easily with the Warp tool. You can choose from 15 different warping options in the Warp Text dialog box. Within this dialog box, you can adjust the amount of the bend in the type, as well as the horizontal and vertical distortion.

Even after you've warped your text, it's still completely editable, and you can make additional formatting changes to it at any time. But because the warp effect is applied to the entire type layer, you can't warp individual characters—it's all or nothing. The Warp Text Style Gallery that follows this section includes a few examples of the results you can get with this addictive tool.

To warp text:

1. Select a type layer on the Layers palette.

2. From the toolbar, select a type tool (so that the type options appear on the options bar) and click the Create Warped Text button (**Figure 9.38**).

   The Warp Text dialog box appears.

3. Pick a warp style from the drop-down menu (**Figure 9.39**).

4. Choose either Horizontal or Vertical orientation for the effect (**Figure 9.40**).

Figure 9.38 Click the Create Warped Text button on the options bar to experiment with various type distortions.

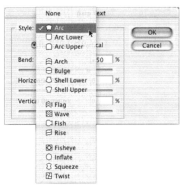

Figure 9.39 You can select from 15 different text warp options and make additional adjustments for each.

Horizontal orientation

Vertical orientation

Figure 9.40 The Horizontal and Vertical orientation options make a huge change in the results.

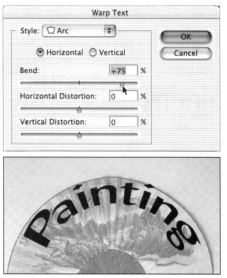

Figure 9.41 In this example, the Bend slider was used to get the type to match the curve of the fan.

Figure 9.42 To remove text warp, just select None from the Style pop-up menu.

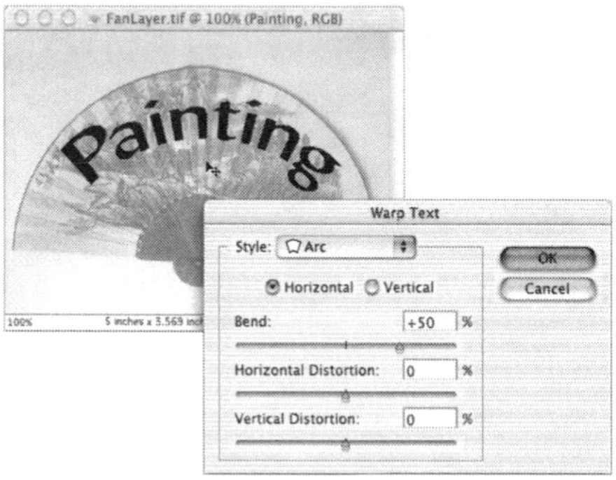

Figure 9.43 You can even move your text around while experimenting with the various warping options.

5. If you want, you can modify the amount of Bend and Horizontal or Vertical distortion with the sliders (**Figure 9.41**).

6. Click OK to apply the effect.

To remove text warp:

1. On the Layers palette, select a type layer that's been warped.

2. Select a type tool and click the Warp button on the options bar.

3. Choose None from the Style drop-down menu (**Figure 9.42**).

4. Click OK to remove the effect.

✔ Tip

■ As you experiment with the various warping options, your text can undergo some pretty dramatic changes. For this reason, you might want to move your text around to see how it looks in different parts of your image. Luckily, you can do this without closing the Warp Text dialog box. If you move your pointer into the image area, you'll see that it automatically changes to the Move tool so you can move your text around while adjusting the warping effect (**Figure 9.43**).

Warping Text Style Gallery

Original text	Arc	Arc Upper	Arc Lower
Arch	Bulge	Shell Lower	Shell Upper
Flag	Wave	Fish	Rise
Fisheye	Inflate	Squeeze	Twist

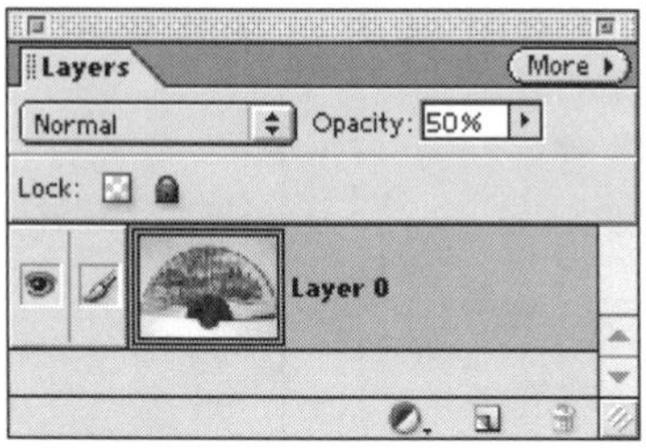

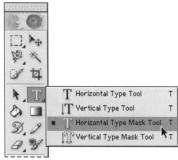

Figure 9.44 To create a type mask, first select the layer you want it to appear on.

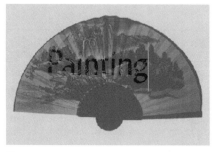

Figure 9.45 You can choose either the Horizontal or Vertical Type Mask tool.

Figure 9.46 Your type appears reversed out of the colored mask.

Figure 9.47 After you confirm the type, it appears as a selection with the typical selection border.

Creating Text Effects with Type Masks

Sometimes the text effects you want to create are better done with a type *selection*, not the actual, editable type itself. The Horizontal and Vertical Type Mask tools let you enter text, which is automatically converted to a selection in the *shape* of type. Since it's a selection, you can do everything you can do to any other selection—you can paint or fill the type or transform its geometry by skewing it or applying perspective. Unlike the previous type tools we've mentioned, the type mask tools do not create a unique layer. The type selection appears on whatever layer you have active at the time you use this tool. The bottom line: a type selection is just like any other selection, but in the shape of text.

To create a selection with the type mask tools:

1. Make sure that your active layer is the one where you want the text selection to appear (**Figure 9.44**).

2. Select either the Horizontal or Vertical Type Mask tool (**Figure 9.45**).

3. Set the type options (such as font, style, or size) on the options bar.

4. Enter your text on the image.

   The text will appear reversed out of the colored mask overlay (**Figure 9.46**).

5. Confirm your text selection by clicking the Commit Current Edits check mark on the options bar.

   Your text is selected (**Figure 9.47**). You can now apply additional changes to your type selection.

To fill a type selection with an image:

1. Create a type selection following the steps in the preceding task.

   Make sure to position the selection over the image that you want to show through the text.

2. Copy the selection to the clipboard (**Figure 9.48**).

3. Choose File > New from Clipboard (**Figure 9.49**).

   Your text selection appears in its own file, with the image peeking through (**Figure 9.50**).

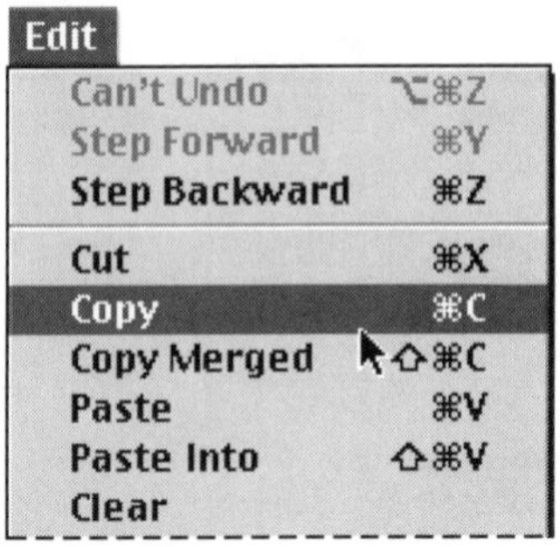

Edit

Can't Undo	⌥⌘Z
Step Forward	⌘Y
Step Backward	⌘Z
Cut	⌘X
Copy	⌘C
Copy Merged	⇧⌘C
Paste	⌘V
Paste Into	⇧⌘V
Clear	

Figure 9.48 To fill a selection with an image, first copy the selection to the clipboard.

File

New...	⌘N
New from Clipboard	
Open...	⌘O
Browse...	⇧⌘O
Open Recent	▶

Figure 9.49 When you select File > New from Clipboard, a new file is created that contains your text selection.

Figure 9.50 You can create all sorts of interesting text effects by filling type with images.

Figure 9.51 To fill text with a gradient, start by making a type selection.

Figure 9.52 Click the Gradient tool on the toolbar and then pick any gradient you want.

To apply a gradient to a type selection:

1. Create a type selection following the steps in the task "To create a selection with the type mask tools" (**Figure 9.51**).

2. Click the Gradient tool on the toolbar and choose any gradient style on the options bar (**Figure 9.52**).

3. Drag across your type selection to establish the direction of the gradient (**Figure 9.53**).

4. Deselect the type selection.

   Your text now appears with the gradient fill (**Figure 9.54**).

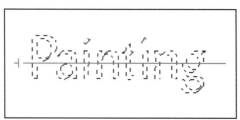

Figure 9.53 Drag in the direction you want the gradient to appear inside your type.

Figure 9.54 This example uses the Linear gradient.

CREATING TEXT EFFECTS WITH TYPE MASKS

Applying Layer Styles to Type

Since the Horizontal and Vertical Type tools create a unique text layer, you can use layer styles to make all sorts of unusual and interesting changes to your type. The significant advantage of using layer styles with your text (as opposed to using type masks) is that your text remains editable.

When choosing a font, it's a good idea to go with simpler sans-serif typefaces. This way, your type is more likely to remain readable after you've applied the style. Take a look at the text layer style gallery to see just a few examples of the different styles available.

To apply a layer style to type:

1. Enter text in your image using either the Horizontal or Vertical Type tool (**Figure 9.55**).

2. Make sure that the appropriate type layer is selected on the Layers palette, and choose a style from the Layer Styles palette (**Figure 9.56**).

   The style is automatically applied to your type (**Figure 9.57**).

✔ Tip

- If you're not quite getting the look you want, remember that you can set lighting angle, shadow distance, and other options by selecting Layer > Layer Style > Style Settings.

Figure 9.55 To use layer styles with your type, first enter text with one of the type tools.

Figure 9.56 You can use any of Photoshop Elements' dozens of layer styles on your type. The example here uses a drop-shadow layer style.

Figure 9.57 The drop-shadow layer style adds depth and substance to the type selection, making it appear to pop out of the screen.

Text Layer Style Gallery

Original text

Bevels >
Simple Sharp Outer

Drop Shadows > Low

Inner Glows >
Heavy Noisy

Inner Shadows > Low

Outer Glows > Fire

Visibility > Ghosted

Complex > Rivet

Complex > Molten Gold

Glass Buttons >
Black Glass

Image Effects > Snow

Patterns > Diamond Plate

Photographic Effects >
Bevel Edge

Wow Chrome >
Shiny Round Bevel

Wow Neon >
Aqua Blue Neon

Wow Plastic >
Clear Plastic

PREPARING IMAGES FOR THE WEB 10

The odds are pretty good that at some point you're going to want to post your images on a Web page, or e-mail a few photos to friends and family. And whether you decide to post a snapshot of an old push mower to an Internet auction site or just want to send vacation photos to your Aunt Ruth, the considerations are pretty much the same.

Size and speed influence most decisions regarding image preparation for the Web, and they are the central themes of this chapter. The goal of virtually every step of every procedure that follows is to make your images as small and compact as possible. That's not to say that we're abandoning aesthetics altogether—after all, what's the purpose of a photograph or illustration that's too fuzzy or distorted to be seen clearly, or e-mailing a photo if it's too large to be opened? So although this chapter focuses on creating small, easy-to-download images, it's also about creating compact files that look *good*.

Understanding Image Requirements for the Web

Preparing images for publication on the Web or for distribution via e-mail presents its own unique set of challenges. Because the vast majority of Internet users still depend on dial-up connections (as opposed to high-speed DSL or cable connections), an image's file size is of primary concern. Your image needs to be small enough to download quickly, while retaining enough information to display the colors and details of your original image.

Photoshop Elements helps you accomplish this digital sleight-of-hand through a process called *optimization*. Optimization pares down and streamlines an image's display information based on variables that you select and control. By limiting the number of colors in an image or by selectively discarding pixels that are less critical than others, Photoshop Elements simplifies an image and reduces its file size. Once an image has been simplified in this way, it is said to be *optimized* (**Figure 10.1**).

Photoshop Elements offers four file format options for optimizing an image: JPEG, GIF, PNG-8, and PNG-24. Generally speaking, JPEG and PNG-24 are most appropriate for images that contain subtle transitions of tone and color (like photographs), while GIF and PNG-8 are best for graphics or illustrations containing a lot of flat color or typography (**Figure 10.2**).

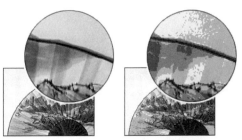

Figure 10.1 The original illustration of the Chinese fan (left) contains a great deal of detail and subtle gradations of tone and color. The optimized version (right) is greatly simplified and contains far less color and image information.

Figure 10.2 The photograph on the left, with its subtle and varied tones and color, is a good candidate for JPEG optimization, while the flat, bold colors and use of typography in the version on the right make it more appropriate for GIF optimization.

About the Save for Web Dialog Box

The Save for Web dialog box might be more appropriately called the "Prepare Web Images" or "Optimization" dialog box. Within it, you'll find all the tools, pop-up menus, and text fields necessary to transform any digital photograph, painting, or illustration into a graphic suitable for distribution on the Web. The original and optimized image previews, the heart of this dialog box, provide instant visual feedback whenever even the smallest setting adjustment is made, while information fields below the image previews constantly update to reflect the current optimization format, file size, and download times. And at any time in the optimization process, you can preview and verify exactly how your image will appear in any Web browser loaded on your computer.

Choosing File Formats

JPEG is the most common file format for images on the Web. Because it supports 24-bit color (which translates to over 16 million colors), it's the ideal format for optimizing photos without sacrificing too much image quality. However, because it *does* discard a small portion of image information as it optimizes, it's not the best choice for images where detail and sharpness is critical, such as scanned line art, vector graphics, or images containing a lot of type.

If you want to keep the detail in your images as sharp as possible, try using the **GIF** format. The GIF format sacrifices subtle gradations of tone and color, but retains the sharpness and image detail that can be lost with the JPEG format, making it a good choice for animations, images with transparency, vector graphics, and images with type.

In the pages that follow, we don't go into a lot of detail with regard to the two **PNG** formats. It's not that we have any qualms with the format or its capacity for optimizing different types of images—which by the way, can be impressive, indeed. It's just that the PNG format does have a couple of limitations significant enough that we don't recommend using it yet.

Foremost among those limitations is its relative newness. PNG hasn't been around all that long, and since the majority of browsers still don't support the PNG format, GIF and JPEG are simply more reliable formats for viewing over a wide range of browsers.

And though in some cases PNG-8 images can be slightly smaller than comparable GIF images, PNG formats (particularly PNG-24) tend to produce images markedly larger than their GIF and JPEG counterparts. Keeping with the goal of controlling file size, we recommend sticking with GIF and JPEG formats for optimizing your images.

Optimizing an Image for the Web

With the Save for Web command, Photoshop Elements provides a simple, automated method that not only saves an optimized *copy* of your original image, but also preserves the original high-resolution image, untouched and intact. Simply choose from a list of 12 predefined settings, and your image is instantly optimized for the Web. You may want to experiment with the custom optimization settings, but the 12 predefined settings should accomplish most of your optimization tasks.

To save an image for the Web:

1. Open the image you want to optimize.

2. From the File menu, choose Save for Web (**Figure 10.3**), or press Alt+Shift+Ctrl+S/ Option+Shift+Command+.

   The Save for Web dialog box opens on top of the active image window, display-ing the image in side-by-side original and optimized previews (**Figure 10.4**).

Figure 10.3 Open the Save for Web dialog box from the File menu.

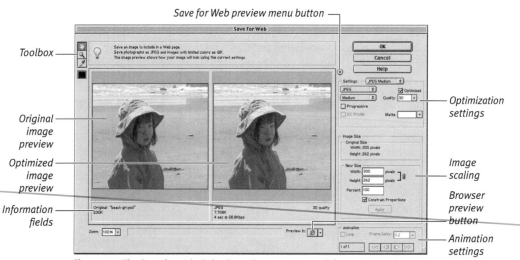

Figure 10.4 The Save for Web dialog box. The image on the left shows the original image. The image on the right shows a preview of what the same image will look like after it's been optimized.

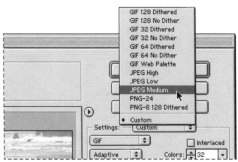

Figure 10.5 Choose from the list of predefined settings for JPEG and GIF or PNG optimization formats.

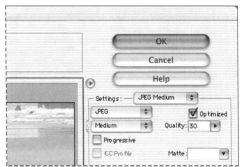

Figure 10.6 Once you've chosen a predefined optimization setting, the rest of the options change accordingly. Here, the options have automatically changed to reflect the Medium JPEG optimization format.

Figure 10.7 Click OK in the Save for Web dialog box to save your optimized image.

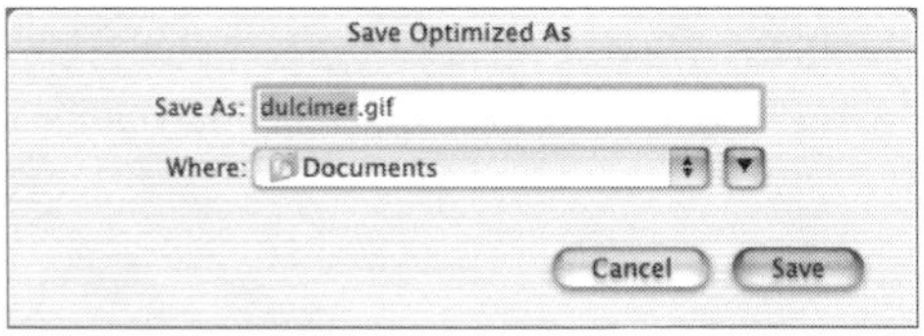

Figure 10.8 Enter a name and destination for your optimized file in the Save Optimized As dialog box.

3. From the main Settings pop-up menu in the Save for Web dialog box, choose a predefined optimization setting (**Figure 10.5**).

   The various pop-up menus within the Settings portion of the dialog box change to reflect the setting you've selected (**Figure 10.6**), as does the optimized preview in the center of the dialog box,

4. Click the OK button in the Save for Web dialog box (**Figure 10.7**).

5. In the Save Optimized As dialog box, type a new name for your file and verify that the file type matches the optimization format you chose in the Save for Web dialog box (**Figure 10.8**).

6. Choose a location for your file and click Save.

   The Save Optimized As and Save for Web dialog boxes will automatically close, and your optimized image will be saved to the location you specified.

The Save for Web Preview Menu

The Preview menu (**Figure 10.9**), which you can find by clicking the triangle button to the right of the optimized image in the Save for Web dialog box, is one of those easy-to-overlook tools in a space already packed with check boxes, palettes, and pop-up menus.

As its name implies, the Preview menu works with the image preview (the optimized side of the image preview, to be exact) and establishes parameters for the way that the image preview is displayed. Depending on the color space you select in the top portion of the Preview menu, you can view your image as it would appear in a browser on your own monitor, on a standard Macintosh or PC monitor, or see a preview of how it would appear if it were saved with its color profile.

The bottom portion of the menu offers a variety of standard dial-up and high-speed Internet connection settings. Whatever connection speed you choose here determines the estimated connection speed value displayed in the information box below the optimized preview image (**Figure 10.10**). So, by doing nothing more than selecting from a handful of menu options, you can get a good idea of how much time it will take anyone, with any number of connection speeds, to download and display your image.

None of the settings you choose from the Preview menu affect the actual image file itself in any way at all. They're for the purpose of previewing only and are completely independent of the attributes you actually apply to an image in the Settings portion of the dialog box. For instance, there's no way to include a setting for connection speed with an image, since connection speed is completely dependent on the modem and Internet provider of whoever it is out there in the world that may want to view or download that image.

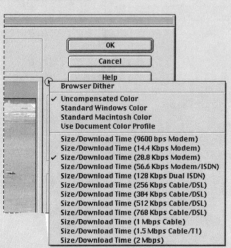

Figure 10.9 It's a little hard to find, but you can use the Preview menu to control the appearance of the optimization preview and the information displayed below it.

Figure 10.10 After you've chosen a connection speed from the preview menu, the Save for Web dialog box uses that input, along with the optimization format you've selected, to estimate the size the file will be when optimized and the time it will take to download. That information is displayed below the optimized preview, at right.

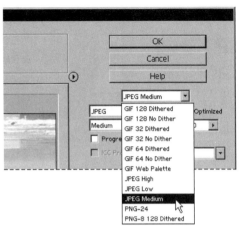

Figure 10.11 If you like, you can choose one of the predefined JPEG settings to use as a baseline for your own custom settings.

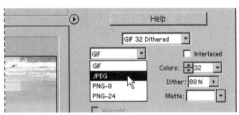

Figure 10.12 Optimization formats can be changed at any time from the pop-up menu.

Adjusting Optimization Settings

You're not limited to using predefined settings to optimize your images. You can fine-tune these settings further by using the collection of pop-up menus, check boxes, and sliders available in the Settings portion of the dialog box. For example, if you want your JPEGs to retain a little more image quality as they're compressed for the Web, you can change the default quality setting for a Medium JPEG image from 30 to 45, and, depending on the image, improve its sharpness and detail without increasing its download time. As you make adjustments, refer to the optimized image preview to the left of the Settings column. There, you can see how your changes affect the image, as well as its file size and download time.

To apply custom JPEG optimization settings to an image:

1. Open the image you want to optimize, then choose File > Save for Web to open the Save for Web dialog box.

2. From the main Settings pop-up menu, choose one of the predefined JPEG settings (**Figure 10.11**).

   You don't have to choose one of the predefined JPEG settings, but they can serve as a good jumping-off point for building your own settings For instance, if you decide that small file size and quick download time are priorities, you might want to start with the predefined JPEG Low setting and then customize the settings from there.

3. Verify that JPEG is selected from the Optimized file format pop-up menu, or if you've decided to skip step 1, choose JPEG from the Optimized pop-up menu (**Figure 10.12**).

continues on next page

4. To set the image quality, *do one of the following:*

▲ From the Compression quality pop-up menu, choose a quality option (**Figure 10.13**).

▲ Drag the Quality slider while referring to the optimized preview (**Figure 10.14**).

The Quality slider has a direct impact on the Quality pop-up menu, and vice-versa. When the slider is set between 0 and 29, the level in the Quality pop-up menu will be Low. A setting of 30 through 59 registers as Medium, 60 through 79 as High, and 80 through 100 as Maximum. Just remember that a quality setting in the Maximum range will usually create a file six to eight times larger than one saved in the Low range.

5. Select the Progressive check box if you want your image to build from a low-resolution version to its final saved version as it downloads in a Web browser (**Figure 10.15**).

This option is more critical for large, high-quality images with download times in the tens of seconds. Rather than leaving a blank space, the low-resolution image appears almost immediately, giving your Web page visitors *something* to look at until the complete file is downloaded.

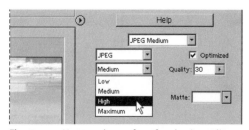

Figure 10.13 You can choose from four basic quality options for JPEG images: Low, Medium, High, and Maximum.

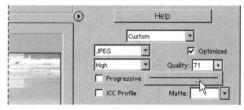

Figure 10.14 Once a quality option has been selected, use the slider control to fine-tune it.

Figure 10.15 The Progressive feature draws your image incrementally on a Web page as it downloads, eventually displaying the image in its final state.

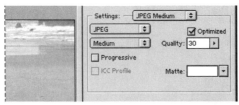

Figure 10.16 Check the Optimized box to reduce the file size of your image just a hair more.

6. Select the ICC Profile check box if you've previously saved a color profile with your image and want that information preserved in your optimized image.

   Unless your photo or art contains some *critical* color (a logo with a very specific corporate color, for instance), you should leave this box unchecked. Not all Web browsers support color profiles, and the inclusion of the profile information can increase a file's size significantly.

7. If it's not already selected, select the Optimized check box (**Figure 10.16**).

   This is the default selection for all of the predefined JPEG settings and helps to trim just a little more off the file size with little or no sacrifice of image quality.

   Note that if you selected the Progressive option (in step 4), Optimized is dimmed and unavailable. You'll need to uncheck Progressive if you want to take advantage of the Optimized option.

8. If your original image contains transparency, see "Making a Web Image Transparent" later in this chapter.

9. Click the OK button in the Save for Web dialog box to rename and save your optimized image.

To apply custom GIF optimization settings to an image:

1. Open the image you want to optimize, then choose File > Save for Web to open the Save for Web dialog box.

2. From the main Settings pop-up menu, choose one of the predefined GIF settings, or choose GIF from the Optimized file format pop-up menu (**Figure 10.17**).

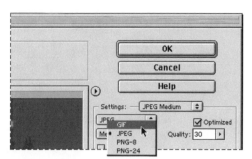

Figure 10.17 Choose the GIF setting to optimize illustrations, vector art, or type.

3. From the Color Reduction Algorithm pop-up menu, choose the color lookup table that you want applied to your image (**Figure 10.18**). (For more information, see the sidebar "About Color Models and Color Lookup Tables" later in this chapter.)

4. From the Colors pop-up menu, choose the maximum number of colors that will be displayed in your image by specifying the number of colors that the image's palette will contain (**Figure 10.19**).

   You can choose from the list of eight standard color palette values, use the arrows to the left of the text box to change the values in increments of one, or simply enter a value in the text box and press Enter/Return.

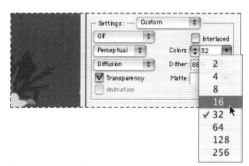

Figure 10.18 The GIF format offers several schemes for interpreting and displaying the color in your image.

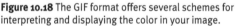

Figure 10.19 A GIF image can contain from 2 to 256 colors.

Figure 10.20 This illustration was optimized with three GIF color palettes containing progressively fewer colors. From left to right, the illustrations were saved with palettes of, 16, 8, and 4 colors, creating file sizes of roughly 32K, 19K, and 12K respectively.

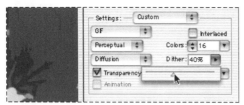

Figure 10.21 Three different dithering schemes determine the type of pixel pattern that is used to define and display your image.

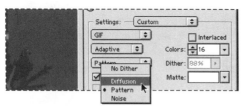

Figure 10.22 If you choose the Diffusion option, you can control the amount of dithering that occurs in your image, from 0 to 100 percent.

Figure 10.23 The Interlaced feature works like JPEG's Progressive option to draw your image incrementally on a Web page as it downloads.

When formatting GIF images, the number of colors you specify will have a larger impact on final file size and download time than any other attribute you set. Naturally, the fewer colors you select, the smaller the image file size will be, so experiment with different values, gradually reducing the number of colors, until you arrive at a setting you find acceptable (**Figure 10.20**).

5. From the Dither pop-up menu, choose a dithering scheme to apply to your image (**Figure 10.21**). (For more information, see the sidebar "Choosing Dithering Options" later in this chapter.)

6. Use the Dither slider to specify a percentage for the dither (**Figure 10.22**).

    Higher percentages create finer dither patterns, which tend to preserve more detail in images where limited color palettes have been specified. The Dither percentage slider is active only when Diffusion dither is selected.

7. If you want your image to build from a low-resolution version to its final saved version as it downloads in a browser, select the Interlaced check box (**Figure 10.23**).

    Interlacing a GIF image works in much the same way as applying the Progressive option to a JPEG image. If you choose not to select the interlace option, your image won't display on a Web page until it's completely downloaded.

8. If your original image contains transparency, see "Making a Web Image Transparent" later in this chapter.

9. Click the OK button in the Save for Web dialog box to rename and save your optimized image.

continues on next page

✔ Tip

- If you want to save an image in the PNG-8 format, you'll find that it uses all the same options as for GIF, and the procedures for applying custom PNG-8 settings will be exactly the same as those for GIF. The only options available for PNG-24 are transparency and interlacing.

About Color Models and Color Lookup Tables

Though you certainly don't have to be proficient in Web color theory to successfully save images for the Web, a little background information on the different color models might will help you to make more informed decisions as you make color choices for your Web images. When you optimize an image using the GIF format, Photoshop Elements asks you to pick a *color model* from the Color Reduction Algorithm pop-up menu. Since GIF images are limited to just 256 colors, color models help to define which colors—from the vast spectrum of *millions* of colors—will be used in any individual optimized image. Sets of colors are given priority over others depending on the color model chosen, as follows:

Perceptual color leans toward colors to which the human eye is most sensitive.

Selective color draws from the largest possible range of colors, incorporating colors from the Web-safe palette as much as possible. Selective is the default option.

Adaptive color favors those colors that appear most often in a particular image. For instance, a seascape may contain colors primarily from the blue spectrum.

Web color is limited to the standard 216 Web colors and typically produces color the least true to the original image. Since most browsers and personal computer monitors are capable of displaying in thousands and millions of colors, you'll probably have very little occasion to use this option.

Once you've selected a color model and chosen a maximum number of colors from the Colors pop-up menu, Photoshop Elements builds a *color lookup table* specific to the image you're optimizing.

A color lookup table can be thought of as a palette of color swatches. If an original image contains more colors than you specify for its GIF version's color lookup table, any missing colors will be recreated as best they can, using the existing number of colors in the color palette. If the original image contains *fewer* colors than you've specified, then the color lookup table will shrink and will contain only the colors in the image.

Either way, no unnecessary color information is included in the color lookup table, meaning that your image's file size is kept to a minimum.

Choosing Dithering Options

Because a GIF image works with a limited color palette, it's impossible to reproduce most of the millions of colors visible to the human eye, much less subtle gradations of tone and color. GIF optimization employs a little visual trick called *dithering* to fool the eye into perceiving more colors and softer transitions than are actually there. By reorganizing pixels of different hues and values, dithering can do a surprisingly good job of simulating thousands of colors with a palette of a hundred colors or less (**Figure 10.24**). Dithering works, quite simply, by mixing two available colors to create the illusion of a third. Blue and yellow pixels mixed together will blend to create green. Black and white pixels mixed in varying proportions will simulate a graduated fill or soft-edged drop shadow.

Photoshop Elements gives you a choice of three dithering schemes.

Diffusion is the default scheme for any of the predefined GIF settings; it creates a random pattern that usually yields the most natural-looking results. Diffusion is the only option that allows you to control the percentage of dither present in your image.

Pattern, as its name implies, lays down pixels in a uniform grid pattern. It can have the effect of a very coarse halftone screen such as you might see in low-resolution newspaper photography.

Noise creates a random pattern similar to Diffusion, but attempts to blend color transitions further by allowing color from one area to spill over slightly into an adjoining one. It occasionally produces an interesting effect, but will rarely be your first choice.

Figure 10.24 The original image (left) relies on thousands of subtle tonal and value changes to define the faces of the little girls. The GIF-optimized version (right) shows the close-up results of dithering. Since GIF optimization uses a limited palette of colors, it gathers together pixels of whatever colors are available to reproduce an approximation of the original image.

Making a Web Image Transparent

In just a few simple steps, you can preserve the transparency of any image using options available in the GIF formatting settings. Once transparency has been set, an image of any shape (even one with a transparent cutout) can be placed on a Web page and made to blend seamlessly with its background (**Figure 10.25**).

To apply transparency to an image:

1. Open the image you want to make transparent, then choose File > Save for Web to open the Save for Web dialog box.

2. In the Settings portion of the Save for Web dialog box, make sure that the Optimization format is set to GIF.

3. If it's not already selected, click to select the Transparency checkbox (**Figure 10.26**).

   The image in the optimized preview area will be displayed against a transparency grid pattern (**Figure 10.27**).

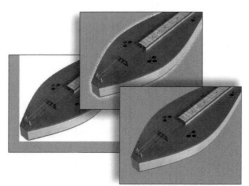

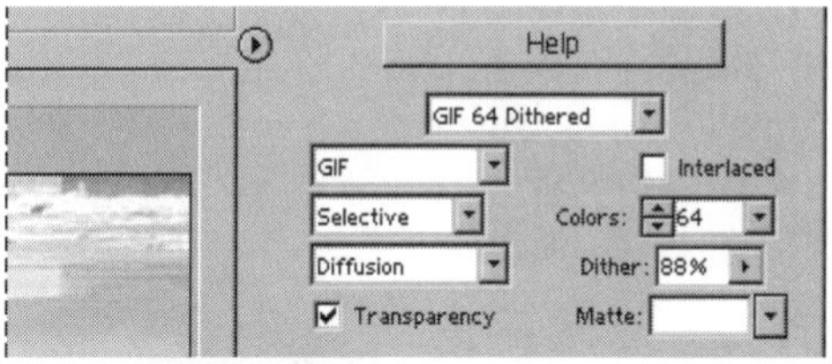

Figure 10.25 The image at left was saved with no transparency and displays with a solid, white background. The center image was saved with transparency, but since its matte color was set to the default of white, it appears to have a ghosted halo around its edge. The image at right was saved both with transparency and with its matte color matching that of the Web page background.

Figure 10.26 GIF optimization offers the added bonus of preserving transparency in your Web-bound images.

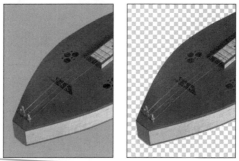

Figure 10.27 If the Transparency box is unchecked, the image is displayed on a solid, colored background (left). If the Transparency box is checked, the image is displayed on a transparent background (right).

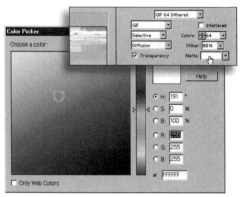

Figure 10.28 Choose a matte color from the Color Picker to match your intended Web page background.

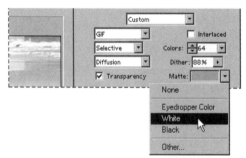

Figure 10.29 The Matte pop-up menu offers a limited number of color options.

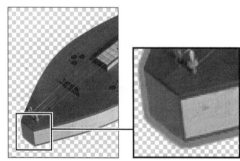

Figure 10.30 The color you select from the Matte pop-up menu or color box fills in the semitransparent pixels around your image, helping to maintain a smooth edge and creating a seamless transition when the image is placed on a Web page of the same color.

4. To select the color that will be used to blend your image with the Web page background color, *do one of the following:*

▲ Click the Matte color box to open the Color Picker; then select a color from the main color window or enter color values in either the HSB or RGB color space text boxes (**Figure 10.28**).

▲ From the Matte pop-up menu, choose a color option (**Figure 10.29**).

Only the semitransparent pixels around the edges of the image are filled with the matte color. If the matte color matches the color of the Web page background, the transition between the transparent image and its background will be seamless (**Figure 10.30**).

✔ Tip

■ The JPEG format doesn't support true transparency, but as long as your image is placed on a Web page with a solid, colored background, you can simulate transparency by filling the original transparent spaces with a background color. Follow the steps in the procedure "To apply custom JPEG settings," then click the Matte color box to open the Color Picker. Select a color, then click OK. When you close the Color Picker, any areas that were transparent in the original image will be filled with the matte color.

MAKING A WEB IMAGE TRANSPARENT

305

Identifying Web Page Background Colors

You'll need to do a little homework to identify the color of your Web page background before you can precisely assign a matte color to your transparent GIF images in Photoshop Elements.

The most accurate method of determining the color of the Web page is to identify the color values in the Web page's source code. This isn't nearly as intimidating as it sounds. Open any Web page, then from the browser's main menu, find the command to view the source code. (In Internet Explorer, you simply choose View > Source). A window will open, with code describing everything from the location of graphics and text to the background color.

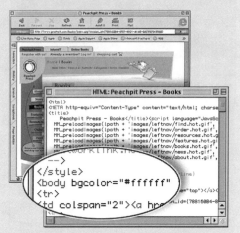

Once you have the source code window open, scan down the entries for the one that begins with <body>. (You'll typically find it within the first dozen entries or so.) On the same line, directly to the right, it will say, bgcolor= followed by either a 6-digit Web color code (something like #E2A6A6) or RGB color values (**Figure 10.31**). The "bg" of course, stands for *background*, and the color code describes the color for that background. Simply jot down the color values from the Web page source code, then return to Photoshop Elements and enter those same values in the bottom field of the Color Picker to assign the matte color.

Figure 10.31 In this example, we've opened the source code for a page from Peachpit's Web site. On the <body> line is the color code for the Web page background—bgcolor="#ffffff". "#ffffff" translates to white. So in this case, the background color code could also have read as either bgcolor=white or bgcolor=255,255,255 (the RGB values for white).

Placing Transparent Images on Patterned Backgrounds

You may want to place your transparent GIF image on a patterned background rather than a background with a solid, colored fill. If you try to assign any matte color at all, even one similar to a color in the patterned background, you're likely to be disappointed by a halo that appears around the edges of the image (**Figure 10.32**). Instead, set the Matte option to None (**Figure 10.33**). The transparent edges will become hard and jagged, particularly on curved and angled edges (**Figure 10.34**), but when placed on the patterned background, the edges should be barely noticeable and will blend much more naturally than if you use the halo-edged alternative.

✔ Tip

■ Since the Eyedropper tool can sample color only from the two preview boxes in the Save for Web dialog box, the **Eyedropper Color** option is helpful only if the color of your Web page background also happens to be present in your image. The **Other** option simply opens the Color Picker. You're better off using the Matte pop-up menu only when selecting the **White**, **Black**, and **None** options.

Figure 10.32 When a transparent GIF with a matte color is placed on a patterned background, a colored "halo" may appear around its edges (left). When the matte is set to None, the halo effect disappears and the image appears to blend with the patterned background (right).

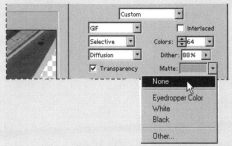

Figure 10.33 Select None from the Matte pop-up menu to create a hard-edged transparent image ideal for placing on a patterned background.

Figure 10.34 When None is selected from the Matte pop-up menu, a hard, aliased edge is created around a transparent image.

Previewing an Image

Before you commit to saving your optimized image, you may want to see exactly how the image will appear in a Web browser window. Although the Save for Web optimized preview gives you a good approximation of how the final image will look, there's no substitute for seeing the image displayed in its natural environment.

Additionally, you can remain within the Save for Web dialog box to preview your image as if it were viewed on an older, lower-end system, limited to just 256 colors. This can be helpful, as it allows you to design primarily for most current computer systems while giving you the opportunity to fine-tune your settings to accommodate the limited display capabilities of older systems. Note that this is only a preview, and has no effect on your actual image file and its settings.

To preview an image in a Web browser:

1. Open the image you want to preview, then choose File > Save for Web to open the Save for Web dialog box.

2. At the bottom of the Save for Web dialog box, choose a Web browser or click the current browser icon on the Preview In pop-up menu (**Figure 10.35**).

   The browser opens displaying the optimized image plus its dimensions and the settings you specified (**Figure 10.36**).

3. Close the browser window to return to the Save for Web dialog box.

Figure 10.35 Using one of two options in the Preview In portion of the Save for Web dialog box, you can open your optimized image directly in a browser.

Figure 10.36 When your image opens in a browser, it's accompanied by all of the settings you specified in the Save for Web dialog box.

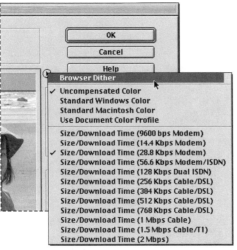

Figure 10.37 Select Browser Dither from the preview menu if you want to view your image using a limited Web-safe palette.

To preview an image as it would display on older monitors:

1. From the preview menu in the Save for Web dialog box, choose Browser Dither (**Figure 10.37**).

   The image in the optimized preview window appears just as it would on an 8-bit (256-color) monitor, allowing you to anticipate what this image will look like on older computer systems (**Figure 10.38**).

2. To turn off the browser dither preview, choose Browser Dither again from the preview menu.

Figure 10.38 When you select Browser Dither, the optimized preview (right) changes to display your image as it would appear on an older, 256-color monitor.

Sending Images by E-mail

With the new Attach to E-Mail feature, Photoshop Elements streamlines the process of sending digital photos to family and friends. If your photo is too large or is in the wrong file format, Photoshop Elements can automatically resize your image and save it as a JPEG file, if you prefer. But it's all up to you—you can send photos and images in any file size or format, so long as you have the bandwidth for it.

To attach a photo to e-mail:

1. Open the photo or image you want to send.

2. From the File menu, choose Attach to E-mail (**Figure 10.39**).

   If Photoshop Elements determines that your photo is ready to send, it automatically launches your default e-mail program (if it's not already open) and attaches a copy of your photo to your e-mail (**Figure 10.40**).

   If a warning dialog box appears on the screen, skip to step 4.

3. Type a recipient's e-mail address in your e-mail program's To field; then click the Send or Send Now button on your e-mail program's toolbar.

   Every e-mail program is slightly different, so check your e-mail program's Help menu or user instructions if you're not sure how to send your e-mail.

Figure 10.39 From the File menu, choose Attach to E-mail.

Figure 10.40 If Photoshop Elements determines that your image is an acceptable size and format, your default e-mail program launches, then attaches a copy of your photo to an outgoing e-mail message.

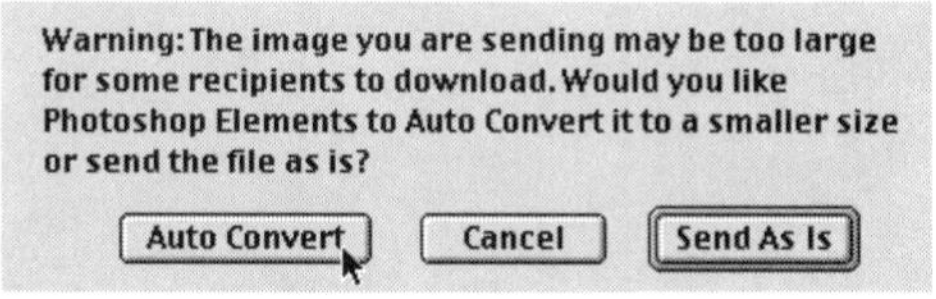

Warning: The image you are sending may be too large for some recipients to download. Would you like Photoshop Elements to Auto Convert it to a smaller size or send the file as is?

[Auto Convert]   [Cancel]   [Send As Is]

Figure 10.41 If your photo's file size is too large, Photoshop Elements offers to resize it for you.

You must save your file before you can attach it to e-mail.

[Cancel]   [Save As and Continue]

Figure 10.42 You'll need to save any changes to your image before you can send it.

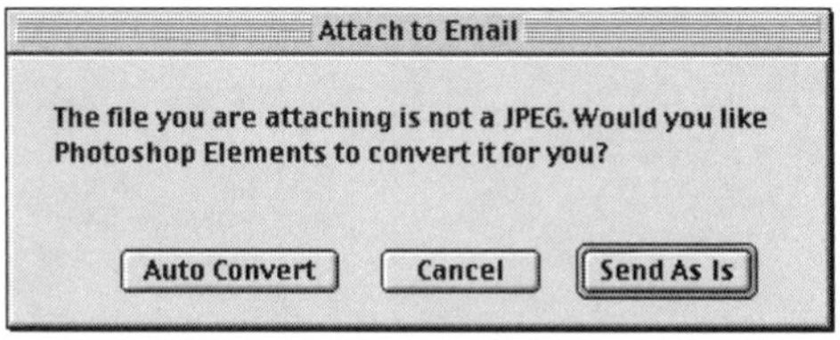

Attach to Email

The file you are attaching is not a JPEG. Would you like Photoshop Elements to convert it for you?

[Auto Convert]   [Cancel]   [Send As Is]

Figure 10.43 Photoshop Elements offers to convert your image to JPEG format. If you want to reduce your image's file size, this is a good idea.

4. If Photoshop Elements considers your photo to be too large, a dialog box appears, asking you if you want to auto convert a copy of your image to a smaller size or to send it as is (**Figure 10.41**).

If you want to reduce its size, click Auto Convert. If you don't want to reduce its size, click Send as Is.

or

If you've made changes to your photo and haven't saved them, a dialog box informs you that you must save your image if you want to attach it to e-mail (**Figure 10.42**). Click Save As and Continue.

or

If your image isn't in JPEG format, a dialog box appears asking you if you want to convert your image to JPEG (**Figure 10.43**). If you want to convert it to JPEG, click Auto Convert. If you don't want to convert your image, click Send as Is.

Depending on the dialog boxes that appear, Photoshop Elements resizes, reformats, or saves your image, then attaches it to an e-mail message, ready for you to send.

SAVING AND PRINTING IMAGES

With Photoshop Elements, you can save images in a number of file formats, each with its own set of specialized uses and limitations. In this chapter, we'll begin with a discussion of those formatting options and then move on to other considerations for saving your image files and preparing them for printing. We'll look at how to format and save multiple images (known as *batch processing*) and then look at tools you can use to lay out, organize, and catalog your image files. Last, we'll look closely at all of the steps necessary to get the best prints from all of your digital images, whether you're printing them at home, or uploading your files to an online photo service.

Understanding File Formats

Photoshop Elements lets you save an image in any of 15 different file formats, from the native, information-rich Photoshop format to optimized formats for the Web, such as GIF and JPEG. Among these is an extremely specialized collection of formats (PCX, PICT Resource, Pixar, PNG, Raw, Scitex CT, and Targa, if you must know) that you'll rarely ever need to use and so won't be described here. What follows, then, are descriptions of the most common file formats, presented in the order that they appear in the Format pop-up menu, in the Save As dialog box.

Photoshop

Photoshop is Photoshop Elements' native file format, meaning that the saved file will include information for any and all of Photoshop Elements' features, including layers styles, effects, typography, and filters. As its name implies, any file saved in the Photoshop (PSD) format can be opened not only in Photoshop Elements, but also in Adobe Photoshop. Conversely, any Photoshop file saved in its native format can be opened in Photoshop Elements. However, Photoshop Elements doesn't support all of the features available in Photoshop, so while you can open any file saved in the PSD format, some of Photoshop's more advanced features (such as layer sets) won't be accessible to you within Photoshop Elements.

A good approach is to save every photo you're working on in the native Photoshop format and then, when you're finished, save a copy in whatever format is appropriate for that image's intended use or destination. That way, you always have the original, full-featured image file to return to if you want to make changes or just save in a different format.

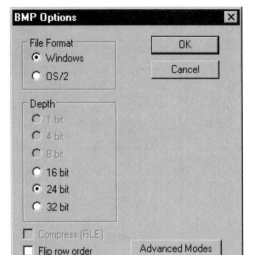

Figure 11.1 The choices available in the BMP Options dialog box vary, depending on the color or tonal content of the particular image.

BMP

If you're a Windows user, you may recognize the .bmp file extension, which identifies a bitmap file. BMP has long been Windows' standard graphics format, and it's the one you'll want to use if you're creating images for screensavers or computer wallpaper.

Radio buttons in the BMP options dialog box (**Figure 11.1**) offer you bit-depth options (you can set the maximum number of colors or values), but Photoshop Elements does a pretty good job of selecting the appropriate settings for any particular image. So, unless you know that you have a special requirement (like keeping file size to a minimum in order to conserve disk space, for instance) you can leave these options alone.

A *compression* (or optimization) scheme is available when certain combinations of file format and bit depth are selected. However, if you plan to use this format to save an image for wallpaper or a screensaver (and that's about the only practical purpose for BMP images any more), *don't* select this compression. If you do, the Windows operating system won't recognize your file.

Photoshop EPS

Photoshop EPS is actually a format you'll probably *not* want to save to. Although EPS (Encapsulated PostScript) files are compatible with a host of graphics and page layout programs, they're not the best choice for saving raster, bit-mapped images, which are what Photoshop Elements creates. The EPS format adds layers of PostScript code to describe everything from the way an image appears in preview to the way it's color managed, which translates into overhead in the form of bloated file size and slower display time. Any advantage this format holds for displaying and printing vector art and typography is lost on Photoshop Elements' raster art.

UNDERSTANDING FILE FORMATS

Photoshop PDF

PDF, which stands for Portable Document Format, is the perfect vehicle for sharing images across platforms or for importing them into a variety of graphics and page layout programs. PDF is also one of only three file formats (native Photoshop and TIFF are the other two) that support an image file's layers, meaning that layer qualities (like transparency) are preserved when you place a PDF into another application like Adobe Illustrator or InDesign. The real beauty of this file format, though, is that any document saved as a PDF file can be opened and viewed by anyone using Adobe's free Acrobat Reader software, which Adobe bundles with its applications and makes available as a free download from its Web site.

PDF offers two compression schemes for controlling file size: ZIP and JPEG (**Figure 11.2**). ZIP removes whatever extraneous file information it can without the loss of any image quality and so is referred to as *lossless* compression. Since some degree of image fidelity is lost in the JPEG compression process, it's known as a *lossy* compression. With either compression scheme, you should turn off Image Interpolation, as it tends to blur low-res images in an attempt to smooth their edges.

PICT File

The PICT file format (**Figure 11.3**) is used for onscreen images on the Macintosh platform. You'll want to avoid this file format if you're planning to share images across platforms. If you're creating images specifically for the Macintosh, however, PICT can be a valuable, if somewhat limited, format. Though it doesn't print particularly well from some applications, it does look nice on the screen. And because the file size of PICT images can be controlled with JPEG compression, the PICT format is good for creating placeholder images when you're working on complex page layouts or on designs that might slow down your computer

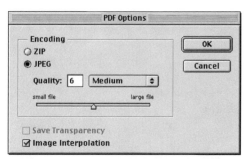

Figure 11.2 When you save your work as a PDF file, you can apply JPEG compression, which dramatically reduces file size at the expense of a little image quality.

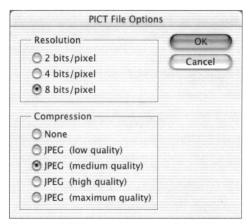

Figure 11.3 PICT-formatted images can be reliably displayed and printed only from Macintosh operating systems.

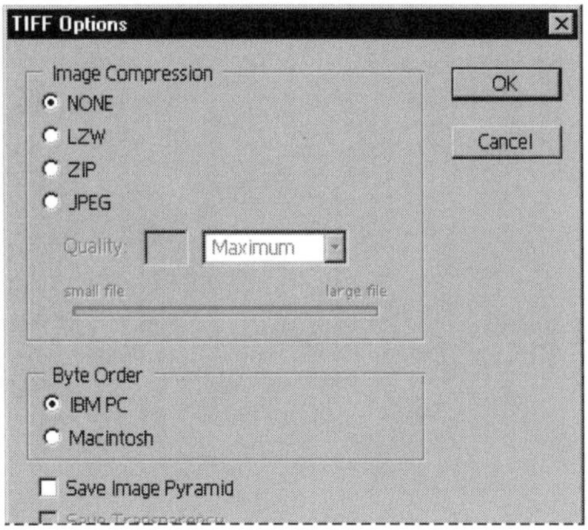

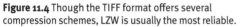

Figure 11.4 Though the TIFF format offers several compression schemes, LZW is usually the most reliable.

under the weight of numerous megabyte-sized images. Once the design work is done, you can replace the low-resolution PICT files with high-resolution TIFF or native PSD files of the same images just before you print your work.

On the Macintosh, Photoshop Elements also offers a PICT Resource file format option. You'd only use this option if you were developing system graphics for the Mac. The splash screen that appears as the Mac version of Photoshop Elements loads is an example of a system graphic saved as a PICT Resource file.

TIFF

TIFF, or Tagged Image File Format, is the one true workhorse among the file formats. The TIFF format was designed to be platform independent, so TIFF files display and print equally well from both Windows and Macintosh machines. Additionally, any TIFF file created on one platform can be transferred to the other and placed in almost any graphics or page layout program.

You can optimize TIFF files to save room on your hard disk using one of three compression schemes, or you can save them with no compression at all (**Figure 11.4**). Of the three compression options, LZW is the one supported by the largest number of applications and programs.

The Byte Order option encodes information in the file to determine whether it will be used on a Windows or Macintosh platform. On rare occasions, TIFF files saved with the Macintosh option don't transfer cleanly to Windows machines. The Mac has no problem with files saved with the IBM PC byte order though, so we recommend you stick with this option, no matter what platform you're using.

continues on next page

UNDERSTANDING FILE FORMATS

Checking the Save Image Pyramid check box saves your image in different tiers of resolution, so that you can choose to use the full-resolution image or a lower-resolution version. However, not many applications (Photoshop Elements included) support the Image Pyramid format as yet, so you should leave this box unchecked.

JPEG and GIF

The two major Web file formats (JPEG and GIF) are covered in detail in Chapter 10, "Preparing Images for the Web," so we'll look at them just briefly here. Of particular note is that you can indeed use the Save As command to save an image as a GIF or JPEG file, with virtually all of the same file options as in the Save for Web dialog box—so the obvious question is why use one saving method over the other when saving for the Web?

The Save for Web dialog box offers several features that the individual GIF and JPEG Save As command dialog boxes don't. For one, the Save for Web dialog box provides a wonderful before-and-after preview area, displaying side-by-side comparisons of your original and optimized images while an information area displays the optimized version's file size and projected download time.

No less valuable is the flexibility you have to change and view different optimization formats on the fly. An image just doesn't appear the way you expected in GIF? Try JPEG. Additionally, with the click of a button, you can open and preview your optimized image in any browser present on your system.

Choosing Compression Options

As you save images in the various formats available, you're presented with a variety of format-specific dialog boxes, each containing its own set of options. One of those options, present in most of the dialog boxes, is a choice of compression settings. Compression, which is just another term for optimization, makes an image's file size smaller, so the file will download faster when you attach it to an e-mail or post it to a Web page, for example. Following is a brief rundown of the compression schemes you can save to in Photoshop Elements.

JPEG: Yep, JPEG is presented in Photoshop Elements as a formatting option, but at its core, it's just a very powerful, flexible compression scheme. JPEG works best with continuous-tone images like photographs. It compresses by throwing away image information and slightly degrading the image and is therefore a lossy compression.

LZW: This is the standard compression format for most TIFF images. Though it works best on images with large areas of a single color, it will help reduce file size at least a little for nearly any image it's applied to. Since it works behind the scenes, throwing out code rather than image information (and so doesn't degrade the image), LZW is a lossless compression.

RLE: This is a lossless compression similar to LZW, but it's specific (in Photoshop Elements) to BMP compressed files. It's particularly effective at compressing images containing transparency.

ZIP: This compression scheme is also similar to LZW, but it has the advantage of adding a layer of protection to files that makes them less susceptible to corruption if they're copied between systems or sent via e-mail. Zip files are common on the Windows platform, although Macintosh systems can open Zip compressed files if they have Stuffit Expander installed.

Setting Preferences for Saving Files

The Saving Files portion of the Preferences dialog box provides a number of ways to control how Photoshop Elements manages your saved files, including options for displaying file extensions and thumbnail previews. There are some subtle (and not so subtle) differences in the features included in the Windows and Macintosh dialog boxes, but you'll see those platform-specific features flagged within the procedure.

To set the Saving Files preferences:

1. From the Edit menu, choose Preferences > Saving Files (Windows and Mac OS 9).

   or

   From the Photoshop Elements menu, choose Preferences > Saving Files (Mac OS X).

   The Preferences dialog box opens with the Saving Files window active (**Figure 11.5**).

2. From the Image Previews pop-up menu, choose an option to either save or not save a preview with the file (**Figure 11.6**).

   When an application supports them, images saved with a preview will appear with a thumbnail version in that application's Open or Place dialog box.

3. (Mac OS only) Select the check boxes for the Image Preview options you want included with your file (**Figure 11.7**).

   Icon includes an icon as the file graphic on your desktop.

   Macintosh and **Windows Thumbnail** include the thumbnail that would appear in an application's Open or Place dialog box.

   Full Size saves a low-resolution (72 pixels per inch) version of the file for applications that accept only low-resolution files.

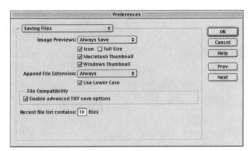

Figure 11.5 The Saving File window of the Preferences dialog box.

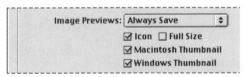

Figure 11.6 You can save an image preview with your images that will display a thumbnail of your image in the Open dialog box of some applications.

Figure 11.7 The Macintosh version of the Image Previews dialog box lets you save the image preview for a number of different uses.

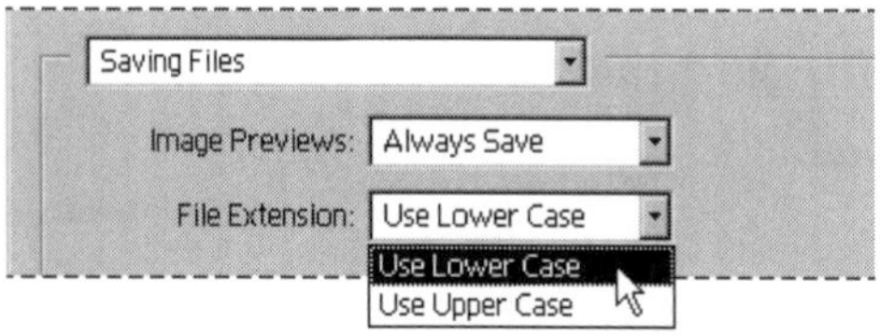

Figure 11.8 The Windows version of the Image Previews dialog box lets you determine how you want file name extensions displayed.

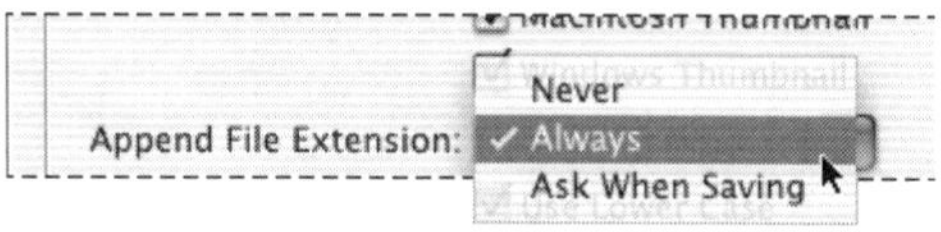

Figure 11.9 On the Macintosh, you can choose whether or not to include extensions with your file names.

Figure 11.10 The number of save options that the TIFF format dialog box displays can be controlled from the Saving Files preferences.

Figure 11.11 Specify the number of file names that are displayed when you choose Open Recent from the File menu.

We suggest leaving this last option unchecked, as it only adds overhead in the form of increased file size, and it's the rare application that won't accept high-resolution graphics files.

4. (Windows only) From the File Extension pop-up menu, choose whether you want your file extensions in uppercase or lowercase characters (**Figure 11.8**).

5. (Mac OS only) From the Append File Extension pop-up menu, choose an option to specify when you want file extensions added to your file names (**Figure 11.9**); then use the check box below to indicate whether or not to use lowercase characters.

6. In the File Compatibility portion of the dialog box, ensure that the Enable Advanced TIFF Save Options check box is selected (**Figure 11.10**). (In Mac OS X, you'll see that the Ask Before Saving Layered TIFF files and Maximize Compatibility for Photoshop PSD Files check boxes are already selected.)

   This is a Photoshop Elements default and ensures that the maximum number of compatibility and saving options is always available to you.

7. In the Recent File List Contains text box, enter a number from 1 to 30 (**Figure 11.11**).

   This designates the number of file names available to you when you select Open Recent from the File menu.

8. Click OK to close the dialog box and apply your preferences settings.

SETTING PREFERENCES FOR SAVING FILES

Adding Personalized File Information

With any Photoshop Elements file open, choose File Info from the File menu to open the File Info dialog box (**Figure 11.12**). Within this simple dialog box, you can add personalized information specific to any file, including title, author, caption, and copyright information. Though most of the information entered here is accessible only by opening the dialog box from within Photoshop Elements, some of it does have practical uses both inside and outside the application. Entries from the Title, Author, Caption, and Copyright Notice text fields can be included when you create a Picture Package (see "Creating a Photographer's Picture Package" later in this chapter). Also, the Caption field can be included with any saved image (see "Setting Additional Printing Options" later in this chapter). And if you select Copyrighted Work from the Copyright Status pop-up menu, a copyright symbol appears in the Image Window title bar, alerting anyone who receives a copy of your file that it's copyright protected (**Figure 11.13**).

The File Info dialog box is also useful for *retrieving* information. Many digital cameras include EXIF annotations (such as date and time, resolution, exposure time, and f-stop settings) in each digital photo. To access this information from within Photoshop Elements, just open the photo file and choose EXIF from the Section pop-up menu. Any EXIF information exported with the photo from your digital camera will be displayed in the File Info dialog box (**Figure 11.14**). You can use this information to record exposure and f-stop settings from your more successful photos, a handy reference for future photography outings. You can also view EXIF annotations in the Information area of the File Browser.

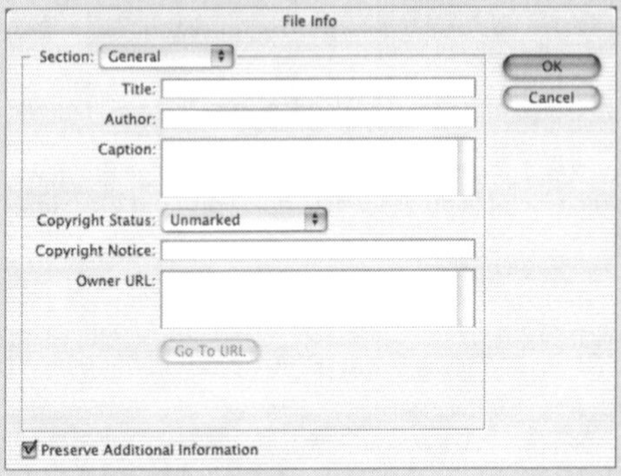

SETTING PREFERENCES FOR SAVING FILES

Figure 11.12 Use the File Info dialog box to add title, copyright, and other information to any specific file.

Figure 11.13 When a file is assigned copyright status in the File Info dialog box, a copyright symbol appears next to the file name at the top of the image window.

Figure 11.14 The File Info dialog box displays EXIF information included with photos exported from digital cameras.

Formatting and Saving Multiple Images Automatically

You've just finished a prolific day of shooting pictures with your digital camera, and as a first step to sorting through and cleaning up all those images, you'd like to convert them to Photoshop Elements' native Photoshop format and then change their resolution to 150 dpi. You could, of course, download them from your camera, open each one individually, and apply the desired formatting and resizing changes. But Photoshop Elements' Batch Processing command saves you all that tedious, repetitive work by doing it for you. Just enter a few parameters in the Batch dialog box and sit back. Within seconds, your images are converted and saved to a location of your choice.

To batch process multiple files:

1. From the File menu, choose Batch Processing to open the Batch dialog box (**Figure 11.15**).

continues on next page

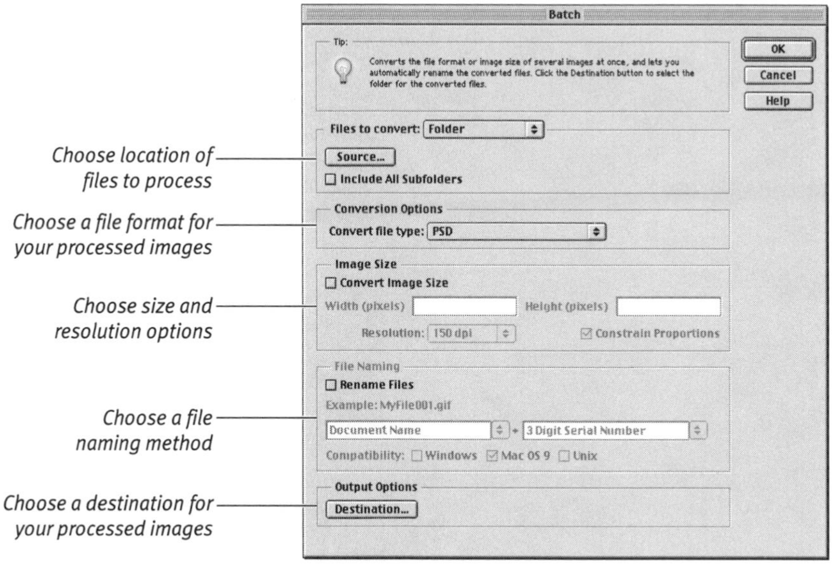

Choose location of files to process

Choose a file format for your processed images

Choose size and resolution options

Choose a file naming method

Choose a destination for your processed images

Figure 11.15 The Batch dialog box.

2. From the Files to Convert pop-up menu, (**Figure 11.16**), *do one of the following*:

   ▲ To select images within a folder on your hard drive, choose Folder, click the Source button, and then browse for and select the folder containing the images you want to convert (**Figure 11.17**). If there are folders within the folder you select that *also* contain files you want to convert, click the Include All Subfolders check box in the Batch dialog box.

   ▲ To select images stored in a digital camera, scanner, or PDF, choose Import; then select the appropriate source from the From pop-up menu (**Figure 11.18**). The choices in the From pop-up menu will vary depending on the hardware connected to your computer.

   ▲ To select files that are currently open within Photoshop Elements, choose Opened Files.

3. From the Convert File Type pop-up menu, choose the desired format type (**Figure 11.19**).

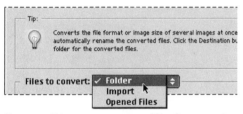

Figure 11.16 You can save groups of files from a number of different sources.

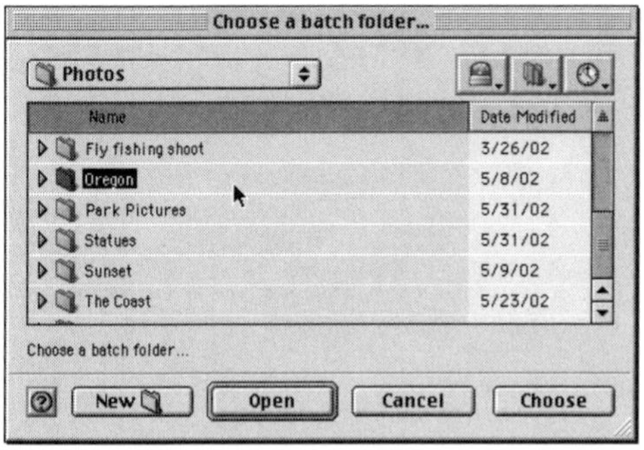

Figure 11.17 Select a folder containing all of the images you want to save at one time.

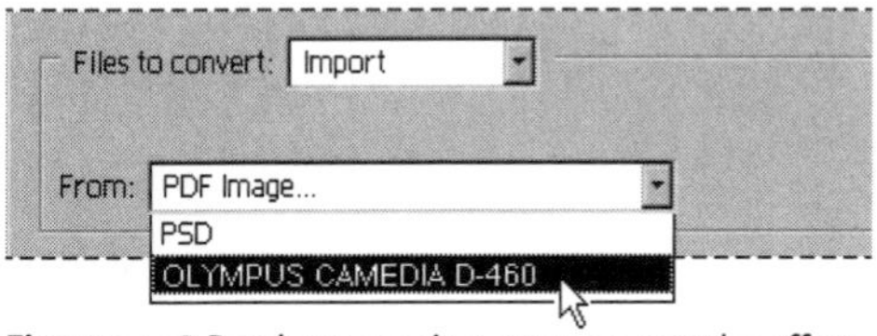

Figure 11.18 Batch processing can save you the effort of renaming and formatting images one by one. Import them from your digital camera or scanner, and then apply the changes.

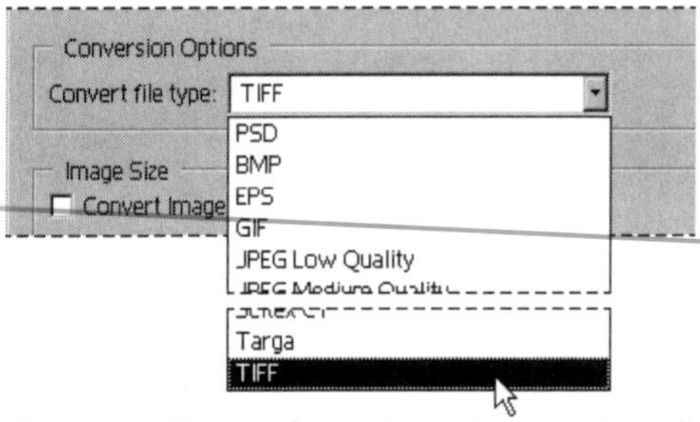

Figure 11.19 Choose a formatting option to apply to all the files in your selected group.

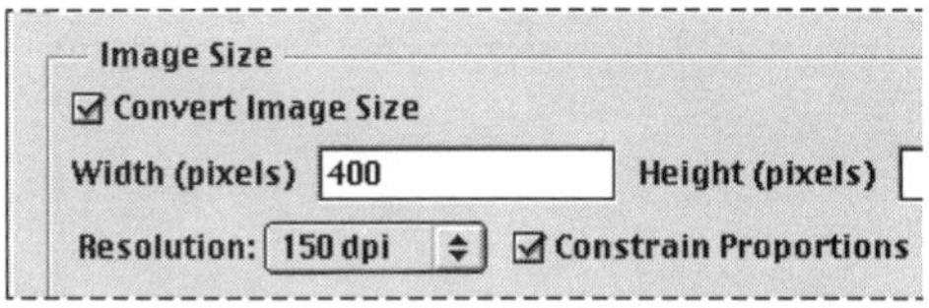

Figure 11.20 You can resize entire groups of images to the same width or height dimensions.

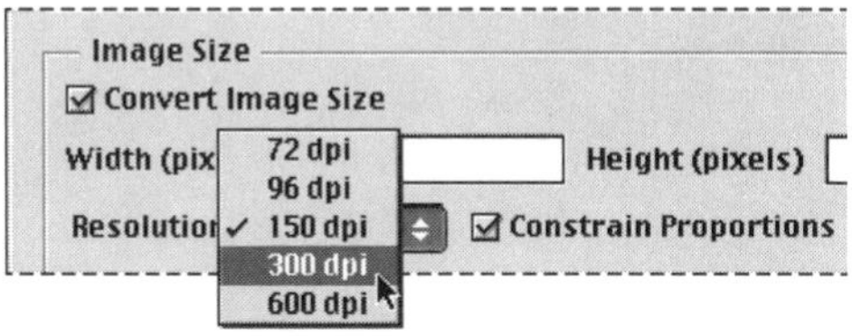

Figure 11.21 Choose a resolution to apply to all of the files in your selected group.

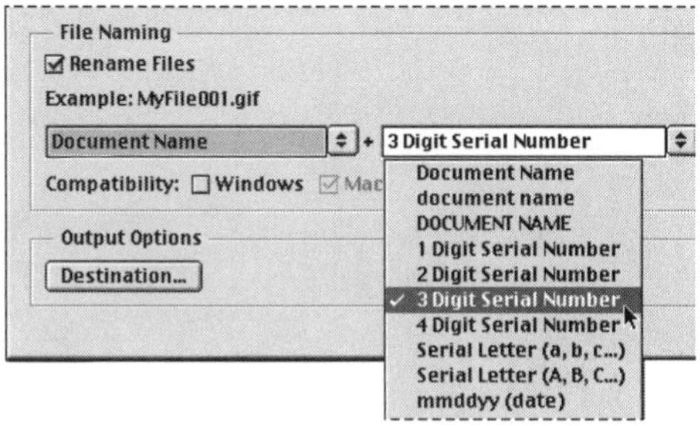

Figure 11.22 You can pick from a number of file naming options to arrange your images in consecutive order.

4. If you want to change either the physical dimensions of your image or its resolution, click the Convert Image Size check box, *then do one or both of the following:*

▲ To convert all of your images to a specific size, enter the width *or* height (in pixels) in the appropriate text box; then select the Constrain Proportions check box (**Figure 11.20**).

▲ From the Resolution pop-up menu, choose a resolution in dots per inch (dpi) to change the resolution of all your images (**Figure 11.21**).

Since the resolution setting in this dialog box is in dots per inch (print resolution) rather than pixels per inch (screen resolution) changing just the resolution here will do nothing to alter your image, or change its file size. It changes only the dimensions of the final printed image, but has no effect on the size it displays on screen. (For more information on image resizing, see "Changing Image Size and Resolution" in Chapter 2.)

5. If you want to add a file naming structure to your collection of converted images, select the Rename Files check box; then select naming options from the two pop-up menus (**Figure 11.22**).

Refer to the Example text (located below the Rename Files check box) to see how the renaming changes will affect your file names.

continues on next page

FORMATTING AND SAVING MULTIPLE IMAGES

6. Select the Compatibility check boxes for whatever platforms you want your file names to be compatible with.

A good approach is to select all three of these, just to be on the safe side. Notice that the platform you're working on (whether Macintosh or Windows) is pre-selected for you and dimmed.

7. Click the Destination button; then browse for and select a location to save your converted files to.

In the Browse for Folder (Windows) or Choose a Destination Folder (Mac OS) dialog box that appears, you're also offered the option of creating a new folder for your converted files.

8. Click OK to close the dialog box and start the batch process.

The selected files are opened, converted in turn, and then saved to the folder you've chosen.

If you've chosen one of the import options, an additional series of dialog boxes will appear, guiding you through the selection of images you want to import. For example, if you've chosen PDF, you'll first be asked to select a PDF file from which to import the images, then you'll be presented with a dialog box to choose the images you want to import (**Figure 11.23**). Once you've made your image selections, the files are opened, converted, and saved to the destination folder you assigned in step 7.

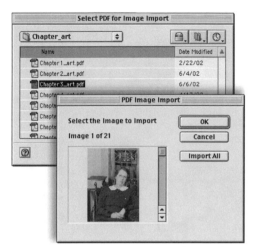

Figure 11.23 When you import a batch of images from a PDF file, you first select the PDF and then select the files you want to import.

✔ Tips

- The import options within the Batch dialog box are also accessible by choosing Import from the File menu. But the Import command offers no options for image sizing, resolution, or file naming (not to mention the ability to save to specified destination folders). So even if you're importing just one image at a time (as would normally be the case when importing from a scanner, for instance) you may find that the Batch dialog box still holds a decided advantage over the File menu's Import command.

- Using a little simple math can help you to convert pixel dimensions to inches. Just multiply the resolution you've selected by the number of inches (of either height or width) that you want your final image to be. For example, if you've selected a resolution of 72 dpi, and you want the width of your images to be 4 inches; simply multiply 72 by 4, then enter the total (288) in the width text box.

- You can enter width and height values for your images *without* constraining to the proportions of the original images, though this approach isn't recommended. Unless you know the exact dimensions of your original images (and unless they all share the same dimensions or proportions), you run the probable risk of distorting your converted images.

FORMATTING AND SAVING MULTIPLE IMAGES

Cataloging Your Images

You may have lots of photographs downloaded from your digital camera, but because they have unhelpful file names like 102-0246_IMG.JPG, organizing and sorting them can be a difficult task. And although Photoshop Elements' File Browser window lets you view and sort through your images, sometimes it's nice to have a printed hard copy to study and mark up. In traditional photography, *contact sheets* are created from film negatives and provide a photographer or designer with a collection of convenient thumbnail images organized neatly on a single sheet of film or paper. Photoshop Elements' Contact Sheet feature works in much the same way, allowing you to create your own collections of thumbnails, drawn from the contents of any folder on your desktop.

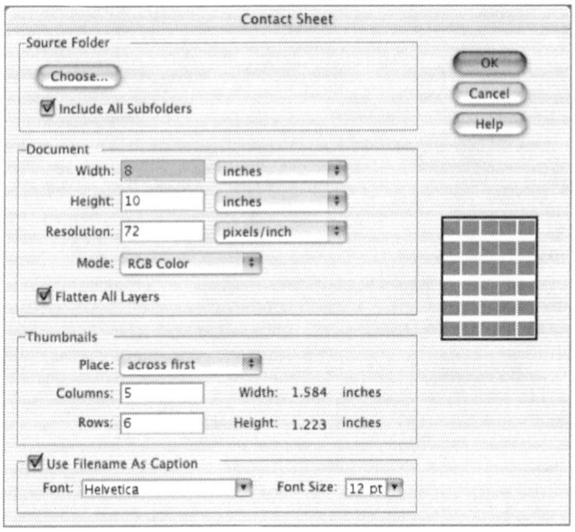

To make a contact sheet:

1. From the File menu, choose Print Layouts > Contact Sheet to open the Contact Sheet dialog box (**Figure 11.24**).

2. Click the Browse (Windows) or Choose (Mac OS) button; then browse for and select the folder containing the images you want to include on your contact sheet.

   If there are folders within the folder you select that also contain files you want to include, select the Include All Subfolders check box.

3. Select a width and height value for your contact sheet images.

   The page preview to the right updates to reflect the values you enter (**Figure 11.25**). The default setting of 8 x 10 inches allows your images to be contained with a standard 8.5 x 11 sheet of paper, which works best for most users.

   Note that these values specify the actual area that the images will occupy, not the page size itself.

Figure 11.24 The Contact Sheet dialog box.

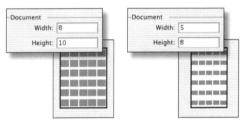

Figure 11.25 If you change the size of your contact sheet, the image layout will automatically accommodate the change.

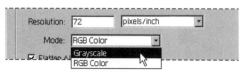

Figure 11.26 Choose from two different color modes for your contact sheet.

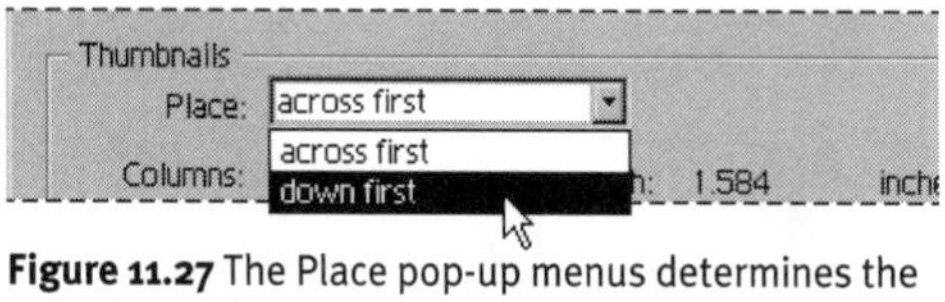

Figure 11.27 The Place pop-up menus determines the order in which the contact sheet thumbnails are placed on the page.

Figure 11.28 You can choose to place nearly any number of thumbnails on a page.

4. Enter a resolution value for your images.

Since you are simply preparing a sheet of thumbnails for reference, the default resolution of 72 pixels per inch should work just fine for most images and will help to keep the file size of your contact sheet reasonably small.

5. From the Mode pop-up menu, select a color mode for your contact sheet (**Figure 11.26**).

6. Make sure that the Flatten All Layers check box is selected.

Again, this helps to reduce file size.

7. From the Place pop-up menu, choose whether you want your thumbnails to appear in order starting from the top left and running across or down the page (**Figure 11.27**).

8. In the Columns and Rows text boxes, enter the number of thumbnails that you would like to appear down and across the page.

Again, the page preview to the right will update to reflect the values you enter (**Figure 11.28**).

9. If you want a file name to appear below each image on the page, see that the Use Filename as Caption check box is selected; then choose a font and size for the file.

continues on next page

10. Click OK to close the dialog box and build the contact sheet.

A new Contact Sheet file is created, and the files from the selected folder are automatically opened and placed in the new file (**Figure 11.29**).

✔ Tips

■ You can reset the Contact Sheet dialog box at any time by holding down Alt/Option and clicking the Reset button that appears below OK in the upper right corner.

■ The number of columns and rows you choose to display your cataloged images will vary depending on the types of images involved and your reasons for creating the contact sheet in the first place. If all you want are small thumbnail versions of your photos to help with sorting or organizing, then you may be able to group a large number of images on one page. On the other hand, if you have a series of similar images you want to study for the purposes of comparing subtle differences in exposure settings or picture composition, you may want to limit the number to just four or six. Then you'll be able to more clearly see the qualities of each individual photo.

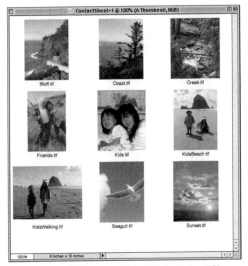

Figure 11.29 This is a completed Contact Sheet file as it appears in a new document window.

Figure 11.30 The Picture Package dialog box.

Figure 11.31 Choose among the Use pop-up menu options to determine the source of the image for your picture package.

Creating a Photographer's Picture Package

Photoshop Elements' Picture Package creates a page with multiple copies of the same image, just like the kind you'd receive from a professional photographer's studio. Photos can be arranged in a number of layouts and sizes, from a sheet made up only of wallet-sized images to a variety pack of different sizes and quantities. Printing images this way is also more economical, as you waste less photo paper.

To make a picture package:

1. From the File menu, choose Print Layouts > Picture Package to open the Picture Package dialog box (**Figure 11.30**).

2. From the Use pop-up menu, select the location of the image for your picture package (**Figure 11.31**).

   If you select either File or Folder, click the Browse (Windows) or Choose (Macintosh) button; then browse for and select the image or folder of images you want to create your picture package from.

   Note that if you choose a folder of images, only the first image in the folder will appear in the Picture Package preview, but when you click OK to start the process, a picture package will be created from every image in the folder.

   Note also that if you have an image open before you open the Picture Package dialog box, the Use pop-up menu will automatically set itself to Frontmost Document, and the image will appear in the preview on the right side of the dialog box.

continues on next page

3. From the Page Size pop-up menu, choose a page size compatible with your printer.

   The page preview to the right will update to reflect the values you enter.

   Note that as in the Contact Sheet dialog box, these values specify the actual area that the images will occupy, not the page size itself.

4. From the Layout pop-up menu, choose a layout template.

   The selection of layout templates varies depending on the page size you choose (**Figure 11.32**). Again, the page preview to the right updates to reflect the selection you make (**Figure 11.33**).

5. Enter a resolution in the Resolution text box; then from the Mode pop-up menu, choose either RGB Color or Grayscale.

   If your original images are RGB, you can select Grayscale, if you'd like, and create a contact sheet of grayscale rather than color images. Choosing grayscale here will have no affect on your original RGB images.

6. Choose whether or not to flatten layers using the Flatten All Layers check box (**Figure 11.34**).

   When Flatten All Layers is left unchecked, every individual image and line of type (if a label is applied) is assigned to its own layer. The inclusion of up to 20 or 40 layers in your final contact sheet will increase its file size accordingly, but will also provide you some flexibility to hide, delete or even rearrange all those picture and text objects. If file size and disk space aren't concerns, we recommend leaving this box unchecked. You can always choose to flatten the contact sheet file later, if you like.

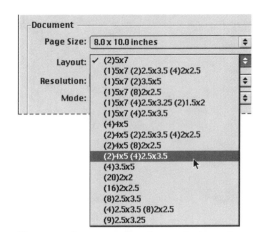

Figure 11.32 Layout templates let you display and print a variety of image sizes and orientations.

Figure 11.33 The default layout template (left) and one of the many selections from the Layout pop-up menu (right).

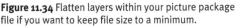

Figure 11.34 Flatten layers within your picture package file if you want to keep file size to a minimum.

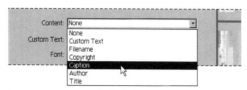

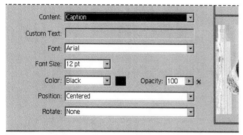

Figure 11.35 You can include descriptive text, such as captions or copyright information for your images. The selected text is placed directly on top of each individual image in the picture package.

Figure 11.36 Customize your picture package labels in the lower portion of the dialog box.

7. From the Content pop-up menu, choose a label option to apply to your images (**Figure 11.35**).

   You can choose to include no label information, enter custom text in the Picture Package dialog box, or pick text from any one of the fields in a picture's Image Info dialog box. (See the "Adding Personalized File Information" sidebar earlier in this chapter.)

8. Enter text attributes for the label, including font, size, color, and position on the image (**Figure 11.36**).

9. Click OK to close the dialog box and create the picture package.

   A new Picture Package file is created, and the selected image (or folder of images) is automatically placed in the new file according to the layout template you selected, ready for you to print.

CREATING A PHOTOGRAPHER'S PICTURE PACKAGE

Setting Up Your Computer for Printing

If you're completely unfamiliar with printing from your computer, you'll want to follow these steps for selecting your printer. If you *are* familiar with the steps for selecting a printer, you can probably skip ahead to the next topic.

Setting up your computer to print from Photoshop Elements is a simple process, providing you've installed the proper printer driver that you received with your printer. If you stumble at all through this section, refer to the documentation for your particular printer. It will probably also cover the same material as in this topic, but if not, you can return here once your printer is properly installed.

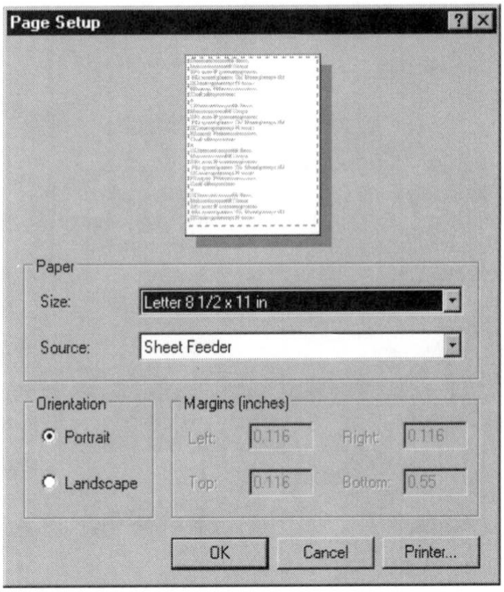

To select a printer in Windows:

1. From the File menu, choose Page Setup to open the Page Setup dialog box (**Figure 11.37**).

2. In the Page Setup dialog box, click the Printer button to open a second Page Setup dialog box (**Figure 11.38**).

3. In the Name pop-up menu (in the topmost dialog box), confirm that the printer you want to use is visible.

   If the printer you want to use *isn't* visible, select it from the list of printers in the Name pop-up menu.

4. Click OK to close the topmost Page Setup dialog box; then click OK again to close the remaining dialog box.

   Your Windows system is ready for printing.

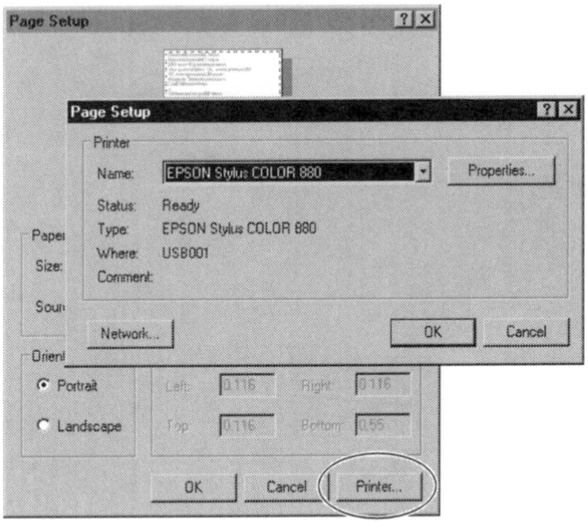

Figure 11.37 The Page Setup dialog box (Windows).

Figure 11.38 Select a printer by clicking the Printer button in the first dialog box.

Figure 11.39 Open the Chooser from the Mac OS 9 Apple menu.

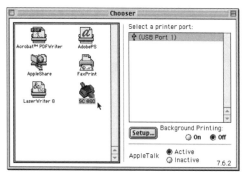

Figure 11.40 In Mac OS 9; select a printer from the Chooser.

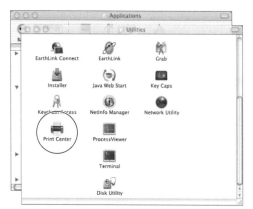

Figure 11.41 In Mac OS X, click the Print Center icon to launch the Print Center program.

To select a printer in Mac OS 9:

1. From the Apple menu, select Chooser (**Figure 11.39**) to open the Chooser window.

2. In the Chooser's left window, click the icon representing the printer you want to use (**Figure 11.40**).

   If you've installed a printer driver for a desktop inkjet printer, it will be represented by its own icon. If you are printing to a PostScript printer, select either the LaserWriter 8 or AdobePS icon. You'll need to check your printer's documentation to see which PostScript driver is most appropriate for that individual printer.

3. Click the Close box to close the Chooser window.

   Your Mac OS 9 system is ready for printing.

To select a printer in Mac OS X:

1. Click the Applications icon in the toolbar of any Finder window.

2. Open the Utilities folder.

3. Locate and double-click the Print Center icon (**Figure 11.41**).

continues on next page

SETTING UP YOUR COMPUTER FOR PRINTING

The Printer List dialog box opens (**Figure 11.42**). If you've installed driver software for any printers and have previously set them up for use, they'll appear here in the list. If you've installed a printer driver but haven't yet used it to print, you may need to add it to the list.

4. Click the Add Printer button at the bottom of the Printer List dialog box.

   A window will appear from out of the Printer List title bar.

5. Choose a source for your printer connection from the pop-up menu at the top of the window (**Figure 11.43**).

   Most likely, you'll select either USB or AppleTalk. If your printer is properly connected to your computer, it will appear in the printer list below (**Figure 11.44**).

6. Click to select the printer; then click the Add button at the bottom of the dialog box.

   The printer you selected will now be included in the master printer list.

7. If more than one printer is displayed in the list, click to select the one you want to use; then click the Close button to close the Printer List dialog box.

   Your Mac OS X system is ready for printing.

✔ Tip

- If you're using Mac OS X and find yourself switching between different printers, drag the Print Center into the Dock on your desktop. That way, you can save yourself the trouble of navigating through all those layers of folders every time you want to change printers.

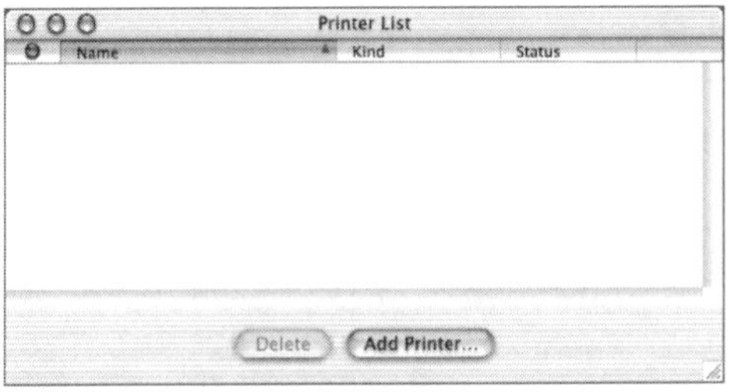

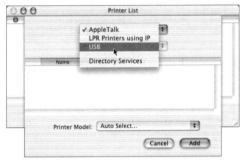

Figure 11.42 The Printer List dialog box is empty until you select a printer.

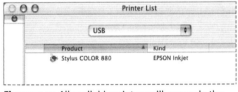

Figure 11.43 Choose the correct connection setting for your printer.

Figure 11.44 All available printers will appear in the printer list.

Setting Up Your Computer for Printing

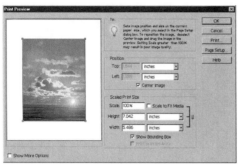

Figure 11.45 The Print Preview dialog box.

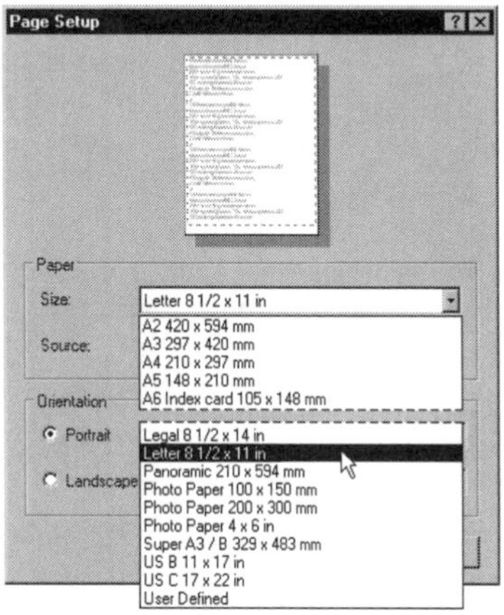

Figure 11.46 In the Page Setup dialog box, confirm that the paper size matches the paper in your printer.

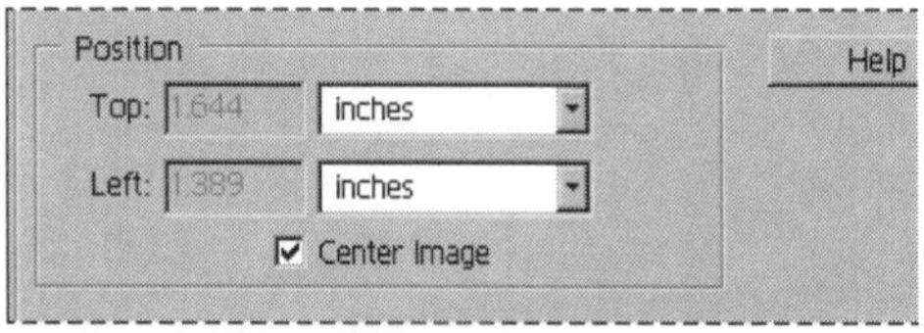

Figure 11.47 The Center Image check box perfectly centers your image on the page.

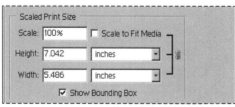

Figure 11.48 The Show Bounding Box check box must be selected before you can reposition your image.

Preparing an Image for Printing

Photoshop Elements offers a simple, elegant, intuitive tool to help you print your images. From the Print Preview dialog box, you can choose paper sizes, and you can position your image on the page, scale it, and even make some last minute modifications.

To reposition an image on a page:

1. Select an image you want to print, then open it in Photoshop Elements.

2. From the File menu, choose Print Preview to open the Print Preview dialog box (**Figure 11.45**).

3. In the right column of the dialog box, click the Page Setup button to open the Page Setup dialog box.

4. From the Size pop-up menu in the Page Setup dialog box, choose a paper size (**Figure 11.46**).

   The default paper size is Letter, 8.5 x 11.

5. Close the Page Setup dialog box.

   The page preview on the left side of the dialog box reflects the page size in proportion to the image you want to print.

6. If you want your image printed in the center of the page, confirm that the Center Image check box is selected (**Figure 11.47**).

   Center Image is Photoshop Elements' default.

7. If you want to move your image to a different area of the page, first uncheck Center Image; then make sure that the Show Bounding Box check box is selected in the Scaled Print Size portion of the dialog box (**Figure 11.48**).

   Show Bounding Box is Photoshop Elements' default setting.

continues on next page

PREPARING AN IMAGE FOR PRINTING

8. To move the image to a new area on the page, *do one of the following*:

▲ Move the pointer into the center of the image until it becomes a crossed-arrow cursor; then drag the image to a new spot on the page (**Figure 11.49**).

▲ Enter new values in the Top and Left text boxes. You can change the measurement system from the default of inches by selecting a different unit from the pop-up menus (**Figure 11.50**).

Note that in either case, the position displayed in the text boxes is measured from the upper left corner of the page to the upper left corner of the image. In other words, if you enter 0 in both the Top and Left text boxes, your image will be positioned in the upper left corner, directly on the top and left margins of the page.

To resize an image by entering size or percentage values:

To resize, *do one of the following*:

◆ In the Scale text box, enter a new percentage value. The default is 100 percent.

◆ Enter either a new Height or Width value in the respective text box. Just as when positioning, you can change the measurement systems for both height and width from the accompanying pop-up menus (**Figure 11.51**).

Note that the Scale, Height, and Width text boxes are linked together, and that a change to any one of the boxes will be reflected in the other two.

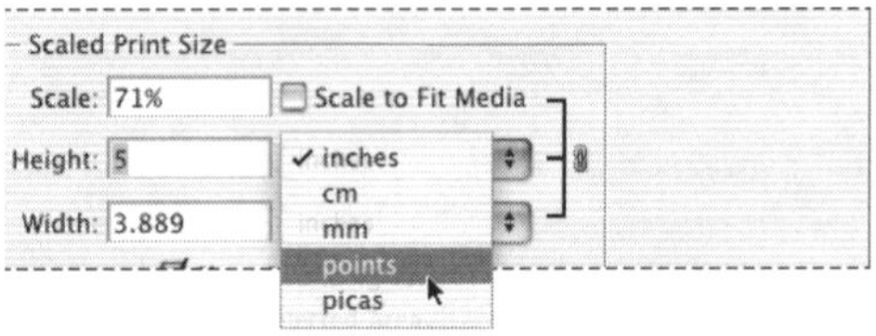

Figure 11.49 Drag to manually move your image to a new location on the page.

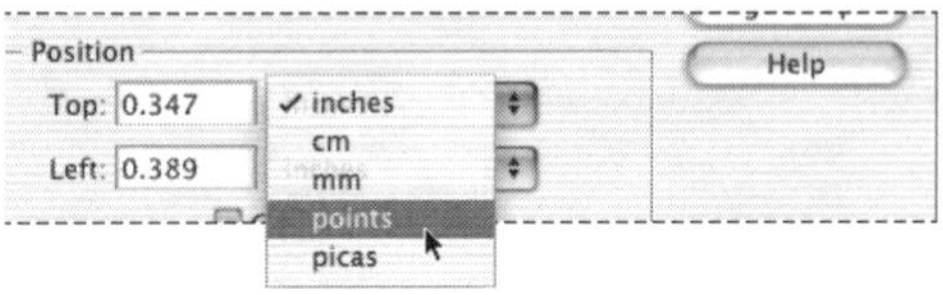

Figure 11.50 To reposition your image on the page, choose a measurement value for your document.

Figure 11.51 Choose a measurement system; then enter either a scale or a height or width value to resize an image numerically.

Figure 11.52 The Scale to Fit Media check box scales an image to precisely fill out the dimensions of a page.

Figure 11.53 Drag to manually resize your image.

To resize an image to fit the dimensions of your page:

◆ Select the Scale to Fit Media check box.

The image is sized proportionally to most efficiently fill the page (**Figure 11.52**).

The Scale to Fit Media option is best used if the original image is too large to fit on the page and needs to be reduced. For that matter, remember that when rescaling an image, it's best to avoid scaling up (upsampling) whenever possible.

To resize an image manually:

◆ See that the Show Bounding Box check box is selected; then in the image preview, drag any of the four bounding box handles (**Figure 11.53**).

The image is resized, and its new scale and dimension values are displayed in the Scaled Print Size text boxes.

Note: If your image's file size is significantly large (over 1 MB), you won't be able to resize it manually. From the File menu, choose Image > Resize > Image size to resize it.

✔ Tip

■ Remember that the changes you make to an image from within the Print Preview dialog box have no effect on the actual image itself—that is, the image's file size and physical dimensions don't actually change. Any repositioning, scaling, or other modifications you perform in the Print Preview dialog box affect only the way that the image appears on the printed page.

PREPARING AN IMAGE FOR PRINTING

Setting Additional Printing Options

At the bottom of the Print Preview dialog box, you'll find a set of features that you can use to modify the printed output of your image. A couple, like the Background and Border options, can be particularly handy if you want to experiment with adding color and stroke elements to your images without the risk of harming the actual image files.

To add a background color:

1. Select the Show More Options check box at the bottom of the Print Preview dialog box (**Figure 11.54**).
   The dialog box expands to reveal the additional features.

2. Click the Background button to open the Color Picker.

3. Select a color in the Color Picker; then click OK.
   The Color Picker closes, and the background of the page preview fills with the color you selected (**Figure 11.55**).

4. If you want to change the background color, repeat steps 2 and 3, selecting a different color.

5. To delete the color altogether, repeat steps 2 and 3, choosing white for the color in the color picker.

To add a stroked border:

1. Click the Border button to open the Border dialog box.

2. In the Width text box, enter a size value for the border (**Figure 11.56**).
   You can change the measurement system for the width value from the accompanying pop-up menu (**Figure 11.57**).

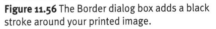

Figure 11.54 The Show More options check box displays some hidden functions in the Print Preview dialog box.

Figure 11.55 You can select a color to fill in the space around your printed image.

Figure 11.56 The Border dialog box adds a black stroke around your printed image.

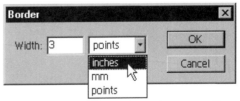

Figure 11.57 The stroked border can be measured in inches, millimeters, or points.

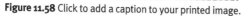

Figure 11.58 Click to add a caption to your printed image.

Figure 11.59 A caption appears as a simple gray bar in the Print Preview's page preview.

Figure 11.60 Click to add crop marks around your printed image.

Figure 11.61 Crop marks are automatically positioned around the margins of an image.

3. Click OK to close the Border dialog box.

The image in the page preview is stroked with a black border.

4. If you want to change the size of the border, repeat steps 1 through 3, entering a different width value in the Border dialog box.

5. To delete the border altogether, repeat steps 1 through 3, entering 0 for the border width.

To add a caption:

◆ Select the Caption check box (**Figure 11.58**).

If a caption was entered for the image in the File Info dialog box, it will be represented below the image in the page preview as a gray bar (**Figure 11.59**). (See the sidebar "Adding Personalized File Information" earlier in this chapter.)

When the image is printed, the caption will appear below it in 9-point Helvetica type.

To add crop marks:

◆ Select the Corner Crop Marks check box (**Figure 11.60**).

Crop marks appear outside the corners of the image in the page preview (**Figure 11.61**).

SETTING ADDITIONAL PRINTING OPTIONS

Printing an Image

Photoshop Elements offers a couple of different ways to print your images. The Print command on the File menu sends you directly to the Print dialog box where printing is as simple as confirming your choice of printers and clicking OK. But the Print Preview dialog box will direct you to that same Print dialog. And you may want to have it open anyway (to verify or modify your image's position and scaling), you may prefer to print straight from the Print Preview dialog box.

Figure 11.62 After you've applied print settings to your image, click the Print button in the Print Preview dialog box.

To print an image:

1. From the File menu, choose Print Preview to open the Print Preview dialog box if it's not already open.

2. Confirm the image's position, scaling, page size, and other applicable options, as described in the two previous topics.

3. Click the Print button to open the Print dialog box (**Figure 11.62**).

4. In the Print dialog box, set the desired options.

   Print dialog boxes vary from one printer to another, so you should refer to your printer's documentation if you have any questions regarding options.

5. Click OK (Windows) or Print (Mac OS) to close the Print dialog box and send your image file to the printer.

   Your image prints just as it was displayed in the page preview area of the Print Preview dialog box.

Choosing Paper

You can pick from a wide range of papers for your inkjet printer. For most photos, you'll want to print on either photo paper or glossy photo paper (glossy photo paper is thicker, and a little more durable). Quality matte paper is often preferred for high-resolution photographs, and you can even find archival-quality paper that won't fade for 100 years. If you just want to print a quick proof, your regular inkjet printer paper will do, in a pinch.

Before you start buying paper, it's a good idea to review the documentation that came with your printer (or check out your printer manufacturer's Web site) to see a list of recommended paper choices.

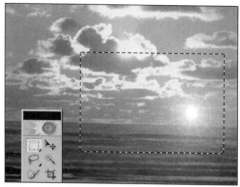

Figure 11.63 Drag a selection around a specific area of an image you want to print.

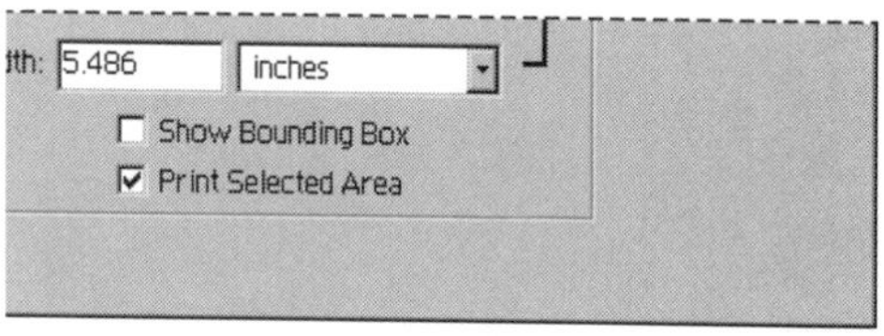

th: [5.486]   [inches ▾] ⌐
　　□ Show Bounding Box
　　☑ Print Selected Area

Figure 11.64 Select the Print Selected Area check box to print just the portion of the image you selected.

To print a selected area of your image:

1. Select the Rectangular Marquee tool from the toolbox; then in the image window on your desktop, select the area of your image that you want to print (**Figure 11.63**).

2. From the File menu, choose Print Preview to open the Print Preview dialog box.

3. In the Print Preview dialog box, select the Print Selected Area check box (**Figure 11.64**).

4. Click the Print button; then follow steps 4 and 5 in the previous procedure.

Though it doesn't appear in the page preview area of the Print Preview dialog box, only the selected area of your image will be printed.

Using Online Photo Services

While it's satisfying to print your photos from your own inkjet printer, it's not a fool-proof process. You may find it slow to print your photos one by one. Your printer may run out of ink, and the cost of coated photo paper can quickly add up. If you have a large selection of digital photos that you want to convert to prints, it's worth looking into online photo services. Most of these services allow you to upload your digital photos, store them on a public Web page for friends and family to see, and order prints in different sizes. Photoshop Elements' Online Services feature lets you connect directly to Shutterfly.com, a popular and affordable online photo service. At this writing, Shutterfly offers 4x6 prints for about 49 cents apiece—and you can get the first 15 free, if you're a new Shutterfly user.

To upload your photos to an online photo service:

1. From the File menu, choose Online Services (**Figure 11.65**).

    To use this feature, your computer must be connected to the Internet. If this is your first time accessing this feature, an Adobe Terms of Use dialog box appears. If you agree to these terms, click OK to continue.

    The Online Services Assistant dialog box appears.

2. In the Online Services Assistant dialog box (**Figure 11.66**), select Upload Images to Shutterfly (if it's not already selected), then click Next.

    A Shutterfly dialog box appears, asking you to sign in (**Figure 11.67**).

Figure 11.65 From the File menu, choose Online Services.

Figure 11.66 The Online Services Assistant dialog box appears. Select Upload Images to Shutterfly.

Figure 11.67 To upload your photos, you must log in. If you're not already a registered Shutterfly member, click Sign Up (it's free) to register at the Shutterfly.com Web site.

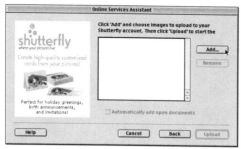

Figure 11.68 Click Add to browse for photos you want to upload.

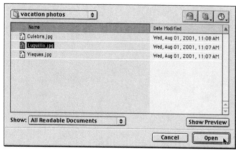

Figure 11.69 When you find an image you want to upload, select it, then click Open to upload it to Shutterfly. If you have multiple images to upload, repeat as many times as you need.

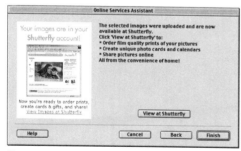

Figure 11.70 Once you've uploaded your images, a new dialog box appears, informing you that your images are ready for viewing. Click View at Shutterfly to view all your images at Shutterfly's Web site.

3. If you have an existing Shutterfly account, type in your e-mail address and your password, then click Next.

or

If you don't have a Shutterfly account, click the Sign Up button to go to Shutterfly's Web page, and sign up for an account following the on-screen instructions.

4. In the Online Services Assistant dialog box, click the Add button to browse your hard drive for photos you want to upload (**Figure 11.68**).

To add photos that are already open in Photoshop Elements, click the Automatically Add Open Images check box.

5. Once you've found a photo you want to upload, select it, and then click Open (**Figure 11.69**) to return to the Online Services Assistant dialog box.

Repeat until you've selected all the photos you want to upload.

6. In the dialog box, click Upload to send your photos to Shutterfly.

Your computer connects to Shutterfly.com and quickly uploads each image. Depending on the size and number of your photos, this could take a few minutes.

A new dialog box appears (**Figure 11.70**), informing you that your images have been uploaded and are available for viewing at Shutterfly.

continues on next page

7. In the dialog box, click Finish if you are done uploading.

or

In the dialog box, Click the View at Shutterfly button to go to your customized Shutterfly Web page, where you can view your photos, organize them into albums, order prints, and create photo-based gifts.

You can also view your uploaded digital photos at any time by navigating to www.shutterfly.com and clicking on the Sign In banner. Simply enter your login name and password to access your online photo collection.

✔ Tip

■ Shutterfly isn't the only online photo service available, but it's the only one that you can connect to within Photoshop Elements. Other services, like Ofoto (www.ofoto.com) or Snapfish (www.snapfish.com), can also store and print your digital photos, but you'll need to navigate to their individual Web sites to upload your images.

CREATIVE
TECHNIQUES

If you've read through earlier chapters of this book, you've learned how to use specific formatting, retouching, and painting tools in Photoshop Elements. In this chapter, you'll explore a few new Photoshop tools and techniques and see how to combine several Photoshop Elements tools to create your own projects. First we'll take a look at Photomerge, a feature that automates much of the work required to stitch together multiple images into a single panorama. Then we'll look at two different ways of delivering sets of images: using PDF slideshows and Web photo galleries. Next, we'll explore a couple of techniques for creating animation using the Layers palette and the Save for Web dialog box. And we'll look at a couple of methods for using the power of transparency and layers for creating compelling composite images.

Creating Panoramas

With Photoshop Elements, you can create wide, panoramic images that would be difficult to capture with a single shot from a standard camera. If you've ever taken a series of photographs and tried "stitching" them together with tape or glue to assemble a continuous panoramic photo, you know how frustrating this can be. The Photomerge command does this for you automatically, letting you save your scissors and tape for other projects. Photomerge analyzes your individual photos and automatically assembles them into a single image (**Figure 12.1**). From there, you can manually move and rotate your images, adjust for slight exposure differences, and correct for distorted perspective—all problems particular to merging images together.

Taking pictures for panoramas

If you're getting ready to snap some scenic photos and know you want to assemble them into a panorama later, making a few camera adjustments will make it easier to assemble a seamless panorama.

◆ Use a consistent zoom level when taking the pictures.

◆ Use a consistent focus. If your subject matter is far away, set your camera's focus to infinity, if that option is available.

◆ Use consistent exposure. A panorama with widely varying lighting will be difficult to merge seamlessly. Set your camera's exposure manually or lock the exposure setting if possible. Photomerge can make slight adjustments for images with different exposures, but it is not as effective when the image exposure varies greatly (**Figure 12.2**).

Figure 12.1 Photomerge combines several separate photos into a single panoramic picture.

Figure 12.2 Images with different lighting exposures can be more difficult to merge than series of images with consistent exposures.

Figure 12.3 Photomerge does its best to merge images that are rotated slightly. When shooting panoramic photos, try using a tripod to ensure that all your shots have consistent angles.

Figure 12.4 The more your images overlap, the better your chances of successfully merging them together. Try for an overlap of between 15 to 40 percent.

◆ If possible, use a tripod. You can take pictures for a panorama with a hand-held camera, but you might find it difficult to keep all of the images perfectly level (**Figure 12.3**).

◆ Overlap sequential images by about 15 to 40 percent (**Figure 12.4**). Photomerge looks for similar detail in the edges of your images to match consecutive pictures. Try to capture as much detail throughout the frame to give Photomerge more reference points to match up. A large area of clear sky will be difficult to merge automatically, whereas an image containing unique, discernable shapes like peaked rooflines or the boats in our example make the best candidates.

✔ Tips

■ Try taking *two* versions of your panorama images: one with the camera held horizontally and one with the camera held vertically. See which option makes a better panorama.

■ You're not limited to creating horizontal panoramas. You can also create vertical panoramas of tall subjects, such as skyscrapers or redwood trees.

CREATING PANORAMAS

Assembling images into a panorama

To create a panoramic image, you select the images you want to merge and then let Photomerge work its magic. You may end up with a perfectly seamless image on the first try, but chances are good that you'll need to make some additional adjustments before you're completely satisfied. (See the color plate section of this book for a full-color example of creating a panorama.)

To create a panorama:

1. Open the images you want to merge together to create your panorama.

   The File Browser is handy for selecting multiple images and even rotating them if necessary. If you want to make any adjustments, such as tonal corrections or cropping, make your corrections first, *before* you begin assembling the images together.

2. From the File menu, choose Create Photomerge.

   A preliminary Photomerge dialog box appears (**Figure 12.5**). Any images that are open in Photoshop Elements will appear in the Source Files list. If you need to delete a file from the list, select it and then click the Remove button.

3. If you want to add more images, click the Browse button to open the Open dialog box; then navigate to the folder containing the images that you want to merge.

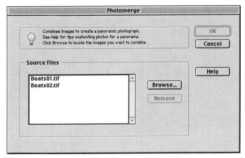

Figure 12.5 Browse for photos to merge in the first Photomerge dialog box.

CREATING PANORAMAS

Figure 12.6 The names of the image files you choose appear in the Source Files section of the first Photomerge dialog box.

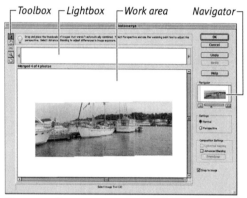

Figure 12.7 The main Photomerge dialog box provides a work area, where you adjust your images, and a Lightbox, where Photoshop Elements stores images that you aren't yet using. You'll also find additional tools and navigational aids on both sides of the dialog box.

4. Press Ctrl/Shift, and then click to select the files you want to appear in your panorama.

If it isn't already active, click the Show Preview button in the Open dialog box to see a thumbnail preview of your image files as you select them. If you select multiple images, the preview thumbnail will display just the last image you selected.

5. Click Open.

The files appear in the Source Files list in the preliminary Photomerge dialog box (**Figure 12.6**).

6. When you have all of the images you want in the Source Files list, click OK.

Photoshop Elements automatically opens the images you listed, and with a little behind-the-scenes trickery, merges them into a single panorama in the Photomerge dialog box (**Figure 12.7**).

Don't panic if your panorama isn't perfect. Photomerge has tools to adjust your images.

7. If your images aren't matching up correctly, or if they appear in the Lightbox rather than the work area section of the dialog box, see "To reposition images in the Panorama" later in this chapter.

You may also see an alert message telling you that some images can't be assembled. If Photomerge can't find enough common details in your images, it will place some images in the Lightbox section of the dialog box. It may also place images off to the side of the panorama.

continues on next page

CREATING PANORAMAS

8. If your images have matched up correctly and you want to explore different perspective or blending options, see "Enhancing Perspective in a Panorama" later in this chapter.

9. When you are satisfied with your merged composition, click OK.

Photoshop Elements creates a new image file of your panorama, leaving your original files unaffected (**Figure 12.8**).

Figure 12.8 When you click OK to save a new Photomerge composition, your merged images open in a new Photoshop Elements file.

✔ Tips

- As a general warning, be aware that some panoramas will take longer to process and render than others. In particular, if you're working on a computer with an older, slower processor, or if your original images are particularly large, it's not uncommon for rendering time to take well over a minute. That can seem like an awfully long time when you're staring at a motionless screen, so be patient. The payoff of the rendered panorama is usually worth the wait.

- Once you click OK to create your panorama, there's no returning to the Photomerge dialog box to make further adjustments. If you're not happy with the way your panorama rendered, you'll just need to start over from the beginning. Refer to the following topics for further instruction on how to make additional adjustments to your panorama before you press the OK button.

- If seams are still visible in the panorama, try touching up those areas with the Clone tool.

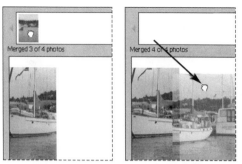

Figure 12.9 Drag or double-click an image in the Lightbox to move it to the work area.

Figure 12.10 The Select Image tool in the Photomerge dialog box.

Figure 12.11 When you drag one image over another, the top image becomes semitransparent, allowing you to align the images.

Adjusting images within a panorama

After your images have been rendered, the Photomerge dialog box opens again to reveal your newly assembled panorama. However, the Photomerge function doesn't always work as promised. You may find the separate images loosely arranged or even scattered in the work area. Some images may have not made it into the panorama at all, but may have been placed in the Lightbox instead. Photoshop Elements tries its best to merge the images automatically, but sometimes it needs a little help. Fortunately, the Photomerge dialog box makes it fairly easy to adjust your images.

To reposition images in the panorama:

1. If one of your images is in the Lightbox area, add it to the work area by dragging it from the Lightbox (**Figure 12.9**) or by double-clicking its thumbnail.

   If you want to remove an image from the panorama, you can also drag images from the work area into the Lightbox.

   Once all the images are in the work area, they still may not be lined up perfectly.

2. Check that the Select Image tool is high-lighted in the Photomerge dialog box (**Figure 12.10**).

3. Drag the image over the image it should merge with.

   As you drag, the image becomes transparent so that you can more easily line it up with the one below it (**Figure 12.11**).

   continues on next page

4. When the two images match up, release the mouse button.

If Snap to Image is selected in the dialog box, any two overlapping images will automatically try to match up with one another (**Figure 12.12**). If Snap to Image is not selected, Photomerge allows you to match up the overlapping image manually.

Turning off Snap to Image allows you to move the images in small increments if they are not matching up exactly. You may also need to rotate an image slightly to make it match up with its neighbor correctly.

Figure 12.12 Images that share similar detail merge together automatically when the Snap to Image option is selected.

5. Select the Rotate Image tool in the Photomerge dialog box, then drag to rotate the selected image (**Figure 12.13**).

6. If you need to undo an action, click the Undo button in the dialog box.

To redo an action, click the Redo button.

The Photomerge dialog box offers several options for moving through its work area while working on your panoramas, including its own built-in navigator.

Figure 12.13 You can rotate images to help align them in the work area.

Figure 12.14 The Move View tool in the Photomerge dialog box.

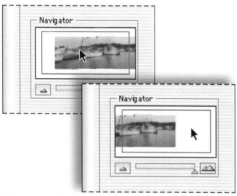

Figure 12.15 Drag the view box in the Navigator to change the view in the work area.

7. To navigate through the work area, *do one of the following:*

▲ Select the Move View tool in the dialog box and drag in the work area (**Figure 12.14**).

▲ In the Navigator, drag the view box. This changes the view in the work area (**Figure 12.15**).

▲ Use the scroll bars at the bottom and left edges of the work area.

8. To change the zoom level in the work area, *do one of the following:*

▲ Select the Zoom tool in the dialog box and click in the work area to zoom in.

Hold down Alt/Option while clicking to zoom out.

▲ Move the slider under the thumbnail in the Navigator (**Figure 12.16**).

▲ Click the Zoom icons under the thumbnail in the Navigator section of the dialog box.

Enhancing Perspective in a Panorama

You may find that some panoramas you create appear a little flat, or just not quite right, particularly as they progress out toward the edges. That's because even the most sophisticated camera lens has a tendency to flatten what little depth or perspective is present in the landscapes or objects they capture. Photomerge lets you add back that lost perspective to create a more natural looking panoramic image. In addition, you can adjust the vanishing point (the point where natural perspective recedes into the distance) to create a help draw attention to a specific area or object in your panorama. Photomerge even provides an option to correct unwanted distortion that may appear as a result of using the Perspective feature, and another that will adjust for minor exposure differences between images that sometimes become more noticeable when you apply perspective.

To add perspective to a panorama:

1. In the Settings section of the dialog box, select the Perspective option (**Figure 12.17**).

   The outside edges of the panorama become distorted, creating a more dramatic, and sometimes more realistic, perspective view (**Figure 12.18**).

   The middle of the center image is designated as the vanishing point, and the outside images appear to recede into its center. The center (vanishing point) image is identified by a blue outline when it's selected.

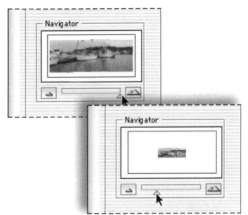

Figure 12.16 Move the slider under the Navigator window to zoom in and out in the work area.

Figure 12.17 Click the Perspective button to add exaggerated perspective to your merged composition.

Figure 12.18 When you select the Perspective setting, Photomerge adjusts and distorts the images to create the illusion of a vanishing point. Here, the vanishing point image is identified by the blue outline.

Figure 12.19 The Set Vanishing Point tool in the Photomerge dialog box.

Figure 12.20 When you change the Vanishing Point image, the other images adjust and distort in response to change the perspective.

Figure 12.21 The Cylindrical Mapping check box helps even out some of the distortion caused by the Perspective setting.

2. To make a different image the vanishing point image, first select the Set Vanishing Point tool (**Figure 12.19**).

3. Click a different image in the work area.

   The panorama changes the perspective to make it look as if the other images now recede into the new Vanishing Point image (**Figure 12.20**).

4. If the perspective option doesn't give you the effect you'd hoped for, select the Normal option in the Settings section of the dialog box to return your panorama to its original state.

   You can also remove the perspective from your panorama by dragging the Vanishing Point image to the Lightbox.

Sometimes the perspective effect can be a little severe, creating more distortion in your image than you think is acceptable. Use the Cylindrical Mapping feature (described in the following task) to reduce this distortion.

To make further adjustments to your panorama:

◆ To compensate for any distortion created by the Perspective setting, click the Cylindrical Mapping box; then click the Preview button (**Figure 12.21**).

   The panorama is adjusted again, this time removing the shape distortion created by the Perspective check box.

   Note that any adjustments you make with the Cylindrical Mapping check box are visible only in Preview mode. Note also that you can't work on the panorama while in Preview mode, and that the cylindrical mapping isn't applied to your panorama until you click OK in the Photomerge dialog box.

continues on next page

CREATING PANORAMAS

- ◆ To compensate for slight variations in exposure or lighting in the separate images, click the Advanced Blending box; then click the Preview button.

  Photoshop Elements attempts to even out the color differences. As with Cylindrical Mapping, this setting is visible only in Preview mode.

Figure 12.22 After you have rendered the panorama in the Photomerge dialog box, you can use the Crop tool in Photoshop Elements to trim the image.

✔ Tips

- Even after you've used the cylindrical mapping feature to correct some of the perspective distortion, you may still find that your image's edges are a little raggedy. Use Photoshop Elements' crop tool to remove those rough edges and give your panorama a nice, crisp rectangular border (**Figure 12.22**).

- Before you print your final panorama, take the time to examine its size in the Image Size dialog box (From the File menu, choose Resize > Image Size). Depending on the size and resolution of the images you've used, your panoramas can quickly grow to exceed the standard paper stock sizes for your printer (which are usually no larger than 8.5 x 14 or 11 x 17 inches). Once you've determined the final image dimensions, use either the Image Size dialog box or the controls in the Print Preview dialog box to resize your image so that it will fit on whatever paper stock you have available.

CREATING PANORAMAS

Figure 12.23 When you create a slideshow, you can specify how your slideshow transitions from one image to the next. Here, this slideshow displays the Wipe Down transition, where a new image rolls down over the previous image's slide.

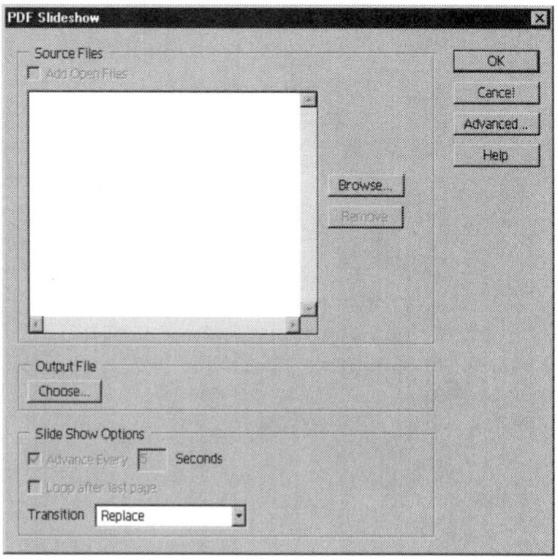

Figure 12.24 The PDF Slideshow dialog box.

Making Your Own Slideshow

With Photoshop Elements, you can create a self-contained, portable slideshow—a useful and elegant way to share your photos and images with friends and family.

Photoshop Elements saves the slideshow as an Adobe Acrobat PDF (Portable Document Format) file. The operative word here is portable. You can view a PDF file on nearly any Windows or Macintosh computer, as long as Adobe's Acrobat Reader is installed. Acrobat Reader, a small program that Adobe offers as a free download, is one of the most widely used helper applications available and can be downloaded from Adobe's Web site at www.adobe.com. Additionally, the Acrobat Reader installer is included on a variety of software installation disks, including Photoshop Elements.

When you open the slideshow file in Acrobat, the slideshow automatically opens in full-screen mode. Slides change with a transition you select when creating the PDF (**Figure 12.23**). In an automatic slideshow, the slides change at preset intervals you set when you generate the file. Alternatively, if you prefer to advance each slide manually, you can create a slideshow that changes slides with keyboard commands.

To create a slideshow:

1. From the File menu, choose Automation Tools > PDF Slideshow.

The PDF Slideshow dialog box opens (**Figure 12.24**).

continues on next page

2. Click the Browse button.

The Open dialog box appears. If the images you want to put in the slideshow are currently open in Photoshop Elements, simply click the Add Open Files box in the PDF Slideshow dialog box. All open files will automatically be added to the Source Files list.

3. Navigate to the folder containing the image files you want to put in your slideshow.

4. Press Ctrl/Shift to select the files you want to appear in your slideshow, then click Open

The files you have selected appear in the Source Files list in the PDF Slideshow dialog box (**Figure 12.25**).

If you have image files in different folders, repeat steps 3 and 4 as needed for each folder.

5. You can rearrange the files in the Source Files list by dragging the file names. You can also remove a file from the list by selecting the file name and clicking the Remove button.

6. In the Output File section, click the Choose button to navigate to the folder where you want to save the PDF file.

7. Additionally, you can select from the following options:

▲ To have the slideshow run automatically, select the Advance Every check box in the Slideshow Options section. Enter the number of seconds to delay between each slide (**Figure 12.26**).

▲ To advance each slide manually, make sure the Advance Every check box is not selected.

▲ If you want the slideshow to loop continuously instead of playing just once, select the Loop after Last Page check box.

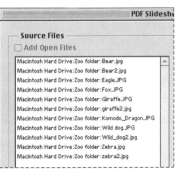

Figure 12.25 When you select images for a PDF slideshow, the file names appear in the Source Files section.

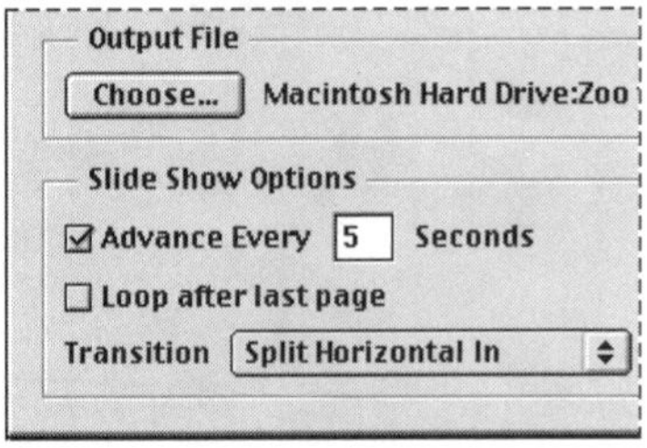

Figure 12.26 If you want the slideshow to change slides automatically, enter the number of seconds that you want each slide displayed on the screen.

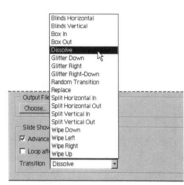

Figure 12.27 Choose your slide transitions from the Transition pop-up menu.

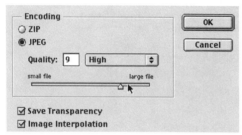

Figure 12.28 In the PDF options dialog box, you can reduce or enlarge the file size of your slideshow by choosing a compression file type and by adjusting the sliders.

8. Choose a transition from the pop-up Transition menu (**Figure 12.27**).

   This option defines how each new slide replaces the slide before it. For example, the Wipe Down transition literally "wipes" a new slide over the previous slide, while the Glitter transition dissolves each slide into tiny pixels.

9. If desired, click the Advanced button to open a dialog box that allows you to choose different compression options for the PDF file (**Figure 12.28**).

   If you need to keep your slideshow's file size small (this is especially useful if you want to e-mail it) choose a Zip or JPEG format, then drag the slider to the left to reduce the file size.

10. When you are finished setting your slideshow options, click OK.

    Photoshop Elements creates a single PDF slideshow file, saving it to the location you selected.

✔ Tips

■ You can also use Photoshop Elements' type tools to create professional-looking title slides. Just enter text in a series of separate files, save them, and then include them along with the image files when you build your slideshow. This is a useful way to create an artist's portfolio, a school report, or a quick business presentation.

■ Using more than one or two different transitions within the course of a slide-show can grow tiresome. You'll probably want to stick with the collection of more conservative transitions. The simple wipe and split transitions in the lower portion of the Transition pop-up menu will give you cleanest, most elegant results.

MAKING YOUR OWN SLIDESHOW

Using the File Browser to Arrange Your Slides

When creating a slideshow, you normally use the Source Files list in the PDF Slideshow dialog box to arrange the order of your slideshow images. This works fine if you have a limited number of images. But if you have a lot of images and the file names aren't very descriptive, it can be difficult to arrange your slides in the exact order you want.

Instead, use the File Browser to visually arrange your slides and rename them in numeric order. Place all of the images you want to include in the slideshow in one folder. (You should make copies of these images, since you'll be renaming them.) In the File Browser, ensure that Large Thumbnail is selected for the view option, so you can see your images clearly. Then click the names of the image files and rename them numerically (01, 02, 03) in the order you want them to appear (**Figure 12.29**).

Refresh the display order of the images by choosing Filename from the Sort By pop-up menu (**Figure 12.30**). You may have to refresh the sorting more than once. This gives you a visual preview of the entire slideshow order. Now, when you add the images to your slideshow via the PDF Slideshow dialog box, they are already in the correct order.

Figure 12.29 If you're working with multiple images, it's often easier to rename the images numerically. That way, they'll sort in the order you want them to appear in your slideshow.

Figure 12.30 When you sort by file name, you see a visual preview of the slide order in the Browser window.

To view a slideshow:

1. Make sure that Adobe Acrobat Reader is installed on your computer.

   If it's not installed, install it from the Photoshop Elements installation disk, or download it free from www.adobe.com.

2. In Acrobat Reader, open the PDF slideshow you created in Photoshop Elements.

   The slideshow appears, taking up the full screen. If the slideshow is set to run automatically, each image will be displayed

MAKING YOUR OWN SLIDESHOW

for the time you set in the PDF Slideshow dialog box.

3. To navigate through your slideshow in Acrobat Reader, use the following keyboard commands:

▲ Move forward one slide by pressing Enter/Return, or press the right arrow key.

▲ Move back one slide by pressing Shift+Enter/Shift+Return, or press the left arrow key.

▲ Exit Full Screen view and access Acrobat Reader's interface by pressing Ctrl+L/Command+L.

✔ Tip

■ The transitions and auto advance features of your PDF slideshow will only work in Acrobat Reader 5.0 or later. The slideshow will open and display with older versions of Acrobat, but you'll need to navigate through the slides manually using the keyboard commands listed above.

MAKING YOUR OWN SLIDESHOW

About Web Photo Galleries

Preparing a gallery of photos for use on the Web can be repetitive, tedious work. You have to resize and format each image, one at a time—a lengthy process. Luckily, Photoshop Elements eliminates this drudge-work for you with its automated Web Photo Gallery feature (**Figure 12.31**). When you create a Web photo gallery, Photoshop Elements instantly opens a group of image files, resizes them to identical dimensions, and creates smaller thumbnail versions. Photoshop Elements also creates HTML code for each Web page in the gallery. (HTML stands for Hypertext Markup Language, and is the code that describes the size, location, color, and other attributes of any and all objects and text on a Web page.) All of the images and HTML files are stored in a desig-nated folder on your hard drive. Once the photo gallery is completed, you can then view the gallery on your hard drive or on the Web. If you have a digital camera full of images that you can't wait to share over the Web, this feature can help you get them posted online quickly. (See the color plate section of this book for a full-color view of a Web photo gallery.)

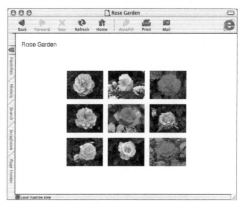

Figure 12.31 Create a Web gallery of your favorite digital photos with Photoshop Elements' automated Web Photo Gallery feature.

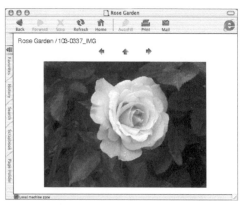

Figure 12.32 In a Web gallery, you can navigate backward or forward through the images or go back to the main page.

Figure 12.33 In the Vertical Frame gallery, thumbnails are in one frame, and full-sized images appear in the other frame.

You can create two main types of Web galleries, each with different ways of navigating through the images. All of the photo gallery styles available in Photoshop Elements fall into one of these two types:

◆ One gallery type consists of a main Web page with a *grid* of image thumbnails. To navigate, you click on a thumbnail to display the full-sized image on its own page. Each full-sized image page contains buttons to move to the previous image, the next image, or back to the main gallery page. The Simple gallery style is an example of this type (**Figure 12.32**).

◆ The other gallery type consists of a main page divided into two areas, or *frames*. When you click on a thumbnail, the full sized image displays in the other frame. To view different full-sized images, you click on the different thumbnails. The Vertical Frame style is an example of this type (**Figure 12.33**).

When you launch the Web Photo Gallery command, Photoshop Elements creates the following items and assembles them into one main folder:

◆ A main HTML page (index.htm)

◆ A folder of full-sized JPEG images

◆ A folder of thumbnail images

◆ A folder of linked HTML pages

◆ Navigation buttons for your HTML pages

To create a Web photo gallery:

1. Move (or copy) any images you want to appear in the Web photo gallery into one folder.

2. From the File menu, choose Create Web Photo Gallery to open the Web Photo Gallery dialog box (**Figure 12.34**).

3. Choose a gallery type from the Styles pop-up menu (**Figure 12.35**).

   When you choose a gallery style, a pre-view appears on the right side of the dialog box, and options for that style (if available) appear in the lower portion of the dialog box.

4. If you want an e-mail address to appear in the gallery, enter it in the E-mail field (**Figure 12.36**).

   Not all gallery styles will display an e-mail address.

5. In the Folders section of the dialog box, click Browse (Windows) or Choose (Mac OS) to open the Select Image Directory dialog box.

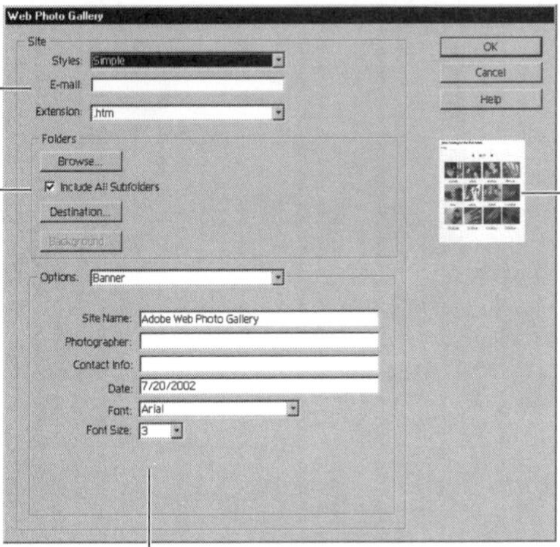

Select a source and destination for your gallery files in the Folders area

Define the gallery type in the Site area

Gallery preview

Customize your Web gallery in the Options area

Figure 12.34 The Web Photo Gallery dialog box.

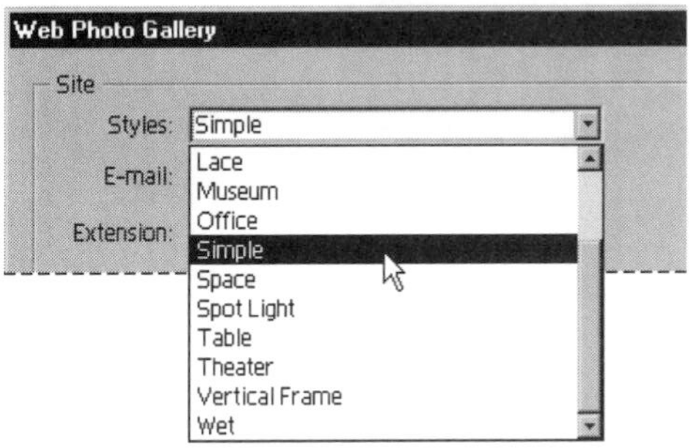

Figure 12.35 You can choose from more than 10 different styles of preformatted Web galleries in the Web Photo Gallery dialog box.

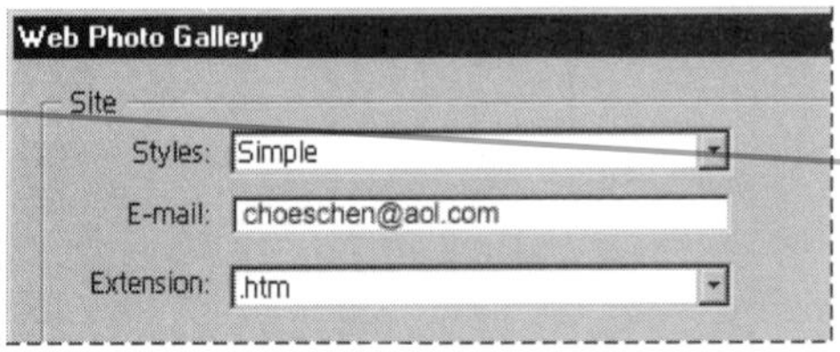

Figure 12.36 If you like, you can enter an e-mail address to appear on your Web gallery pages.

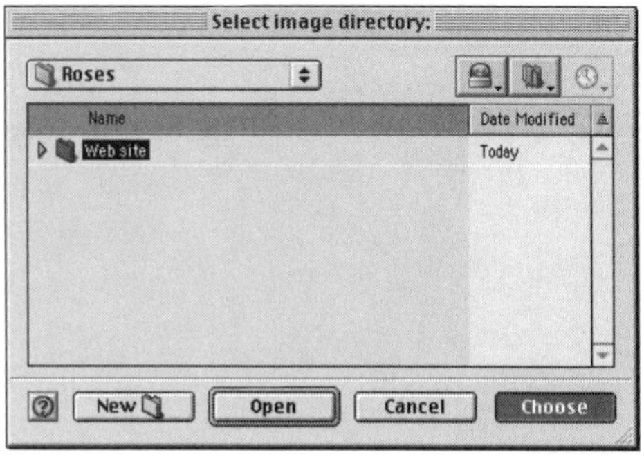

Figure 12.37 In the Select Image Directory dialog box, you choose the folder of images from which to build your Web gallery.

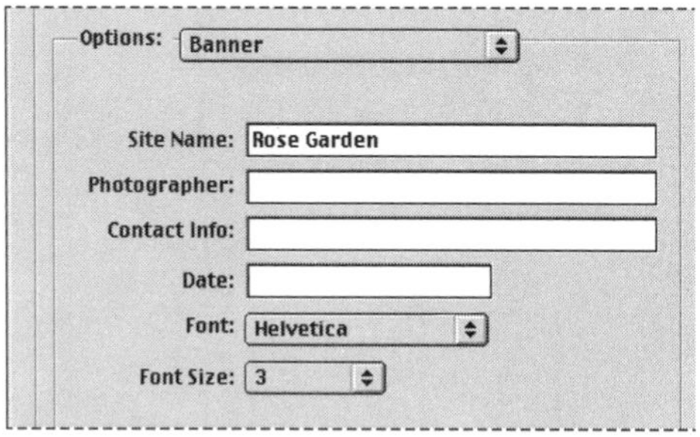

Figure 12.38 The Banner options in the Web Photo Gallery dialog box.

6. Navigate to the folder containing the images you want to display in the Web photo gallery; then select the folder and click OK (Windows) or Choose (Mac OS) (**Figure 12.37**).

   All of the images in the folder are imported into the gallery. If you selected Include All Subfolders, any images in subfolders will also be included.

7. Back in the Web Photo Gallery dialog box, click the Destination button; then select a folder (or create a new folder) to store your final gallery HTML files and images. Click OK (Windows) or Choose (Mac OS).

   Many of the Web Gallery styles offer limited (or no further) options, and so the Options portion of the dialog box may be dimmed. The Simple, Table and Frame gallery styles offer additional options for controlling the appearance of the title banner at the top of each page, the display size of the images, and even the color of the text and background.

8. Choose Banner from the Options pop-up menu to enter a title for your Web page, the name of the photographer, contact information, and the current date. You can also assign the font and font size for any text on the page. Any banner information will appear on every page of the gallery (**Figure 12.38**).

continues on next page

ABOUT WEB PHOTO GALLERIES

9. Choose Large Images from the Options pop-up menu to modify the appearance of the full-sized versions of your images. You can also add borders and titles (**Figure 12.39**).

The Titles Use check boxes all link to text you've entered for individual images in their File Info dialog boxes. (For more on the File Info dialog box, see "Setting Preferences for Saving Files" in Chapter 11.)

If you don't want your full-sized images resized, make sure that the Resize Images check box is not selected.

10. Choose Thumbnails from the Options pop-up menu to manage the size of the thumbnail images, as well as their borders and titles (**Figure 12.40**).

11. Choose Custom Colors from the Options pop-up menu to set background and text colors (**Figure 12.41**).

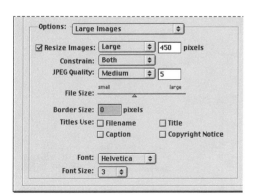

Figure 12.39 The Large Images options in the Web Photo Gallery dialog box.

![Thumbnails options dialog]

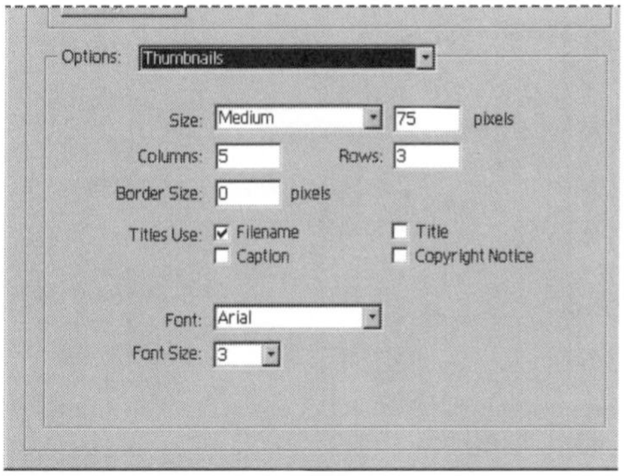

Figure 12.40 The Thumbnails options in the Web Photo Gallery dialog box.

![Custom Colors options dialog]

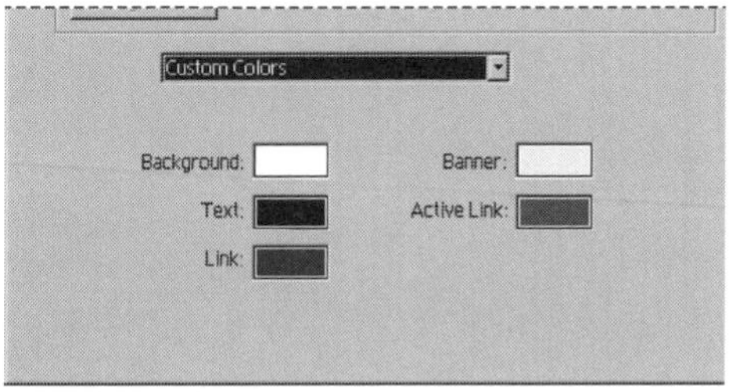

Figure 12.41 The Custom Colors options in the Web Photo Gallery dialog box.

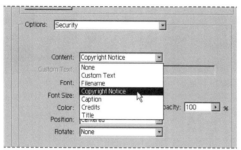

Figure 12.42 The Security options in the Web Photo Gallery dialog box.

12. Choose Security from the Options pop-up menu to superimpose text over the full-sized images (**Figure 12.42**).

This is especially convenient if you'd like to place copyright information directly on the faces of your images.

13. Once you've set the options you want applied to your gallery, click OK.

Photoshop Elements automatically creates your Web gallery. Be warned, however: depending on how many images your gallery contains, this process could take a few minutes. Once the process is finished, Photoshop Elements displays the gallery within your Web browser.

✔ Tips

■ The small thumbnail views of the different galleries in the Web Photo Gallery dialog box aren't really big enough to give you a good idea of what the final gallery will look like, but you can quickly create a series of galleries with just one or two images and then save them to use as a visual reference when creating your final galleries.

■ Once you create and save your Web gallery, all of the images and HTML files are stored in a folder on your hard drive. Since all ISPs (Internet Service Providers) operate in a slightly different fashion, you'll want to contact your ISP directly before you try posting your gallery to the Web. They should be able to provide you with complete instructions and parameters for uploading and displaying your Web gallery files.

ABOUT WEB PHOTO GALLERIES

Creating Animated GIFs

In Chapter 10, we discussed GIF files but decided to wait until this chapter of special techniques to delve into one of the more interesting uses of GIFs—animation. GIF animations are widely used on Web pages as a device to help draw special attention to particular icons, graphics or logos. But they can also be used as a way to deliver compact little "movies" from a limited number of video images, or from a single still photo. In addition to posting animated GIFs to the Web, you can also share them with friend by including them as e-mail attachments. To view your animation, all your recipient need do is to open the GIF file from within their Web browser.

Animated GIFs contain a sequence of images that are displayed sequentially, like a flip book, creating the illusion of motion (**Figure 12.43**). Like all GIF files, they can be displayed in most Web browsers and have a relatively small file size because of their compression and limited color palette.

Photoshop Elements creates the individual frames of an animated GIF file from the individual layers in an image file, so you'll need to create your animation in a file with multiple layers. The bottom layer on the Layers palette is always the first frame of the animation, so you'll build your animated GIF file from the bottom up (**Figure 12.44**). (See the color plate section of this book for a full-color example of creating animated GIFs.)

Figure 12.43 Animated GIFs create the illusion of motions by displaying a series of frames over time.

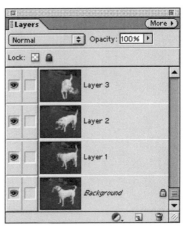

Figure 12.44 The bottom layer of the Photoshop Elements Layers palette becomes the first frame of an animated GIF file.

Figure 12.45 Collect all of the files you want to use to build your animation; then choose the image file that you want to use as the first frame.

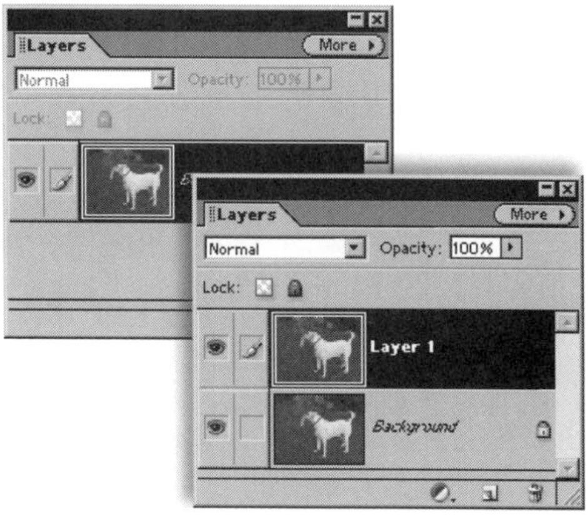

Figure 12.46 When you paste a selection into an image, it creates a new layer on the Layers palette.

To prepare a layered file for animation:

1. Open all of the images you want to use as frames for your animated GIF file.

2. Select the image that you want to use as the first frame of the animated GIF file (**Figure 12.45**).

3. Choose File>Save as and save the image as a Photoshop Elements file with a new name.

   This will be the layered "source" file for creating your animated GIF

4. Click to select the image window of the image that you want to use as the next frame in your animation; then, from the Select menu, choose All, or press Ctrl+A/Command+A.

5. From the Edit menu, choose Copy, or press Ctrl+C/Command+C.

6. Select the image with the first frame; then, from the Edit menu, choose Paste, or press Ctrl+V/Command+V.

   The second image is pasted on top of the first image and is represented by a new layer on the Layers palette (**Figure 12.46**).

7. Repeat steps 4 through 6 for each additional frame, continuing to add layers to the first image.

8. Save your image.

✔ Tip

■ With animated GIFs, less can be more. You may be surprised at how few frames you need to convey motion. Start with a small number of frames (5 or 6 are probably adequate) and then add more only if you think they're needed.

To create an animated GIF:

1. Open the layered file you've built as the source for your animation.

   (If you don't have a layered file ready, see the preceding task, "To prepare a layered file for animation.")

2. From the File menu, choose Save for Web, or press Alt+Shift+Ctrl+S/ Option+Shift+Command+S to open the Save for Web dialog box (**Figure 12.47**).

3. Choose GIF in the Settings area of the dialog box; then select the Animate (Windows) or Animation (Mac OS) check box (**Figure 12.48**).

4. Click the Play button to move the animation one frame forward (**Figure 12.49**).

   You can use the Play button and the other control buttons to step through the animation, but the animation will not show in real time.

5. In the Animation section of the dialog box, set the options for frame delay and looping (**Figure 12.50**).

   Frame delay sets the amount of time that each frame is displayed before the next frame appears. You can set the frame delay for as short as one-tenth of a second and as long as 10 seconds.

   When the Loop check box is selected, your animation will play continuously. If Loop is not checked, your animation will play once through all of its frames and then stop.

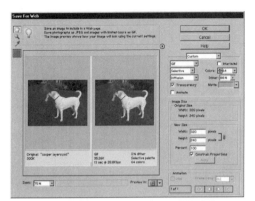

Figure 12.47 Open the Save for Web dialog box to make additional changes to your animated GIF file.

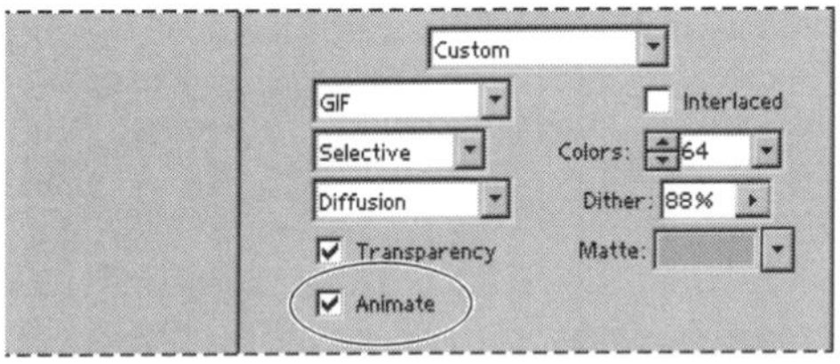

Figure 12.48 Select a GIF setting; then click the Animate check box.

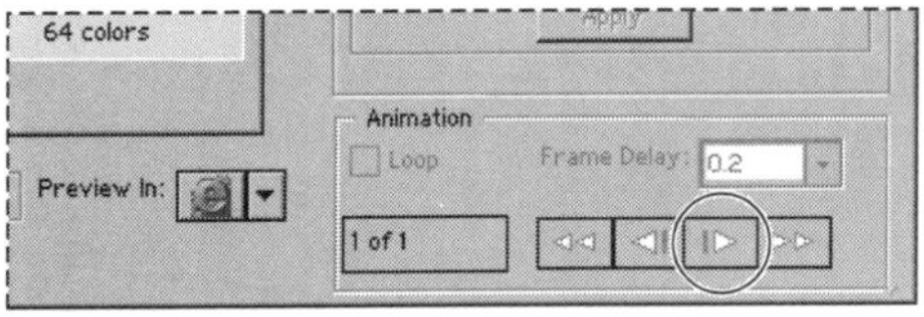

Figure 12.49 Click the Play button to step through the frames of your animation, one frame at a time.

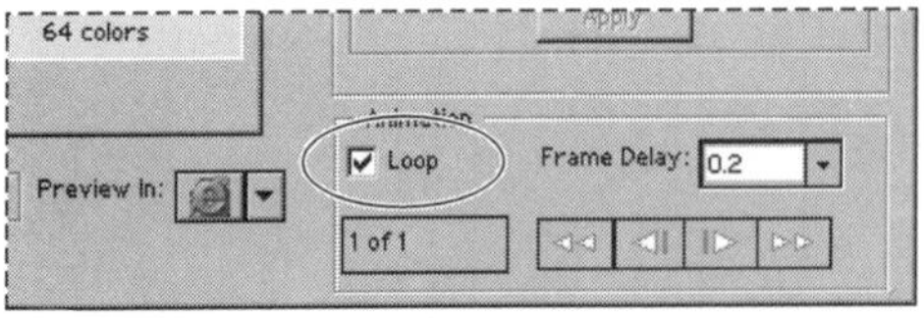

Figure 12.50 You can choose to have your animation loop, so that it will play continuously, over and over again.

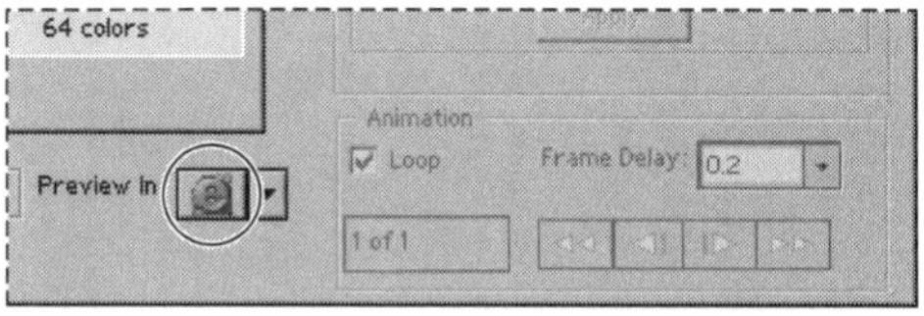

Figure 12.51 When you click the Preview In button, a Web browser opens and plays the animated GIF file.

6. Click the Preview In button to view the animated GIF file in a Web browser (**Figure 12.51**).

   You may need to return to Photoshop Elements and adjust your settings and preview again. When you are satisfied, close the browser.

7. Still in the Save For Web dialog box, click the OK button.

   The Save Optimized As dialog box opens.

8. In the Save Optimized As dialog box, type a new name for your animation and verify that GIF is selected for the optimization format.

9. Choose a location for your file, then click Save.

   The Save Optimized As, and Save For Web dialog boxes automatically close, and your animated GIF is saved to the location you specified.

Animating GIF Images from Video Files

One way to create frames for an animated GIF file is to use frames you've captured from a video file. You can use Photoshop Elements to capture individual frames from video, combine them in a single layered file, and then convert the layers to an animated GIF by following the steps in this section. (For detailed information on capturing frames from video footage, see "Importing Images from Cameras and Scanners" in Chapter 2)

Many digital cameras also have the ability to capture short movies, so even if you don't have a video camera, you may still be able to gather digital video. Check the specifications and documentation that came with your camera.

Creating animation from a still image

Another method for creating the illusion of motion in Photoshop Elements is to start with a single still image, duplicate the image onto a series of separate layers, and then slightly shift each layer either horizontally or vertically. When saved as an animation, it will appear as if a camera is slowing panning through a scene. You've probably seen this technique used in documentaries, where for lack of film or video footage, the camera pans slowly over an archival photograph.

In this example, we'll shift successive frames horizontally to create the illusion of panning past a ship at rest in a harbor. You can use this same technique with photos of large family groups or any other instance when you want to control exactly where your viewer's attention is drawn. This technique can be particularly effective when used along with the wide panoramic images you create using Photomerge.

To mimic camera movement in an animated GIF file:

1. Open the image you want to use as the source file for your animation.

2. Create a new file with either the width or height dimensions (or both) smaller than those of your source image.

   Since we'll be panning from side to side across our image, we've made the width of our new file about half that of the source image (**Figure 12.52**).

3. Drag the large image into the file you just created (**Figure 12.53**).

   A new layer is created on the Layers palette.

4. On the Layers Palette, drag the Background layer to the trash (**Figure 12.54**).

Figure 12.52 Start with a source image that is larger than the final size of the animated GIF image.

Figure 12.53 Drag the larger source image into the final animated GIF project image window.

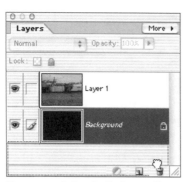

Figure 12.54 Delete the Background layer by dragging it to the Delete Layer icon on the Layers palette.

Figure 12.55 Position the first (bottom) image layer for the first frame of your animation.

Figure 12.56 Duplicate the bottom image layer to create an image for the second frame of your animation.

The new image layer becomes the only layer in the file.

Remember that the bottom layer always becomes the first frame of an animated GIF file. Since the first layer in any new file is empty, we'll delete it so as not to include a blank frame in our animation.

5. Select the Move tool and drag the image to compose your first frame.

In our example, we dragged the image all the way to its left edge, since we want to create the illusion of panning from left to right (**Figure 12.55**).

Notice that even though you can see only a portion of the original, source image, it's all still there, hidden outside the borders of the image window.

6. On the Layers palette, drag the layer to the Create a New Layer icon.

A duplicate of the new, first layer is created (**Figure 12.56**).

continues on next page

CREATING ANIMATED GIFS

7. With the Move tool still selected, move the new layer a little to the left in the image window.

A portion of the image that had been hidden beyond the right edge of the image window comes into view, while a portion originally visible, disappears beyond the left edge (**Figure 12.57**).

8. On the Layers palette, drag the new top layer onto the Create a New Layer icon; then drag this new layer a little farther to the left in the image window.

Continue to repeat the process, creating successive layers and gradually moving the image through the image window (**Figure 12.58**).

9. Choose File > Save for Web and follow steps 3 though 9 from the "To create an animated GIF," task earlier in this chapter.

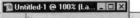

Figure 12.57 Move the new layer in the image window. Since the layer is larger than the final image size, it still contains information beyond its frame.

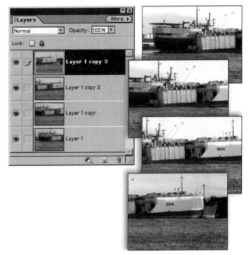

Figure 12.58 Create as many layers as you need. Each layer will become a frame in the animated GIF file.

CREATING ANIMATED GIFs

Compositing Images

Combining multiple images together to create a single merged image is called *compositing*, and the possibilities for compositing are endless. You can combine different digital photos or scanned images to create effects that range from subtle to spectacular. For example, you can create realistic-looking photo collages, add your face to the Mona Lisa, insert President Bush into a family photo, or place an architect's drawing of a skyscraper into the photo of an existing skyline. We'll explore just a few of the ways you can composite images with Photoshop Elements.

Photoshop Elements lets you combine pictures in ways that would be difficult or even impossible to accomplish in the darkroom. The selection tools let you isolate the parts of an image you want to use, and the Layers palette provides a powerful and elegant tool for combining and merging different image elements. Though you can do some compositing without the aid of the Layers palette (cloning parts of an image from one file to another, for example), layers give you much more flexibility to move and adjust and modify one area of an image while leaving other areas untouched.

In the following example of an image for a travel agency brochure, we want the composite image to look as if it were an original unretouched photograph.

COMPOSITING IMAGES

To replace part of an image with another image:

1. Open an image that contains an area you want to replace.

   We'll call this the "target" image.

   In the example here, the sky isn't very interesting, and we want to add a more dramatic background (**Figure 12.59**). Even though the sky and the ship are both blue, the edges are well defined, and so the image is a good candidate for the Background Eraser tool.

2. From the toolbox, select the Background Eraser tool; then adjust its brush size and tolerance values.

   We set the tolerance value fairly low because the sky and the ship both contain a lot of blue. If we set the tolerance value higher, a broader range of pixels may be selected, and some parts of the ship might be erased. (For more information on using the Background Eraser tool, see "Erasing Backgrounds and Other Large Areas" in Chapter 8.)

3. Position the Background Eraser tool along the outside edge of the foreground shape (the ship). Making sure that the brush crosshairs are over the background (sky), drag along the edge to erase the background. Continue to erase the background until the area is completely transparent (**Figure 12.60**).

4. Open the image that you want to use to replace the transparent pixels in your original image.

   We'll call this the "source" image.

Figure 12.59 We'll enhance this image by replacing its lackluster background.

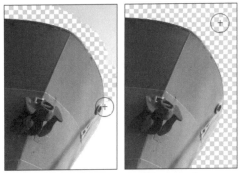

Figure 12.60 Use the Background Eraser tool to remove the sky and create a transparent background.

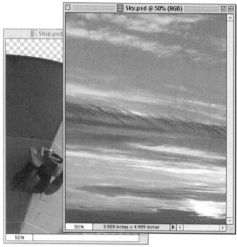

Figure 12.61 Drag the source image (the sky) into the target image (the ship).

Figure 12.62 Move the sky layer below the ship layer on the Layers palette and adjust the position in the image window.

5. Select the Move tool and drag the source image into the target image (**Figure 12.61**).

In our example, the sky image is larger than the empty background area, which allows flexibility in positioning the new sky in the composition.

If you like, you can also use the selection tools to select just a portion of the source image, then drag just that selection into the target image.

6. On the Layers palette, drag the source layer below the target layer (**Figure 12.62**).

7. In the image window, use the Move tool to adjust the position of the source image until you're satisfied with the composition.

If you want, you can use the image adjustment tools on each layer to create a more natural-looking composition.

✔ Tip

■ It's always good practice to save a copy of your composition retaining the layers, in case you want to make further adjustments. Layered files should be saved as Photoshop Elements (PSD) files.

COMPOSITING IMAGES

Creating whimsical composite images

In many cases, as in the previous example, you composite images to improve them in a way that isn't obvious to the viewer. You don't want to draw attention to your work; you just want to improve the image (as in our ship and sky example). But sometimes you want your audience to wonder how you created that cool special effect. This composite for an elementary school astronomy fair poster is an image that looks pretty realistic, if a little fantastical (**Figure 12.63**). (See the color plate section of this book for a full-color view of this task.)

To combine images:

1. Open two images that you want to composite (**Figure 12.64**).

2. Use the selection tools and/or eraser tools to isolate part of the source image.

   In this case, we used the Background Eraser tool to erase the background from the boy, leaving the area around him transparent (**Figure 12.65**). This way, he'll insert nicely into the target image, with no messy halos or edges around his body.

3. Copy the area of the source image that you want to composite.

Figure 12.63 This final composite image was created from two separate images.

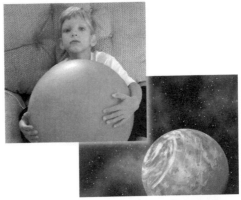

Figure 12.64 Here, we used a picture of a boy and a photograph of space to create an otherworldly image.

Figure 12.65 Use the Background Eraser tool (or any other selection tool) to isolate your source image.

Figure 12.66 After pasting the source image (the boy) into the target image, the source image is placed on a new layer above the target image. That makes it easy to drag the image of the boy into its proper position.

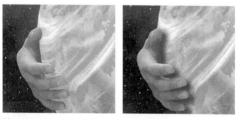

Figure 12.67 The original composite lacked a little realism (left), so we added a drop shadow layer effect below the boy's hands (right) to complete the effect.

4. Paste that selection into the target image (**Figure 12.66**).

   This creates a new layer.

5. Using the Move tool in the image window, position and resize the source image (top layer) to match the target image (bottom layer).

6. If you like, you can add layer styles to enhance the image.

   In this example, we chose the Low option in the Drop Shadow section of the Layer Styles palette to create an effective drop shadow on the boy's hand (**Figure 12.67**).

COMPOSITING IMAGES

Creating new composite images

In the previous examples, we simply combined different objects we'd photographed in order to enhance those objects. In these types of compositions, the source images (the ship and little boy) were still recognizable; they were just composited into new backgrounds or environments.

A second compositing technique combines digital photos or scanned objects to create something entirely new, while in the process the individual replacement images used become barely recognizable. (A classic example of the old adage, "the whole is better than the sum of its parts.") In the next example, we'll combine multiple layers to create a collage for a quilting Web site (**Figure 12.68**). We'll use the Custom Shape tool to create a layer group, and then we'll apply layer styles to a text layer.

To create a layered photo collage:

1. Open the two images you want to combine (**Figure 12.69**).

    We're going to combine scans of two contrasting fabrics to create the look of a quilt.

2. Select the Custom Shape tool and choose a shape from the menu on the Options bar.

    We chose the Tile 4 option, since it looks like a diamond quilt pattern (**Figure 12.70**).

3. In the background image file, drag the Custom Shape tool to create the shape pattern. Hold down Ctrl/Command and drag in the shape to reposition it if necessary.

    A new layer with the shape is created (**Figure 12.71**).

    Now we'll use the shape to create a mask for the other fabric layer.

Figure 12.68 This image is a composite of two image layers: a shape layer and a text layer with layer styles applied.

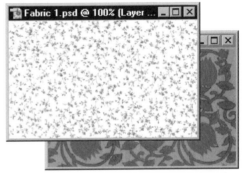

Figure 12.69 Open the images you want to composite.

Figure 12.70 Select a custom shape that you'll use to define the shape of one of your composite layers.

Figure 12.71 Draw the Custom Shape so that if fills a large portion of the image window.

COMPOSITING IMAGES

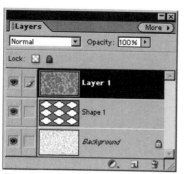

Figure 12.72 Paste the layer you want to composite above the custom shape layer.

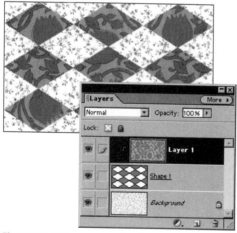

Figure 12.73 When you create a layer group, the bottom layer acts as a mask, allowing the layer above to show through only those areas in the bottom layer that are opaque.

Figure 12.74 Create a new text layer on top of the other layers.

4. Copy and paste the foreground image into the Background image file.

The foreground image creates a new layer in the Background image file, immediately above the shape layer we just created (**Figure 12.72**).

5. Make sure that the foreground image is selected; then, from the Layer menu, choose Group with Previous, or press Ctrl+G/Command+G.

A layer group is created. The foreground image now shows only within the area of the custom shape below it. The fabrics look like they have been quilted together in a pattern (**Figure 12.73**).

6. Select the Text tool, then click in the image and enter your text.

Select the Move tool and position the text if necessary.

For our example, we used a bold typeface and set the text color to white (**Figure 12.74**).

continues on next page

COMPOSITING IMAGES

7. With the text layer selected on the Layers palette, click the Layer Styles tab in the palette well; then choose one of the styles from the pop-up menu.

   We chose Simple Pillow Emboss from the Bevels styles (**Figure 12.75**).

8. Click the Layer Styles tab again; then choose Visibility from the pop-up menu.

9. Select the Ghosted option (**Figure 12.76**).

   The text looks like it has been quilted into the fabric.

10. To make further adjustments to the embossing effect, click the Layer Style icon on the text layer on the Layers palette.

    The Style Settings dialog box appears, where you can make adjustments to the Layer style you have applied (**Figure 12.77**).

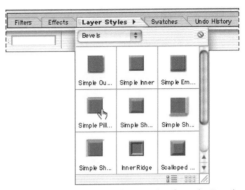

Figure 12.75 Choose an Emboss option from the Bevels section of the Layer Styles menu.

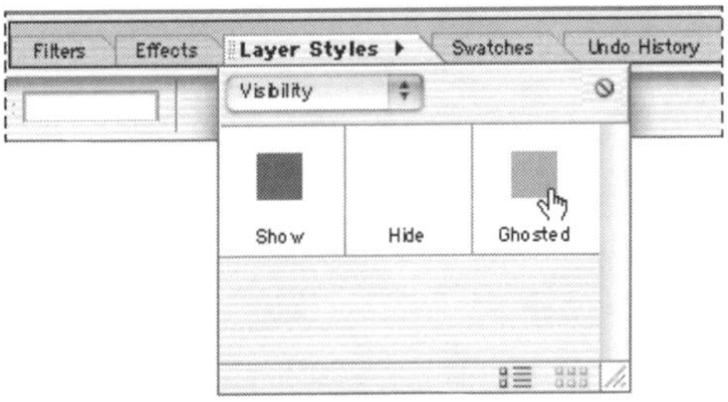

Figure 12.76 Choose an option from the Visibility section of the Layer Styles menu.

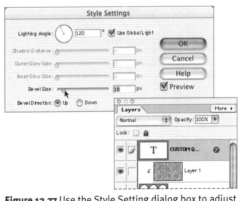

Figure 12.77 Use the Style Setting dialog box to adjust your layer styles.

KEYBOARD SHORTCUTS

To choose a tool		
TOOLS	WINDOWS	MAC OS
Marquee	M	M
Move	V	V
Lasso	L	L
Magic Wand	W	W
Selection Brush	A	A
Crop	C	C
Custom Shape	U	U
Type &Type Mask	T	T
Paint Bucket	K	K
Gradient	G	G
Brush	B	B
Pencil	N	N
Eraser	E	E
Red Eye Brush	Y	Y
Blur	R	R
Sharpen	P	P
Sponge	Q	Q
Smudge	F	F
Dodge	O	O
Burn	J	J
Clone Stamp	S	S
Eyedropper	I	I
Hand	H	H
Zoom	Z	Z

To cycle through tools

TOOLS	WINDOWS	MAC OS
Marquee tools	Shift +M	Shift +M
Lasso tools	Shift +L	Shift +L
Shape tools	Shift +U	Shift +U
Type &Type Mask tools	Shift +T	Shift +T
Brush	Shift +B	Shift +B
Eraser	Shift +E	Shift +E
Clone Stamp	Shift +S	Shift +S

Working with tools

MARQUEE TOOL	WINDOWS	MAC OS
Draw marquee from center	Alt +drag	Option +drag
Constrain to square or circle	Shift +drag	Shift +drag
Draw from center and constrain to square or circle	Shift + Alt +drag	Shift + Option +drag
MOVE TOOL	**WINDOWS**	**MAC OS**
Constrain move to 45 °	Shift +drag	Shift +drag
Copy selection or layer	Alt +drag	Option +drag
Nudge selection 1 pixel	Arrow key	Arrow key
Nudge selection 10 pixels	Shift +arrow	Shift +arrow
Nudge layer 1 pixel	Ctrl +arrow	Ctrl +arrow
Nudge layer 10 pixels	Shift + Ctrl +arrow	Shift + Ctrl +arrow
LASSO TOOL	**WINDOWS**	**MAC OS**
Add to selection	Shift +click, then draw	Shift +click, then draw
Delete from selection	Alt +click, then draw	Option +click, then draw
Intersect with selection	Alt + Shift +click, then draw	Option + Shift +click, then draw
Change to Polygonal Lasso	Click, then Alt +drag	Click,then Option +drag
POLYGONAL LASSO TOOL	**WINDOWS**	**MAC OS**
Add to selection	Shift +click, then draw	Shift +click, then draw
Delete from selection	Alt +click, then draw	Option +click, then draw
Intersect with selection	Alt + Shift +click, then draw	Option + Shift +click, then draw
Draw using Lasso	Alt +drag	Option +drag
Constrain to 45 ° while drawing	Shift +drag	Shift +drag
MAGNETIC LASSO TOOL	**WINDOWS**	**MAC OS**
Add to selection	Shift +click, then draw	Shift +click, then draw
Delete from selection	Alt +click, then draw	Option +click, then draw
Intersect with selection	Alt + Shift +click, then draw	Option + Shift +click, then draw
Add point	Single click	Single click
Remove last point	Backspace or Delete key	Delete key
Close path	Double-click or Enter	Double-click or Enter or Return
Close path over start point	Click on start point	Click on start point
Close path using straight line segment	Alt +double-click	Option +double-click
Switch to Lasso	Alt +drag	Option +drag
Switch to Polygonal Lasso	Alt +click	Option +click

Working with tools		
Crop Tool	**Windows**	**Mac OS**
Rotate crop marquee	Drag outside crop marquee	Drag outside crop marquee
Move crop marquee	Drag inside crop marquee	Drag inside crop marquee
Resize crop marquee	Drag crop handles	Drag crop handles
Resize crop box while maintaining its aspect ratio	Shift+drag corner handles	Shift+drag corner handles
Shape Tools	**Windows**	**Mac OS**
Constrain to square or circle	Shift+drag	Shift+drag
Constrain Line tool to 45 °	Shift+drag	Shift+drag
Transform shape	Ctrl+T	⌘+T
Distort	Ctrl+drag	⌘+drag
Skew	Ctrl+Alt+drag	⌘+Option+drag
Create Perspective	Ctrl+Alt+Shift+drag	⌘+Option+Shift+drag
Type Tool	**Windows**	**Mac OS**
Select a word	Double-click in text	Double-click in text
Select a line	Triple-click in text	Triple-click in text
Select all characters	Ctrl+A	⌘+A
Left align text	Ctrl+Shift+L	⌘+Shift+L
Center text	Ctrl+Shift+C	⌘+Shift+C
Right align text	Ctrl+Shift+R	⌘+Shift+R
Increase by 2 points	Ctrl+Shift+.(period)	⌘+Shift+.(period)
Decrease by 2 points	Ctrl+Shift+,(comma)	⌘+Shift+,(comma)
Scroll through fonts	Select font in menu +up/down arrow	Select font in menu +up/down arrow
Paint Bucket Tool	**Windows**	**Mac OS**
Change color of area around canvas	Shift+click outside canvas	Shift+click outside canvas
Brush and Pencil Tool	**Windows**	**Mac OS**
Decrease or increase size by 10 pixels (or by 1 pixel when size is less than 10 pixels)	[(key) or] (key)	[(key) or] (key)
Smudge Tool	Windows	Mac OS
Smudge using Foreground color	Alt+drag	Option+drag
Eyedropper Tool	**Windows**	**Mac OS**
Choose Background color	Alt+click	Option+click

Display Shortcuts

CHANGE VIEW	WINDOWS	MAC OS
Zoom In	Ctrl+Spacebar+click/ drag or Ctrl++(plus)	⌘+Spacebar+click/ drag or ⌘++(plus)
Zoom out	Alt+Spacebar+click/ drag or Ctrl+-(minus)	Option+Spacebar+click/ drag or ⌘+-(minus)
Zoom to 100%	Double-click Zoom tool	Double-click Zoom tool
Zoom to fit window	Double-click Hand tool	Double-click Hand tool
Fit on screen	Ctrl+0	⌘+0
Actual pixels	Ctrl+Alt+0	⌘+Option+0
Show/hide edges of selection	Ctrl+H	⌘+H
Show/hide ruler	Ctrl+R	⌘+R
HAND TOOL	WINDOWS	MAC OS
Toggle to zoom in	Ctrl	Z
Toggle to zoom out	Alt	Option
Fit image on screen	Double-click tool	Double-click tool
ZOOM TOOL	WINDOWS	MAC OS
Zoom out	Alt+click	Option+click
Actual size	Double-click tool	Double-click tool
MOVE IMAGE IN WINDOW	WINDOWS	MAC OS
Scroll up one screen	Page Up	Page Up
Scroll down one screen	Page Down	Page Down
Scroll left one screen	Ctrl+page up	⌘+page up
Scroll right one screen	Ctrl+page down	⌘+page down
Scroll up 10 pixels	Shift+page up	Shift+page up
Scroll down 10 pixels	Shift+page down	Shift+page down
Scroll left 10 pixels	Ctrl+Shift+pageup	⌘+Shift+page up
Scroll right 10 pixels	Ctrl+Shift+page down	⌘+Shift+page down
Move view to upper left	Home key	Home key
Move view to lower right	End key	End key

Menu Shortcuts

FILE MENU	WINDOWS	MAC OS
New	Ctrl+N	⌘+N
Open	Ctrl+O	⌘+O
Browse	Ctrl+Shift+O	⌘+Shift+O
Open As	Ctrl+Alt+O	⌘+Option+O
Close	Ctrl+W	⌘+W
Save	Ctrl+S	⌘+S
Save As	Ctrl+Shift+S	⌘+Shift+S
Save for Web	Ctrl+Alt+Shift+S	⌘+Option+Shift+S
Page Setup	Ctrl+Shift+P	⌘+Shift+P
Print Preview	Ctrl+P	⌘+P
Print	Ctrl+Alt+P	⌘+Option+P
Exit	Ctrl+Q	⌘+Q

EDIT MENU	WINDOWS	MAC OS
Undo	Ctrl+Alt+Z	⌘+Option+Z
Step Forward	Ctrl+Y	⌘+Y
Step Backward	Ctrl+Z	⌘+Z
Cut	Ctrl+X	⌘+X
Copy	Ctrl+C	⌘+C
Copy Merged	Ctrl+Shift+C	⌘+Shift+C
Paste	Ctrl+V	⌘+V
Paste Into	Ctrl+Shift+V	⌘+Shift+V
Color Settings	Ctrl+Shift+K	⌘+Shift+K
Preferences > General	Ctrl+K	⌘+K

ENHANCE MENU	WINDOWS	MAC OS
Auto Levels	Ctrl+Shift+L	⌘+Shift+L
Auto Contrast	Ctrl+Alt+Shift+L	⌘+Option+Shift+L
Auto Color Correction	Ctrl+Shift+B	⌘+Shift+B
Adjust Lighting > Fill Flash	Ctrl+Shift+F	⌘+Shift+F
Adjust Color > Hue/Saturation	Ctrl+U	⌘+U
Adjust Color > Remove Color	Ctrl+Shift+U	⌘+Shift+U
Adjust Brightness/Contrast > Levels	Ctrl+L	⌘+L

LAYER MENU	WINDOWS	MAC OS
New > Layer	Ctrl+Shift+N	⌘+Shift+N
Group with Previous	Ctrl+G	⌘+G
Ungroup	Ctrl+Shift+G	⌘+Shift+G
Arrange > Bring to Front	Ctrl+Shift+]	⌘+Shift+]
Arrange > Bring Forward	Ctrl+]	⌘+]
Arrange > Send Backward	Ctrl+[	⌘+[
Arrange > Send to Back	Ctrl+Shift+[	⌘+Shift+[
Merge Down	Ctrl+E	⌘+E
Merge Visible	Ctrl+Shift+E	⌘+Shift+E

KEYBOARD SHORTCUTS

Menu Shortcuts

SELECT MENU	WINDOWS	MAC OS
All	Ctrl +A	⌘+A
Deselect	Ctrl +D	⌘+D
Reselect	Ctrl +Shift +D	⌘+Shift +D
Inverse	Ctrl +Shift +I	⌘+Shift +I
Feather	Ctrl +Alt +D	⌘+Option +D
Nudge selection marquee 1 pixel	Arrow key	Arrow key
Nudge selection marquee 10 pixels	Shift +Arrow key	Shift +Arrow key
LIQUIFY FILTER	WINDOWS	MAC OS
Warp tool	W	W
Turbulence tool	A	A
Twirl Clockwise tool	R	R
Twirl Counter Clockwise tool	L	L
Pucker tool	P	P
Bloat tool	B	B
Shift Pixels tool	S	S
Reflection tool	M	M
Reconstruct tool	E	E
Zoom tool	Z	Z
Hand tool	H	H
Reverse direction for Shift Pixels and Reflect tools	Alt +tool	Option +tool
Increase/decrease brush pressure by 1	Up and down arrow keys	Up and down arrow keys
Increase/decrease brush size by 1	Up and down arrow keys	Up and down arrow keys

INDEX

Stylize, 194
Texture, 195, 214–217
See also effects
Filters palette, 180–183
  changing the view of, 182–183
  displaying filters in, 181
  viewing, 180
Flashlight lighting style, 210
flattening images, 129, 332
Flip Orientation button, 280
floating selections, 116
Floodlight lighting style, 210
font family and style, 275
Frame From Video dialog box, 42, 43
frames, 365
Frames effects, 196
Free Rotate Layer command, 260
Free Transform Shape command, 261
full tonal range, 76
Fuzziness slider, 85, 87

G

galleries
  of effects, 196–198
  of filters, 189–195
Gaussian Blur filter, 203
Geometry Options palette, 256, 257
GIF file format, 293, 318
GIF images
  color options, 300–301, 302
  custom optimization settings, 300–302
  dithering options, 301, 303
  placing on patterned backgrounds, 307
  preserving transparency, 304–305
  See also animated GIFs
Global Light checkbox, 145
Gloss light property, 211
glossary of terms, xi
Gradient Editor dialog box, 229–234
gradient picker, 227
Gradient tool, 227–228, 287
gradients
  applying gradient fills, 227–228
  creating new gradients, 229–232
  editing gradient sets, 233–234
  saving gradient sets, 233
  text filled with, 287
  types of, 234
grayscale mode
  converting images to, 64
  explained, 62
grid, 56–57
Grid Preferences dialog box, 56

grouping/ungrouping
  layers, 139–140
  palettes, 21
Grow command, 104

H

Hand tool, 27, 206
Hardness slider, 243
Help menu, 31
help system, 31–32
  Hints palette and, 29
  shortcuts bar and, 32
hidden tools, 15, 16
hiding
  grid, 56
  layers, 121
  options bar, 18
  palettes, 20, 21
  rulers, 54
  selection borders, 110
  shortcuts bar, 18
  toolbox, 16
  See also displaying
Hints palette, x, 29
histograms, 76, 79–80
How To palette, x, 30
HSB color model, 63
hue, 63
Hue slider, 86, 177
Hue/Saturation dialog box, 175, 176–177

I

I-beam pointer, 270
ICC Profile check box, 299
Image effects, 197
Image Size dialog box, 46, 358
images, 33–57
  batch processing, 323–327
  blending elements of, 170
  blurring parts of, 168, 199–203
  cataloging, 328–330
  color cast removal, 83–84
  color saturation adjustment, 173
  color tints added to, 176
  composite, 377–384
  copying between pictures, 159
  creating, 37–38
  cropping, 152–154
  darkening portions of, 172
  displaying, 36
  distorting, 204–207
  downsampling, 47

T

U

INDEX

WWW.PEACHPIT.COM

Quality How-to Computer Books

Visit Peachpit Press on the Web at www.peachpit.com

- Check out new feature articles each Monday: excerpts, inter-views, tips, and plenty of how-tos

- Find any Peachpit book by title, series, author, or topic on the Books page

- See what our authors are up to on the News page: signings, chats, appearances, and more

- Meet the Peachpit staff and authors in the About section: bios, profiles, and candid shots

- Use Resources to reach our academic, sales, customer service, and tech support areas and find out how to become a Peachpit author

About

News

Books

Features

Resources

Order

Find

Welcome!

Peachpit.com is also the place to:

- Chat with our authors online
- Take advantage of special Web-only offers
- Get the latest info on new books